LOWER YOUR YOUR TAXES—

BIG TIME!

Wealth-Building, Tax Reduction Secrets from an IRS Insider
2019-2020 Edition
including updates for the Tax Cuts and Jobs Law
Protecting Americans from Tax Hikes Act

Sandy Botkin, CPA, J.D.

New York   Chicago   San Francisco   Athens   London
Madrid   Mexico City   Milan   New Delhi
Singapore   Sydney   Toronto

1 2 3 4 5 6 7 8 9 LCR 23 22 21 20 19 18

ISBN 978-1-260-14381-2
MHID 1-260-14381-3

e-ISBN 978-1-260-14382-9
e-MHID 1-260-14382-1

This publication is designed to provide accurate and authoritative information in regard to the subject matter covered. It is sold with the understanding that neither the author nor the publisher is engaged in rendering legal, accounting, securities trading, or other professional services. If legal advice or other expert assistance is required, the services of a competent professional person should be sought.

—*From a Declaration of Principles Jointly Adopted by a Committee of the American Bar Association and a Committee of Publishers and Associations*

McGraw-Hill Education products are available at special quantity discounts to use as premiums and sales promotions or for use in corporate training programs. To contact a representative, please visit the Contact Us pages at www.mhprofessional.com.

Contents

Introduction: Rich or Poor—Your Choice   ix

Part 1. Wealth-Building Tax Secrets for Small and Home-Based Business Owners   1

Chapter 1. Why You Would Be Brain Dead Not to Start a Home-Based Business (If You Don't Already Have One)   3

This chapter explains why everyone who is employed should have some kind of business, preferably a home-based business. If you don't have one, you are losing thousands each year.

Chapter 2. How to Deduct Your Meals and Some Employee Outings   8

How to deduct your meals during business and sales presentations—and audit-proof all these deductions. You will learn some IRS inside secrets and find out about the great $75 exception to keeping receipts, as well as exceptions for entertaining employees and for employee parties. You will be having twice as much fun if you know it's deductible!

Chapter 3. How to Turn Your Vacation into a Tax-Deductible Write-Off   21

This chapter deals with how to deduct your travel and vacation expenses. It will put thousands of dollars in your pocket.

Chapter 4. Income Shifting and Income Splitting: One of the Greatest Single Wealth-Building Secrets

37

How would you like to completely deduct the equivalent of your kids' college education, room and board at college, and their weddings? You can, with income shifting. This chapter also deals with a great tax planning technique called the gift-sale technique and the "Botkin Trust," which allows a double deduction for equipment—and has been approved in numerous Supreme Court cases. I love this chapter!

Chapter 5. How to Turn Your Car into a Tax-Deductible Goldmine

53

Learn the five methods of IRS-bulletproofing your automobile deductions. This is a must if you use your car for business. With the passage of the new Tax Cuts and Jobs Law, certain vehicles can become big winners that can save you hundreds of thousands of dollars over your business career.

Chapter 6. Home Office: The Misunderstood Key to Saving $15,000 Every Five Years

78

This chapter explains how to convert your home into a tax-deductible money machine, using little-known audit-proofing strategies. One of my students told me that this chapter reduced her taxable income by $100,000. This chapter also covers the methods used to get around the property tax and debt limits imposed by the latest tax reform law.

Chapter 7. Beating the Dreaded IRS Audit

98

What do you do when you get a letter from the IRS "inviting you in for a chat"? This chapter covers what your chances are of being audited, your audit rights, how to reduce your chances of being audited, what to do if you don't have the money to pay the IRS, and much more. This is a great chapter and you should read it carefully.

Chapter 8. How to Shield Yourself from the IRS Weapon of Classifying a Business as a Hobby

112

This chapter illustrates the practical steps necessary to withstand any "hobby attack" by the IRS. I have been so successful with clients who have used this information that many accountants have asked me for copies of this book because of this chapter alone. If you are running a business out of your home, this chapter could save you a bundle and prevent lots of IRS problems. This problem becomes particularly acute as a result of the new tax reform law. Every small business and home based business will need to both understand and apply the tips found in this chapter.

Part 2. How to Incorporate to Shelter Your Wealth 123

Chapter 9. Finding the Best Corporate Entity for Your Business 125

Here's a great overview of the pros and cons of incorporating vs. being a sole proprietor or being a Limited liability company. In addition, with the new tax rate changes for corporations, many small businesses will need to reevaluate the entity used to run their business.

Chapter 10. Forming a Nevada Corporation or a Limited-Liability Corporation in Nevada 150

Many well-known, wealthy personalities (and many con artists) incorporate in Nevada. You will learn exactly why. This has been a well-kept secret—until now!

Chapter 11. How to Eliminate up to 40 Percent of Your Social Security and Medicare Tax with an S Corporation 155

This technique works especially well for Middle America businesses.

Chapter 12. How to Get Assets and Money into a Corporation Tax-Free 159

This chapter explains what should and what should not be transferred to a corporation. It also covers a crucial topic that has killed many businesses: dealing with co-owners and partners. Finally, if you terminate your corporation at a loss, it explains a method that will give you an ordinary loss rather than a less-valuable capital loss.

Part 3. Every Fringe Benefit Available to Small and Home-Based Businesses as Amended by the New Tax Cuts and Jobs Act Legislation 165

Chapter 13. Fringe Benefits You Will Love, Part 1 171

This chapter deals with most of the wonderful tax-free fringe benefits that you can have in almost any small business that are not covered in other chapters. I will discuss such perks as payment for parking, transportation, exercise equipment, employee achievement awards, and much more.

Chapter 14. Fringe Benefits You Will Love, Part 2   200

This chapter continues the discussion of tax-free fringe benefits
from Chapter 13, with parking, transit passes, cafeteria plans,
qualified profit-sharing plans, SEPs, SIMPLE IRAs,
and more.

Part 4. Miscellaneous Tax Strategies   219

Chapter 15. The Four Most Overlooked Real Estate Tax Deductions in America   221

Here are the big four: (1) the large deduction for mortgage
points, (2) choosing to make "repairs" vs. "improvements" on
your property, (3) the new universal exclusion that will allow
you to avoid up to $500,000 of gain on your properties every two
years, (4) one of the biggest tax deduction mistakes in divorce
situations. In fact, do not get divorced without reading
this chapter!

Chapter 16. Making Colleges Less Expensive with Tax Planning   234

This chapter highlights qualified tuition plans for your kids'
future education,which will enable you to pay for college with
tax-free savings. This chapter also explains the benefits of
both the Lifetime Learning Credit and the Opportunity Tax
Credit, both of which result in a dollar-for-dollar reduction in
your taxes. The chapter also covers the rules of deducting
student loan interest.

Chapter 17. Tax Planning for Stock and Bond Investments   247

This chapter deals with many of the most important tax issues for
investors so that they can substantially reduce their taxes on these
investments.

Chapter 18. Trader versus Investor: The Best-Kept Secret Around   260

This chapter will discuss the little known benefit of being a stock
and commodities trader.

Chapter 19. Tax Scams and Other Shams   272

This chapter deals with some of the latest tax and other scams
that are being perpetrated today.

Chapter 20. Highlights of the new Tax Cuts and Jobs Act Legislation 287

This chapter will give an overview on what has changed as a result of this new groundbreaking legislation, and most importantly, how to plan for the changes. This discussion will also include an analysis of the new 20 percent pass-through deduction.

Chapter 21. The Top 10 Tax Questions 308

This is one chapter you don't want to miss.

Appendix A: 2018 Tax Rates 317

Appendix B: How to Find a Good Accountant 319

Appendix C: Health Savings Account 322

Index 324

Introduction

Rich or Poor—Your Choice

When a person with money meets a person with experience, the person with experience will get some money and the person with money will get some experience.

—Harvey MacKay,
How to Swim with Sharks Without Being Eaten Alive

This is not a financial planning book or a book about money. However, it will probably put more money in your pocket *each year* than any other book you've read. This is also not a book about investing or wealth building. However, the information contained here could probably create more wealthy people than any wealth-building book. Finally, this is also not a book that will show you how to do your own taxes. In fact, there are no tax forms in this book. However, it will probably help you reduce your taxes more than any idea that an accountant has given you and more than any idea that you may have read about in any other book.

Lower Your Taxes—Big Time! is a practical book on tax strategies and IRS audit-proofing techniques. You will not only learn to significantly reduce your taxes with proven strategies developed over many years, you will, at the same time, lower your chances of being audited and make your tax return "IRS-bulletproof." This sounds contradictory, but I promise you that these statements are true.

Read the quote at the beginning of this chapter again. I intend to give you the experience you need so you can become both "a person with money" and "a person with experience." There are costly ways to gain experience, as anyone who has been thoroughly audited will tell you, and not-so-costly ways. This book is the not-so-costly way for you.

The idea for this book began to develop when I was a trainer of IRS attorneys. While working at the IRS, I realized that many people were overpaying their taxes because of a lack of knowledge or lack of information. In fact, the turning point of my life occurred as a result of reviewing a friend's tax return. My friend knew that I was an attorney for the IRS and asked me to review his tax return for omitted deductions. Although his return had been prepared by a major accounting firm, I recommended that he file an amended return and get back over $16,000! As a result of this refund, my friend and his wife had their first vacation outside the U.S.

This experience led me to start my own company, TRI Seminars, Inc. (Tax Reduction Institute) of Germantown, Maryland, which teaches people how to significantly and legally reduce their taxes and, at the same time, IRS-bulletproof their records.

The Problem

I have seen time and again many people spending hours fighting over a $200 over-charge by their credit card company, yet spend little or no time learning how to reduce their tax bite by thousands of dollars, which would be very easy to do. I often have 100 people in a seminar where I can guarantee to show tax savings of at least several thousand dollars a year, unlike some motivational speakers who have thousands of participants with few or no guarantees. I used to wonder why most people don't understand the importance of tax strategies. As a result of many interviews, studies, and phone conversations, I came to realize that there were several myths that were impoverishing a great majority of people in this country.

Myth 1: I didn't make a lot of money this year so I don't need to know about tax planning. This is absolutely false. If you are a consultant or have a small or home-based business, you have access to the last great tax shelter left in this country. (If you don't have a home-based business, read Chapter 1, where I'll convince you why you should start one!) If your deductions in your business exceed your income, you can use that business loss against any form of income that you or your spouse have, such as rents, dividends, pensions, or even wages.[1]

Example: John and Mary earned $40,000 in salary but had a side home-based business that generated a loss of $15,000. They may use this loss to offset their salary in computing their taxable income. Thus, they only pay tax on $25,000 of income.

If your business losses exceed your whole year's income, don't fret. The government will allow you to deduct all losses from your business against any other form of income. If your losses exceed your income, they can be now carried over forever against up to 80 percent of future taxable income.[2]

Example: John has a net loss from his business of $10,000. If John has $40,000 of earnings from a job this year, can use this $10,000 loss and reduce his taxable income to $30,000. This is treated as if he only earned $30,000. If he didn't have any taxable income this year to offset the loss, can can carry over the loss forever and offset up to 80% of future earnings until the loss is used up.

Isn't life grand! My point is, knowing about tax planning strategies is important regardless of your income level.

Myth 2: My home-based/small business has to have a profit at least three out of five consecutive years. Did you believe this myth too? Hundreds of people, including accountants, have said this to me. This is absolutely false. Congress simply wants you to run your business like a business and not like a hobby. If you do, you can have losses for many years.[3] This will be discussed in depth in Chapter 8.

Myth 3: My accountant takes care of my taxes. A similar myth is **"My spouse takes care of my taxes."** This is the biggest myth of all. These seven words impoverish more people than any other myth. It's like saying, "My doctor takes care of my body." Wouldn't it be great if we never had to exercise and could eat all the fattening foods and, once a year, our doctors would give us a "Roto-Rooter" job? The point is that the tax savings your accountant can find for you after December 31 are small compared with what you can save if you are pursuing your own tax strategies before December 31.

Myth 4: Tax knowledge won't save me that much money anyway. Did you know that taxes are the number one expense in this country? If you add up your federal, state, and Social Security taxes, you may find that what you pay in taxes rivals or exceeds what you pay for food, lodging or mortgage payment, transportation, and clothing combined![4]

In a great book entitled *The Millionaire Next Door: The Surprising Secrets of America's Wealthy,*[5] the authors analyzed the mindset of multimillionaires in order to determine what makes them tick. They found a number of interesting correlations among millionaires. First, most millionaires are frugal and live beneath their means. Sam Walton, for example, drove a pickup truck. Second, most millionaires believe that if you want to get rich, you must get your taxes down to the legal minimum. They know that we have two tax systems in the U.S. You may be thinking, "Right—one for the rich and one for the poor." No, that's not correct. There is one tax system for employees and for those who don't know the rules. This system is designed to take your wealth. The second tax system is for self-employed people who know the rules. This tax system is designed to create economic growth.

It has been estimated that small businesses generate the majority of job growth in the U.S. It isn't IBM or Microsoft, but small and home-based businesses. Thus, when lobbyists come to Congress to get some good tax laws passed for small businesses (and there are good tax laws), the small business lobbyists can sometimes get what they want. The reason is that Congress knows that small business is the economic engine behind our economy. In fact, states that have low taxes on business tend to be more economically successful because they attract business and jobs. The key is to take advantage of these good tax laws, which means that you have to know about them. The problem is, as a professor of mine many years ago said, "We don't know what we don't know." This is, unfortunately, especially true about tax knowledge.

The authors of *The Millionaire Next Door* concluded that most people who became millionaires didn't win a lottery, inherit a lot of money, or make a big stock market gain. They were, for the most part, average folks who saved a little bit each year, probably from the taxes saved with good planning, and invested the money in an average investment for 30 or more years.

At first I didn't believe this, so I ran some numbers. If Tom invests $10,000 annually into his retirement plan for 30 years (assuming that he has no initial savings), he will have $790,582 in his retirement plan, such as a Roth 401(k), at retirement, at the end of 30 years.[6] This all assumes that he deposited his $10,000 yearly contribution at the end of each year, which is what most folks do. *However*, if he had the foresight to make these yearly contributions at the beginning of each year, his total at retirement would rise to $838,017! This is almost $48,000 more at retirement on the same contributions! Thus the very important point is this: The earlier in the year you make your contributions, especially for all retirement plans, the more you will have at retirement. This point cannot be overstated. Notice that if the investment were to be made for five more years, which would be 35 years, at the beginning of each year, your projected amount at retirement would be $1,181,208. Thus a measly five more years, putting away $10,000 per year, would get you an extra $343,191. If you were to put away $10,000 per year for 40 years instead of the original 30 years, you would have $1,640,477 at retirement, which is almost double what you would have had after 30 years!

What This Book Will Cover

We will be covering a wide area of tax knowledge.

Chapter 1. Why You Would Be Brain Dead Not to Start a Home-Based Business (If You Don't Already Have One) explains why everyone who is employed should have some kind of business, preferably a home-based business. If you don't have one, you are losing thousands each year.

Chapter 2. How to Deduct Your Meals and Some Employee Outings deals with deducting various types of meals and employee events and how to audit-proof all these deductions. You will also learn some IRS inside secrets and learn about the great $75 exception to keeping receipts. You will love the information in this chapter, since you will be having twice as much fun by deducting your meals and some fun.

Chapter 3. How to Turn Your Vacation into a Tax-Deductible Write-Off deals with how to deduct your travel expenses and how to convert almost any vacation into a deductible business trip. This chapter will put thousands in your pocket.

Chapter 4. Income Shifting and Income Splitting: One of the Greatest Single Wealth-Building Secrets is for anyone who is married or who is single with children, whether young or adult, or people with friends. How would you like to completely deduct the equivalent of your kids' college education, room and board at college, and their weddings? You can, with income shifting. This chapter also deals with a great tax planning technique called the "gift-sale" technique. In fact, if everyone in the country knew about this one technique, it could reduce the IRS treasury legally by billions of dollars! No kidding. Finally, we will cover the "Botkin Trust," which allows a double deduction for equipment and has been approved in numerous Supreme Court cases. I love this chapter.

Chapter 5. How to Turn Your Car into a Tax-Deductible Goldmine is a must if you use your car for business or incur automobile expenses for the job. Automobiles are the area that the IRS audits most frequently because they are big-ticket items. You will learn how to make your car into a tax-deductible goldmine and learn the five methods of IRS-bullet proofing your automobile documentation. This chapter becomes especially important because of the significantly improved write offs available to business vehicles that came about from the Tax Cuts and Jobs Act.

Chapter 6. Home Office: The Misunderstood Key to Saving $15,000 Every Five Years explains how to convert your home into a tax-deductible money machine. It focuses heavily on little-known audit-proofing strategies required by the IRS and shows a great way to claim a home office year after year and pay very little tax on the sale of the home. One of my students told me that this chapter reduced her taxable income by $100,000. It is a very important chapter for anyone who works out of the house.

Chapter 7. Beating the Dreaded IRS Audit deals with a situation that worries far too many taxpayers. What do you do when you get a letter from the IRS "inviting you in for a chat"? This chapter will cover what your chances are of being audited, what your audit rights are, how to reduce your chances of being audited, what to do if you don't have the money to pay the IRS, and much more. This is a great chapter and should be read carefully.

Chapter 8. How to Shield Yourself from the IRS Weapon of Classifying a Business as a Hobby deals with an IRS tactic that has become a major issue nationwide. The IRS can eliminate virtually all business losses if you don't run your endeavor correctly. This chapter will illustrate all the practical steps necessary to withstand any "hobby attack" by the IRS. I have been so successful with clients who have used this information that many accountants have asked me for copies of this book primarily because of this chapter alone. If you are running a business out of your home or have a side business, this chapter could save you a bundle and prevent lots of IRS problems. It is well worth reading this chapter several times.

Chapter 9. Finding the Best Corporate Entity for Your Business will give you a great overview of the pros and cons of incorporating vs. being a sole proprietor or being a limited liability company. You will learn the inside secrets of what to look for in deciding whether incorporating is right for you.

Chapter 10. Forming a Nevada Corporation or a Limited-Liability Corporation in Nevada provides some little-known information. Many well-known, wealthy personalities (and many con artists) incorporate in Nevada. You will learn exactly why. This has been a well-kept secret until now!

Chapter 11. How to Eliminate up to 40 Percent of Your Social Security and Medicare Tax with an S Corporation deals with one of the best-kept secrets among accountants and wealthy clients for years. Now you can learn exactly what the rich have known for years and learn a great way to substantially reduce those pesky, large Social Security and Medicare taxes.

Chapter 12. How to Get Assets and Money into a Corporation Tax-Free deals with avoiding some of the pitfalls of forming a corporation. It will also emphasize what should and, as important, what should not be transferred to a corporation. It covers a *very* widespread and crucial area that has killed many businesses: dealing with co-owners and partners. Finally, if you terminate your corporation at a loss, it explains a method that will give you an ordinary loss rather than a less-valuable capital loss.

Chapter 13. Fringe Benefits You Will Love, Part 1 deals with most of the wonderful, tax-free fringe benefits that you can have in almost any small business that are not covered in other chapters. I will discuss such perks as payment for parking, transportation, exercise equipment, employee achievement awards, and much more.

Chapter 14. Fringe Benefits You Will Love, Part 2 deals with some of the drawbacks to being a corporation, such as personal service corporations, accumulated earnings taxes, and more. It's essential for every person who's thinking of incorporating to be aware of these hidden congressionally mandated tax traps.

Chapter 15. The Four Most Overlooked Real Estate Tax Deductions in America deals with four major real estate problems that affect almost every American at some point in their lives. It explains the large deduction for mortgage points, deals with the new universal exclusion that will allow you to avoid up to $500,000 of gain on your properties every two years, describes ways to dramatically increase your return on investments with the right choice of repairs and improvements, and finally reveals one of the biggest tax mistakes in failing to plan for loan costs as a result of home purchases.

Chapter 16. Making Colleges Less Expensive with Tax Planning addresses frequently asked questions concerning the deductibility of educational expenses and details great tax credits available for education. This chapter will also cover the prepaid tuition plans that will enable you to save money for your kids' education on a tax-free basis.

Chapter 17. Tax Planning for Stock and Bond Investments deals with many of the most important tax issues for investors in order to substantially reduce your taxes on these investments. It also deals with some of the biggest mistakes that accountants and financial planners have seen with clients.

Chapter 18. Trader versus Investor: The Best-Kept Secret Around discusses the little-known benefit of being a stock and commodities trader. Traders can get many of the benefits available to investors without suffering the disadvantages of reducing their investment-related expenses. It is really a good chapter to read if you do a lot of short-term trading in the market.

Chapter 19. Tax Scams and Other Shams deals with some of the latest tax and other scams that are being perpetrated today. Millions of Americans each year seem to be caught by some of these. This chapter also deals with identity fraud and how to both stop it and handle it if you become a victim.

Chapter 20. Highlights of The New Tax Cuts and Jobs Act Legislation: This will give you a great overview of the many tax benefits that apply to small buisnesses as well as discuss the new passthrough deduction and how to max out its benefits.

Chapter 21. The Top 10 Tax Questions addresses some of the most universal tax issues in America. I've also chosen some questions due to their inherent appeal. It will undoubtedly address some questions that you have asked yourself at some point or are currently wondering about. This is one chapter that you don't want to miss.

When I started writing this book, I had several goals in mind. First, I wanted to show readers, especially consultants, small business owners, and home-based business owners how to save thousands of dollars on their taxes. Second, I wanted to present the material in a simplified format without any of the "accountant jargon" or "gobble-dygook." Finally, I wanted to emphasize the little-known, audit-proof documentation strategies needed to survive any IRS audit. As you will see, practicality is the theme of this book, which includes hundreds of practical tips and suggestions that will save you a bundle each year.

This book is a product of thousands of lectures I have delivered to more than 100,000 students over the years. In these lectures I constantly ask my students to evaluate what was scary to them or what they didn't understand. Thus, *Lower Your Taxes—Big Time!* is the result of an evolutionary process of 25 years of work.

I have also provided all the IRS annotations, which are the legal footnotes for everything that will be discussed. Everything in this book will be supported with the appropriate documentation; thus, there will be nothing that will trigger any audit. If there were any "gray" areas, I omitted them from the discussion.

Finally, throughout the book, you will find icons that look like the one here: These indicate a concept, strategy, or action you can take to lower your taxes—big time!

I hope that you get as much enjoyment from reading this book as I got in writing it.

Dedication and Acknowledgment

I would like to dedicate this work to my wife, Lori, and my children, Jeremy, Matthew, and Allison, for their endless patience, and to my many students who have helped craft this work with feedback and suggestions. I wish to thank Amy Li, and Diana Penikas, my editor at McGraw-Hill, for her input and timely suggestions. Finally, I also want to dedicate this book to the U.S. Congress, which makes this work not only possible, but necessary.

Notes

1. Section 162 of the Internal Revenue Code (IRC) and Regulations.
2. Section 172 of the IRC as amended by the 2017 Tax Cuts and Jobs Act (Sec 13302(a)(1).
3. Section 183 of the IRC and Regulations thereunder.
4. The Tax Foundation and *The Tax Adviser* (American Institute of Certified Public Accountants), May 2000.
5. *The Millionaire Next Door: The Surprising Secrets of America's Wealthy* by Thomas J. Stanley and William D. Danko (Longstreet Press, 1996).
6. From the Vanguard prospectus, the Growth and Equity Fund had a 10-year rate of return of 12.90 percent. I should note that I am not necessarily recommending Vanguard. There are many good funds, such as Fidelity, AIM, Janus, T. Rowe Price, and others.

Part 1

Wealth-Building Tax Secrets for Small and Home-Based Business Owners

1

Why You Would Be Brain Dead Not to Start a Home-Based Business (If You Don't Already Have One)

There are really two sets of tax laws in this country. One is for employees; it allows deductions for normal employee items, such as individual retirement accounts, 401(k)s (if you have one set up by your company), interest and property taxes on your home, and charity. Then there are the laws for small and home-based business people who conduct their business either full or part time. In addition to the tax deductions employees can get, small business people can deduct, with proper documentation, their house, their spouses (by hiring them), their business vacations, their cars, and food with colleagues. They can also set up a pension plan that makes any government plan seem paltry by comparison and deduct most of their "vacation" trips if they combine them with an appropriate amount of business. (See the discussion in Chapter 3.) Moreover, under the new Tax Cuts and Jobs Act, small businesses and independent contractors can now effectively pay tax on only 80 percent of their net income from their business (not counting investment earnings).

> **Chapter Overview**
> - You will *never* get rich until you learn to get your taxes down to the legal minimum.
> - There are two tax systems in this country—one for salaried employees, one for small/home-based business owners.
> - A home-based business will make you better off than a second income.
> - Traditional job security has declined over the years and will continue to do so, making home businesses more attractive.
> - You will probably save $2,000–$10,000 per year by starting your own part-time business.

The example below shows how a woman named Lori, who earned a $20,000 salary, took home only $1,001 after she deducted all her work-related expenses. Yet she could have netted the entire $20,000 had she earned it in a home-based business. This is an increase of almost 18 times her take-home pay as an employee.

It illustrates why having more than one job in a family does not produce any major effect on most people's bank accounts because of the tax laws.

Let's assume a husband earned $40,000 per year, which is $3,400 per month, and his wife (I'm calling her Lori) wasn't working. They had more month than money. (Sound familiar?) Lori subsequently got an administrative job for $20,000 per year. When examining the economics of getting this extra income for the family, the results were startling!

Lori had to pay federal and state taxes on her new income. Since they filed jointly, the family's combined income was what established their tax bracket. She paid $4,845 in new federal and state taxes, most of which were nondeductible.

Lori had Social Security withheld from her paycheck at the rate of 7.65 percent, which amounted to an additional nondeductible amount of $1,530 being extracted from her. She also had to commute to work 10 miles a day round trip, which is probably conservative for most people. This results in nondeductible commuting costs of $1,337 in 2018.[1]

Lori also had child care expenses that give a partial tax credit. Quinn figured that the amount spent over and beyond the tax credit was $6,250 per year.

Lori also ate out each day with colleagues, spending an average of $7 per day for lunch, five days per week. This results in a nondeductible expense of $1,750 a year.[2] (I would love to know where she ate for only $7!)

Now that Lori has a job, she has to have better clothing and much more dry cleaning. Let's assume Lori's increased expenses here were an extra $1,200 per year, nondeductible, of course.

Finally, with both spouses working, Lori wasn't in the mood to cook, somewhat akin to my own life. Thus, there were more convenience foods and more eating out. This resulted in increased food costs of a nondeductible $2,000 per year at the minimum.

Add it all up and Lori's take-home pay was a paltry $1,001 a year, for which she had to put up with the commute and the boss and the corporate hassles. (See the following summary of all these numbers, so you can do the math yourself.)

Gross Income *LESS:*	$20,000
State and federal taxes	($4,845)
Social Security taxes	($1,530)
Car expenses (at 53.5 cpm—50 miles per week, for 50 weeks)	($1,337)
Child care (net of the credit)	($6,250)
Lunches at the job	($1,750)
Business clothing and dry cleaning	($1,287)
Higher food expenses (eating out, snack foods, etc.)	(<u>$2,000</u>)
Net take-home pay as an employee:	$1,001 per Year

No wonder more and more people are starting up home-based and consulting businesses. In fact, according to author David D'Arcangelo, there are currently an estimated 37 million people working from their homes, "representing a 20-fold increase over the last 10 years. What's more is that number is expected to grow by 15 percent annually and keep on growing!"[3] This has become and will continue to become one of the greatest mass movements in the U.S.

If Lori started a home-based business, she would not be spending dramatically more money then she is currently spending. She would eat out anyway, go on trips, and have the same car expenses for repairs, gas, and insurance as she did before. If she has a home-based and/or consulting business, however, many of her expenses become deductible. This concept is known as "redirecting expenses." With a home-based or consulting business, she can now deduct some of the expenses that she is incurring anyway.

More Reasons to Start a Home-Based Business

In recent years, the era of large corporate profits and economic growth came to an end. Moreover, many economists believe things won't be getting better any time soon.

Remember the American Dream? You worked hard for one employer, saved your money, and retired with dignity and security. Today, young and middle-aged alike are realizing that their dream of having a job with a company forever is an illusion. Just pick up any national paper and you will see companies downsizing, rightsizing, and capsizing. (Remember Enron and WorldCom.)

If this isn't bad enough, under recent tax laws, employees are shafted more than ever with the total elimination of employee business expenses and higher Social Security tax limits. This results in more couples working than ever before and, on many occasions, working at more than one job. It is now almost impossible to have only one job in the family and make ends meet!

Finally, with both spouses away from the home most of the day, we have more children fending for themselves until their parents get home and less discipline in the home. (I wonder if some of the shootings that occur in school today aren't caused, in part, because many parents aren't home to take care of their children and supervise them properly.)

The reasons so many people are going into a home-based business or becoming consultants rather than joining a traditional business are many. There is no commute (unless you have a really big home), no boss, little if any chance of lawsuits, much less overhead, and no employees or very few employees. In addition, the new tax law effectively reduces the tax on net business income or on income earned by contractors to 80 percent of their net business income. It is for these reasons, according to *Entrepreneur Magazine*, that 95 percent of the home-based businesses succeed in their first year and achieve an average income of $50,250 per year, with many earning much more.

I should note that, in addition to all the benefits noted above, Congress will subsidize you while you're growing your small business. If your business produces a loss in the first year or so, you can use that loss against any other income that you have.

> **Strategy**
> If you don't have a home-based or small business, start one immediately!

It can be used against wages earned as an employee, dividends, pensions, or interest income, or against your spouse's earnings if you filed a joint return. If the tax loss exceeds all your and your spouse's income for the year, no problem. If the loss exceeds your income, you can now carry forward all business losses forever and use these losses to offset up to 80 percent of your future taxable income until the losses are used up. Yes, you read this correctly, the losses can be carried forward forever.

Example: Mike earns $50,000 in a job with the government. If he starts a home-based business that generates a tax loss of $10,000, he pays tax on only $40,000.

In fact, if everyone in America who is employed full-time got a part-time business and used the strategies suggested in this book, each employee could easily reduce his or her taxes from $2,000 to $10,000 or more each year. If all the employees and small business people applied this information, the tax bite in the U.S. would be reduced by a whopping estimated $300 billion each year. (Of course, Congress would have to change the laws if this occurred.)

Finally, I want to note that you should *not* set up a business just to save taxes. Tax savings should be the icing and not the cake. Otherwise, you could run afoul of the hobby loss statutes (see Chapter 8).

> **Hot Tip**
> You can probably save $2,000–$10,000 a year by starting your own part-time business.

What Types of Businesses Should I Consider?

This is one of the questions asked most frequently of me. Actually, starting a business is not as hard as most people think. In most cases, there is little or no licensing required and you can operate it out of your home with few or no overhead costs. The key is deciding what type of business is right for you.

The best business for most people is the one that excites them and/or about which they have substantial knowledge. Consider the things that you are good at or really like to do. Consider your hobbies. I know one person who became an antique dealer because he and his wife loved collecting antiques. Perhaps you like writing and want to be a freelance writer or freelance editor. Tutoring and training such as giving SAT lessons or music lessons from the home are becoming fast-growing businesses.

Many people become distributors of products or services out of their homes. If you are good with people, you should also consider one of the many good network marketing companies. Why? These companies have proven products and sales literature and you usually don't have to store or finance inventory or even ship it to customers. The company does all that for you. It will even give you an account of all your sales and of all your distributors' (downline) sales. There is no overhead, such as rent and employees, so there's no liability exposure, which can occur in traditional businesses. Moreover, just about every product that you can think of is currently being marketed using the network marketing approach.

In addition, most network marketing companies provide some form of residual income that provides a continual stream of income from your distributors from year to year and month to month. Finally, you get the same or even better tax benefits with network marketing than you would with any traditional business.

The only downside to network marketing is that some of these operations are shaky. If you go this route, you want to associate with a company that has been around a while and has a proven track record of success and proven marketing programs. Many of these companies have a very high failure rate within the first two years of operation. I would recommend that you consider only companies that have been around and continuously successful for at least two years. Check out the various distributors that you want to be associated with. You want successful people who will teach you and support you. Your best friend may or may not be the ideal person.

Research has constantly shown that it is rarely the business that determines success or failure. It is usually the business owner. Why does one person succeed and another fail at the same business? Two words: *knowledge* and *action*. Some people want the benefits of having their own business, but they don't take action. The result is business failure. Then there are the people who are always working. They take action all day but still fail. The reason is that they are not taking the correct actions, the knowledgeable actions that will bring the desired results. Again, the result is business failure.

It's like drilling for oil. If you set up a drilling rig in your backyard, it's going to fail to produce oil unless your backyard is in Texas or Alaska. The same rig in a good oil field will produce a gusher because it was placed where oil was known to exist.

The point is that most people who start businesses or become consultants do so without all the necessary knowledge. Consequently, many people quit before they acquire through experience the knowledge that they need—and also without realizing that they are getting substantial tax breaks.

The choice between being rich and being poor, for you and for millions of others, is the opportunity that starting your own consulting or small business offers. If you have one going already, then you need to make sure that you're enjoying the many tax advantages your brilliance in so doing offers you.

Summary

- Job prospects are declining and will continue to do so.
- You will never get rich unless you get your tax affairs down to the legal minimum.
- There are two tax systems in this country: one is for employees and one is for small businesses, consultants, and home-based businesses.
- Everyone should have a home-based business immediately!

Notes

1. This allowed figure for 2018 is 53.5 cents per mile.
2. This assumes a two-week vacation.
3. David D'Arcangelo, *Wealth Starts at Home* (McGraw-Hill, 1997), p. 13.

2

How to Deduct Your Meals and Some Employee Outings

Taxes are the price that we pay for civilization.
—Oliver Wendell Holmes, Jr.

I'm proud to be paying taxes in the United States. The only thing is, I could be just as proud for half the money.

—Arthur Godfrey

You are going to love this chapter. It deals with deducting your meals and audit-proofing your records for the Internal Revenue Service (IRS). It also will cover some exceptions that most people and even most accountants don't even know about. It will apply to you if you have a small business but also if your job requires you to entertain prospects or subordinates in order to obtain more business or to help motivate employees.

Prior to 2018, small businesses could deduct 50 percent of meals and 50 percent of their entertainment and fun. In fact, both were always treated the same under tax law, which is why we accountants spoke of "mealsandentertainment" as if they were one and the same.

> **Chapter Overview**
>
> - Deduct your meals.
> - Learn when you need a receipt and when the IRS doesn't require receipts.
> - Deduct theater tickets, golf, plays, and other associated entertainment.
> - Deduct season tickets.
> - Know when a spouse's meals would be deductible.
> - Know how to audit-proof all entertainment for the IRS.
> - Deduct home entertainment.
> - Learn about a special exception for parties at home.
> - Learn how to deduct large parties without ever discussing business.
> - Provide lunches for employees.
> - Deduct business club dues and dues to civic organizations.
> - Find out about the "sales seminar at home" exception.

Starting in 2018, all of this has changed! All deductions for entertainment have been eliminated. Thus, you can no longer deduct fun activities with clients and prospects such as movies, plays, theater, sporting events, and golf.

Sandy's note: I wonder what the NFL and NBA will do with their box seats and whether firms will still rent them.

Before I get into the meals deduction, I want to discuss a question that comes up frequently in my seminars, which is, "When do I have to keep receipts?" The IRS has been very taxpayer-friendly lately with respect to receipts. No receipts are needed for entertainment expenses under $75 per expense.[1]

Example: John takes Mary out for a prearranged lunch and discusses business. John spends $25 on pretzels. (Hopefully, they're good pretzels!) John does not need a receipt because the cost of the entertainment is under $75.

Example: If John spent $85 for lunch, which includes drinks, he then would need a receipt.

Author's note: Although you technically don't need meal receipts for under $75, I would keep them anyway. IRS agents love seeing receipts, and it will avoid most problems. If you lose a receipt or forgot to get one, you can always use this IRS regulation in an audit.

Meals: Under the new Tax Cuts and Jobs Act legislation, Congress carved out various categories for meal deductions. Most are only deductible at 50 percent of the cost and some are 100 percent deductible. Here is a handy comprehensive chart for you to use in understanding the new, more complicated rules:

Business Meals and Entertainment		2018 Deduction Amount		
		100%	50%	Zero
	Entertainment with clients & prospects			X
	Year-end party for customers			X
	Golf, spa, sporting event, or theatre with customer			X
Type 1	Meals with clients or prospects*		X	
	Meals with your business partner, officers, or directors*		X	
Type 2	Meals while traveling outside of a normal commute		X	
	Meals while traveling away from home overnight		X	
Type 3	Employee meals for convenience of employer		X	
	Employee meals for required business meeting		X	
	Meal paid for at Chamber of Commerce meeting		X	
	Food in the office for employees (e.g., donuts & coffee)†		X	
Type 4	Year-end party for employees and spouses†	X		
	Team building recreational activity with employees†	X		
	Meals for general public at marketing presentation	X		
	Food at "open house" when selling property	X		
	Food as a cost of goods sold in your business (ie. restaurant)	X		

* On 1/25/18, Veena Murthy, legislation counsel for the Joint Committee on Taxation said that under the TCJA, "There is still a 50% deduction permitted for meals. That is generally the case. However, meals that are considered entertainment are no longer deductible".

† Employees are defined as non-owners, non-officers, non-directors, or non-highly compensated employees. For example, the majority of those attending a year-end party, team building activity, or eating the in-office food, must be employees as defined in the preceding sentence.

How are business meals with prospects and clients treated under the new Tax Cuts and Jobs Act? When the new law was passed, the deductibility of business meals with clients and prospects was uncertain. However, based on the legislative intent of the new law, the IRS has notified tax professionals that they will still allow a 50 percent deduction for business meals with prospects and clients as long as they are ordinary and necessary to their business and aren't too lavish.[2]

In the case that business meals are combined with entertainment, only the meal portion would be deductible. If there is no separation between the expense for the meal and that of the entertainment, none of the cost would be deductible. Here are some examples that should explain this:

Example: Jim entertains a prospect at a baseball game, paying for both the tickets and food. The food would be 50 percent deductible but the cost of the game would not be.

Example: Jim has a sky box that sends him one combined bill for both the game and the food provided to to the skybox. Since the bill doesn't state what portion is food, the entire cost would be non-deductible.

Documentation required for meals and business gifts:

There are several legal requirements for you to deduct your meals with prospects. First, tax law requires that a business meal be arranged for the purpose of conducting business or for acquiring business. Your prospect must reasonably expect a business reason for the meal.[3]

Strategy 1
Discuss specific business when you eat.

Example: Sam went to Greasy Lloyd's Restaurant for lunch and happened to discuss business with the waitress. This would not be a deductible business meal because Sam didn't have business intent to meet with the waitress, nor did she reasonably expect to discuss business with Sam as part of the lunch.

Example: Let's assume the same facts as above, but the waitress was Sam's neighbor and told Sam to stop by the restaurant where they could discuss Sam's services as a financial consultant. As part of the discussion, Sam also orders lunch while he is talking with her. This would be a deductible business meal because this was clearly a prearranged meeting with an actual business discussion.

A second requirement of the tax law is that you must discuss business before, during, or after a business meal to qualify for the business meal deduction.[4] This was put in because before the tax simplification law (1986 Tax Reform Act), you could have a quiet business meal and not say anything.

As long as your prospect was a legitimate prospect, this meal was deductible. The law was changed to require you to discuss some specific business. *The key is that you must have and document a clear and specific business discussion.*

The third requirement is that the meal must take place in surroundings conducive to a business discussion.[5] The IRS presumes that the active business discussion requirement is not met if the business meal occurs under circumstances in which there is little or no possibility of engaging in business.[6] Eating dinner in a nightclub with a continuous floor-show is an example of a nonbusiness setting; the same would be true for a large cocktail party.[7] Food purchased at the theater would not be a business meal either.

The final requirement is that you must substantiate your meal adequately even if a receipt is not required.[8] Here are the exact six questions that you will need to audit-proof your meal forever:[9]

- Who *was entertained (business relationship)?* The IRS wants you to identify the person or persons entertained, with names, occupations, official titles, and other corroborative information to establish the business relationship.
- Where *did the business meal take place?* The nature and place of the entertainment (dinner at Greasy Lloyd's) must be described. When a charge slip or receipt is obtained, the nature and place usually are self-evident.
- When *did the business meal take place?* The definition of time is usually the date when the entertainment takes place. When entries are made in a diary-type of document, the date on the diary page is adequate support for time.
- Why *did the business meal take place (business purpose)?* Of the five elements, this is the most important. State the exact nature of the business discussion or activity. Be brief but specific—very specific. If you simply say "prospect" or "goodwill," this will not be enough.[10] You must be more specific. For example, it would be good enough if you said, "Tried to get a listing or referral," "Talked about using my services," "Talked about disability insurance needs or financial needs," or "Talked about opportunity or healthcare needs."
- What type of meals or expense was involved? Was it for breakfast, lunch, or dinner, or for drinks? Was it a business gift, or was the expense for employee seminars etc.?
- How much *did the meal cost?* The cost of the entertainment must be recorded someplace. As I noted earlier, when the cost is $75 or more, you must retain documentary evidence, such as a receipt, voucher, or credit-card copy.

There is also one other requirement for all entertainment expenses that was not included in the preceding list. You must record the answers to these six IRS questions in a timely fashion, which means at or near the time of the expenditure[11] in some kind of notebook, diary, or tax organizer. You don't need to do this daily, but the closer in time you document your deductions, the better IRS agents will like it.[12]

Author's note: If you follow everything that I noted above, you will never have to worry about an IRS audit. You will have peace of mind in the face of any audit.

Author's tip: I have found that if people don't have something to trigger them to write down these things each day after each expense, they forget to do it, which results in no deduction. A tax diary or organizer is not only required by the IRS but also quite useful. Think of a tax diary as audit insurance or life insurance.

An interesting case happened when I was working at the IRS. There was a consultant who was being audited for his 1985 expenses in 1987. His accountant told him that he needed to keep some form of tax organizer. He thus converted his appointment book into a diary by backdating all his mileage and entertainment and travel questions using six pens of different colors. Some of the pages looked like they were dragged through the mud. Agatha Christie would have been proud! However, he made one mistake: He used a 1987 diary for his 1985 expenses!

Don't wait until you get audited. Get into the habit of filling out a tax organizer or daily diary, and you will save thousands—and you will have that peace of mind of never worrying about an IRS audit.

Generally, Congress and the IRS want you to discuss business in surroundings conducive to a business discussion. Thus, when you discuss business at a theater, on a golf course, and in a nightclub, this is not deemed conducive surroundings.[13]

Author's tip: Not only should you keep track of your business meals, but I recommend that you keep track of any expenditures incurred for entertaining a business prospect even though the entertainment is no longer deductible. Why? First, everyone should keep track of their business expenditures regardless of the deductibility of these expenses in order to track where their money has been spent. Moreover, tracking expenses incurred for business will help in establishing that you are conducting your business like a business and not like a hobby.

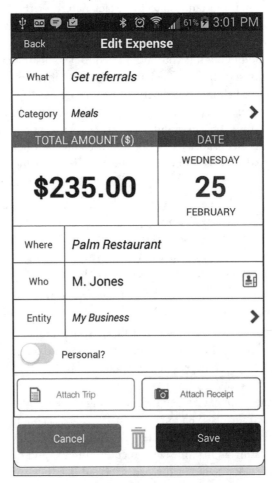

Figure 2-1. Documentation of a business meal.

Charity Events

There is one interesting IRS twist to this: If you buy tickets for a charitable event, you are not limited to the face value of the ticket if the following three conditions apply:[14]

- The event is organized for the primary purpose of benefiting a tax-exempt charity.
- All the net proceeds of the event are contributed to the charity.
- The event uses volunteers for substantially all the work performed in carrying out the event.

Thus a charitable golfing event where all the net funds raised go to the Heart Fund or the United Way, for example, would be a qualifying event. (I should note that no matter how needy you may feel that you are, you, personally, are not a qualifying charity.)

> **Strategy 2**
> Deduct for feeding and entertaining your spouse.

One big question that most people have is whether they can deduct the cost of a meal alone with a spouse. The answer is very clear-cut: Absolutely not! The IRS has what is known as a "closely connected" spouse rule.

Author's note: At least the government acknowledges that your spouse is closely connected to you. This rule prevents you from deducting meals out alone with your spouse. Is there a way to deduct the cost of a spouse? The answer is yes! The closely connected spouse rule allows you to bring your spouse and deduct his or her costs whenever you are entertaining another couple.[15] In other words, if your business guest brings a spouse or a guest, you are entitled to bring yours.[16] In addition, if you are not married, you may bring your "significant friend" to help entertain the other couple. Naturally, you must be entertaining the business guest during the ordinary course of your business, and you must meet the business discussion and documentation requirements that I noted earlier in this chapter. I guess that if you are single but living with someone or dating someone, this would be classified as the "closely connected significant friend rule."

Author's elaboration: In case you are curious as to why this deduction for your spouse or significant friend is allowed when your guest has a companion, the rationale for this distinction is that your spouse or significant friend can keep the companion busy while you have a one-on-one conversation with your guest. The key is to note in your tax organizer or diary the name of the other couple and what you discussed. Moreover, this rule can be carried another step. If the other couple brings their children, you probably could bring your kids to keep the prospect's kids busy. This is probably one of the least understood areas for most people and even for accountants. In fact, when I have lectured to accountants and ask about this, very few have heard of this issue.

The general rule is that if you pay for the meal for you and your guest(s), you can deduct 50 percent of the total cost of the meal. If you split the bill, you could presumably deduct 50 percent of your share of the bill.

The IRS may at its whim invoke the *Sutter rule*. The Sutter rule allows the IRS to disallow a portion of your business meals when such meals absorb substantial amounts of your typical living expenses.[17]

Strategy 3
Avoid the
Sutter rule.

Author's note: There was a case that a former IRS colleague had that involved a doctor who claimed $35,000 in meals in one year. This doctor was the biggest example of what we CPAs call the "P-I-G rule." His lawyer argued at a hearing that "he only eats for business reasons." Obviously, all his deductions were disallowed under the Sutter rule. Practically speaking, IRS doesn't try to impose the Sutter rule unless you are deducting a lot of meals for entertainment. Also, it is questionable whether it is still applicable since Congress changed the entertainment deduction from 100 percent to 50 percent to take into account that there was some "personal element" in entertainment. Thus, you may be able to argue that the Sutter rule does not apply due to the congressional action taken to reduce the deduction for entertainment.

Note: As I noted above, meals with spouses and prospects might be considered non-deductible entertainment as a result of the Tax Cuts and Jobs Act. However, as noted above, most accountants feel that this deduction has not been affected by the new law and, therefore, would be deductible. This is the position that I would recommend unless IRS rules to the contrary.

Exceptions to the 50 Percent Deduction Rule

Strategy 4
Some
entertainment
can be deemed
business
promotion.

There are a couple of exceptions to the 50 percent rule for deducting meals. In these exceptions, you can deduct 100 percent of the meal cost.

Employee year-end events and recreational parties with employees are 100 percent deductible. Realtor's open houses are considered promotion and are likewise 100 percent deductible. Meals served at sales or marketing seminars are 100 percent deductible.[18]

Travel agents would be another example of people who would fall into this category on some expenses. If you were a travel agent and went to various cities to check out the hotels, restaurants, accommodations, and meeting facilities, you would be able to deduct all your expenses and not be subject to the 50 percent rule. Obviously, it would be important to document that you send clients to these places on vacations, document who you met with (such as the director of catering or the convention service), document that you had made some appointments in advance to meet with these people, etc.

Tax law limits your maximum deduction to $25 for business gifts to any one person during the year.[19] This limitation applies to gifts of tangible personal property and not money,[20] and even worse, a husband and wife are deemed to be one taxpayer for purposes of the $25 limit.[21]

Note: Gifts of food items where the business owner, partner or company employee isn't present aren't deductible according to a recent IRS notice. If you want to deduct a meal with clients or prospects, a company employee or owner must be present during the meal discussion.

Example: Alan, a consultant, gives a client a housewarming gift of flowers and a giant vase that cost him $300. He may deduct only $25 of the cost of this business gift. Ugh!

One interesting exception is that gifts made to a business where there is no single person designated to receive or benefit from the gift have no limit.[22]

Example: I do a lot of programs for Tony Robbins' Wealth Mastery seminars. Every year I send to the marketing department and the production department of Robbins Research big vases of flowers that cost several hundred dollars each. Since they are sent to each department without mentioning any names, the entire cost of the baskets is deductible and not subject to the $25 limitation.

As a result of the tax simplification law (remember that this term means you have been shafted by Congress), gifts or meals are no longer allowed if you are not present.[23] You are entitled to a tax deduction for a business meal only if you are present during the meal.[24]

Without question, the most overlooked type of entertainment is home entertainment. This is just as deductible as having a business meal in a restaurant and in some cases even more deductible.

Your home is already deemed to be a setting conducive to a business discussion.[25] If you have a couple in your home for dinner, it's easy to have a one-on-one conversation. You do not need to spend more time trying to conduct business than you spend on entertaining your guests.[26] In fact, there's no time limit for the business discussion.

> **Strategy 5**
> Deduct your meals at home business presentations.

Example: Sam and Mary entertain Bob and Alice. Sam has a five-second discussion about getting referrals, and the party lasts four hours. Bob may deduct the cost of the party. There is no time limit to the business discussion.

Moreover, if you entertain at home and have only a few people for dinner, you probably won't spend more than $75 and thus won't need a receipt.

Author's tip: You have to discuss business to deduct any meals. Here's one suggestion that I give: Most people will start out the discussion with some variation of "How's business?" You should respond, "Business is unbelievable," because this response covers the state of your business either way! However, you need to add one other line, which is, "However, I never have enough business" or "I never have enough referrals" or "I never have enough clients." This is quick and to the point, and it suffices as an appropriate business discussion if it's clear that you're asking for business or referrals.

> **Hot Tip**
> Don't have all your home entertainment be $74.99!

Your home business meal deductions are secure when you discuss specific business with guests.[27] You don't even need to discuss business with your spouse or closely connected significant friends to deduct them too.[28] Keep the guest list small (fewer than 12 people). Then you can talk to everyone with whom you need to discuss business. With small groups, you can easily discuss business with everyone there.

Strategy 6
Give small
parties at home.

When you invite 12 people or more to your home, you will be hard-pressed to prove to the IRS that you had specific business discussions with everyone in attendance. Therefore, you must establish some other type of commercial motivation. It's not that you can't talk business with everyone and document this fact in your diary. It's just that it would be difficult to do.

One approach to this problem is to display products on the wall. If you entertain a group for the purpose of showing a display of your business products or services, commercial motivation generally is deemed to be clearly established.[29] When you combine the display of products with an invitation that invites the guests for a specific business reason, you greatly improve your chances for deductibility.[30] It is also best that you have little social or personal relationship with the guests—the less social the better.[31]

Strategy 7
Deduct meals
for large groups.

One note of caution if you want to deduct business meals incurred at home entertainment: Never, never combine a personal event with a business meal event. A birthday party for your 10-year-old with business guests in attendance won't cut the mustard with the IRS.[32] The bottom line is that home entertainment, especially when large groups are involved, is deductible only when you can firmly establish a business motive.[33]

Example: Wanda (I've changed the person's name for privacy reasons), a real estate professional, invited 100 people over to her home for cocktails to celebrate being in real estate 20 years. This establishes a business agenda for the party. At the party, she has a buffet with pictures of properties above the food. She then has her husband take a picture of people looking at the displays while they're getting their food. This establishes a clear business setting and motive. Finally, when she goes shopping, she obtains two receipts from the grocery store: one for the party food and one for the general household. She staples them together and labels which is which. She clearly would be allowed to deduct the entire cost of the party (multiplied by the 50 percent limitation).

Strategy 8
Give sales
seminars and
presentations in
your home.

Normally, food provided in your home as part of a business discussion is only 50 percent deductible, as with the general rule for meals deductions. However, food served at a seminar would be an exception to the rule—100 percent deductible.[34] In addition, there was a tax court decision[35] that noted that all food and beverages served to prospects are 100 percent deductible if provided at home during a sales presentation or sales seminar.

Example: Juan holds sales presentations in his home for his network marketing business. If Juan provides food and drinks, he may deduct 100 percent of the cost of this entertainment.

Author's note: The key to this 100 percent deduction is documentation. Again, you have to show the who, where, when, why, and how much of the entertainment, as discussed earlier. You should note in your diary or tax organizer who attended (or have your guests sign a register), the date, what was discussed, what was served, and the cost of the food.

The reasonable cost of providing social or recreational parties for employees, year-end holiday parties, or a summer outing that is primarily for employees and their families is 100 percent deductible.[36] You must, however, invite all employees. No discrimination is allowed.[37] Thus, if you have several workers and have a year-end celebration that they, their families, and you and your spouse attend, you may deduct the whole cost of the party. If it were just you and your spouse, it would not be deductible. The key is that the social outing be primarily for employees rather than for the owners and their families.

> **Strategy 9**
> Give parties for employees.

If you have any employees, you may provide lunches to your staff on a tax-free basis if you provide lunch for over half the employees and any one of the following conditions holds:[38]

> **Strategy 10**
> Provide lunches for employees.

1. There is a short lunch period[39] (generally no more than 45 minutes in length).
2. The employees are available for emergencies (such as ambulance services).[40]
3. There are insufficient eating facilities nearby.

Also, meals must be furnished on normal workdays.[41]

Sandy's note: Under the new law, it appears that these meals would be 50 percent deductible.

You deduct dues paid to business clubs when such payment is in the ordinary and necessary course of business.[42] The terms *ordinary* and *necessary* mean that the expenses are customary, usual or normal, and helpful or appropriate.[43] Dues to your local Chamber of Commerce almost always would be appropriate.[44] Dues paid to your professional societies, such as the Board of Realtors, Life Underwriters, enrolled agents societies, consultant societies, etc., are deductible.[45] Trade association dues also would be deductible if the association's purpose is the furthering of the business interests of its members.[46] Dues to community clubs organized to attract tourists and new members to your locality are deductible.[47] Dues to civic organizations such as the Rotary Club, Kiwanis, and Lions Club are deductible.[48]

> **Strategy 11**
> Deduct dues to business and civic organizations.

Author's note: A good tax tracker or diary that I would recommend is Taxbot. It not only requires what you need to be fully compliant but also is one of the few trackers that will read receipts and automatically insert most of the required questions. You can get Taxbot from the iphone app store or the Google play store for droids.

Country Club and Health Club Dues

As a result of tax simplification, Congress eliminated the deduction for country clubs and health clubs.[49] However, strange as it may seem, you can get a deduction for these kinds of clubs if the company reimburses the employees for the dues to the extent that they are used for business as a working-condition fringe benefit.[50]

Example: Cornell's consulting company provides Peter with a country club membership worth $20,000, which he does not record as compensation. If he substantiates that

60 percent of the time that he uses the club is for business, he may exclude 60 percent of the $20,000 cost of the club and be taxed on only $8,000. Cornell's company may deduct the entire cost of the membership. I should note that this would work for your employees regardless of what entity you conduct your business under and should work for you if you are incorporated.

Author's tip: The key here is documentation. You must show when you or your employee used the club and to what extent it was used to entertain prospects and discuss business. A tax diary or tax organizer is a necessity here. A little documentation goes a long way.

Author's tip: Regardless of the deductibility or nondeductibility of the club dues, any meal would be deductible (at 50 percent) if you discuss business during the meal. Again, the key is documentation and writing down the five elements of substantiation.

Summary

- **Strategy 1:** Discuss specific business when you eat—and document everything with the five elements of documentation—who, where, when, why, and how much.
- **Strategy 2:** Deduct for feeding and entertaining your spouse.
- **Strategy 3:** Avoid the Sutter rule.
- **Strategy 4:** Some entertainment can be deemed business promotion.
- **Strategy 5:** Deduct your meals at home business presentations.
- **Strategy 6:** Give small parties at home.
- **Strategy 7:** Deduct meals for large groups.
- **Strategy 8:** Give sales seminars and presentations in your home.
- **Strategy 9:** Give parties for employees.
- **Strategy 10:** Provide lunches for employees.
- **Strategy 11:** Deduct dues to business and civic organizations.

Notes

1. Section 1.274-5(c) of the Income Tax Regulations (ITR hereunder); IR 95-56; notice 05-50, 1995-42 IRB.
2. Notice 2018-76, 2018-42 IRB; IR 2018-195.
3. Section 274 (a) of the IRC; 1.274-2(c)(4) of the ITR and *J. Flaig v. Commissioner*, 47 TCM 1161.
4. Section 274 (a) of the IRC.
5. Section 1.274-2(f)(2)(i)(a) of the ITR.

6. Section 1.274-2(c)(7) of the ITR.

7. Ibid.

8. Section 1.274-5T(c) of the ITR.

9. Ibid.

10. Section 1.274-2(d)(3) of the ITR; *J. B. Walliser v. Commissioner*, 72 TC 433 (1979); *P.H. Leon v. Commissioner*, 37 TCM 1514 (1978).

11. Section 1.274-5T(c)(1) and (2) of the ITR.

12. Section 1.274-5T(c)(2) of the ITR.

13. Section 1.274-2(c)(7) of the ITR.

14. Section 274(l)(1)(B) of the IRC.

15. Section 1.274-2(d)(4) of the ITR; Revenue Ruling 2000-45, IRB 2000-41; 46 RIA Weekly Alert, No. 39 (9/21/2000).

16. Ibid.

17. Revenue Ruling 63-144, Q&A 31, 1963-2 C.B. 129; *Sutter v. Commissioner*, 21 TC 170 (1953), acq. 1954-1 C.B. 6.

18. Section 274 as amended by Tax Cuts and Jobs Act.

19. Section 274(b)(1) of the IRC.

20. Section 274(j)(3)(A) of the IRC.

21. Section 274(b)(2)(B) of the IRC.

22. Section 1.274-3(e)(2) of the ITR.

23. Section 274(K)(2) of the IRC.

24. Section 274(K)(1)(B) of the IRC.

25. Section 1.274-2(e)(2) of the ITR.

26. Section 1.274-2(f)(2) of the ITR.

27. Section 1.274-2(d)(4); Revenue Ruling 63-144, cited above, Q&A 26-28.

28. Ibid.

29. Section 1.274-2(c)(4) of the ITR.

30. Ibid.

31. *Steel v. Commissioner*, 28 TCM 1301 (1969).

32. Sections 1.274-2(c)(4) and 1.274-2(c)(7)(ii) of the ITR.

33. Section 1.274-2(c)(4) of the ITR.

34. Sections 274(n)(2)(A) and 274(e)(8) of the IRC.

35. *Robert Matlock v. Commissioner*, TC Memo 1992-324.

36. H. Rept, 99-842, P. II-28, Section 274(e)(4) of the IRC and Section 1.274-2(f)(2)(v) of the ITR.

37. Ibid.

38. Section 119(b)(4) of the IRC and Section 1.119-1(a)(2) of the ITR.

39. Section 1.119-1(a)(2)(ii)(b).

40. Section 1.119-1(a)(2)(ii).

41. Section 1.119-1(a)(2)(i) of the ITR.

42. Section 274(a)(2)(C) of the IRC.

43. Section 162(a) of the IRC and regulations thereunder.

44. Section 274(a)(2)(C) of the IRC.

45. Section 1.274-2(e)(3)(ii) of the ITR.

46. Section 1.274-2(e)(3)(ii) and 1.274-2(f)(2)(i) of the ITR.

47. Roland J. Hymel, Jr., 86-1 U.S. TC Section 9419 (5th Cir. 1986).

48. Section 1.274-2(a)2)(iii)(b) of the ITR.

49. Section 1.274-2(a)(2)(iii)(a) of the ITR.

50. Section 1.132-5(s) of the ITR.

3

How to Turn Your Vacation into a Tax-Deductible Write-Off

The politicians' promises of yesterday are the taxes of today.

—Mackenzie King

Read my lips, no new taxes.

—George H. W. Bush

I have no intention of raising taxes.

—Bill Clinton

A t my seminars people often ask whether they can deduct their meals while eating alone. The answer is yes, if you are on business travel, because that will allow a deduction for meals for each day that you are traveling on business. So, when are you traveling on business?

You are on business travel, according to the IRS, when you are traveling from home, overnight, or for a period of time sufficient to require sleep.[1] For example, assume that you live in Washington, DC, fly to New York City in the morning, and return that evening. You would not be deemed on business travel since you were not away from home overnight on

Chapter Overview
- Understand when you are on business travel.
- Understand the difference between business transportation and "on the road" expenses.
- Know how to deduct your spouse's or significant friend's expenses to any business convention and have the IRS bless those expenses.
- Know how you can maximize your business car usage with conventions travel, especially when you take family members with you on the trip.
- Understand the IRS dry cleaning rule.
- Learn how to avoid the congressional trap of taking courses on the wrong ships!
- Learn how to deduct the expenses for all weekends without doing any work on the weekends.

business. The IRS would classify this trip to New York as a non-travel trip. On this trip you would be allowed to deduct only your transportation costs of getting to the city.[2]

Although the IRS doesn't specifically state that you must sleep overnight on your business trip, for all practical purposes, this is usually required. You may be able to get around this if you take a daily trip to a job location for several weeks that might be 170 miles away, for example.[3] In this situation, even if you didn't sleep overnight somewhere, the IRS may deem this to be business travel. However, to save yourself any uncertainty or challenge, you are better off sleeping somewhere overnight.

Author's elaboration: I call this the "strange bed" rule. I encourage people who want to establish "business travel" status to stay overnight in a strange bed … conducting business. This can be a hotel, a friend's home, or a family member's home. The key is that you rarely stay there and that you are sleeping at your business location.

Notice, however, that it doesn't have to be in a hotel. If you choose to stay with friends or a relative, this would be "staying overnight," as long as you were on a business trip with a business motive. You should document in your tax organizer where you stayed and deduct any out-of-pocket expenses that you incurred.

I should note that there is no geographic limit to the business travel. For example, I gave a seminar in Gaithersburg, Maryland, that is about six minutes from my home. However, I stayed in the hotel the evening before the meeting to avoid potential car and traffic problems. I was considered to be on business travel.

I should note at this juncture that there is a lot of confusion between *transportation* expenses and *on-the-road* expenses. Many people and many accountants seem to combine this under one set of rules. However, they are treated differently; each category has its own separate rule base. It is possible to take a business trip where transportation expenses are not deductible but on-the-road expenses are deductible.

What are the differences? Transportation expenses are those costs that you incur in getting to and from your destination.[4] The actual cost of your airfare or car costs, if you drove to your destination, would come under this category. The on-the-road expenses include all costs necessary to sustain life while on your trip.[5] These expenses comprise lodging, meals, laundry, dry cleaning, and similar expenses.[6]

Author's tip: Not only are your dry cleaning and laundry expenses deductible while you are on business travel, but you can deduct the first laundry and dry cleaning expenses you incur when you get home, as long as your clothing was soiled on the business trip. You do not need to get your clothes dry-cleaned and laundered while away on the trip.[7]

The tax law rule is that, for every day you are on business travel, you may deduct 100 percent of your on-the-road expenses[8] but only 50 percent of your meal costs.[9] An example will illustrate this.

Example: Allison incurs the following on-the-road costs while on business travel:
$400 for hotels
$50 for dry cleaning
$20 in tips
$300 in food

She may deduct all of the hotels, dry cleaning, and tips but only $150 of the meal costs, which are limited to 50 percent.

You may *not*, however, deduct the cost of any entertainment in which there was no business motive or prospecting.[10] Thus, if you were to go to a movie alone while on the business trip, the movie would not be deductible. (Darn!)

Moreover, the IRS has a convenient ruling for travel-related receipts that I mentioned in a previous chapter. The IRS has stated[11] that you don't need receipts for travel if the expenditure is less than $75 per expense.

Example: Kim spends the following on her business trip:
$6.00 for drinks on the plane
$4.00 in skycap tips
$6.95 for breakfast
$12.00 for lunch
$50.00 for a fabulous dinner
$300.00 for airfare

She would only need to keep a receipt for the airfare, which is the only expense that was $75 or more. She would, however, need to have to document these expenses in some diary or tax organizer.

Strategies to Increase Travel Deductions and Add More Fun

Hire your spouse or significant friend. If you want to take trips with your spouse or significant other and deduct the travel expenses for both of you, you must have a legitimate business reason for bringing along that person.[12] If he or she is in an entirely different business than you, taking your spouse to one of your business conventions would not result in tax deductions for your spouse. He or she would need to have a business reason for being on the trip, independent of being your spouse.

If you want to take your spouse or significant friend on a business trip or to a convention, you can do so if he or she is licensed in your business (such as real estate or securities or insurance) or—and you will like this—can make money for you at the convention! But what does "make money for you" at the convention or on the business trip mean?

Interestingly, Congress actually defined what this means. Starting in 1994:

- Your spouse or significant friend must be a bona fide employee of your business, and
- Your spouse or significant friend must be traveling for a bona fide business purpose, and
- The expense would otherwise be deductible.

Let's examine what all this means to you. If your spouse helps in marketing, computer work, or management of your business, it certainly would be important to take him or her to a convention where courses were given in these areas. If your spouse is your accountant, on the other hand, you would not be able to take him or her to the convention unless there were some programs relating to what he or she does, such as tax planning.

Take your business car for family travel. Tax law allows you to deduct the cost of your business trip.[13] If you travel with nonbusiness family members, you are allowed to deduct the cost that you would have incurred had you taken the trip alone.[14] Since traveling with a full car costs no more than traveling alone, all of your business car expenses are deductible, even if you have nonbusiness passengers. What this means is that you could deduct your gas and tolls and increase your business mileage for your car.

Author's tip: For consultants and small business owners who normally don't have a lot of business mileage on their vehicles (such as medical or legal professionals), this point of taking your car to a convention or out-of-town seminars becomes crucial. This one trip could increase your business use to a significant extent, which would allow you to depreciate a large portion of your vehicle and deduct a larger portion of some big expenses, such as insurance and repairs. As we will discuss in Chapter 5, your deduction for various car expenses is a ratio of your business mileage to your total mileage. One out-of-town business trip could make a big difference.

Lodging and meal expenses. One common question I get concerns lodging and meals. If you take someone on the trip, your food costs will be more and your room costs may be more than what you would have spent had you gone alone. The rule is that you deduct all of your costs as if you had taken the trip alone.[15] Thus, if a motel costs $100 for one occupant and $120 for the family, you deduct $100. The $20 difference is a personal, nondeductible expense. What I recommend for documentation is either to ask the hotel what the single room rate would be or to remove the rate card from behind the door. (If you are ever in a room where the rate card is missing, I probably stayed in that room!)

Drive 300 miles a day toward your business destination. The federal government reimburses IRS employees a full day's per diem for each 300 miles of travel.[16] Take advantage of this rule. Plan your trips to cover 300 miles a day in direct route to your business destination. Each such day will count as a full business day and also allow you to deduct your on-the-road expenses for the day. This 300-mile rule also will determine the maximum amount of travel days that IRS will allow with your car. You would divide the amount of mileage for your trip by 300 and round up if there is a fraction. This will determine the maximum number of travel days allowed.

Example: Tom drives 800 miles to a convention in Orlando, Florida. He takes his time in seeing the sights and takes 14 days to go the 800 miles. The IRS will allow only three business days as travel days (800/300).

Take courses on U.S. cruise ships. There are a lot of organizations recently that are encouraging people to take courses on cruise ships with the promise of deductibility of those courses. Are all these claims true? The answer is clear-cut: it depends!

If you're looking for a vacation cruise ship subsidy, this is it—but only if you meet the four requirements below. You, and possibly your spouse, can deduct up to $2,000 each year for attending cruise ship conventions directly related to your business, provided:[17]

- The cruise ship is a registered U.S. vessel.
- All ports of call are in the U.S. or U.S. possessions.
- You submit two supporting statements with your tax return. One statement signed by you should give the days of transportation, number of hours of the trip, and the program of the scheduled business activity. In addition, you need a statement signed by an officer or official of the course or ship showing the number of hours of the business seminar and how many hours you attended.
- More than 50 percent of your total days should be spent on business. Thus, if the course is for one day but the cruise is for 14 days, you would not get a deduction for the cruise. See the discussion below on transportation.

Make weekends deductible. How would you like to treat Saturday and Sunday as business days without ever working on the weekend? Believe it or not, you can treat weekends as business days—if you know what you are doing.

Generally, because it's so attractive, foreign travel has stricter rules than domestic travel.[18] If you meet these rules, you will satisfy any IRS challenge and lock in your travel deductions. I will, therefore, focus on the foreign rules for deducting travel expenses, since this will protect you when traveling both in the U.S. and abroad.

When you're traveling to a foreign destination, you may count as business days all weekends and legal holidays that fall between business meeting days.[19] Thus, you want to sandwich your weekend days and/or holidays between business days. This is important to you for two reasons:

- You deduct all the on-the-road expenses for the weekend and holidays.[20]
- You add these days for purposes of determining if your transportation expenses are deductible.

Example: Thelma leaves for a business meeting in Hawaii on Thursday with a business meeting on both Friday and Monday and returns home on the following Tuesday night. Saturday and Sunday would be considered business days since they are sandwiched in between business days (Friday and Monday).

Author's note: If Friday or Monday is a federal holiday, you can sandwich the weekend and the holiday between business days. Thus, if the holiday is on a Monday, you would set up meetings on Friday and Tuesday, thus sandwiching in three days without doing any work on those three days. They would all be deemed business days for the on-the-road expenses and for transportation. We really have some great tax laws; it's just that most people aren't aware of them!

A second approach to deducting weekends surprisingly comes from an unlikely source—the IRS! In a private ruling,[21] the IRS allowed Saturday and Sunday to be considered business days if the costs of staying over were less than the savings on airfare of traveling after Saturday, which is usually the case. The following example will illustrate this point.

Example: Thelma leaves for a convention in Hawaii on Sunday and would have returned home on Thursday, which would have cost her $1,200. If, however, she stays over in Hawaii Friday and Saturday and leaves on Sunday, her cost would be $400 (thus saving $800). As long as her food and lodging for Friday and Saturday and Sunday are less than $800, she may count Friday, Saturday, and Sunday as business days. She may also count as business days each convention day and each travel day.

Count travel days as business days. This is an idea most people often overlook. Days in transit are considered business days provided that the travel to your business destination is by reasonably direct route and does not involve substantial nonbusiness diversions.[22] Remember that when a day is classified as a business day, you can deduct all your on-the-road costs for that day and the day is counted toward satisfying the business trip test for transportation, which will be discussed later.

Example: Sam leaves New York for a convention in Vancouver, BC, on Thursday. He has a seminar on Friday and sets up referral meetings on Monday with various military base personnel. On Tuesday he leaves to return to New York; however, due to the time zone change, he doesn't arrive until Wednesday. Thursday is a business day (travel). Friday is a business day (seminar). Saturday and Sundays are business days because they were sandwiched between business days. Monday was a business day because it was a workday. Tuesday and Wednesday are business days due to being travel days.

Although you need to take a reasonably direct route, this requirement does not affect the mode of transportation that you use. Thus, you may take the trip by automobile, train, plane, or boat.[23] Thus, even if flying to your Hawaii destination would have cost only $400, you could take a boat to Hawaii that costs $1,400. The cost is not relevant.

There is, however, a special rule for luxury boats. The allowable deduction for cruise ships may not exceed twice the highest amount generally allowable per day to a low-ranking White House employee traveling in the U.S. multiplied by the number of days on the ship.[24] In addition, if you are simply using the cruise ship as a means of transportation to your business appointment or seminar, then it does not have to be a U.S. ship and you don't need any signed statements, as you would if you took a course on the ship.[25]

Note: Normally the highest federal per diem rate with the lower 48 states is found in Manhattan; however, this can change based on the time of the year changes from year to year. You need to do a search of per diem rates or ask your tax professional.

Author's note: It amazes me that someone would even bother to think about trivial guidelines like this. So much for tax simplification!

Example: You take a six-day cruise from New York City to London on the Queen Mary 2. Your deduction may not exceed twice the highest federal per diem rate. If the highest federal per diem rate is $366, your deduction for a six-day trip may not exceed $4,392 per person ($732 per day × six days).

Combine some fun with a business day without losing any deduction. If your presence is required at a particular place for a specific and bona fide business purpose, that day is counted as a business day, even if your presence is required for only part of the day.[26] This applies even if you spend more time sightseeing during normal working hours than participating in business activities.[27] Thus, if you were to deliver a document to a client in Washington, DC, or attend a meeting that lasted 30 minutes, you could spend the rest of the time having fun in Washington. The key is to set up in advance at least one business appointment.

Attend a convention or a seminar. If a convention or seminar has at least six hours of scheduled business activities during the day and you attend at least two-thirds of those activities, your day is considered a business day.[28] I call this the "four hour and one minute rule." Thus, if you spend the majority of the working hours (generally four hours and one minute) pursuing your trade or business by attending a convention or seminar, the day is counted as a business day.

When you are prevented from engaging in the conduct of your trade or business due to circumstances beyond your control, the day is still counted as a business day, even if you spend the day playing in the sand and enjoying the sun.[29]

Example: Todd was meeting a prospect in Hawaii with whom he had made an appointment in advance. If the prospect gets sick and cancels the meeting while Todd is in Hawaii, the entire day would still be deemed a business day. The same result would occur if Todd was expecting to fly home but the airline cancelled the flight because of mechanical difficulties and scheduled him to fly home the next day.

Caretake your rental property. Necessary travel to caretake your rental property is deductible.[30] The key is that it must be necessary, which is determined by the facts and circumstances. If you collect the rents and actively participate in the day-to-day operations of the rental property, you will obviously have to take some trips to make sure that the property is in good condition. You will also have to check on rents in the area, make repairs, and speak with certain vendors.

Even if you engage a management company to look after the property, you must check on their work. Are they maintaining the property? Is the rent reasonable? How do the tenants feel about the management company, and how does the company feel about the tenants? It could take several days to get the answers to all these questions and would certainly justify your trip. The key, again, is to document in your tax diary or tax organizer what you did and with whom you met.

If you spend any days repairing and maintaining the property on a full-time basis, those days would be deemed business days and not personal days.[31] Moreover, even if people related to you use the property for recreation on the same day, the day is not a personal day.[32]

 Visit colleagues and improve your skills and get referrals. The rationale is that you can learn new business skills from your colleagues. Therefore, you can design combined business and pleasure trips to make the rules work for you. Again, the key is to make appointments in advance and document them (with whom did you meet and for how long?). In addition, give a short description of the business discussion, such as "discussed sales or marketing techniques."

Example: You live in Washington, DC, and take a trip to Dallas, Phoenix, San Francisco, Denver, Minneapolis, and Pittsburgh. At each location, you spend a few days visiting with colleagues to learn new business skills or attempting to get referrals for any prospects who move to Washington, DC. You take the trip by automobile and drive at least 300 miles each or more each day toward the next visit. Assuming that you made no side trips for pleasure, all the days would be business days. You would deduct all of your on-the-road expenses and all days would be business days for the transportation deduction.

 Get educated out of town. Most people mistakenly believe that if a course is offered in your hometown it would be unreasonable to take the same course elsewhere, such as Hawaii. The fact is that you are allowed deductions for travel to and from educational facilities, meetings, seminars, and conventions that improve your business—regardless of where the events are held.[33] Thus, if the exact same seminar is held both in your hometown and at a nice out-of-town resort, there is no requirement that you stay at home. At the Tax Reduction Institute, we always allow our participants to enroll in courses taken anywhere in the country or to transfer to any course and even encourage exotic locations. Famed speaker Tony Robbins takes this concept one step further: most of his courses and seminars are in Hawaii, Las Vegas, Florida, and Anaheim, California (where Disneyland is located). Nice planning, Tony!

 Hunt for a job anywhere in the U.S. The IRS allows deductions for all expenses directly related to a search for employment in the same trade or business. It makes no difference if the search is successful or unsuccessful.[34]

Author's note: Do not take all your job-hunting trips to the same place every year! Also, to audit-proof a trip, you need documentation of your intention to search for a job *prior* to your trip. You should maintain in your files correspondence before the trip. In addition, you should maintain in your tax organizer or diary correspondence after the trip as to whom you met, when you met them, how long the meeting lasted, and a brief description of the discussion.

Maximize your deductions for travel in the U.S. As was discussed, you are allowed to deduct on-the-road expenses for each day that you are on "business travel status." Transportation, however, has a completely separate set of rules, as illustrated by the flowchart in Figure 3-1.

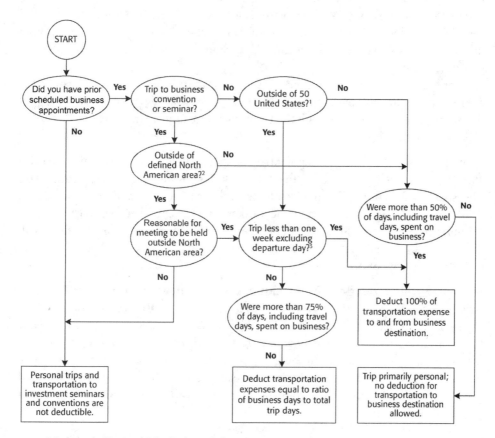

1. Includes the District of Columbia but excludes U.S. possessions and territories.
2. Trip outside Canada, Mexico, Jamaica, Barbados, Grenada, the U.S., its possessions, the Trust Territory of the Pacific, the Marshall Islands, the Federated States of Micronesia, Jarvis Island, Johnston Island, Kingman Reef, Costa Rica, Dominica, Dominican Republic, Guyana, Honduras, Saint Lucia, Trinidad, Tobago, and Palau. See Section 274(b)(3) and Rev. Rul. 87-95, 1987-2 C.B. 79 and Rul 94-56, 1994-36 IRB.
3. Assuming one deductible business day during the trip; Reg.§ 1.274-4(c).

Figure 3-1. Flowchart for deducting transportation expenses when trip combines business with pleasure.

As I discuss the rules, I encourage you to follow along on the flowchart. Understanding this chart will enable you to determine exactly how many days must be business days for you to deduct all of your transportation.

It is essential that your primary purpose of the trip be for business.[35] Thus, you *must* have clear business intent before you leave for the trip. This is a crucial point that has caused a great deal of deductions to be lost without proper planning. You should document your intent by sending letters to confirm your appointments or keep copies of e-mails. You don't need to have all your appointments set up in advance, but at least a few must be prearranged.

Example: Connie is a network marketing consultant out of Sacramento, California. She wants to go to New York. She advertises for prospects in *The New York Times* and keeps a copy of the ad. She also sends confirming letters to her appointments, noting the day, time, and place for the meeting. This should be more than enough to satisfy the "intent" test.

For trips within the U.S., your primary purpose must be for business. Although the courts and the IRS have based this on "facts and circumstances,"[36] most cases interpret this to mean that you spend more than one-half your time attending to business and appointments.[37]

Example: Jim meets with some potential clients or distributors in Hawaii on Friday and Monday and returns home the following Friday. If he travels to Hawaii on Thursday, six days out of the nine would be business (Thursday and Friday for travel, Friday and Monday for work, and the weekend sandwiched between business days counts as business days). Since six out of nine is more than one-half, Jim may deduct all of his travel to Hawaii. However, because he has only six business days, he may deduct only those six days of his on-the-road expenses.

Maximize your deductions for foreign travel. Like most things in tax law, there is very little simplification. Foreign travel has its own rules that make it different from domestic travel. The general rule is that when you leave the U.S., you can deduct your transportation as a ratio of business days to total days.[38] Thus, if you take a 13-day trip of which 8 were deemed business days, 8/13ths of your transportation would be deductible. There are, however, two notable exceptions to this rule where you would be able to deduct 100 percent of your transportation without spending 100 percent of your days on business.

The first exception is known as the one-week loophole.[39] You'll like this! Congress allows a 100 percent deduction for transportation even if you work on business only one or two days *if* you are back home within one week. Thus, if you have a meeting in London on Monday and you leave for that meeting the previous Sunday, you can deduct all of your transportation if you are back home by Saturday. If you leave on Saturday, you must be back home by Friday. Remember: this applies only to foreign trips and you must be home within one week to qualify for this exception.

The second exception to the general rule for foreign travel is if your total business days equal or exceed 75 percent of the total days away from home, you may deduct 100 percent of your transportation.[40]

Example: Sue has some distributors in Italy. She spends 12 days away from home and meets with her distributors or provides seminars for them or their customers for eight days. If she has two travel days, she may deduct 100 percent of her transportation under this exception because she spent 75 percent or more of her days on business (eight work days and two travel days).

Maximize your seminar and convention travel. The final type of trip that has its own rules is seminar and convention travel. As with the general rule for domestic travel, you can deduct a percentage of your transportation costs based on the ratio of business days to the total days.[41] However, if you travel outside of what is defined as "the North American area," the rules are a lot stricter. You must have a reasonable basis for being at those conventions,[42] which is a much tougher standard than for domestic conventions or seminars or going within the North American area.

This North American area comprises the U.S. and its possessions, the Trust Territory of the Pacific Islands, Canada, and Mexico. Puerto Rico is considered a U.S. possession and thus is within the North American area.[43] In addition, the U.S., as a result of treaties, has added the Caribbean Basin countries to this area.[44] These countries are Barbados, Bermuda, Dominica, the Dominican Republic, Grenada, Guyana, Honduras, Jamaica, Trinidad and Tobago, Saint Lucia, and Costa Rica. (There must have been some members of Congress who wanted to visit these countries!)

Example: Carol and Nick attend a convention for U.S. makeup artists. If the convention is held in the defined North American area, it would be deductible; however, if held outside this area, it probably would not be deductible.

Author's note: If you are attending a convention or seminar outside of the defined North American area, you must have a strong reason for being there. Thus, for example, if you're a lawyer who deals in international law, you normally can't take a seminar or attend a convention in France. If, however, a seminar in France covers some specialized French law topic to which your practice relates and you can't get this training anywhere within the defined North American area, you could probably deduct the seminar in France.

Just to get you used to using the flowchart, we'll start off with the first question: "Was it a business trip?" If you didn't have business intent before you left for the trip, you would get no transportation deduction.

Let's use some examples to pull all these rules together and to get you to use the flowchart.

Example: Sam takes a 10-day trip to San Diego for a convention. The convention lasts five days, but he also has two travel (business) days. Thus, there are seven business days out of 10. It was a business trip. We proceed to the box, "Trip to business convention or seminar?" The answer would be yes. The next box asks, "Outside of the defined North American area?" The answer would be no, since San Diego is within that area.

The next box asks, "Were more than 50% of the total days, including travel days, spent on business?" The answer would be yes (seven business days out of 10). Thus, Sam can deduct 100 percent of his transportation. In addition, because he has seven business days, he can deduct seven days of on-the-road expenses.

Author's note: If this trip were outside the area, such as France, he would have to have a good reason to be there for his business.

Example: Sam wants to set up a distributor network in Hawaii. He spends three days meeting with people and two travel days out of a 14-day trip. How much of his transportation can he deduct? Let's examine the flowchart. Was it a business trip? The answer would be yes. The next box asks, "Trip to business convention or seminar?" This would be no, since he's meeting prospects and not attending a seminar or convention. The next block asks, was the trip "Outside of 50 United States?" Last time I looked, Hawaii was clearly a state; thus, the answer would be no. The next block asks, "Were *more* than 50% of the days, including travel days, spent on business?" Is 5 out of 14 total days more than 50 percent? The answer would be no: Sam would get no deduction for transportation! He did, however, have five business days and would be able to deduct five days' worth of on-the-road expenses. Here is a good example of being able to deduct on-the-road expenses but not any transportation costs. He would have to have at least three more business days to deduct the whole transportation, with eight business days out of 14, which is more than half. I hope you finally understand how useful this flowchart is and hope that you can use it. Feel free to play around with it and try various types of trips.

Documentation and Audit-Proof Techniques

As I mentioned before, there is a great receipt rule: you do not need receipts for any travel expenses under $75 per expense.[45] Lodging, however, is an exception. If you pay for any lodging, you must get a receipt.[46] If you do not keep a good diary or tax organizer, you will need receipts for any travel expenses, even for those under $75. You may not simply make approximations while traveling.

Example: Janet stays in the Bates Motel, where the cost was only $22. (Apparently she hasn't seen the movie *Psycho*.) She would need a receipt, since the expense is for lodging.

Author's note: Frequently, to save money on the trip, people stay with their friends or relatives. Unless you pay them for lodging, which isn't a bad idea, you wouldn't need a receipt, since you get no lodging deduction when you don't pay anything. You can, however, deduct on-the-road expenses that you incur. In addition, as I suggested, it might be wise to pay your relative a lodging fee. The IRS and Congress have a provision that anyone who receives less than two weeks of rent does not have to report this rent as income,[47] but you would still get a deduction for the rent.

Example: Sue attends a convention in Phoenix, but stays with her son while she is there. If she pays her son $100 per day for her week's stay, she can deduct the full $700 and her son does not report this $700 as income. What a great country!

The IRS allows self-employed taxpayers to use their per diem rates for meals and incidental expenses without having to keep receipts.[48] This amount varies generally between $30 and $46 per day, depending on location.[49] The IRS also has a per diem for lodging, but it can't be used for self-employed individuals.[50]

Author's note: Although it may seem "nice" of the IRS to not require receipts for your meals and incidental expenses and give you a daily deduction of between $39 and $64, however, it really isn't recommended to use this method. Frankly, if you hear that something is the IRS method, would you think that it's good for you? You don't need receipts anyway, if the expense is under $75 per item! Thus, the IRS is, in effect, giving you "snow in the winter."

The travel expense documentation rules are easily summarized. Either write down the expense properly on the day it happens or lose it. Congress continually reemphasizes that the IRS is not to use or allow approximations of travel expenses.[51] In addition, when you have the right documentation in a daily log, diary, or tax organizer, the IRS spends much less time looking at your records.

You are to keep your on-the-road expenses separate from your transportation expenses. As a reminder, on-the-road expenses are deductible for a business day[52] and transportation expenses are deductible for a business trip.[53]

In addition, as explained above, in order to deduct 100 percent of transportation costs, your transportation must meet one of three tests:

- 51/49 test for U.S. trips, conventions, and seminars (more days business than personal)
- 76/24 test for foreign travel (more than 76 percent of your days for business)
- less than one week test for foreign travel

Thus, what type of documentation do you need to audit-proof your travel? To deduct your travel expenses, your records must prove all of the following:[54]

- The amount that you spend daily for such things as transportation, meals, and lodging
- The dates of your departure and return home from each trip and the number of days spent on business while away from home
- Where you traveled, described by name of city, town, or similar designation
- Why you traveled, including the business reason for your travel or the business benefit derived or expected to be gained (as specific as possible)

Author's note: Although not specifically required by the Internal Revenue Code, it would be important to also document preexisting business intent for the trip. You can solidify this proof with copies of correspondence sent to prospects, e-mails, and documented phone calls. The key is to have business intent by making appointments in advance of the trip. Simply knocking on doors and giving out your card won't work.

Keep a Good Diary/Tracker

The Internal Revenue Code and IRS regulations both require that travel expenditures be recorded "at or near the time" that the expenses are incurred.[55] IRS agents are trained to require you to have contemporaneous records, since they have a "high degree of credibility" not present with respect to a subsequent statement when you generally lack adequate recall.[56]

In short, if you make your appointments in advance, have enough business days to satisfy the transportation tests noted on the flowchart found on page 29, and keep the right documentation with a tax diary or tax organizer, you will never have to fear an IRS audit on travel and will generate thousands of dollars in deductions that you probably weren't taking before you read this book.

Summary

- Know what the IRS considers "business travel." Use strategies to increase your travel deductions and add more fun:
  - Hire your spouse or significant friend.
  - Take your business car for family travel.
  - Track your lodging and meal expenses.
  - Drive 300 miles a day toward your business destination.
  - Take courses on U.S. cruise ships.
  - Make your weekends deductible.
  - Count travel days as business days.
  - Combine some fun with a business day without losing any deduction.
  - Attend a convention or a seminar.
  - Caretake your rental property.
  - Visit colleagues and improve your skills and get referrals.
  - Get educated out of town.
  - Hunt for a job anywhere in the U.S.
  - Maximize your deductions for travel in the U.S. and abroad.
  - Maximize your seminar and convention travel.
  - Know about documentation and audit-proof techniques.
  - Keep a good diary.

Notes

1. *U.S. v. Correll*, 389 U.S. 299 (1967); Revenue Ruling 54-407, 1954-2 CB 75, superseded in part by Revenue Ruling 75-432, 1975-2 CB 60; Revenue Ruling 75-170, 1975-1 C.B. 60.
2. *K. Waters*, 12 TC 414, Dec. 16,873; *C.M. Scott*, 110 F.Supp. 819.
3. Ibid.
4. Sections 162(a)(2) and 62(2)(B) of the IRC; section 1.162-2 of the ITR.
5. Ibid.
6. Ibid.

7. Section 1.162-2 of the ITR and IRS Pub 463. See also CCH Federal Tax Service Section G 8:41 and Revenue Ruling 63-145, 1963-2 C.B. 86.

8. Ibid.

9. Section 274(n)(1) of the IRC.

10. *Clarke Fashions, Inc. v. Commissioner*, 20 TCM 589, Dec. 24,812(M), T.C. Memo, 1961-121.

11. Sections 1.274-5° and 1.274-5T(c)(2)(iii) of ITR; IR 95-56, Notice 95-50, 1995-42 IRB.

12. *Giordano v. Commissioner*, 36 TCM 430 (1977); *Howard v. Commissioner*, 41 TCM 1554 (1981). See also section 274(m) of the IRC.

13. Section 162(a)(2) of the IRC and section 1.162-1 of the ITR.

14. Revenue Ruling 56-168, 1956-1 C.B. 93; Section 1.162-2(c) of the ITR.

15. Ibid.

16. *IRS Manual*, Handbook HB 1763 314 (4).

17. Section 274(h)(2) of the IRC.

18. Sections 274(c)(1) and 274(c)(2) of the ITR; Section 1.274-4(d) and 1.162-2(b) of the ITR.

19. Section 1.274-4(d)(2)(v) of the ITR.

20. Section 1.162-2(a) and (b)(1) of the ITR.

21. Private Letter Ruling 9237014.

22. Section 1.274-4(d)(2)(i) of the ITR.

23. Ibid. and IRS Publication 463.

24. Section 274(m)(1)(A) of the IRC.

25. Ibid.

26. Section 1.274-2(d) of the ITR.

27. Ibid.

28. Sections 1.274-4(d)(2)(iii) and 1.162-2(b)(1) of the ITR.

29. Section 1.274-4(d)(2)(iv) of the ITR.

30. Section 162(a)(2) of the IRC. See also *J.S. Kopunek*, 54 TCM 239, Dec. 44,136(M), T.C. Memo 1987-417.

31. IRS Publication 17.

32. Ibid.

33. Section 274(h)(1) of the IRC.

34. Revenue Ruling 75-120 1975-1 CB 55.

35. *C. Harris*, 37 TCM 1370 (1978); *P.P. Irwin v. Commissioner*, 72 TCM 1148.

36. Section 1.162-2(b)(1) of the ITR.

37. Section 1.162-2(b)(2) of the ITR and *K.E. Fairey v. Commissioner*, 43 TCM 1169 (1982); *A.F. Habeeb v. Commissioner*, 35 TCM 1134 (1976).

38. Section 274(c)(1) of the IRC.

39. Section 274(c)(2)(A) of the IRC.

40. Section 274(c)(2)(B) of the IRC.

41. Section 1.162-2(d) of the ITR and Section 274(h) of the IRC.

42. Section 274(h) of the IRC.

43. Revenue Ruling 94-56, 1994-2 CB 37.

44. Sections 274(h)(3)(A), 274(h)(6)(B), and 274(h)(6)(A) and Ibid.

45. See footnote 11.

46. Section 274(d)(1) of the IRC.

47. IRS Publication 527.

48. Section 1.274-5(j)(1) of the ITR; Revenue Procedure 2000-39, 2000-41 IRB 340; Revenue Procedure 2001-3, 2001-1 IRB 11.

49. Ibid.

50. *J.L. Christian*, 80 TCM 902 (2000); *P.H. Duncan*, 80 TCM 283 (2000).

51. Section 274(d) of the IRC.

52. Section 1.162-2(a) of the ITR.
53. Ibid.
54. Section 274(d) of the IRC.
55. Section 1.274-5(c)(1) of the ITR.
56. Ibid.

4

Income Shifting and Income Splitting: One of the Greatest Single Wealth-Building Secrets

The only time that the average child is as good as gold is April 15.

—Ivern Boyett

There's nothing wrong with the younger generation that becoming taxpayers won't cure.

—Dan Bennett

This chapter is about income shifting. It's what the wealthy know that you don't. Who is going to benefit from this chapter? Anyone who is married or who is single with children, whether they are adult or small children, or who has friends will benefit. This should cover everyone.

Hire Your Spouse in Your Business and Save a Bundle!

Whenever you hire a spouse, you have to take out Social Security.[1] Thus the key here is to pay your spouse minimum wage and give as many tax-free fringe benefits as possible.

Chapter Overview
- Know how to hire your spouse.
- Find out how to deduct all medical expenses and insurance premiums for your family.
- Learn how to deduct the equivalent of your children's education and weddings.
- Know how to audit-proof relatives' wages against the IRS.
- Discover the one strategy that could reduce the IRS treasury by over $2 trillion if everyone in the country knew about it.
- Learn about the Botkin Trust and get a double deduction for all your equipment. (No kidding!)
- Learn about the number-one financial planning strategy among physicians: the sale-leaseback.
- Learn how to completely deduct the cost of buildings as well as the underlying land.

Thus let's discuss some of the tax-free fringe benefits. (There will be a much greater discussion in Chapter 13.)

The main benefit of hiring your spouse is to enable you to deduct medical expenses that ordinarily would not be deductible unless they exceeded a high threshold amount[2] of 7.5 percent of your adjusted gross income.[3] [*Adjusted gross income* means your salary, pensions, net rents (net of rental deductions), and net income from businesses minus certain deductions, such as moving and pension contributions.] Thus, if your adjusted gross income is $50,000, you can deduct only medical and dental expenses in excess of $3,750. If you're making $100,000, this figure would be $7,500. All this was a result of various tax reform and "tax simplification" bills.

Despite these rules, how would you like to be able to potentially deduct all your medical expenses without any threshold?

Sadly, self-employed people normally are not allowed to be covered under this plan.[4] However, where there's a will, there's a lawyer. You can be an exception to the "normal rules" either by hiring your spouse or by forming a regular corporation and creating a self-insured medical plan in addition to your regular medical insurance. It will cover the holes that your policy doesn't cover, such as deductibles, coinsurance, braces, dental, mileage to and from the doctor, hearing aids, and nontraditional forms of medicine such as chiropractic and acupuncture.

The Internal Revenue Service (IRS) allows a medical reimbursement plan for even one employee.[5] In addition, the IRS was even more generous when it ruled that you could hire your wife and cover your family and yourself under the self-insured medical reimbursement plan.[6] Thus, if your only employee is your spouse, you still can qualify for a medical reimbursement plan.

You, as a sole proprietor, can pay for medical expenses that the insurance policy doesn't cover for your employees and their families if they *legitimately* work in the business. This would be in addition to any medical insurance that you would have and would cover expenses that are *not* covered by insurance.[7]

You even have full control of the design of this plan and can make it as broad or as narrow as you wish. For example, you can cover such expenses as deductibles, coinsurance, braces and dental, mileage to and from the doctor, preexisting conditions, routine physicals, psychiatric treatment, and nontraditional medicine such as acupuncture, chiropractic, etc. that are not covered by insurance. Your company would reimburse you and your family for all these out-of-pocket expenses.

You can get around this problem with hiring your spouse in your business and having him or her elect family coverage. In this way, you are deducting the medical expenses not as employee fringe benefits.

Here are the steps required to set up a self-insured medical reimbursement plan:

- If you're married and your business is a sole proprietorship or a limited-liability corporation, hire your spouse. If you're not married, form a regular corporation and have the corporation approve the plan in the board of directors' minutes.
- Have the self-insured medical reimbursement plan drafted.

- If you've hired your spouse, make him or her the primary insured on the plan, and elect family coverage, which means that you will be covering yourself and the kids.
- Either pay the doctor or dentist directly or reimburse the family member for any medical expense incurred. The bottom line is that you get a deduction, and your family gets the money tax-free!
- Keep the plan in existence for at least three years.
- The IRS has taken the position that payments made to a self-insured medical plan are subject to reasonable compensation. This means that the total salary and payout under the plan must be reasonable for the hours and work performed. Meet with your accountant to have a yearly per-employee maximum payout from the plan.

Hot Tip
How Self-Employed Taxpayers Can Use the Medical Reimbursement Plan.

Author's note: If you're the sole stockholder in your corporation, you shouldn't have any problems getting this plan approved, should you? In addition, this tax strategy can be instituted for a sole proprietorship or a limited-liability corporation. However, if you own more than 2 percent of an S corporation's stock or are a partnership, you will not be able to benefit greatly from the self-insured medical reimbursement plan. Any reimbursements made to you will be included in your taxable income.[8] This also applies to partners in a partnership.[9]

In addition, the self-insured medical reimbursement plan is only for expenses incurred after implementation of the plan.[10]

Example: Ann incurred some medical and dental expenses in 2018. She also has some upcoming medical expenses in 2019. If she were to set up the plan in January 2019, she may benefit from the plan only for expenses incurred after the plan went into effect, which is 2019.

Author's note: S corporations get most of the benefits provided to sole proprietorships, which will be discussed in later chapters. Only owners of more than 2 percent of the S corporation's stock and partners in a partnership don't get the benefits of the medical reimbursements.

Note: Keep all receipts for medical expenses that will be reimbursed.[11]

Sandy's Tip: You should generally use a good fiduciary to establish and operate a health reimbursement plan. The charges for managing the plan and for providing you the plan are very, low especially considering that the benefits can result in tens of thousands in a year. To find out about recommened fiduciaries and to get more information on this, go to HRA.Taxbot.com.

Discrimination Requirements for a Self-Insured Medical Reimbursement Plan

A self-insured medical reimbursement plan has one drawback: It must not discriminate in favor of the owners or highly compensated employees. In addition, you must cover all full-time employees.[12] Thus there are three key questions:

- What constitutes "discrimination"?

- Who are "highly compensated employees"?
- Who are "full-time employees"?

These are good questions and I am glad that you asked them.

The definition of discrimination seems complicated, but it's really easy to understand it and avoid discrimination. A plan is deemed discriminatory *unless*[13]

- it covers 70 percent or more of all employees, or
- 70 percent or more of all employees are eligible to participate and 80 percent of those eligible actually participate, or
- the IRS finds eligibility nondiscriminatory based on the facts and circumstances.

Example: David has 10 employees, but only 5 are full-time workers. To avoid discrimination, David must cover at least 7 of his workers or make at least 7 workers eligible.

Author's note: You can worry yourself and your accountant about all these statistics, or you can do what I did with my corporation, which is to cover all full-time employees. This eliminates any problems.

Example: Tom hires Carey, who is both his wife and only full-time worker, in his self-employed business. Tom sets up a medical reimbursement plan covering all full-time employees' medical expenses that aren't covered by insurance and elects family coverage. Tom may deduct all medical expenses covered by the plan for Carey and her family, who are Tom and the kids.

The next question is, Who is considered "highly compensated"? Congress says that a highly compensated person is one of the five highest-paid stockholders or among the highest-paid 25 percent of all employees.[14] If there is discrimination, then the highly compensated people are taxed on the amount that is deemed discriminatory.[15] An example will explain this.

Example: Alan's corporation provides a self-employed reimbursement plan for those who aren't officers. If one of the officers receives $4,000 of the reimbursement, he or she would have to report $3,000 as taxable income, the amount in excess of what would be allowed those who aren't officers.

Author's note: It truly is amazing that there are people in Congress thinking of this stuff. Why they can't simply allow all owners to benefit without having to put in this complexity is beyond understanding.

Exceptions to the Rules

Now that I have informed you of all the discrimination rules, I should point out that the IRS and Congress have noted several groups of people who don't have to be covered. The following is a list of employees who are exempt:[16]

- Employees who are part time. This means employees who normally work less than 25 hours per week.

- Employees who have not reached age 25. (This exception seems very odd. As you probably know, age discrimination isn't allowed in this country, yet the IRS and Congress encourage us to hire people under age 25 without giving them this fringe benefit! You might wonder why this discrimination exists. The reason is that we don't have any tax policy in this country. Our policy is based on the short-term interests of those whom we elect to Congress.)
- Employees who are seasonal. This is defined as anyone who works for you less than nine months during the year. This exception was put in to encourage hiring college and high school children.
- Employees covered under a collective-bargaining agreement.
- Employees with less than three years of service. Thus you can make workers wait three years before they get these benefits—or you can fire them, which is another option (only kidding!).
- Employees who are nonresident aliens.

One further interesting allowable discrimination is for routine physicals.[17] You are allowed routine physicals and diagnostic procedures for officers or employees and highly compensated employees, and you can discriminate on providing this benefit. You just can't provide this to dependents of officers or employees without providing it to dependents of employees who are not highly compensated.

Example: Acme, Inc., provides a self-insured medical reimbursement plan for all its senior officers that provides reimbursement only for routine physicals and diagnostic procedures such as a complete MRI body scan. Even though only highly compensated people are getting this benefit, it would not be taxed to them because of this exception.

Hire Your Children and Deduct the Equivalent of Their Education and Weddings

If you were to send your kids to college, would the college tuition be deductible? The answer is no! You may get a little tax credit, but that's it. If you pay for their room and board and provide a car, would that be deductible? The answer would be no. If you were to pay for your daughter's wedding, would that be deductible? No! But how would you like to be able to deduct the equivalent of all of this?

The answer is to hire your children in your business. Wages paid to an assistant are deductible. If your kids use this money to pay for college, room and board, and weddings, aren't you getting the equivalent of a deduction for all of these? Yes!

The tax rules on hiring kids are that wages paid from a parent to a child under the age of 18, if hired in either a self-employed business or a limited-liability company, are exempt from Social Security and unemployment taxes.[18] This exemption does not apply to incorporated businesses, which must take out Social Security and unemployment tax on everyone. You also can hire kids who are 18 or older, but it doesn't work as well unless you are in a fairly high tax bracket. The reason is that once the kids reach age 18, you must take out Social Security and federal unemployment tax.

In 2018, the first $12,000 of earned income (i.e., wages) is tax-free because your children receive a standard deduction of this amount on their own tax return.[19, 20] Now we're talking! If you pay your kids more than $12,000, they would pay some income tax, but only at the 10 percent bracket on the first $9,525 earned above this deduction in 2018.[21]

Example: You pay your child $12,000 in wages for the year 2018 in your self-employed business. You deduct the $12,000 in wages on your Schedule C (Schedule E if hired in conjunction with rental property), assuming that the wages were reasonable for the time and services performed. You pay no Social Security or unemployment taxes. Your child reports the $12,000 as income from wages on IRS Form 1040 and then deducts the $12,000 as his or her standard deduction. If you're in the 35 percent tax bracket, the $12,000 produces a tax refund of $4,200 from federal taxes alone, plus a potential savings of $348 (plus a potential 2.9 percent surcharge) from the Medicare surcharge in addition to any state tax savings. Above the $12,000 in wages, you would save at the 25 percent rate (35 percent minus 10 percent bracket of the child).

In addition, your child could put away $5,500 per year of his or her earnings into a Roth IRA that would allow the interest and appreciation to be tax-free to the child if used for college. In effect, by hiring your children, Uncle Sam underwrites the education, weddings, and other uses to which the children put their money.

Author's note: The maximum contribution to a Roth IRA for those under age 50 is 100 percent earned income up to $5,500.

A common question I get at seminars is, "At what age can I hire my children?" There is a tax court case that held that you could hire a child who is at least age 7. The IRS, which had fought the case, acquiesced (agreed to follow the case), effectively approving the employment of 7-year-olds.[22] This legitimates hiring children who are at least age 7. The problem is what happens if you want to hire your children who are under age 7. Some tax planners are urging people to put their child's picture on their business cards and pay a modeling fee, even if the child is under age 7. Will this work? Unfortunately, no one knows for sure. We do know that a child can be hired at age 7. If you hire a child under age 7, you are taking a risk. If you wish to be a trailblazer, maybe we can have a case named after you.

Unlike hiring a spouse, who is subject to Social Security, children under age 18 are exempt if hired in a self-employed business. Thus you want to pay them as much as possible. However, there's one major issue when you hire family members: The wages must be reasonable for the hours and work that they perform.[23] It certainly would be unreasonable to pay a child $40,000 to answer phones occasionally!

Although there has been lots of litigation on this issue,[24] it really isn't that hard to do it right. A salary is considered reasonable if an unrelated employer would pay the same employee under the same circumstances and preferably in the same business.[25] When setting a salary, be sure to allow for the experience or inexperience and ability of your child. The more experience and ability, the more you can pay per hour. Also consider the nine factors that the IRS uses to examine wages for reasonableness:[26]

- Duties performed
- Volume of work
- Type and amount of responsibility
- Complexity of work
- Amount of time required for work
- General cost of living in the area
- Ability and achievements of the employee
- Comparison of amount of salary with amount of business income
- Pay history of the employee

Author's note: In order to make your life easier, what I recommend at my seminars is to find out what you would pay to a comparable agency that does the type of work that you need and then pay your child less per hour than that agency. Thus, if you want your 12-year-old son to do some filing and bookkeeping, call a temporary agency such as Kelly Services or Manpower and find out what they charge per hour. If the charge is $15 per hour, you would pay your child $12, and this should be deemed reasonable. If you want to have your 24-year-old daughter mow the lawns on your rental properties, you would call a landscape service and get a quote. You also would need to document what hourly rate you were quoted. It would be ideal to get this documentation in writing in the form of a written quotation from the organization.

Documentation Strategies Necessary When Hiring Any Relative

Be honest! If you were an IRS auditor, would you believe that your child or spouse was a bona fide employee? You would only if you saw adequate proof. In most cases, it's absolutely essential that your relatives fill out time sheets or a tax diary at the end of each week. To get your deductions for wages, you must be able to prove what work actually was performed.[27] Each day that the relative works, the time sheet or diary should show

- The date worked
- A description of the tasks performed
- The hours worked

At the end of each day or week, you should approve the time sheet or diary for payment. Payment to either your spouse or your children always should be made by check. Even if your child is too young to have a checking account, you should pay by

Month July		Child's Name I. M. Child	
Day of Week (Mon, Tues, etc.)	Date	Description of Tasks Performed	Hours Worked
Mon.	7	Sorted files & made 3x5 cards	4
Tues.	8	Cleaned office & emptied trash	2
Thurs.	10	Addressed brochures	2
Sat.	12	Arranged business trip files	2
Sat.	12	Typed business letters	2
Total Hours Worked			12
X Hourly Rate			5
Total Wages Paid with Check No. 164			60

Figure 4-1. Dependent child's business services and wage sheet.

check. In this circumstance, establish a custodial checking account at your local bank. This would require your signature for the child to withdraw any money! The check completes the audit trail by establishing two things: that you paid the relative and that the relative actually received the payment. The time sheet establishes the validity and reasonableness of the payment. Together you will be audit-proof from the IRS.

In addition, have your attorney draft up an employment contract noting the pay rate, duties, benefits, etc. The pay should be based on the hours worked.[28]

Finally, you want to file the appropriate IRS forms required for hiring any employee. The first step in hiring—relatives or others—is to obtain a taxpayer ID number from the IRS and from your state. Next, you want to complete the necessary payroll paperwork. There's paperwork even on your child under age 18, who, as an employee of his or her parents, is exempt from Social Security and unemployment taxes.[29] However, even if no taxes are due, you must complete the following federal paperwork:

- **IRS Form W-4.** This simple form must be completed by your employee and stored in your files.[30]
- **IRS Form W-2.** If you pay your spouse or child $600 or more, you must give your employee a copy of IRS Form W-2 and file it along with IRS Form W-3 with both the IRS and the Social Security Administration.[31]

- **IRS Form 941.** Use this form to report on a quarterly basis withheld income taxes and to make a deposit.[32]
- **IRS Form 940.** Although you are not liable for unemployment taxes on wages paid to your child if he or she is a dependent and under age 21, you must file IRS Form 940 anyway at the end of the year.[33] If your child is your only employee, you simply enter your child's wages as "exempt" from unemployment tax and return the form to the IRS.[34]

The bottom line is this: Stop paying allowances, tuition costs, and wedding costs. Instead, hire your children in your business, and pay them a reasonable wage. Let them use the money for their tuition, room and board, and weddings.

Miscellaneous Income-Shifting Strategies

Gift and Shift-the-Tax Technique

Here's one strategy that you will *really* like. In fact, the good news is that if everyone in the U.S. understood this strategy, we could legally reduce all taxes paid into the IRS by over $2 trillion! The bad news is that the IRS has nothing to worry about because over 99.9 percent of taxpayers in this country have never heard about it. However, it clearly is one of the most powerful techniques available.

With this strategy, you gift property rather than cash to a person in a lower tax bracket. The test on who would qualify for this is simple. Take a mirror, and put it in your freezer overnight. The following day, take the mirror out of the freezer and place it under the nose of anyone with whom you wish to use this technique. If the mirror fogs, the person passes the test. You can use this strategy with virtually anyone—your kids, grandchildren, nephews, nieces, parents, or even significant friends who are not related to you.

You simply give away the property to these relatives who are in a lower tax bracket than you, and then they sell the property one day later and pay the tax at their bracket.[35] This must be done without a prearranged resale.[36] Thus you must do this before any contract for the sale of the property occurs. The result is that both you (the donor) and the person to whom you give the property (the donee) have more cash to spend because the IRS took less tax from the person in the lower tax bracket.

Think about how this works. Here is a great example from someone I met on an airplane. He was a successful lawyer, and he also was successful in the stock market. He had three kids, and he was paying $20,000 a year for each of his kids to go to college. A smart person was doing a dumb thing. He ought to have been giving each of his kids stock. They then could sell their stock and be taxed on the gain at their brackets and pay their own tuition. Now this lawyer was easily in the 50 percent tax bracket (counting federal taxes, state taxes, and Medicare taxes), and his kids were in the 10 to 15 percent tax bracket. He could have cut his taxes by 70 percent (35 percent savings divided by 50 percent)! This can be done with anything—stocks, bonds, valuable collectibles, or real estate. As you can see, the savings from this one strategy alone can be massive.

Interestingly, there are no income-tax consequences to making a gift (although there are gift-tax consequences that we will discuss shortly). This means that any recipient doesn't pay income taxes on the gift (and you get no deduction for it).[37] The donee takes the same basis and holding period that you had, increased by any gift tax paid.[38] I should note that this discussion applies to gifts and not if you inherit property as a result of death. With inheritances, you get a fair-market-value basis as of the date of death, and the holding period begins on the date of death.[39]

Example: Jackie receives some stock from her parents as a gift. The parents bought the stock two years ago for $20 per share, and it's worth $50 when they give it to her. (I wish this happened to me!) Jackie would get a $20 basis, the same basis as her parents had, and the same two-year holding period. (In contrast, if Jackie inherited the stock and it was worth $50 at the time of her parents' death, her basis would be $50, the fair market value.)

Author's note: I have assumed that the basis of the gift is less than the fair market value. If, however, the fair market value is less than the basis paid, the recipient won't be able to get a loss when he or she sells the property. The basis is always either the basis when the property was purchased or the fair market value as of the date of the gift, whichever is lower! Thus no loss would be allowed if you sell the property shortly thereafter.

Congress wants part of our profits but as little as possible of our losses. This is illustrative of the "Golden Rule": He who has the gold makes the rules.

The key is to never use this technique with property that would produce a loss. Use only with appreciated property.

As mentioned earlier, there are gift-tax consequences in making a gift. If you're single, you can give away up to $15,000 in 2018 per person per year gift-tax-free.[40] If you're married, you can give double this, which is $30,000 in 2018 per person per year, free of gift tax, by consenting to treat one-half the gift as made by each spouse.[41] This may not seem fair, but there are two people involved instead of just one. In addition, you get a lifetime exemption from gift taxes of $11.18 million per person in 2018.[42] A couple would thus get double this amount, which is $22.36 million without an estate or gift tax. Thus, you can give away a lot of gifts without paying any tax. An example will illustrate how financially rewarding this strategy can be.

Example: Melissa owns some real estate that is worth $200,000 and has appreciated $90,000 since she purchased it. If she sells the real estate, she will pay at least $21,510 in capital gains tax plus any state income tax. This also doesn't take into account any depreciation that she took, which would be taxed as ordinary income. If she transfers this property to her three children, who, in turn, sell the property shortly thereafter,

Melissa would owe no gift tax owing to the annual exclusions and lifetime exclusion. The children each would pay tax on one-third of the gain, $3,409 each at their bracket. Thus Melissa would have saved 50 percent of the tax, or $11,283! This savings alone could almost pay for the tuition for one child at a state school.

Beware of the Kiddie Tax

Congress was aware of how powerful this gift-tax technique, and the following gift-leaseback technique, could be, even though it is not used by most Americans. Congress tried to kill off or at least limit its benefits with what is now known as the "kiddie tax." Sadly, starting in 2008, the kiddie tax applies to a lot more people than just kids.

The kiddie tax applies to unearned income for children under the age of 19 and college students under the age of 24. Unearned income is income from sources other than wages and salary, like dividends and interest. Taxable income attributable to net unearned income will be taxed according to the brackets applicable to trusts and estates (which has the highest tax rates in the Internal Revenue Code).[43] With respect to earned income, the rules are the same as before. As mentioned, the kiddie tax applies only to investment income, such as dividends, capital gains, rents, royalties, etc., and not wages.[44]

Note: The kiddie tax also doesn't apply to other relatives age 24 or older (such as your mom).

Author's note: Generally due to the high trust tax rates, you want to limit this shifting in investment income to under $9150 if you are in the top tax brackets and under $2,550 if you are not in the top tax brackets.

Author's elaboration: Using prepaid tuition plans and section 529 plans to save for your kids' college tuition is now even more important than putting money in their names. All interest and gains in these plans are tax-free to the extent the funds are used for college tuition.

Double-Deduct All Your Equipment Plus Protect It from Judgments!

How would you like to double-deduct all the equipment that you use in any business or real estate venture and make your assets lawyer-proof from judgments? Sounds too good to be true, doesn't it? Well, you can, and it isn't that hard to accomplish. This is far and away one of the top financial planning strategies in the country, especially for physicians.

You start by giving away property that you are using in business, preferably after it has been depreciated, either to your relatives or to an irrevocable trust set up for your relatives. You then would lease it back from them in trust and pay monthly lease payments. You've already depreciated the equipment, and now you're deducting the monthly lease payments, which, in effect, gives you a double deduction for the equipment. Moreover, if you're sued thereafter, you have no business assets in your name and thus have liability-proofed your assets. This strategy is known as the *gift-leaseback technique.*

The gift-leaseback technique involves several steps:

- *Give away property that you own.* To put the gift-leaseback strategy to work, you first must own the asset. You as an individual would give away the asset to your children or to any other person who passes the "mirror test" described earlier.[45] If you have a corporation, however, your corporation may not make such gifts.[46]
- *Give away property that you've depreciated.* Fully depreciated property produces the maximum deductions for the gift-leaseback strategy. By using fully depreciated assets in a gift-leaseback, you actually create new deductions. Fully depreciated property produces no depreciation deductions. However, the gift-leaseback technique creates a rent deduction from the fully depreciated equipment.

Example: You own and use in your business a Cadillac. The car is fully depreciated. It has a retail value of $10,000, as published by the National Automobile Dealers Association in its *Official Used Car Guide,* which is available on the Internet (www .nadaguides.com). According to the IRS Annual Lease Value Table, the annual rent on the Cadillac is $3,100 for the next four years.[47] Thus you set up an irrevocable trust for your 14-year-old daughter, give the Cadillac to the trust, and then lease it back.

The result is that you get a yearly tax deduction for the $3,100 of rent that you pay to the trust, which will own the property.[48] Assuming that you're in the 45 percent federal and state tax bracket, your taxes are reduced by $1,395. Your daughter receives $3,100 from the trust and pays a tax of roughly $235. The family unit—you and your daughter or son—receive a net benefit of $1,160 from a car that otherwise would have produced no tax benefit. Remember, however: Do not give away property that would produce a deductible loss if you sold it.

- *Give the property to an irrevocable trust rather than directly to your son or daughter, and use an independent trustee.* Although you may be able to give the property directly to your son or daughter if they are not minors, some cases, and especially if you live in the fifth circuit (Louisiana, Texas, and Mississippi), require you to use a trust and have an independent trustee.[49] In addition, if your kids or grandkids get sued, the creditors can't touch the property held in trust if the trust document is drafted correctly. Finally, if your children are minors, they can't own a car or real estate directly; thus a trust becomes mandatory. In short, regardless of where you live, I would advise setting up a trust for this technique. It will greatly protect you in a wide variety of ways.
- *Pay a reasonable rent.* All cases in the area require a reasonable rental for the property used. With cars, you can use IRS Publication 15-B, Annual Lease Value Table. Just plug in your vehicle's fair market value, and the publication

will tell you how much a reasonable rental would be. If you want to lease equipment other than vehicles, you have several ways of tracking down what a reasonable lease payment would be. One method would be to get a quotation from an equipment leasing company for similar equipment. The IRS also has taken in its litigation the position that you can charge 40 percent of the fair market value of the property as of the beginning of a three-year lease.

Example: Mary has a top-of-the-line computer. If the computer is worth $2,000 today, she could lease it back from her son's or daughter's trust for 40 percent of its value, or $800 per year, for the next three years.

Author's note: Go to your local newspaper and clip out an ad that looks similar to your equipment. This would establish a fair market value. (By the way, you can't be the one who places the ad in the newspaper!)

- *Document your nontax business reason.* Another requirement of some courts is to have a nontax reason for the gift-leaseback or sale-leaseback (which will be discussed below).[50]

With what property can you use this technique? It will work for any tangible property, such as computers, printers, desks, file cabinets, chairs, cars, copiers, and shredders. (In Washington, DC, we have a lot of shredders.) Moreover, you can do this with anyone who passes the mirror test. Thus anyone is eligible. Get a letter from your lawyer outlining a nontax reason for the gift-leaseback. (See my discussion of the sale-leaseback below.)

Deduct 100 Percent of Your Real Estate—Even the Land

One interesting twist with this technique is with real estate. Buildings are depreciable, but land is not. You thus have to make some allocation of the purchase price for any rental property between land and buildings. If you don't, the IRS will make the allocation for you, which you will not like.

How would you like to make your rental properties 100 percent deductible—even the portion allocated to the land? You can by using this technique. When you purchase a property, you would divide the title between the land and the building. The building would be in your name, but the land would be in the name of a trust for your children. You would then lease back the property from the trust. The result is that you can depreciate the building *and* can get a deduction for the land in the form of ground rent. Thus you are now effectively able to deduct 100 percent of your purchase price. Isn't this a great strategy?

Even if you already own some rental property, you can accomplish this. Just have your lawyer transfer the title to the underlying land to a trust set up for your children or relatives. (Get an appraisal on the land.) You then would pay ground rent to the trust.

Sale-Leaseback Technique

A final way to shift income is with the sale-leaseback technique. This technique has been around for many years. It puts the friend or relative in the leasing business but allows you to select the asset. It has the same requirements and steps necessary for the gift-leaseback, but this is a sale and not a gift. You would use this technique when you want to cash out or you want to help your children or grandchildren with some great risk-free estate planning. A great example of how this works follows.

Example: Sam lives in his home, which is completely paid off. He gets few tax benefits from the home because there's no interest and no depreciation since it is his home. Although Sam paid $130,000 for his house 20 years ago, it's worth $380,000 based on an appraisal. Sam now sells the home to his three children for the full fair market value but gives them great terms: $3,000 down, and he finances the rest of the purchase price with an installment note for the remaining $377,000 at 7 percent interest. Subsequent to the sale, Sam's children rent the house back to Sam at fair market rent. The results are startling:

- Sam has no capital gain because his total gain is under $250,000. (As you will learn in Chapter 6, a principal residence can be sold with no capital gain consequences if the gain is less than $500,000 for a married couple and $250,000 for a single person.)
- There is a relatively even cash flow because the mortgage payment is just a little more than the rent payment.
- Sam's children now can depreciate the home because it is rental property.
- Sam's children can deduct any repair costs because it is rental property.
- If the house appreciates before Sam dies, all appreciation is out of Sam's estate because his kids own the house.
- Finally, the children can visit Sam and the property once a year and deduct their trip as a caretaking expense.

This is one technique for which you will need a good lawyer because it must be done correctly.[51] The lease should be relatively short term and not exceed the seller's life expectancy. The rent and sale price should be at fair market value; there can be no "deal" given. An independent appraisal for both the sale price and the rent should be obtained. All payments should be made to the appropriate parties. No forgiveness of any payment should occur, especially in the first two years. In addition, the mortgage payments should not exactly equal the rent. Make one of the payments more than the other.[52]

Finally, as with the gift-leaseback, you will need a legitimate nontax reason for this transaction.[53] Get a letter from a lawyer stating that this transaction is recommended:

- To protect from creditors such as nursing homes
- To avoid any ethical conflicts
- To provide professional management of the property
- To avoid probate fees and to save on estate taxes

Summary

- Hire your spouse and save a bundle deducting medical expenses.
- Hire your son or daughter and deduct the equivalent of their education and weddings.
- Have the right documentation when hiring any relative.
- Use the gift-push and shift-tax technique. It could save you an enormous amount of taxes.
- Beware of the kiddie tax.
- Use the gift-leaseback technique to double-deduct all your equipment.
- Use the sale-leaseback technique to give benefits to your children, cash out, and get some great risk-free estate planning.
- Use the sale-leaseback technique to deduct land.

Notes

1. Sections 3121(b)(3)(A) and 3306(C)(5) of the IRC. See IRS Publication Circular E.
2. Section 213(a) of the IRC as amended by 2017 Tax Cuts and Jobs Act Section 11027(a) for 2018. After 2018, the threshold amount is scheduled to increase to 10 percent of adjusted gross income.
3. Ibid.
4. Section 105(g) of the IRC.
5. Section 1.105-5 of the ITR.
6. IRS Letter Ruling 9409006, ISP Coordinated Issue Paper (UIC-162.35.22); See also Revenue Ruling 71-588, 1971-2 CB 91.
7. Section 105 of the IRC.
8. Sections 1372 and 105(g) of the IRC.
9. Section 707 of the IRC.
10. *W. W. Wollenburg v. U.S.*, 2000-1 USTC 50,156.
11. *Alberz v. Commissioner*, T.C. Memo 2007-144.
12. Section 105(h) of the IRC.
13. Section 105(h)(2) of the IRC.
14. Section 105(h)(5) of the IRC.
15. Section 1.105-11(c) of the ITR.
16. Section 105(h)(3)(B) of the IRC.
17. Section 1.105-11(g) of the ITR.
18. Section 3121(b)(3)(A) and 3306(c)(5); Revenue Ruling 2000-45, IRB 2000-41.
19. Revenue Procedure 2014-61.
20. Omitted.
21. Revenue Procedure 2015-53. See IRC 1 and section 63(c)(7) as amended by 2017 Tax Cuts and Jobs Act Section 11021
22. *Eller v. Commissioner*, 77 TC 934; *acq.* 1984-2 CB 1.
23. Section 162(a)(1) of the IRC.
24. *Mayson Manufacturing Co. v. Commissioner*, 178 F.2d 115 (6th Cir.); *Ridgewood Provisions, Inc. v. Commissioner*, 6 TC 87 (1946) (*acq.*); *Ken Miller Supply v. Commissioner*, 37 TCM 974 (1978) et al.
25. Section 1.167-7(b)(3) of the ITR; *Automotive Investment Development, Inc. v. Commissioner*, 66 TCM 57 (1993); *Giles Industries, Inc. v. United States*, 496 F.2d 566 (Ct. Cl. 1974).
26. IRS Publication 535, Chapter 2 (2001 Edition).

27. Section 1.162-7(a) of the ITR.

28. *R. Haeder v. Commissioner*, 81 TCM 987 (2001).

29. Sections 3121(b)(3)(A) and 3306(c)(5) of the IRC.

30. Section 31.3402(n)-1(b) of the ITR.

31. IRS Instructions for Preparing Forms W-2 and W-3.

32. Section 31.3402(n)-1 of the ITR. See also IRS Instructions for Form 941.

33. IRS Instructions for Form 940.

34. Section 31.3402(n)(1) of the ITR. See also IRS Instructions for Form 941.

35. Section 1015 of the IRC. See also *Taft v. Bowers*, 278 U.S. 470 (1929).

36. Ibid.

37. Sections 102(a) and 2503(b) of the IRC and Section 262 of the IRC. See also *R. Wright v. Commissioner,* 26 TCM 425 (1967) and *J. R. Howard*, 41 TCM 1554 (1981).

38. Sections 1223(1) and 1223(2) of the IRC. See also Section 1.1223-1(b) of the ITR.

39. Sections 2033-2036 of the IRC.

40. Revenue Procedure 2012-41, 2012-45 (10/18/12). See also Section 2513(a) of the IRC.

41. Ibid. See also Section 6019 of the IRC and Section 25.2513-1(c) of the ITR. See also Revenue Procedure 2015-53.

42. Section 2010(c) of the IRC. See Revenue Procedure 2018-18 and 2017 Tax Cuts and Jobs Act Section 11061(c).

43. Sections 1(i) and 1(g) of the IRC as amended by 2017 Tax Cuts and Jobs Act Section 11001. See Footnote 43, IBID

44. IRS Form 8615, Tax for Children Under Age 14 with Investment Income of More than 1,500 (2001 edition). Revenue Procedure 2001-59, 2001-52 I.R.B.

45. Section 2503(b) of the IRC.

46. For example, *Epstein v. Commissioner*, 53 TC 459 (1969), *acq.* 1970-2 C.B. 19.

47. Sections 1.61-2T(d)(2) and 1.61-21(d)(2) of the ITR. See also IRS Publication 15B.

48. Section 162(a)(3) of the IRC.

49. For example, *J. Wiles v. Commissioner*, 59 TC 289, *acq.* by IRS and *aff'd* 74-1 USTC 9379 (5th Cir. 1974); *H. L. Brown v. Commissioner*, 11 TC 744, *aff'd* 180 F.2d 946 (5th Cir. 1950).

50. For example, *Matthews v. Commissioner*, 61 TC 12 (1973), *rev'd* 75-2 USTC Par 967 (5th Cir. 1975); *Frank Lyon Co. v. Commissioner*, 435 U.S. 561 (S. Ct. 1978).

51. *Estate of Maxwell*, 98 TC 39 (1992).

52. Ibid.

53. See note 51.

5

How to Turn Your Car into a Tax-Deductible Goldmine

This is the season of the year when we discover that we owe most of our success to Uncle Sam.
—Wall Street Journal (referring to the period from January to April)

I am often asked at my seminars, "What is the number one business expense that gets audited by the Internal Revenue Service (IRS)?" Most people think that it is entertainment or home office. The answer is your vehicle expense. The reason is that a car is a big-ticket item and is the most used and abused. My purpose in this chapter is not only to increase your automotive deductions significantly but also to lock them in with proper documentation tactics.

Business Use

If you drive only one car for business, what's the maximum business-use percentage that you can achieve? 100 percent. If you drive two

Chapter Overview
- Find out why using two or more cars in business will maximize your deductions.
- Learn why the IRS method of deducting car expenses is generally a bad deal (with one exception).
- Learn when buying or leasing a car is better.
- Know which vehicles can give as much as eight times the normal automobile deduction.
- Learn about some frequently overlooked automotive deductions.
- Learn when it is better to either sell a car or to trade one in.
- Understand why donating a business car is a tax disaster and should almost never occur.
- Know how to maximize your business mileage and some little-known rules that even most accountants don't know.

cars for business, could you drive one car 100 percent for business and another car 100 percent for business? Yes![1] Your business use is based on business miles driven. You calculate your business use by dividing business miles by the total miles driven during the year.[2] You do this for each car driven for business.[3]

Example: Jeremy drives his car 20,000 total miles during the year. If he puts on 15,000 miles for business, he may deduct three-fourths of any automobile-related expenses or three-fourths of his total mileage at the IRS standard mileage rate.

Use Multiple Cars for Business and Increase Your Spendable Cash

The two-car strategy puts extra money in your pocket only when you're converting an otherwise personal asset to business use. In other words, if you have two cars in your family, make them both deductible. But don't buy a second car simply to implement this strategy. See the comparison in Figure 5-1.

In addition, some cases have required you to have some business purpose for using more than one car.[4] This is very easy to establish, however. Can you use one car for rainy days and one for sunny days? Can you use one car for "high sale" prospects and one to look a bit "poorer"? There are lots of reasons for using different cars.

Author's note: I have a friend who is a successful life insurance salesman. He uses his Mercedes when he meets with multimillionaire estate-planning prospects and his older Lexus for nursing home–care insurance sales.

You will notice that by using two cars and switching off between them, you are able to get an extra $6,168 in new deductions each year. Moreover, I based my analysis on cars that cost $28,000. More expensive cars will generate more tax savings.

There's one disadvantage to using the two-car strategy, however: you must keep track of your business mileage during the year on a daily basis. Simplified record keeping using a statistical approach, which will be discussed later, won't work.[5]

Now that you realize that you should use your second car in business, too, the next question becomes, "What basis do I use for depreciation?" Although tax law mandates that you depreciate your car's basis, which is usually your purchase price,[6] there's a slightly different rule if you used the car for personal use first. When you convert your car to business, your basis for depreciation becomes the lower of the cost or the market value of the car on the date it is first used in business (which is usually the lower basis).[7] We accountants call this the *lower of cost or market-value rule.* Although many people do not know this rule, it's applicable to all sorts of property. Thus, if you convert your home to a rental property, the same rule applies.

	One Car	Two Cars	
		Car 1	Car 2
Business/Personal Use			
Total Miles for Business	22,000	18,000	4,000
Total Miles for Year	24,000	20,000	7,800
Business Use Percentage	92%	90%	51%
Deduction Calculations			
Gas and Oil	$4,992	$4,160	$1,622
Insurance	$1,200	$1,200	$1,000
Repairs and Maintenance	$1,200	$1,200	$1,200
Tags and Licenses	$150	$150	$150
Wash and Wax	$230	$230	$230
Other	$50	$50	$50
Total Operating Expense	$7,822	$6,990	$4,252
Business Use Percentage	x92%	x90%	x51%
Business Total	$7,196	$6,291	$2,169
Depreciation	$9,200	$9,000	$5,100
Total Deductions	**$16,392**	**$15,291**	**$7,269**
Extra Deductions		**$6,168**	

Note: The cars in this example cost $28,000 each and are new.
Interest, state, and local taxes are also deductible under both the IRS and
actual methods to the extent the automobile is used for business. IRS Notice 2013-95,
IRS Notice 2018-03. See also sec 164(b)(6) and Committee Reports for Tax Cuts & Jobs
Act paragraph 5016.

Figure 5-1. How the two-car strategy produces extra deductions.

As used here, *cost* is what you paid for the car plus any capital improvements, such as amounts spent to rebuild an engine.[8] *Market value* is the fair market value of the vehicle on the day that you convert it to business use.[9]

Author's note: Generally, you can determine market value using the Blue Book, *The National Automobile Dealer's Association Official Used Car Guide,* which lists two values for used cars: retail and wholesale. You want the higher number, which is the retail value. In addition, there are many Web sites that list this information, such as my site, www.taxreductioninstitute.com.

Example: Assume that you purchased your personal car several years ago for $20,000 and today that car has a retail value of $10,000. (You should be that lucky!) Your basis for purposes of computing depreciation is $5,000, which is the lower of cost or market value.

Deduct the Larger of the Actual Expense or the Optional IRS Standard Rate

Unlike corporations, individuals such as employees and the self-employed have a choice of methods to write off their vehicle expenses.[10] You can use either the IRS optional standard mileage rates or the actual expenses. The actual method allows you to deduct all car expenses based on your business use.[11] This means that you can deduct part of your gas, wash, wax, depreciation, insurance, repairs, tolls, interest, taxes, and other costs related to your car.[12] As an alternative, you could use the IRS standard mileage rates in lieu of all this. Even if you're using the IRS method, however, you can deduct the business use's share of interest, taxes, and tolls.[13]

Author's note: Many people miss this one deduction. Interest and taxes are deductible to the extent a car is used for business. Sadly, many people, including some accountants, don't know this. They've thus taken out home-equity loans in order to deduct the interest on their car payments, which they didn't need to do, and taken a risk if they didn't pay off the loans. Many people are still making this bad mistake owing to a lack of knowledge.

In 2018, the IRS gives you 54.5 cents per business mile, 25 cents of which is depreciation, 14 cents per mile for charitable use, and 18 cents for medical/moving mileage.[14]

Author's Note: Moving expenses are no longer deductible except in the case of a member of the Armed Forces of the on active duty who moves pursuant to a military order and incident to a permanent change of station.[15]

Example: In prior years, you deducted 52,000 miles using the optional IRS standard mileage rate. This year you drove 20,000 miles for business. You may deduct $10,900 (20,000 × 0.545).

Interestingly, the IRS method allows the same 54.5 cents per mile regardless of the cost of the car, regardless of its prior mileage and condition, and regardless of age. Thus the older and more "doglike" the car, the better the method becomes. Consequently, the IRS method is best for cars that cost less than $20,000 and for which you accrue at least 15,000 miles per year.

Author's note: I called a firm that specializes in car costs and helps to develop the numbers for the IRS.[16] According to one of the company specialists, the IRS method assumes that you purchase one of the cheapest cars made in the United States (normally a Ford Escort LX), which costs about $19,000. It assumes that you have no options on the car. It assumes that you drive 10,000 miles per year for three years. Thus, if you have a vehicle that meets these criteria, you may be better off with the IRS method; otherwise, using actual expenses (gas, oil, depreciation, repairs, insurance, etc.) would be the better deal. This is particularly true for vehicles placed in service in 2018 or thereafter because of the substantial increases in depreciation on business vehicles. The IRS method doesn't reflect these new, improved changes.

There are some limitations to the IRS method that you should know about. First, as noted earlier, it can only be used by employees, people who are self-employed, and limited-liability corporations, not corporations.[17] Second, it can't be used in a fleet operation, such as using two cars at once. You can switch cars and you can use the cars in different businesses simultaneously, but you just can't use the cars simultaneously in the same business.[18] You also can't use the IRS method if you took any accelerated depreciation on the car.

Now that you've probably used the wrong method, can you switch? The IRS allows you to switch to the method of actual expenses anytime, with no hassle and no audit.[19] However, going from actual expenses to the IRS method is much tougher. If you used the slower straight-line method of depreciation and not the faster accelerated method of depreciation, you can switch to the IRS method.[20] In addition, if you sell your car and get another car in business, you can start using any method.

Author's note: You might be wondering why the IRS allows you to switch easily from the IRS method to actual expenses but makes it more difficult to go from actual expenses to the IRS method. I don't have the slightest idea why this occurs. This is just one of the quirky rules in tax law.

Depreciating an Automobile

My goal here is not to make you an accountant; thus I am not going to delve into the intricacies of depreciation. However, there are some tax-planning tips and traps that you should know about.

Depreciation is nothing more than a cost-allocation method; therefore, pick the method that gives you the biggest deductions each year.

There are two basic depreciation methods for business vehicles: straight line, the slower method that allows you to deduct in equal amounts, and accelerated, which allows for faster deductions up front. As a result of the "tax simplification" law placing limits on depreciating luxury cars, this is further complicated.[21] The accelerated-depreciation rates (modified accelerated cost recovery system, or MACRS), the straight-line rates, and the luxury limits for passenger cars placed in service in 2018 or thereafter are listed in Figure 5-2.

Year	MACRS	Straight Line	Luxury Auto
1	20%	10%	$10,000
2	31%	20%	$16,000
3	19.2%	20%	$9,600
4	11.52%	20%	$5,760
5	11.52%	20%	$5,760
6	5.67%	10%	$5,760

Figure 5-2. 2018 depreciation limits. The maximum first year depreciation for passenger vehicles is $10,000 plus $8,000 in bonus depreciation.

Author's note: Prior to the implementation of the Tax Cuts and Jobs Act (TCJA), which applies to cars placed in service in 2018 and thereafter, Congress had severe limits on yearly depreciation. They did this in order to stop taxpayers from being able to write off luxury cars. The new law allows for *much* higher yearly limits in years 2 and thereafter. In fact, for most years, the yearly limits have tripled.

Author's note: To give you a great example of how much the tax laws have changed for 2018, let's assume that you purchased a new BMW for $50,000 and use it 100 percent for business. I know that a 100 percent usage is unrealistic but it makes the math simpler. Under the old rules (prior to 2018), it would take you roughly 18 years to full depreciate the car. As a result of the TCJA, if you place the same BMW in service in 2018 or thereafter, you could write it off in 5.3 years! As you can see, the changes are significant. I can just see advertisements say, "buy a BMW, Mercedes or Cadillac and eliminate your taxes." You will also eliminate your cash, but I can see these ads coming.

In addition, tax law requires you generally to treat your car as having been purchased during the middle of the year of purchase.[22] Thus, if you buy your car in January, for depreciation purposes, you're deemed to buy the car on July 1. The same would be true if you purchased the car in September. This is important: Because it's considered to be purchased on July 1, you don't get a whole year's depreciation in the first year.

Thus you would think that you should buy your business vehicle in December, get a half-year depreciation, and probably get a better deal from the dealer too. However, there's a congressional "gotcha." (Someone actually thought of this.)

If you buy over 40 percent of all depreciable equipment for the year during the last three months of the year, then you must treat the purchase as if you made it in the middle of the last quarter of the year, or on November 15. The effect of this is to cut back on your first year's depreciation.[23]

Author's note: This is a great example of needless complexity in our tax laws. The result of this needless complexity is a deferral of your depreciation until a later year. The bottom line is that you should buy most of your vehicles before October 1, unless you can elect to expense the vehicle, which will be discussed below.

In addition, as you can see from Figure 5-2, you're subject to yearly depreciation limits—and you don't even get these if you use your car less than 100 percent for business. An example will illustrate this.

Example: You purchase a $40,000 car and use it 75 percent for business. The personal use reduces your deductions.[24] The depreciation options that you would have are as follows (see Figure 5-2):

- $6,000 under MACRS ($40,000 × 20 percent × 75 percent business use).
- $7,500 under the luxury limits ($10,000 × 75 percent business use).

The maximum depreciation you can claim is $6,000, which is the lower of the MACRS limit or the luxury limit.

Buy "Heavy Metal" Vehicles and Trucks and Get Fast Write-Offs

You should note that all the luxury limits apply only to passenger automobiles. If you can come outside the definition of *passenger automobile,* you have no luxury limits and can write off the entire business use of the car over five years or even less with the expense election. So what is a *passenger automobile?*

Congress defines a *passenger automobile* as a four-wheeled vehicle that is manufactured primarily for use on public streets and highways and has an unloaded gross vehicle weight of 6,000 pounds or less.[25] However, if a vehicle is a truck or a van or has a truck base, as most sports utility vehicles do, then the test changes to having a loaded gross vehicle weight based on manufacturer's suggested carrying weight.[26] I should note that certain commercial vehicles, such as ambulances, hearses, taxicabs, and limousines, are not deemed passenger cars if they're used for commercial purposes.[27]

Example: Sam drives a sports utility vehicle that has a manufacturer's suggested carrying weight of 7,500 pounds. This is not deemed to be a passenger vehicle, so the yearly luxury limits on depreciation do not apply.

Author's note: You might be wondering how you can tell what the manufacturer's suggested carrying weight of a vehicle is. You can either call your dealer or look on the door jam of the driver's side. There is a metal plate that notes your manufacturer's suggested carrying weight.

As a result of the new Tax Cuts and Jobs Act, in 2018 and theereafter, businesses can elect to write off up to $1,000,000 worth of equipment as long as total expenditures are less than $2,500,000. This election applies to trucks and vans if the van can carry nine or more passengers. In addition, both types of vehicles must have a gross vehicle weight over 6,000 pounds and have a truck chassis. Thus, you can write-off 100 percent of the business use of the truck or qualifying van, and this even applies to both new and used trucks. Used trucks, however, must have at least a 6 foot or bigger cargo bed. All sports utility vehicles don't come under this rule because they have a separate rule that applies to them.

Author's note: In 2018 and thereafter, new and used trucks can both be written off in the year of purchase based on your business use. This applies to both new and used qualifying trucks as long as they are new to you.

Sports Utility Vehicles: If you buy a new or used SUV that has a gross vehicle weight over 6,000 pounds and carries passengers and has a truck chassis, you can effectively also write off 100 percent of the business use based on an increase on bonus depreciation to 100 percent.

Example: Scott buys a Cadillac Escalade for $60,000 and uses it 90 percent for business. Thus, his depreciable business use becomes $54,000 (90 percent of $60,000). The way the bonus depreciation works is as follows:

- You would first take the business use of the vehicle,which is based on the business miles divided by the total mileage for the year. Thus, if the Cadillac is driven 9,000 business miles and 10,000 total miles, the vehicles is deemed to be used 90 percent for business

- Secondly, you would multiply the business use by the cost, which is 90 percent of $60,000, which results in a $54,000 deduction. This is what you would deduct in the year that of purchase.

Author's note: I should note that if your business use drops below the business-use percentage during any of the succeeding five years, you will have to recapture or pay back some of the depreciation that you claimed. Thus try to keep the vehicle in your business for at least five years for the same business use. Also, one extra perk that I bet you didn't know: The IRS allows you to deduct the business use of any chauffeur cost.[27] Thus, if you pay a chauffeur $40,000 to drive you everywhere and use the vehicle 80 percent for business, 80 percent of this cost would be deductible.

Also, this applies to any qualified SUV or van that is new to you. It can be a used vehicle as long as it is new to you.

It's Usually Better to Buy than Lease a Vehicle

Since Congress put some limits on depreciation, you would think that leasing would be the better deal; however, Congress thought of this too. Congress made the IRS come up with killer tables that approximate the benefits of what you would have gotten had you purchased the vehicle. You actually would add back some income on your tax return, which is the same as eliminating some lease deductions. Figure 5-3 shows this table. To use it, add back the dollar amounts under "Tax Year During Lease" to your income on your tax return, based on the fair market value of the car and how old the lease is. In later years of the lease, the "add back" to your income is higher; the higher the car value, the greater is the "add back." (Add-back amounts are for automobiles—other than electric automobiles—with a lease term beginning in calendar year 2016.)

If you examine the table, you will see that the more expensive the car, the worse the leasing deal becomes, and the longer the lease, the worse the deal is. Thus four-year leases are worse than three-year leases, which are worse than two-year leases.

After doing a lot of computer analysis, I have found that the best treatment for a business vehicle is to buy it and keep it at least four or more years, with 10 years being ideal. This is particularly true under the new TCJA for vehicles placed in service in

Fair Market Value of Passenger Automobile		Tax Year During Lease				
Over	**Not Over**	**1st**	**2nd**	**3rd**	**4th**	**5th & later**
$19,000	$19,500	6	14	20	23	27
19,500	20,000	7	16	23	27	31
20,000	20,500	8	18	26	30	35
20,500	21,000	9	20	28	35	39
21,000	21,500	10	21	32	38	44
21,500	22,000	11	23	35	42	47
22,000	23,000	12	27	39	47	53
23,000	24,000	14	31	45	54	62
24,000	25,000	16	34	52	61	70
25,000	26,000	18	38	58	68	78
26,000	27,000	19	43	63	75	87
27,000	28,000	21	47	69	82	95
28,000	29,000	23	51	75	89	103
29,000	30,000	25	55	80	97	112
30,000	31,000	27	58	87	104	120
31,000	32,000	29	62	93	111	128
32,000	33,000	30	67	99	118	136
33,000	34,000	32	71	104	126	144
34,000	35,000	34	75	110	133	152
35,000	36,000	36	79	116	140	160
36,000	37,000	38	82	123	147	169
37,000	38,000	40	86	129	154	177
38,000	39,000	41	91	134	161	186
39,000	40,000	43	95	140	168	194
40,000	41,000	45	99	146	175	202
41,000	42,000	47	103	152	182	210
42,000	43,000	49	106	159	189	218
43,000	44,000	50	111	164	197	226
44,000	45,000	52	115	170	204	234

DOLLAR AMOUNTS FOR PASSENGER AUTOMOBILES (THAT ARE NOT TRUCKS OR VANS) WITH A LEASE TERM BEGINNING IN CALENDAR YEAR 2016

Figure 5-3. Lease "add back" table.

Fair Market Value of Passenger Automobile		Tax Year During Lease				
Over	Not Over	1st	2nd	3rd	4th	5th & later
45,000	46,000	54	119	176	211	243
46,000	47,000	56	123	182	218	251
47,000	48,000	58	127	187	225	260
48,000	49,000	60	130	194	232	268
49,000	50,000	61	135	200	239	276
50,000	51,000	63	139	206	246	284
51,000	52,000	65	143	211	254	292
52,000	53,000	67	147	217	261	301
53,000	54,000	69	151	223	268	309
54,000	55,000	70	155	229	275	318
55,000	56,000	72	159	235	282	326
56,000	57,000	74	163	241	289	334
57,000	58,000	76	167	247	296	342
58,000	59,000	78	171	253	303	350
59,000	60,000	80	174	260	310	359
60,000	62,000	82	181	268	321	371
62,000	64,000	86	189	280	335	387
64,000	66,000	90	197	292	349	404
66,000	68,000	93	205	304	364	420
68,000	70,000	97	213	315	379	436
70,000	72,000	101	221	327	393	453
72,000	74,000	104	229	339	407	470
74,000	76,000	108	237	351	421	486
76,000	78,000	111	245	363	436	507
78,000	80,000	115	253	375	450	518
80,000	85,000	122	267	396	474	548
85,000	90,000	131	287	425	511	588
90,000	95,000	140	307	455	546	630
95,000	100,000	149	327	484	581	671

Figure 5-3. Lease "add back" table (continued).

2018 and thereafter. However, there are a few other times when leasing is better than buying, as follows:[29]

Leasing generally becomes better if

- You can't get good financing to buy a car because of bad credit or
- You put on less then 15,000 miles per year and
- You keep your vehicles for three years or less.

This book assumes that you or your spouse have a small business or consulting practice or are considering going into business. If you're solely an employee, the rules are different and, as mentioned, more restrictive. Employees cannot deduct interest and taxes on cars, but they can deduct the business-use portion of their lease payment. Thus, if you are an employee, either pay all cash for the car or lease the car.

Author's note: Considering that a lease payment includes the interest that someone is paying, I find it strange that employees can't deduct interest but can deduct the entire amount of the lease payment based on the business use of the vehicle. This is another example of incongruous tax treatment between employees and small business owners.

Deduct Supplies and Equipment Used to Maintain Your Business Car

If you use the actual method of deducting your car expenses (gas, repairs, depreciation, etc.), you may be missing a bunch of automotive deductions. Go through your garage and basement or wherever you store tools and cleaning supplies. Make a list of the items that you use on your car. You'll probably find a battery charger, battery cables and tester, shammies, wax and wash cans, a pump, a vise, a tire inflator (that plugs into a lighter), sander, small tools, and a car repair manual. (My wife, Lori, fixes my car.) You should have found a number of items that you'd overlooked. Generally, you can deduct the cost of nonequipment items (e.g., shammies, wax cans, and water cans) if they're expected to last less than a year.[30] Most equipment, such as compressors, tools, and tire inflators, must be capitalized and depreciated unless they're considered to be of de minimis value.[31]

Author's note: From my experience with IRS audits, generally an item that is worth under $500 per item without invoices and $2,500 per item supported by invoices or $5,000 per item supported by invoices if your company is subject to and has an audited financial statement, might be allowed as an expense rather than being capitalized and depreciated over time.[32] Since you'll be backtracking through past acquisitions, it's likely you won't have receipts. Take photographs that can represent reasonable substitute evidence and conservatively estimate the value of the items if sold today. This will be less than cost, but it will be better than no deduction.

When to Sell and When to Trade: That Is the Question

There are two ways in which you can dispose of your vehicle: Sell it or trade it. Some people think that donating a business car to a charity after completely writing it off is a good deal. Sadly, this is a tax disaster.

Most people know only half the charitable deduction rules; that is, if you donate a car to a qualified charity, you can deduct the amount received by the charity for the sale of the car. Thus, if your car is sold by the charity for $6,000, you would get a $6,000 deduction. Now for the rest of the story.

You must deduct from this amount any gain that would not be a long-term gain.[33] What this means is that you must subtract any depreciation taken on your vehicle. Thus, if your vehicle was sold for $6,000 and the depreciation taken was $6,000 or more, you would get *zero* deduction—nothing, nada, zip. This is why, from a tax standpoint, you should rarely donate a car or other depreciated property to a charity.

Author's note: I heard in my seminars about two other methods for disposing of a vehicle. One was to park your vehicle in certain shopping malls near Los Angeles where there's a high probability of car theft. The other method was from a New York student who suggested abandoning the vehicle on the highway. Needless to say, these methods aren't legitimate. Now that you understand some of the basics, let's go over the flowchart shown in Figure 5-4.

As you can see, the first question that you need to answer is whether there will be a gain or a loss on the disposal of your vehicle. To do this, you would first need to know your adjusted basis. This is your cost plus any major improvements, such as a new engine,

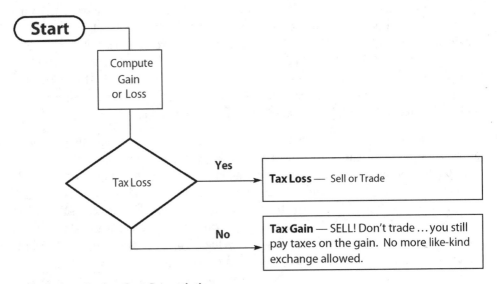

Calculation: **Basis = Cost-Depreciation**

Figure 5-4. Disposing of the automobile, decision flowchart.

minus any depreciation taken.[34] Thus, if you paid $20,000 for a car and got $10,000 in depreciation deductions, your adjusted basis would be $10,000. What this means to you is simple: If you sell the car for more than your basis, $10,000 in this example, you would have a gain, but if you sell the car for less than your basis, you would have a loss.[35] It's really that simple.

Author's note: If you don't know how much depreciation you've taken on your vehicle, you could either ask your accountant or look on your latest tax return. In addition, even if you used the IRS method, depreciation is built into the numbers, with the depreciation portion changing each year. The following are the depreciation amounts that were built into the IRS method from 2007 through 2018:[36]

- For both 2017 and 2018, 25 cents per mile
- For 2016, 24 cents per business mile
- For 2015, 24 cents per business mile
- For 2014, 22 cents per business mile
- For 2012 and 2013, 23 cents per business mile
- For 2011, 22 cents per business mile
- For 2010, 23 cents per business mile
- For 2009, 21 cents per business mile
- For 2008, 21 cents per business mile
- For 2007, 19 cents per business mile

Example: In 2018 you drove your car 20,000 miles for business. You would reduce your basis by 25 cents per business mile, or $5,000 (20,000 business miles × $0.25 for 2018). Once you know your basis, you need to know what your car will sell for. You can go to my Web site at www.taxreductioninstitute.com, which has an appraisal button, or you can go to your classified ads or check out other Web sites. Now, follow the arrows in Figure 5-4. If a loss would result, which is normally the case, you should sell your car and take a deductible loss. Thus, if you used your car 80 percent for business over the last three years and the estimate is that you will have a loss, you can deduct 80 percent of that loss in the year you sell the vehicle!

Author's note: Priot to the passage of the TCJA, if you traded a car, you would have no gain or loss on the trade-in. Thus, if you had a gain, you would avoid the gain on the trade-in. However, if you had a loss and you traded in the car, you would not have been able to deduct the loss. This was a real trap for the unwary. Under the new tax law, however, you recognize both gain and loss on trade-ins. Thus, any trade-in is treated as a sale even though you didn't get any cash.

Example: You have a car that cost you $24,000, and you've taken $8,000 of depreciation. Thus your adjusted basis is $16,000 ($24,000 cost minus $8,000 depreciation). If this vehicle is worth only $10,000 when you sell it, your loss would be $4,800 ($6,000 total loss × 80 percent business usage). If you have a loss, the flowchart recommends that either selling the car outright or trading it to a dealer will still result in the loss.

However, if you were to have a gain, then the flowchart recommends that you sell the vehicle outright since you will want the cash to pay the tax on the gain.[37] Thus, if you have a gain, you want to get enough cash to pay the tax. Trade-ins won't provide you with any cash.

Unfortunately, an estimated 80 percent of all people who use their car in business don't know this information, so they've made tremendous mistakes. If you trade in the car, which happens many times, you won't get any cash to pay the tax that will result from the new TCJA.

I had a physician in my audience who bought a new Cadillac every three years and then traded it in under the old tax law. He did this for all of his 20-plus years of practice. When I ran the numbers, I figured out that he had lost about $16,000 of loss deductions every three years for the full 20 years of practice. That's about $96,000 of lost deductions! How's that for an expensive mistake that an inexpensive book like this could have eliminated? However, under the new tax law, this wouldn't have been a problem since loss is recognized on trade-ins.

Author's note: When I told the physician that all he had to do was sell his current car to deduct the $96,000 of deferred losses, he ran out of the room as if he was running for the goal line. I never saw anyone move so quickly! I guarantee that he got rid of his current car even if he had to blow it up.

What Counts as "Miles Driven for Business"?

After speaking to over 200,000 people over the last 17 years, it still amazes me how little most people know about what trips constitute business mileage and about the documentation needed for the IRS. In fact, I would estimate that well over 95 percent of my students aren't aware of this information. Obviously, both the IRS and accountants aren't doing a good job in disseminating this crucial information, as you'll soon see.

So what are the rules for business mileage? The IRS requires you to separate business use from personal use.[38] Your business-use percentage determines your business automobile deductions.[39]

Example: You drive your car 30,000 miles per year, but only 20,000 of these miles are for business. Thus two-thirds of your car expenses—such as depreciation, wash, wax, interest, repairs, and insurance—would be deductible.

If your corporation provides a car to you or your employees[40] or if you're self-employed and you provide a car to your employees, the personal-use percentage determines additional employee compensation. The compensation to your employees can be based on one of three methods:

- *The annual lease table rule,*[41] for which you would use the IRS Annual Valuation Table. Essentially, you would determine the fair market value of the vehicle on the date of first use and find that number on the IRS Annual Valuation Table found in IRS Publication 15-B(2011), "Employer's Tax Guide to Fringe Benefits." The correct lease amount will be noted. You then would multiply this amount by the personal use.

Example: Your corporation buys a car for $20,000 and provides the car for your use. If you use it 50 percent for business, 50 percent of the lease valuation amount would be taxable to you ($5,600 × 50 percent = $2,800). This is an easy method but very expensive. Although there are other, cheaper methods, they have limited availability, as you'll see.

- *The cents-per-mile rule,* in which you would be taxed a flat 57.5 cents per mile on your personal mileage in 2015. A good tax diary would be essential for you to distinguish between personal and business mileage. As I've said before, the golden rule—"He who has the gold makes the rules"—applies here. The cents-per-mile method works only with a vehicle whose fair market value is under $16,000 and if employees drive it at least 10,000 miles per year.
- *The commuting valuation rule,*[42] which is (as you would guess) for commuting use only. The good news is that this is a great method that probably provides the lowest cost to the employee or to you if you're incorporated. However, it's also the most limited. There are three conditions.

First, you would need a written policy requiring the employee to commute to work. Second, you would need a written policy noting that the car cannot be used for personal purposes other than for commuting. Third, you can't use this for a "control employee." This is the IRS "gotcha." A *control employee* is either a board member or an officer who makes $50,000 a year or more, a director, any employee who makes at least $100,000 a year, or a 1 percent or more stockholder or equity owner.

Author's note: As you can see, the commuting valuation method won't work for you as the owner of your corporation. Also, as a reminder, all these methods apply only if you provide a vehicle to your employees or if your corporation provides you a company-owned vehicle. If you're self-employed or a limited-liability corporation (which is treated like being self-employed anyway), you don't need to worry about this.

When Is the Mileage Business and When Is It Personal?

Before I discuss what constitutes business versus personal mileage, you need to know the difference between a temporary business trip and a regular business stop or trip. A *temporary business stop* is one where you're expected to be for less than a year.[43] A *regular business stop* is one where you're expected to be for more than a year or where your stay will be indeterminate. Thus, if you're going to the bank from your home or to the post office, this would be a regular business stop because you will be going to the bank on a regular basis and not less than a year; on the other hand, if you visit a client or attend a seminar, that would be a temporary business stop.

Most people know that when they go to a business stop from their office, the mileage is business. Thus, going to a client, the bank, or the printer from your office is all business mileage. The real question and confusion arises when you go to a business stop from your home. The IRS says that there are three types of situations that will determine whether your mileage from your home is business or personal.

Situation one: Your home is your principal place of business. If your home is your principal place of business, as defined in Chapter 6, all business stops from your home are deemed to be business mileage, with the exception of a direct commute from your home to your main office where you might have a job.[44] Thus home-based business owners and consultants who make their home their principal office come out ahead here.

Example: Tom is a consultant who works primarily out of his home. He goes to the bank from his home to make deposits on Monday and visits clients Tuesday through Friday. All mileage would be deemed business mileage because his home is his principal place of business.

Situation two: Your home is not your principal place of business, but your business trip takes you outside your "normal geographic area of work." If you're traveling outside the geographic area where you normally conduct business, then all round-trip mileage to these business stops constitutes business mileage, as long as you will not be there more than one year.[45]

Example: You live in Detroit but attend a one-day seminar in Grand Rapids. All round-trip business mileage would be deductible. If, however, you were stationed in Grand Rapids for a project that's expected to last more than a year, this mileage would not be deductible because it wouldn't be a temporary business stop.

Situation three: You travel within your normal geographic area. If your home is not your principal place of business, your business mileage to your office and/or back home would be deductible *if* you went to a temporary business stop on the way to the office or on the way home.[46] All business stops after the temporary business stop also would be deemed business mileage.

Example: You go from your home, which is not your principal office, to meet a prospect for business. You then go to stops A, B, and C and then to your office. All stops would be deemed business mileage.[47]

Example: Instead of the preceding stops, you first go to the post office and then to business stops A, B, and C and then to the office. Your trip to the post office would not be deductible because it's a regular business stop and not a temporary business stop. However, all mileage thereafter would be deductible.[48]

In case you don't remember all these situations and rules, I provide a great flowchart in Figure 5-5. Just read it over. I think that you will find it amazingly simple yet thorough.

Make Your Records Bulletproof from the IRS

When you file your tax return, you or your corporation will have to answer specific questions regarding business vehicles and about having appropriate documentation in writing. The questions are part of your tax return, and you must answer all questions under penalties of perjury.[49]

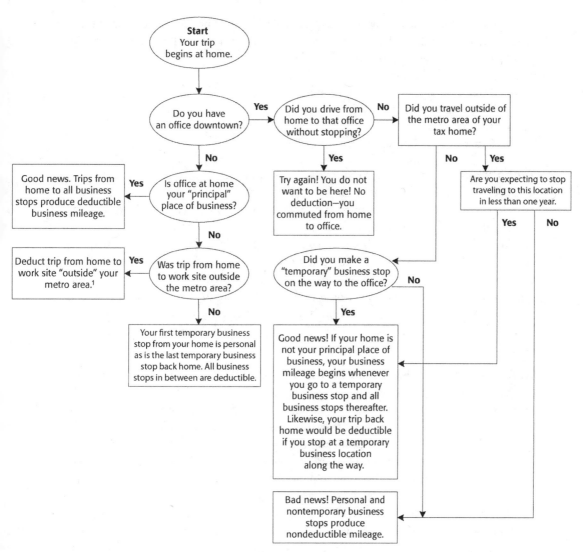

1. A recent case noted that 35 miles away from your normal work area was outside your geographic area.

Figure 5-5. Flowchart for determining business mileage (home business owners should be able to deduct all trips from home to any business stop).

One question you will have to answer is, "Do you have evidence to support business use?"[50] Another question is, "Is the evidence written?"[51] To sustain your business deductions and not be hit with severe penalties, you must be in a position to answer "Yes" to both questions.

Author's note: It is IRS policy to allow electronic documentation.[52] Using a good electronic tracker on your smart phone will thus become both critical and much easier to use than trying to do it manually. Be alert to fact that not all trackers are compliant. I recommend Taxbot that you can obtain through the app store.

There are four other dreaded questions that also must be answered regarding the miles driven during the year. In your tax return, you must report miles driven during the year broken down in the following four categories:[53]

- Total miles
- Total business miles
- Total commuting miles
- Other personal miles (noncommuting)

Author's note: Many people are surprised that the IRS asks for "other personal miles" and are curious what this entails. Other personal miles, other than commuting, are trips to a doctor, a place of worship, charitable functions, and driving children to various activities, such as karate, music or dance lessons.

Your records also must be adequate to support business use.[54] An adequate record[55] is one made at or near the time of business use.[56] *Other sufficient evidence* is acceptable only if you have direct corroborative evidence (such as statements from witnesses) or other documentary evidence.[57] I should note that you don't need to keep your records daily or contemporaneously with each trip, but the log should be completed near or at the time of each event.[58] A weekly log of what you did during the week would be acceptable.[59]

Author's note: What this all means to you is that the IRS clearly states that the log need not be daily. A log of your weekly activities made at the end of the week would suffice. However, I have found (and other accountants concur) that if you don't have something "triggering" you to record your mileage, expenses, tips, and other items daily, you'll probably forget about these expenses and thus lose the deduction. It's crucial to have a good tax organizer or diary. One of the best , easiest to use, and most compliant trackers is Taxbot. You can find out more by going to Taxbot.com or downloading it from the iphone app store or the Google Playstore for droids.

One other point is that although the IRS allows for other evidence such as statements by witnesses, I wouldn't depend on this if I were you. People forget quickly, and having to call in witnesses is a pain. Just keep a good tax diary or organizer and you will simplify your life. If you use the IRS method, you still need adequate records of your business mileage; you just don't need to keep receipts.[60] The IRS standard mileage method eliminates the need to keep gas and oil receipts but, most important, does not eliminate the need for mileage records to be broken down into business, personal, and commuting categories.

Author's note: A careful reading of the IRS regulations seems to indicate that you do not need to keep receipts for automobile expenses such as gas, oil, or tolls that are under $75 per expense.[61]

If you fail to keep the required records, such as a tax diary or organizer, this will expose you to huge penalties. Moreover, Congress wants the IRS to start asking for fraud penalties when taxpayers don't have good records of automobile business use.[62]

Types of Mileage Logs That the IRS Will Accept

The good news is that you have your choice of several types of methods that are acceptable to the IRS. The bad news is that I'll bet that you haven't been doing it right all these years.

The first choice, which is the IRS's favorite method, is the "perfect one-day car log." An example of this is shown in Figure 5-6.

You would list all your appointments, both business and personal, in a tax diary or tax organizer. When you use the car to get to an appointment, you would list the mileage next to the appointment. At the end of the day, you would record your final odometer reading. Finally, you would tally your business, personal, and commuting miles and reconcile those numbers with your beginning and ending odometer readings. The important point is that you would record your business and personal mileage daily for each stop and for each trip. This is clearly the most complicated of all the allowable methods.

The second option is the 90-day log. IRS regulations allow a mileage record for a representative portion of the year to substantiate business use for the entire year.[63] In the first example used by the IRS, it's noted that you can keep detailed daily records of your business and personal mileage, somewhat akin to the "perfect-use one-day log method," for the first three months of the year, to substantiate the entire year, if your business use of the vehicle follows the same pattern for the remaining nine months of the year.[64]

Caution: Despite allowing this statistical (90-day) approach in IRS regulations, some examiners have disallowed it under the theory that people won't go to court to fight it.

Hot tip: A new application/service is available for most smartphones that will allow you to track your business mileage for each stop at the press of a button. Check out www.taxbot.com for more information.

Example: You would keep track of your business and personal mileage for three consecutive months. If your business mileage for the three sample months is 6,000 miles and your personal mileage is 2,000 miles, you may deduct three-fourths of your car expenses for the year, or you may take three-fourths of your total year's mileage and use the IRS standard mileage rate on this amount.

Author's note: Although the IRS regulations use the first three months of the year as an example, you probably can use any normal three consecutive months. They can be January through March, March through May, or (if you've nothing for the year yet) October through December. This method is available only if you use your car on a relatively even basis from month to month. The IRS will want to see that you're not picking your busiest three months. They would check your tax diary or appointment book to see if you had relatively the same number of appointments during the other nine months.

This method assumes that you drive the same car in business during the year. If you switch off cars in the same business, you may not be able to use any statistical approach and may be limited to the "perfect one-day log."

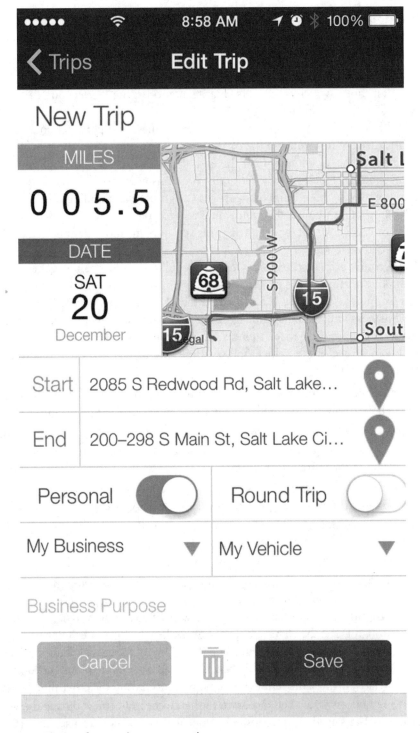

Figure 5-6. The perfect car log. www.taxbot.com

The third approach, which is also a sampling type of approach, is called the *first-week rule*. Here, the IRS assumes that you keep an automobile log for the first week of each month and then can prove by adequate records that your business use for the remainder of each month was consistent with that of the first week.[65]

The key to all the sample approaches listed here is to enter all appointments in your appointment book, tax organizer, or diary—this proves consistent business use. As you can see, these methods are fine but a bit complicated. How would you like a much easier method? I call the fourth approach the *no-hassle approach*.

This method was started by Mr. Frankel.[66] He was told by his accountant to keep track of his automobile using the perfect one-day car log. He did this for one month and wrote down over 600 appointments. He realized that he probably was losing money on all the time spent on documentation. He thus came out with a brilliant approach. He decided to keep track of only his personal and commuting mileage, which was a lot less involved.

This method is somewhat similar to the 90-day log. If you list your daily appointments in your diary or tax organizer, here's how you can make your 90-day test:

- Document your beginning and ending 90-day odometer readings and the odometer readings on January 1 and December 31.
- Record personal miles each day during the 90-day test.
- Record your commuting mileage during the 90-day test.
- Apply the percentages to the test to determine the actual mileage.

Example: For 90 days you would keep track of your personal mileage only and your beginning and ending odometer readings for the test period. Thus you might say, "To office, three miles and to home, three miles," and record all your business appointments without noting the business mileage. If your total mileage for the three-month test is 8,000 miles, of which 2,000 were personal miles, then 6,000 miles were for business. Thus, in this example, you could deduct three-fourths of your car expenses for the year.

Author's note: As a reminder, this method works only if appointments are recorded and they substantiate the business mileage. In addition, you must keep track of your appointments to show that the time period chosen truly represents the business activities for the entire year.[67] Also, as noted earlier, you can't use any sampling method if you use a second car during the year.[68]

Get a good mileage tracker

A good tracker will automatically keep track of your business vs personal mileage and keep track of expenses too. As noted above, I recommend Taxbot as they most complient and easiest to use. It also combines both mileage tracking and expense tracking in one integrated application.

If Your Records Were Lost or Destroyed, Use the Reconstruction Approach

What do you do if you have no records for the prior year? I have a method for you. It's called the *desperation* or *reconstruction approach*. Here you would backdate a tax diary based on your appointment book and, in effect, create the records.

The IRS allows you to reconstruct your records if they were lost owing to circumstances beyond your control.[69] Examples of circumstances beyond your control would be flood, fire, earthquake, theft, or other casualty.[70] You theoretically cannot reconstruct records if they were lost through your own carelessness or negligence.[71]

Author's note: Practically speaking, most IRS agents on audits will let you reconstruct your records if you use a reasonable basis for the reconstruction. You just can't pull the numbers out of thin air. For example, if you keep a diary of your appointment, you probably could write down the estimated mileage next to the appointments.

However, don't use what IRS agents call the *finger in the wind approach*. This is where you estimate your business mileage without a log or some backup support. You'll be hit with substantial penalties for trying to pull the wool over IRS eyes.

At many seminars I get asked about what is a reasonable percentage for business mileage for various professions. I thus did some research and, based on actual cases, and found the following information on various professions and the amount of business mileage allowed for that profession by the court:

Anesthesiologist	39 percent[72]
Attorney	30 percent[73]
Auto dealer	70 percent[74]
Cemetery plot sales representative	80 percent[75]
Dentist (who directed clinics and made outside calls)	80 percent[76]
Doctor	75 percent[77]
Income tax preparer	15 percent[78]
Rental real estate owner	20 percent[79]
Structural engineer	70 percent[80]
Traveling sales representative	80 percent[81]
Wholesale grocer	50 percent[82]

Author's note: These statistics are based on actual cases of people showing the business use allowed for their professions. Certainly, with the right documentation, you may be able to claim much more than was given. You can't, however, use these statistics in lieu of documentation. I offer them here to give you a feel for what was allowed by the courts.

Summary

- Use two or more cars in business and generate a lot more in deductions.
- Deduct the larger of the actual method for your car expenses or the IRS standard rates. Generally, the actual method produces more deductions.
- Buy heavy cars (weighing over 6,000 pounds) and get a fast write-off. The big winners under the "Protecting Americans from Tax Hikes" act are:
  1. With trucks that have a gross vehicle weight (GWV) over 6,000 pounds and new and used trucks with the same GWV and that have cargo areas of 6 feet or more you get to deduct up to $500,000 of the business use by making an election to do so on your tax return.
  2. Second winners are both new and used SUVs with GVW over 6,000 pounds and that have truck chassis. You can elect to write-off $25,000 of the business use.
- Buy your car, rather than lease it, and hold onto it for at least four years.
- Identify and deduct supplies and equipment used to maintain your car.
- Sell cars that produce a deductible loss, but trade cars that produce a taxable profit.
- Generally sell cars if you've used the IRS method of deducting vehicle expenses.
- Rarely donate a car that has been depreciated. You probably won't get any deduction.
- Make your car into a tax-deductible goldmine either by making your home the principal office for your business or by having a temporary business stop on the way to the office and/or on the way home.
- Keep a 90-day daily log of car use, preferably using the no-hassle approach.
- Use a good mileage and expense tax tracker such as Taxbot (www.taxbot.com).

Notes

1. Sections 1.162-1(a) and 1.162-2 of the ITR. See also *Commissioner v. Griner*, 71-2 USTC Par. 9714 (N.D. Fla. 1971) and *Commissioner v. Cavender*, 71-2 USTC Par. 9723 (S.D. W. Va. 1971).
2. Sections 1.274-6T, 1.274-5T(b)(6), and 1.274-5T(c) of the ITR. See also *Reems v. Commissioner*, 67 TCM 3050 (1994) and IRS Publication 17 (2001).
3. See note 1.
4. *On-RI-GA-Medical Professional Association*, T.C. Memo 1978-183.
5. Section 1.274-5T(c)(3) of the ITR.
6. Sections 1001, 1012, and 1016 of the IRC.
7. Section 1.167(g)-1 of the ITR.
8. Sections 1011 and 1012 of the IRC.
9. See note 7.
10. Revenue Procedure 2008-72, 2008-50 IRB 11/24/08.
11. Sections 1.162-1 and 1.162-6 of the ITR.
12. Ibid. and IR Notice 2013-95 (12/06/13).
13. Ibid.
14. Ibid.
15 IRC Section 217 (k) as amended by 2017 Tax Cuts and Jobs Act Section 11049.

16. Runzheimer International.
17. IR Notice 2013-95.
18. Ibid.
19. Ibid. and IRS Publication 463.
20. Revenue Procedure 2015-19.
21. Section 280F(a)(2)(A) of the IRC; Small Business Jobs Act of 2010, 9/27/10.
22. Section 168(d)(3)(A) of the IRC and Section 1.168(d)-1(a) of the ITR.
23. Ibid.
24. Section 280F(d)(2) of the IRC and Section 1.280F-2T(i) of the ITR.
25. Section 280F(d)(5)(A) of the IRC and Section 1.280F-6T of the ITR.
26. Ibid. and Section 280F(a)(1)(C) of the IRC.
27. Section 1.280F-6T(c) of the ITR.
28. *Rodgers Dairy Co.*, 14 TC 66 (1950), *acq.*
29. Research Recommendations, Vol. 54, No. 25, p. 4 (12/3/2001).
30. Section 1.263(a)-1(b) of the ITR. *Cincinnati, New Orleans, and Texas Pacific Railway Co. v. United States*, 424 F.2d 563 (Ct. Cl. 1970); *Metrocorp, Inc. v. Commissioner*, 116 TC 211 (2001).
31. Ibid.
32. IRS Notice 2015-82.
33. Section 170(e)(1)(a) of the IRC.
34. Sections 1001(a)-(c), 1012, and 1016 of the IRC.
35. Section 1001 of the IRC.
36. Revenue Procedure 2009-54; see note 10; and CCH Exp 2002 FED Par. 14,417.043, *Substantiation Requirements and Per Diem Rules;* and IR Notice 2012-95 (supra).
37. Section 1031 of the IRC as amended by the 2017 Tax Cuts and Jobs Act (Public Law 115-97) Section 13303.
38. Section 1.274-5t(b)(6) and (d) of the ITR.
39. Sections 274(d)(4) and 280F(d)(4)(A) of the IRC. See also Sections 1.274-5T(d) and 6T(d) of the ITR.
40. Technically speaking, personal use determines the amount of the fringe benefit reportable by your corporation and includable in your income if either the vehicle cents-per-mile or commuting valuation methods are used for valuing the fringe benefits. See section 1.61-2T(d)-(f) of the ITR. See also IRS Publication 15B.
41. Section 1.61-2T(d) of the ITR.
42. Section 1.61-2T(f) of the ITR.
43. Revenue Ruling 99-7, 1999-5, I.R.B. See also IR 2013-95, PLR 199948019 (12/7/99) and IRS Publication 463, pp. 13-15 (2001).
44. Revenue Ruling 90-23, I.R.B. 1990-11. Modified and superseded by Revenue Ruling 99-7, 1999-5 I.R.B. See also *Curphey v. Commissioner,* 73 TC 766 (1980). Interestingly, the IRS made a mistake in superseding Revenue Ruling 90-23. This ruling was more encompassing and had most of the rules spelled out clearly and simply. Although Revenue Ruling 99-7 was supposed to clarify some ambiguities in Revenue Ruling 90-23, the IRS obsoleted the ruling instead of simply amplifying it (elaborating on the ruling). This has made this whole area very confusing and unclear.
45. Revenue Ruling 99-7, supra.
46. Ibid.
47. Ibid. and IRS Publication 463, pp. 13-15 (2001).
48. IRS Publication 463, pp. 13-15 (2001).
49. IRS Form 1040 and see declaration immediately above the signature line on IRS Form 1040 (U.S. Individual Tax Return) and Form 1120 (U.S. Corporation Tax Return). See IRS Form 2106 and Section 1.274-5T(d)(2)(1) of the ITR.

50. IRS Form 2106. See also Section 1.274-5T(d)(2)(1) of the ITR.
51. Ibid. See also Form 4562 and the instructions thereunder.
52. Revenue Procedure 91-59, 1991-2 C.B. 841.
53. See notes 50 and 51.
54. Section 274(d) of the IRC.
55. Section 274(d) of the IRC and Section 1.274-5T (a) of the ITR.
56. Section 1.274-5T(c)(1) and 1.274-5T(c)(2)(ii)(A) of the ITR.
57. Section 1.274-5T(c)(3) of the ITR.
58. Section 1.274-5T(c)(2) of the ITR.
59. Ibid.
60. Revenue Ruling 2008-50; see footnote 10. See also IRS Publication 463.
61. Section 1.274-5T(c)(2)(iii)(A) of the ITR.
62. Conference Committee Report on P.L. 99-44, as found in 8A Standard Federal Tax Report [CCH 5528.034 (1988)].
63. Section 1.274-5T(c)(3) of the ITR.
64. Section 1.274-5T(c)(3)(ii) of the ITR.
65. Ibid. and see IRS Publication 463.
66. *J. E. Frankel v. Commissioner*, 27 TCM 817 (1968) and *B. W. Moretz*, 36 T.C.M. 1341 (1977).
67. Section 1.274-5T(c)(3)(ii) of the ITR.
68. Section 1.274-5T(c)(3)(ii)(B) of the ITR.
69. Section 1.274-5T(c)(5) of the ITR.
70. *I. A. Murray v. Commissioner*, 41 TCM 337 (1980).
71. *P. L. Luben v. Commissioner*, 37 TCM 550 (1978). "Protecting Americans from Tax Hikes" act.
72. *Edilberto Beltran*, T.C. Memo 1982-153.
73. *Glenn Strother*, T.C. Memo 1957-102.
74. *Harry Canelo*, 41 BTA 713 (1940), *acq.*
75. *Doris Jones*, 11 TCM 529 (1952).
76. *Floyd Bickel II*, T.C. Memo 1966-202 (1966).
77. *T.K. Lewis*, 9 TCM 32 (1950).
78. *Frank Thomas*, T.C. Memo 1969-108 (1969).
79. *Nickolas Barnes*, T.C. Memo 1981-539 (1981).
80. *William Schmidt and Comp.*, 25 A.F.T.R. 2d 70-1353 (7th Cir. 1970).
81. *Reems v. Commissioner*, 67 TCM 3050 (1994).
82. *Harriet Wagner v. Lucus*, 38 F.2d 391 (CA Dist. 1930).

6

Home Office: The Misunderstood Key to Saving $15,000 Every Five Years

Tax reform is taking the taxes off things that have been taxed in the past and putting taxes on things that haven't been taxed before.

—Art Buchwald

I s a home office really worth it? Be honest. Do you believe or have you heard from your accountant that taking a home office deduction isn't worth the risk or hassle? I'll bet your answer to this question is yes!

Without question, the home office area has more myths than any other topic. People have told me that they'd heard that they can't claim a home office because their home is not zoned commercially. The truth is that the Internal Revenue Service (IRS) couldn't care less about your local zoning. I also have heard with more frequency than I would have believed that "you can't claim a home office deduction unless you have a back entrance." I'm not sure what business these people are in!

> **Chapter Overview**
> This will be one of the best and most comprehensive chapters on this subject that you'll ever read. I'll be covering the following:
> - Learn why it's worth taking a home office deduction.
> - Learn how to qualify for a home office deduction using your home as a principal residence.
> - Learn how to qualify for the home office deduction by using the "meet and greet" test.
> - Learn how to qualify for the home office deduction by having a separate structure apart from the home as an office.
> - Learn how to qualify for the home office deduction by storing inventory and product samples.
> - Learn how to qualify for the home office deduction by having a day-care business in the home.

A home office deduction is like having a bunch of pregnant dollar bills—they give birth to many more dollars. If you look at the example for the individual named Snyder, you will see that, based on a $200,000 home, a home office can generate over $15,000 in cash *every five years* (see Figure 6-1). This is based on the fact that you get some new deductions. You can deduct some of your property taxes and mortgage interest as a business expense. You also can increase your business mileage because travel from a qualified home office to a business stop is all business.[1] Finally, you get additional deductions that you aren't normally eligible to get,

> **Chapter Overview (Cont.)**
> - Learn about the little-known IRS strategies needed to audit-proof a home office deduction.
> - Learn how to avoid most taxes on the sale of a home where the home office deduction was claimed.
> - Take the one deduction that normally gets missed—even if you never claim a home office.
> - Understand the rules for the wonderful expensing of assets that could increase your depreciation deductions by over $20,000 per year.

such as depreciation, some repairs on the home, utilities, and some house cleaning.[2] I also have factored in something that most people never think of: interest. I assumed that you could earn a conservative long-term interest rate of 6 percent on your tax savings. My question now is simple: "Assuming that you would qualify for the home office deduction, would an extra $15,000 or more every five years be worth the slight increase in documentation?"

Author's note: Even better, the home office deduction becomes even better after the new Tax Cuts and Jobs Act since it provides a partial way of getting around some of the limitations that the new law implements such as the limitation on $10,000 in state and local income /property taxes and the new interest limitation on up to $750,000 in mortgage debt. This is just another reason why many people should have either a side business or become an independent contractor.

Home Office Rules

The general rule is that you can't deduct your home or dwelling unit insofar as it is used as a residence.[3] However, if you meet the home office rules, you can deduct some expenses related to your residence. The law states that a home office deduction is available only to the extent that a portion of the dwelling unit (your home) is used exclusively on a regular basis as one of the following:[4]

- Your principal place of business
- A place of business that you use to meet and deal with patients, clients, or customers in the normal course of your trade or business
- A separate structure that is not attached to the dwelling unit (residence)
- Part of a day-care business

First-Year Tax Refund

	Total	Home Office Percentage	Home Office Deduction	Tax Benefit Rate	Tax Refund
Mortgage Interest	$10,401	15.84%	$1,648	13.02%	$215
Real Estate Taxes	947	15.84%	150	13.02%[1]	20
Utilities	1,704	15.84%	270	54.02%[2]	146
Homeowner's Insurance	310	15.84%	49	54.02%	26
General Repairs	600	15.84%	95	54.02%	51
Pest Control	400	15.84%	63	54.02%	34
Repairs to Office	200	100%	200	54.02%	108
Depreciation – Furniture	1,886	100%	1,886	54.02%	1,019
Depreciation – Home	2,545	15.84%	403	54.02%	218
Snyder's cash-in-pocket from home-office deduction					**$1,837**

Economic Results

Cash from home-office deducation	$1,837
Cash from extra business mileage	582[3]
Total first-year cash	2,419
6% annuity due factor for 5 years	x5.9753
Net cash after 5 years	$14,454

1. Self-employment tax rate.
2. Self-employment tax rate plus 31% federal tax rate plus 10% state tax rate.
3. Snyder's home business allows him to reduce his personal mileage and increase his business auto expense by $1,077. Thus $582 is refunded by the tax collectors ($1,077 x 54.02%).

Facts: Snyder files a joint tax return with his wife. The Snyders earn $198,000 in taxable income. This puts them in the 33 percent federal and 8 percent state income tax brackets. Mrs. Snyder earns $98,000 from her job as an employee in town. Mr. Snyder works out of his home and earns net taxable income of $100,000, which is reported on Schedule C of Form 1040.

Figure 6-1. How Snyder benefits from the home office deduction.

In addition, in the case of an employee, the home office deduction is allowed only if the exclusive use is for the convenience of the employer.[5] Although this is a factual issue, if you are an employee, the courts generally feel that this test is met if "you are required by the employer to have a home office or to work out of your home." Let's examine these tests.

Qualify by Making Your Home Your Principal Place of Business

What constitutes a principal place of business has been the subject of a great deal of litigation and controversy. The good news is that this issue went all the way up to the Supreme Court to decide.[6] The bad news is that the Supreme Court should never take a tax case because the justices rarely understand what they're doing in this area.

The court provided two tests for determining whether your home is a principal office.

The first and most important test is, "Where are the most important functions conducted for your business?" For most businesses, it's where you would see customers or patients or where you render your services.

Example: Doctor Soliman was an anesthesiologist. He rendered his services in the hospital but billed his patients and kept his books from home. The hospital is where he performs his important services.

The second test is a time test. If you work over 50 percent of your total working hours out of your home, then your home will qualify as a principal place of business.

This is important to you because the IRS requires all businesses first to examine where they do their most important functions for their business. If there's a clear answer, this is the test that is used, and you never resort to the time test.[7] Some examples of major factors that the IRS uses would be where you meet your customers, where you render your services, and where contracts are signed. Some examples will illustrate the application of the *Soliman* decision very clearly.

Example: A sales representative spends 30 hours per week taking orders from clients in various stores and spends 12 hours per week working at home on administration for his business. Visiting with clients and taking orders will be deemed the most important functions for his business, and he would not be eligible for the home office deduction under *Soliman*. Yuck!

Example: Same facts as above, but the orders are placed over the phone, and the sales representative spends 30 hours a week working from his home and 12 hours seeing customers. He would be allowed a home office deduction because the most important business functions occurred at home (selling products and taking orders), and if there was any confusion, he met the 50 percent time test.[8]

Those adversely affected by *Soliman* will be people who really perform most administrative duties out of their home and/or put in over 50 percent of their working hours outside the home. Realtors, insurance professionals, financial planners, and many consultants probably will have their home office deductions disallowed because of where they see clients and where they usually perform most of their working activities. The same would be true for most plumbers, carpenters, and electricians.

Thus who can take a home office deduction under the *Soliman* case? Anyone who truly works out of his or her home and performs his or her most important functions at home. This would include network marketers, freelance writers, musicians who do most of their practicing out of their homes, and consultants who do most of their important work out of their homes.

Because the *Soliman* case eliminated the deduction for many people, Congress passed a great exception to the *Soliman* case. If you meet this exception, you don't need to worry about the *Soliman* requirements. If you don't meet this exception, you're back to trying to fit within the *Soliman* factors.

Exception to *Soliman*

Starting in 1999, Congress passed a new exception to *Soliman* that will help many small-business and home-based business owners. Your home office qualifies as a principal place of business if[9]

- The office is used to conduct administrative or management activities of your trade or business, and
- There is no other office where you conduct substantial administrative activities.

Thus, if you do your logs, contact patients or customers, listen to educational tapes, read business materials, and prepare bills for customers, you're rendering administrative activities.

Example: John, a self-employed plumber, spends most of his time in homes repairing and installing plumbing. He has an office at home that he uses exclusively and regularly for his administrative and management activities, such as billing customers, making appointments, and ordering supplies. His home qualifies as a principal office for the home office deduction.[10]

Example: Eddie, an independent contractor of clothing, meets with clothing store owners in their stores. He shows his new lines and takes the initial orders, which he completes in his home. His home is where he conducts his administrative activities for billing customers, keeping his books and records, ordering supplies, and forwarding orders and reports to his company. Assuming that Eddie uses a room exclusively and regularly for his business, his home office is deemed to be his principal place of business for the home office deduction.

The real congressional "gotcha" is found in the second part of the exception. You can't have another office where you render any significant administrative or management activities.[11] This means that you can have another office, but you just can't do any substantial administrative services there.[12] In fact, even if an office is provided you, you still may claim a home office deduction if you opt to work out of your home and perform all your administrative and management activities out of your home. Thus, if you do some minimal paperwork elsewhere, this won't disqualify you from the home office deduction.[13] This is especially true if you render some administrative or management services at a location that isn't a fixed office or fixed place, such as a hotel while traveling or a car.[14]

Example: Edith is a traveling saleswoman. She occasionally writes up orders and sets appointments from the hotel room during business travel. She has no fixed location for performing her administrative or management activities other than in a set spot in her home. She does all her other administrative activities in her home, including finishing the sales paperwork, preparing reports to her company, keeping her books and records, and billing customers whenever credit was declined or a check bounced. Her home qualifies as the principal office for purposes of the home office deduction.

Author's note: This is a very different result from that of the *Soliman* case, where both Edith and Eddie would have been deemed to perform their most important functions away from the home. Thus this exception has saved their deduction, as it will save the home office deduction for many small-business owners.

I also should note here that the key is that your administrative and management activities must occur out of your home. Other activities can occur from other locations. Thus, if you meet with clients or customers or you render services such as medical, legal, and plumbing away from the home, these services will not disqualify you from the home office exception.[15] The key to the *Soliman* exception is that your administrative or management activities must occur out of a set spot in your home.

One final point that should be noted is that you can have other companies do some administration for you, and this won't disqualify you from the exception.[16] Thus, if you have a billing company bill your customers, this *won't* disallow the deduction.

Qualify by Meeting and Greeting Clients or Customers in Your Home

If you do not use your home office as your principal place of business, another way to qualify for the deduction is to use the home office as a place to meet or deal with clients, patients, and prospects in the normal course of your business.[17] However, this exception applies only if the use of the home office by your clientele is substantial and integral to conducting your business.[18] Occasional meetings are insufficient to make this exception applicable.[19]

Example: A lawyer meets with clients in her office three days a week and in her home two days a week. She qualifies for the exception.

This "meet and greet" test requires a physical presence in your home. You can't just make phone calls, no matter how extensive or frequent the conversations.[20]

Author's note: If you want to use the "meet and greet" exception, I recommend at my seminars that you have your clients, customers, or prospects sign a guest log whenever they come to your home. This log should show who the guest was, the date that he or she visited you, and the reason for the visit. More on this will be discussed below in the section on audit-proofing your home office.

Qualify by Using a Separate Structure

You may qualify for a home office deduction if, in connection with your trade or business, you use a separate structure not attached to your dwelling unit.[21] The separate structure must be used exclusively and on a regular basis for your business.[22] (These requirements will be discussed further below.) It need not, however, be your principal place of business or a place where you meet customers or prospects.[23] Examples of structures that meet the "separate structure" requirement would be an artist's studio, a florist's greenhouse, and a carpenter's workshop.[24]

Qualify by Storing Inventory or Product Samples

A deduction is allowed when you use your home on a regular basis to store either inventory or product samples if you are in the business of selling products at retail or wholesale and if your residence is your fixed location for that business.[25] This exception is available to you even if you sell your products at no fixed locations, such as craft shows, flea markets, or a customer's business premises.

On reading this, you might be tempted to place all your product samples along your hallways and in your bathrooms in order to inflate the deduction (as some tax books and even some companies have recommended). However, the IRS has thought of this trick. The storage of your inventory or product samples must be in a separately identifiable area suitable for storage.[26] Moreover, only this separately identifiable storage area would qualify for the deduction.

Example: Jane runs her network marketing business out of her home, where she sells vitamin supplements. She stores her inventory and product samples in a set part of her basement. She may claim a deduction for the space used to store product samples and inventory.

The space used doesn't have to be used exclusively for storing inventory. It just has to be in a set, identifiable area. Thus, even though Jane uses her basement for occasional personal use, her deduction wouldn't be denied.[27]

Finally, this exception applies only to inventory or product samples and not to other business assets. Thus it doesn't apply to old records,[28] law or business books,[29] or client or business files.[30]

Qualify by Running a Day-Care Center in Your Home

Without question, day care is in big demand and is very encouraged by companies and the government as well. In fact, in terms of deducting home office expenses, day-care business gets slightly better treatment than other small businesses.

The general rule is that a day-care business can deduct a portion of a home that is used regularly in the trade or business of day care for children and adults who are age 65 or older or who are mentally or physically incapable of caring for themselves. The key is that the day care must have applied for or have been granted a state license or be exempt from having a license.[31]

Author's note: If you want to claim a home office deduction for a day-care facility, you must comply with state law requirements.

The nice fact about day-care facilities is that you don't need to use a room or part of a room exclusively for the business.[32] In fact, you can use a room for day care during the day and use it for your family or for personal reasons at night and still get a home office deduction. However, the IRS has developed a formula for prorating your business use among the available hours.[33]

The formula uses two fractions. The first fraction is the square footage used by the day-care facility out of the home's total square footage. The second fraction would be the total hours in the year that the day care uses the home divided by the total hours in the year, which is 8,760 for a normal year and 8,784 for a leap year. Hours used to prepare for the day care or to clean up after the care is over also get treated as day-care hours.[34] Thus it would appear as follows:

$$\frac{\text{Square feet used by day care}}{\text{Total square feet of the home}} \times \frac{\text{total hours in the year for day care}}{\text{hours in a year (8,760)}}$$

This fraction is the portion of home expenses such as interest, taxes, utilities, repairs, and depreciation that can be deducted on the tax return for the day-care business.

Example: Mary runs a day care out of her home for 12 hours a day, 5 days a week, 50 weeks a year. (Thus she runs the day care for 3,000 hours a year.) She uses 1,200 square feet of the home's 1,600 square feet for the day care.[35] Assuming that her total housing expenses for taxes, interest, depreciation, utilities, garbage, etc. totaled $10,000, the following would be her home office deduction:

$$\frac{1{,}200 \text{ sq ft}}{1{,}600 \text{ sq ft}} \times \frac{3{,}000 \text{ hours}}{8{,}760 \text{ total hours}} \times \$10{,}000 \text{ expenses} = \$2{,}569$$

You Must Use Your Home Office for Business Regularly

In addition to one of the business uses that I noted earlier, you must use your home regularly for business. Interestingly, the Internal Revenue Code does not define *regular use*. However, some courts indicate that *regular use* means using your home three to four days a week for 10 to 12 hours a week.[36] Thus, if you use your home for business less than this, such as four hours per week, your use may not be deemed regular, so your deduction may be disallowed.

You Must Use Your Home Office for Business Exclusively

With the exception of storing inventory or product samples or running a day-care facility in your home, you can qualify for the home office deduction only for the parts of your home used exclusively for business. This is a difficult requirement for many people. The term *exclusive use* means just that.[37] No personal or other nonqualifying work may occur in the home office area.[38] A portion of a room can qualify as a home office, but all business items must be located in the same contiguous area, and there should be some physical separation of the business area from the personal area.[39] You must get all personal items out of the home office area other than purely de minimis items such as a radio for music while you're working, etc.

Author's note: I constantly get asked whether the IRS actually will come over to your home and check out whether you're using a portion of the home exclusively for business. The answer is yes, an agent may pay a visit. Get any personal items out of the home office area. Get all nonbusiness books out of the bookshelf in the home office, and don't play games on the computer. An IRS agent that I know was involved in an audit where the taxpayer kept a convertible couch in his home office. When questioned, the taxpayer admitted that his parents sometimes slept there on occasional visits. His entire home office deduction was disallowed.

What Deductions Are Available with a Home Office?

In claiming deductions for a home office, you need to break them into three categories:

1. *Expenses that are directly related to the home office portion.*[40] Examples of these types of deductions are painting of the home office or repairing a water leak in the home office. These would be deductible in full.
2. *Expenses that don't benefit the home office either directly or indirectly.* These expenses are *not* deductible because they are clearly not related to the home office in any way. Some examples of these expenses are repairs or painting in another room, plumbing repairs in an unrelated bathroom, and according to the IRS, lawn care if you don't meet and greet people in your home.[41] These expenses are not deductible at all.

Author's note: Many people believe that in order to take the deduction, you must own your home. This is incorrect. You can deduct the portion of the rent that's attributable to your home office square feet.

3. *Indirect expenses related to the home in general.* These include depreciation, costs for a home security system and for monitoring, utilities, and repairs and painting to the outside of the house. These expenses get allocated using one of three methods noted below.

Methods for Allocating Indirect Expenses

There are three methods that you can use to calculate the amount of indirect expenses that you can deduct.

Method one is based on the amount of home office square feet out of the total usable square footage of the house.[42] Interestingly, only the *usable square feet* count, not the total square footage.[43] You also can ignore square feet outside the house, such as a deck (see Figure 6-2).

Second Floor

Three Choices
1. Number of rooms office occupies, divided by total rooms in house.
2. Total square feet office occupies as a percentage of total square feet in house.
3. Net square feet applicable to office use.

Computation of Net Square Feet
Total square feet 25' x 35' x 2 floors   1,750

Deduct
Common area:		
First floor entry and stairway	128	
Second floor stairway and landing	128	
Second floor common area	24	
Deck (not a living area)	75	355
Net square feet base		1,395

Analysis of Choices Based on:
1. Number of rooms 1/8 = 12.50%
2. Total square feet 221/1,675 (1,750 − 75 for deck) = 13.19%
3. Net square feet 221/1,395 = 15.84%

Figure 6-2. Maximizing home office square footage.

Example: You have 1,675 square feet in your home, and your home office is 221 square feet. The allocation of your indirect expenses would be 221/1,675 = 13.19 percent.

The second method is known as the *number-of-rooms method.* You would take the room used for the home office and divide by the number of rooms in the house.[44] Thus, if you have eight rooms, and you use one room as an office, you may deduct $\frac{1}{8}$, 12.50 percent, of the indirect costs. There's a catch with this method, however. The IRS allows this method only if your rooms are approximately equal in size and you don't use a room that's much smaller than the other rooms.[45]

The final method, which may be the best method of all, is called the *net-square-footage method.*[46] This is similar to the square footage method, but you subtract from your total square feet of common areas, such as hallways, entranceways, landings, and stairways. In the preceding example, you would have 221 square feet in your home office divided by your net square feet, which would be 1,395. This would result in a deduction of 15.84 percent of your indirect expenses.

Author's note: I've discussed these methods in order to alert you and your accountant to take the approach that results in the biggest deduction. As you can see, in our example, the amount of the deduction will vary from 12.50 percent using the number-of-rooms method to 15.84 percent using the net-square-footage method. This could result in thousands of dollars of extra deductions over your duration of use of a home office.

Starting in 2013,[47] the IRS has allowed use of a "simplified method" for keeping track of your home office deductions. If you use this method, you would compute the amount of square feet used in a qualifying home office and multiply this figure by $5. This is your total deduction. Thus, if you use a room that has 250 square feet for business, you would get a deduction of $1,250 (250 feet × $5/sq foot).

The problem with this method is that it gives the worst results for taxpayers for several reasons. First, the simplified method is in lieu of any other home deductions including depreciation. You don't get depreciation. Secondly, the home office rules only allow a home office deduction up to the net income from the business. Any excess can be carried forward to future income. With the simplified method, there is no carryover. Third, you cannot deduct any other home office expenses such as the business use of your interest and taxes in computing your net income from your business. These expenses, however, can still be taken as an itemized deduction. Finally, you must meet all of the home office requirements such as being the principal place of business and use a portion of the home regularly and exclusively. In short, I don't recommend the simplified IRS method.

Audit-Proofing Your Home Office

Take a Picture

Take a yearly, dated picture of your home office to establish that it was used exclusively for business. It's easy to say that you qualified for the home office deduction. However, if you get audited for it, you'll need some planning to prove that you were eligible in the past. Thus one important bit of documentation that you should have is a yearly photograph of your office to prove that it actually existed and that there were no personal items in the office that would disqualify the deduction. It's best to use a digital camera because the date of the photo usually is recorded on the picture.

Author's note: Do *not* send the photo to the IRS with your tax return. One person did this—and in the photo made some "undesirable" hand and arm gestures! Personally, I thought that it was quite amusing, but the IRS higher management didn't, and the person got audited.

Keep Records of the Square Footage

Keep blueprints or other documentation showing the square footage of your home office and the square footage of your home. If blueprints aren't available, make a drawing of your home office showing the relationship of the home office's square footage to the total square footage of the home.

Display Your Address and Phone Number

Use your home office phone number and address on business cards, stationery, and advertising as proof that you actually operated a business from your home. If economically feasible, install a separate business phone in your home. The business phone should be listed in the business's name in both the White and the Yellow Pages. You should have business stationery with your home address on it.[48] If you have two business addresses, they should have equal prominence on the stationary.[49] You also should use your home address on your business cards.[50] If two addresses appear, they should have equal prominence.[51] If you have two phone numbers, they should have equal prominence too.[52]

Author's note: You would be wise to put in a second business line anyway because tax law allows no deduction for the first telephone line into your personal residence regardless of use.[53] Local charges are deductible only if you install a second phone line in your home. Welcome to tax simplification!

I should note that long-distance charges made for business reasons are deductible and should be documented on your bill.

Have Your Business Visitors Sign a Logbook

If you claim a home office deduction because you use the office in the normal course of business to meet and deal with clients, patients, or prospects, have your business visitors sign a guest book each time they come to your office. The guest book need not be formal, just a record of business contacts who meet with you in your home office. It should contain the name of the guest, the date of the visit, and the purpose. Remember: The burden of proof is on you. If you claim use of your home office to see clients and customers, you must be able to prove that clients, patients, prospects, or colleagues were physically present in your home office.

Keep a Work-Activity Log for Time Spent in Your Office

Showing how much time you spent working in the home office is important because it establishes that you put in your substantial administrative time and worked in the office regularly (at least 10 hours per week). Thus a work-activity log, which could be a meticulously annotated daily diary or tax organizer, constitutes an excellent supporting document to establish where you spent your work time. This does not need to be elaborate. You already have a daily diary. Simply use it as an activity log. If you are working in your home office, you simply could write "home office" (or some abbreviation) and note the time spent there.

Author's note: I've also found that some details that indicate the specific type of work you are doing at home help immensely. See the example in Figure 6-3.

Problems with Claiming a Home Office

As I illustrated at the beginning of this chapter, a home office deduction can be worth thousands to you every year. There are three drawbacks to claiming this deduction. However, most of the drawbacks can be eliminated with some planning or knowledge. Remember my favorite saying: "Where there's a will, there's a lawyer."

1. The Home Office Deduction Has a Gross Income Limitation

Your home office deduction is the only business deduction that is limited to the net income from the business that is attributable to your home office.[54]

Example: Alan conducts a home-based business for which he claims a home office deduction. He grosses $6,000 from his business and has $5,000 of business expenses other than for his home office. His home office expenses for his share of the taxes, utilities, interest, depreciation, security monitoring, and garbage collection costs amount to $2,500. He may deduct only $1,000 of these costs because his net income from the home-based business is $1,000 ($6,000 less $5,000 of business expenses). This is the bad news.

The good news is that you don't lose the excess deductions from the home office because you get to carry them over forever.[55] What this means is that you can use the excess deduction against future income from your home business.

Example: In the preceding example, if Alan makes a net profit of $4,000 next year, he may use the unused $1,500 deduction to offset this $4,000 net profit and thus pay tax on only $2,500 in the next year.

2. You Will Have to Pay Tax on Any Depreciation at the 25 Percent Rate

If you claim a home office deduction, you will be depreciating a portion of your home. This means that you take the home office portion of your residence and deduct the cost over 39 years.[56]

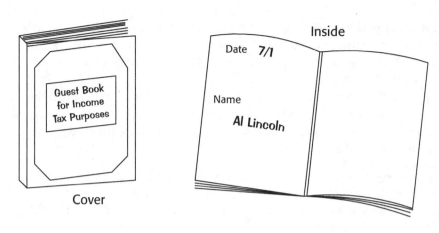

Cover   Inside

Work-activity log for typical morning

1 MONTH _____ May _____ DAY OF THE WEEK S (M) T W T F S			
APPOINTMENTS DAILY	**BUSINESS**	**COMMUTE**	**PERSONAL**
7:00 AM			
7:30			
8:00 Study HTSA Program HO			
8:30			
9:00 Prospect calls			
9:30 Al Lincoln contract			
10:00			
10:30			
11:00			
11:30 Wendy Wilson OO			
12:00 PM			
12:30			
1:00			
1:30			
2:00			
2:30			

HO = Home Office, OO = Other Office

Figure 6-3. Guest book and work-activity log for a typical morning.

Example: You paid $200,000 for your home. If you use 10 percent for your home office, then you deduct $20,000 over 39 years at the rate of approximately $513 per year. Thus, if you were in the 35 percent federal tax bracket over all the 39 years, this would save you $7,000.

If you sell your home, you cannot exclude the entire amount of gain on the sale. As a result of the tax simplification law, Congress makes you pick up this depreciation taken after May 6, 1977, as income and taxes you on it at your normal tax rate, but up to a maximum 25 percent rate.[57]

Example: Karen claims a home office in 1998 and thereafter. If she claims $4,000 in depreciation as a result of the home office, she'll have to report the first $4,000 of gain on the sale of her home at the 25 percent rate of tax, which means that she would pay back $1,000 on the depreciation taken.[58]

Author's note: This may sound bad to you, but it isn't. If you are in the 32, 35, or 37 percent bracket when you take the depreciation but have to pay it back at only the maximum rate of 25 percent, you're certainly coming out ahead!

An Employee Can Claim a Home Office Deduction Only if the Office Is for the Convenience of the Employer

As I mentioned earlier, employees don't get the same benefits from the tax law that self-employed people get. If you're an employee, your home office not only must meet all the rules noted earlier but also must be used for the convenience of the employer.[59] Thus the home has to be more than just helpful and appropriate for you.[60] This means[61] that

- Your company must require you to maintain your home office as a condition of your employment, or
- The home office is necessary for the functioning of your employer's business, or
- The home office is necessary for you to perform your duties.

What all this means is that if your employer provides you with a perfectly good office, you probably can't claim a home office deduction as an employee. If, however, the office is inadequate for you to perform your functions (if there's too much noise, if there's not enough privacy for sensitive work, or if you're a musician and practice is mandatory), then you can claim a home office.

Author's note: Frankly, it's much better for an employee to have a side business and work this business out of the home. However, if you choose not to have a business, at least get a letter from your boss mandating that you work at home and giving the reasons for this directive. Remember: If the IRS feels that the office is for your convenience and not that of the firm, you won't get the deduction.

Depreciate Furniture and Equipment That You Use for Business

A major misunderstanding is that the home office deduction applies to all business equipment, too. This is not true. The deduction applies only to the real estate and related deductions, such as interest, taxes, depreciation, utilities, rent, and maintenance.[62] Furniture and equipment are depreciable to the extent you use these items for business. You do *not* need to claim a home office deduction in order to deduct your furniture.[63]

Example: You work in an office in your home but do not qualify for the home office deduction because the office is not used exclusively for business. Your work adds up to 80 percent of the use. The result is that you may depreciate the furniture and equipment such as the desk, the chair, the computer, the carpeting under the desk, and the lamp lighting up the desk.

Author's note: This applies even if you're an employee taking work home. If you use a desk 80 percent for business, you may depreciate that desk.[64]

Now that you are aware that you can depreciate furniture such as desks, chairs, file cabinets, and computers, the question becomes, "What do you depreciate?" The answer is that if you purchased the desk, the chair, the file cabinet, and the computer several years ago, you may start to depreciate those items under what is known as the *lower of cost or fair market value rule.*[65]

Example: You have an antique desk that you purchased three years ago. It cost you $500 but has a current fair market value of $600. (Antiques tend to appreciate.) If you use the desk 80 percent for business, you may depreciate 80 percent of the original cost of $500, which is the lower of the cost or fair market value.

Required Record Keeping

You'll need to have some reasonable method for determining your business use. With bookcases and file cabinets, it's easy to determine business use. If you have three file drawers, of which you use two strictly for business files and one for personal files, then you can depreciate two-thirds of the file cabinet. Similarly, if you have a bookcase with four shelves, of which three are for business books and one for fiction, then you can depreciate three-fourths of the bookcase.

With desks, chairs, and computers, it becomes tougher. You want to keep records of use for three consecutive months, as you would do with your automobile, by documenting what you or your family members do when using the furniture.[66] The following is an illustration of what I would do for some sample days out of the three months.

On Monday, no one uses the room, so you write down nothing. On Tuesday, you made client calls from 6 to 9 p.m., so you note in your log "made client calls 6 to 9 p.m." On Wednesday, your son plays the game EverQuest from 3 to 7 p.m., so you log "game or personal use 3 to 7 p.m."

Keeping this log will show what percentage you can deduct your desk, your chair, your computer, your rug, and your lamps. Thus, if you use this furniture 150 hours for business out of 200 hours during the three-month test, you could depreciate three-fourths of these items.

Expense New Equipment Instead of Depreciating

There are, in effect, three methods of depreciation. Yes, you read that correctly! You can depreciate computers and monitors over five years and furniture over seven years. The second method, which is known as a Section 179 expense election (named after the code section that allows this), allows you to deduct the cost of the equipment immediately, rather than depreciate, up to $1,000,000 in 2018 and thereafter and $100% of the business useage for sport utility vehicles (SUVs) used in business through an increase in the bonus depreciation.

The equipment must be new to you.[67] It can be used equipment or a used SUV as long as the equipment or SUV is new to you.

Example: You buy a new computer, monitor, and printer for $2,500 and a used shredder for $1,000. (Shredders are popular in Washington and Houston.) You may depreciate the computer equipment over five years and the shredder over seven years, or you may elect to write off the entire $3,500 purchase in the year that you buy the equipment.

Author's note: You may make this election on most items of business equipment but not equipment used for investment purposes. Some examples of equipment used in business include desks, computers, printers, faxes, shredders, lamps, chairs, throw rugs, and cell phones and phone systems.

Warning: If you expense an asset but your business use drops to under 50 percent or less during years that it would have taken to depreciate the asset, you must recalculate the original expense amount as if you had claimed the straight-line depreciation and then report the difference as taxable income.[68] Thus, for computers, you must keep the business use above 50 percent for five years, and for other office equipment, you must keep the business use above 50 percent for seven years.

What if You Purchase over $1,000,000 Worth of Equipment?[69]

Let's say that you want to purchase more than $1 million worth of equipment in 2018. You can elect to write off up to $1 million and depreciate the difference.

Author's note: This may sound like a great benefit, but with tax rates going up, it is questionable whether you want to take the deduction in the year of purchase rather than depreciate over five to seven years. Higher tax rates mean bigger benefits from deductions. One final point that I want to make regarding the expense election is that you actually must elect on your tax return to expense rather than depreciate. You would actually check off a box on your tax return noting that you make an election to deduct up to $1,000,000 of equipment in 2018. You don't just take the deduction without the election. Many people make this mistake—to their dismay when the IRS finds out.

Author's note: If you buy over $2,500,000 of equipment in 2018 or thereafter, the $1,000,000 election phases out dollar-for-dollar over $2,500,000 in equipment purchases.[70] Thus, if you buy $2,600,000 worth of equipment, you can only elect to write-off $900,000

Summary

- A home office deduction is a tax-deductible gold mine. If you're eligible, you should clearly take the deduction. Earning over $15,000 every five years should convince you that it's worth the trouble.
- The best ways to ensure a home office deduction are to use your home as a principal place of business or where you meet and greet customers in the normal course of business, have a separate structure that isn't attached to your home (such as a greenhouse or an art studio), use your home to store inventory or product samples, or run a day-care center.
- Audit-proof your home office by taking yearly pictures, keeping blueprints of the home that clearly show your home office square footage, and having business cards, stationery, and Yellow Pages listings of your home office address and/or phone number.
- Deduct all expenses for equipment that you use in your home for business, even if you never claim a home office deduction.

Notes

1. See Chapter 5 for this discussion and for the footnotes.
2. See IRS MSSP, *Child Care Providers* (3/2000).
3. Section 280(A)(a) of the IRC.
4. Section 280(A)(c)(1) of the IRC.
5. Section 280(A)(c) of the IRC.
6. *Commissioner v. Soliman*, 506 U.S. 168 (1993).
7. Revenue Ruling 94-24, 1994-1 CB 87 and IRS Publication 587 (2001).
8. IRS Publication 587 (1998).
9. Section 280(A)(c)(1) of the IRC.
10. IRS Publication 587 (2001).
11. Section 280(A)(c)(1) of the IRC.
12. Section 280(A)(c)(1) of the IRC and IRS Publication 587 (2001).
13. H. Rept.105-148 (PL 105-34), p. 407.
14. IRS Publication 587 (2001).
15. H. Rept. 105-148 (PL 105-34), p. 407, and IRS Publication 587 (2001).
16. Ibid.
17. Section 280A(c)(1)(B) of the IRC and Section 1.280A-2(c) of the ITR.

18. Section 1.280A-2(c) of the ITR.

19. Section 1.280A-2(c) of the ITR. See also IRS Publication 587 (2001), p. 6.

20. Ibid. See also *Green v. Commissioner*, 707 F.2d 404 (9th Cir. 1983).

21. Section 280A(c)(1)(c) of the IRC and Section 1.180A-2 (d) of the ITR. See also IRS Publication 587 (2001), p. 6.

22. Ibid.

23. Ibid.

24. IRS Publication 587 (2001).

25. Sections 280A(c)(1)(c) and 280A(c)(2) of the IRC.

26. Section 1.280A-2(e)(2) of the ITR.

27. IRS Publication 911 (2000), p. 5, and IRS Publication 587 (2001).

28. *Lloyd Pearson*, T.C. Memo 1980-459.

29. *James Druker*, 77 T.C. 867 (1981).

30. *Thomas L. Borom*, T.C. Memo 1980-459.

31. Section 280A(c)(4)(B) of the IRC.

32. S. Report No. 95-66 (P.L. 95-30), p. 91.

33. Section 280A(c)(4)(c) of the IRC; IRS Publication 587, p. 10. See also Revenue Ruling 92-3, 1992-1 C.B. 141.

34. IRS MSSP, *Child Care Providers* (3/2000), p. 12.

35. This example was taken from Revenue Ruling 92-3, 1992-1 C.B. 141.

36. *Green v. Commissioner*, 78 T.C. 428 (1982) *rev'd* on another issue, 83-1 USTC Par. 9387 (9th Cir. 1983).

37. Section 280A(c)(1) of the IRC.

38. *Hamacher v. Commissioner*, 94 T.C. 348 (1990). See also Section 1.280A-2g(1) of the ITR.

39. *Gomez v. Commissioner*, 41 T.C.M. 585 (1980); Section 1.280A-2(g) of the ITR.

40. Section 1.280A-2(i)(5) of the ITR.

41. IRS Publication 587 (2001).

42. Section 1.280A-2(i) of the ITR and IRS Publication 587 (2001).

43. *Ronald Culp*, T.C. Memo 1993-270.

44. Section 1.280A-2(i)(3) of the ITR. See also *Gene Moretti*, T.C. Memo 1982-552.

45. IRS Publication 587 (2001) and Revenue Procedure 2013-13.

46. IRS Publication 587 (2001).

47. Rev. Proc 2013-13

48. *Jackson v. Commissioner*, 76 TC 696 (1981); *Heuer v. Commissioner*, 32 TC 947 (1959).

49. Ibid.

50. Ibid.

51. Ibid.

52. Ibid.

53. Ibid.

54. Section 262(b) of the IRC.

55. Section 280A(c)(5) of the IRC.

56. Ibid.

57. Section 168(c). See also IR-2008-117.

58. Section 121(d)(6) of the IRC.

59. Section 121 of the IRC.

60. Section 280A(c)(1) of the IRC and IRS Publication 587 (2001).

61. IRS Publication 587 (2001).

62. *Hamacher v. Commissioner*, 94 T.C. 348 (1990).

63. IRS Publication 587 (2001), p. 2.

64. Section 280 of the IRC and *Mulne v. Commissioner*, T.C. Memo 1996-320.

65. Section 1.167(g)-1 of the ITR. See also IRS Publication 551 (1992).

66. Section 1.274-5T(c) of the ITR.

67. Sections 168 and 179 of the IRC. See also 2017 Tax Cuts and Jobs Act Section 13201(b)(1)(A) and Section 13201(c).

68. IRC Section 179(d); and IRS Publication 946 (2010), p. 15). See 2017 Tax Cuts and Jobs Act Section 13101 (a).

69. Section 280F(d)(1) of the IRC.

70. American Taxpayer Relief Law.

7

Beating the Dreaded IRS Audit

We do not have, and never had, and could not have a "voluntary" tax system.

— **Donald C. Alexander,**
former IRS commissioner

I f there is anything that you learn from this book, it is that you should be as aggressive as possible but not cheat!

Did you ever notice that most Internal Revenue Service (IRS) stories about people being jailed usually are announced on television and radio from January 1 to April 15? What are you thinking about during this period? *Taxes!*

My favorite story involves Leona Helmsley. She was convicted of 33 counts of tax evasion August 30, 1989—but not sent to a federal prison until more than two and a half years later, on the morning of tax day, April 15, 1992,

Chapter Overview
- Most taxpayers should be as aggressive as possible.
- Learn your rights on audit. (Yes, you do have some significant rights.)
- Learn the nine ways to reduce your chances of an IRS audit.
- Know the 15 steps that you should take if you are audited. (Going to Mexico for a long vacation is *not* one of the steps.)
- Learn how to collect money from the IRS by ratting on someone. This could be a lucrative opportunity.
- Avoid the scam artists who try to convince you that a tax return need not be filed or that taxes need not be paid.

the busiest filing day. This was *not* a coincidence. The IRS wants you to feel intimidated. The question is whether you should be intimidated or be aggressive with your deductions. The answer, for a number of reasons, is to be aggressive.

Author's note: By *aggressive,* I do *not* mean cheating. I simply mean that you take any deduction that you're reasonably entitled to.

The first reason for you to be aggressive is because of the IRS person that you may encounter. Here's what I mean.

The person who's lowest on the IRS totem pole is called the *taxpayer service representative.* These are the people who answer questions on the telephone. Although they're usually quite courteous, they're usually the dumbest thing on two legs. They're dumber than sheep, cattle, or plant life. Several years ago I conducted my own survey consisting of 27 yes/no answers, and taxpayer service reps only answered 6 questions correctly. You have a better shot asking your friends. At least they have a 50-50 chance of getting the right answer. These representatives aren't even that lucky.

Normally, when the IRS hires them, they must have at least two years of college in any field; there's no requirement for any accounting or tax course. They get training, but it's very limited. As of several years ago, the IRS provided 20 days' worth of training for the people who answer the phones. In many cases these people never worked for the IRS as auditors. Moreover, you take a risk in accepting any answers they give you because the IRS is not bound by their answers. You are just stuck and must pay the proper tax plus interest and penalties.

Author's note: Based on my experience, and based on some conversations with IRS appeals officers, you may be able to get the IRS to waive penalties if you relied on a bad answer from these people. However, you must record in a log the following:

- The name of the person
- The badge number of the person
- The date of the call
- The time of the call
- The question asked
- The answer given

If you record all these items in a log, the IRS ordinarily will waive penalties.

Author's note: I have found that the taxpayer service representatives will give you their badge number for identification, but they say it very quickly. I usually ask them to repeat it slowly because I'm getting older.

The next person on the totem pole is an IRS tax auditor. If you're going down to the IRS office to present your information, you will in all likelihood be visiting a tax auditor. To qualify, a tax auditor must have a four-year college degree—in anything. Tax auditors generally start at a salary of $18,000 to $20,000 and can advance to $40,000-plus. Before advancing to a salary of about $27,000, a tax auditor must have completed at least six semester hours of accounting courses.

The auditors generally are not required to interpret guidelines or engage in research. They're told what to audit, how to audit, and almost what to think. The issues in contention are clearly defined by a classifier before the returns are assigned to individual examiners. The group manager must approve any expansion beyond that.

The next rung on the ladder is the revenue agent. Revenue agents must have a four-year college degree and a minimum of 24 semester hours of accounting. Experience can be substituted for the 24 hours of accounting. The IRS does not recruit many "A" students; they're usually snapped up by the better-paying, big accounting firms. Sadly, many of the revenue agents squeak through college with "C" averages. In fact, one unnamed manager said that some of the people that the IRS was hiring don't understand the tax law; thus the IRS is giving remedial reading courses to some of these people. The bottom line is that, for many audits, you will get a less competent person than found in many accounting firms.

The second reason to be aggressive in your deductions is based on how IRS agents get promoted. Revenue agents are expected to be good soldiers. This is important. For the IRS system to work, revenue agents must believe that it's their IRS, right or wrong. They learn tax law the way the IRS teaches it, as the IRS wants them to see it. Revenue agents go through extensive initial and yearly training to learn the way the IRS wants things done. They can handle some complex returns that require full use of their accounting skills. Unlike a tax auditor, the revenue agent sets the entire scope of the examination. The starting salary, however, lags seriously behind that of most accounting firms and way behind that of the major accounting firms.

The key to the importance of all this is that both revenue agents and tax auditors get promoted based on the number of cases closed and not on the money collected. You might wonder why this is the case. The reason is that about 1 percent of national revenue is obtained through audits. Thus 99 percent of the revenue is gotten through "voluntary" compliance from people who have not been audited. Therefore, the more audits the IRS conducts, the greater the fear is for people who have *not* been audited. So there really is some logic in government.

If you came to my seminar, you would find that because of the need for all agents to close their cases quickly, over 90 percent of students who have been audited in the past either got a refund or no change on an audit, or if they paid anything, there usually was a compromise or settlement. This doesn't always happen, but it certainly happens enough to justify a lot of aggressive treatment of your deductions.

The final reason for being audited is based on what we CPAs call the "audit lottery." The following are the IRS statistics showing your chances of being audited for tax year 2011 based on the type of return and the type of income:[1]

Average Recommended Additional Tax After Examination, by Type and Size of Return, Fiscal Year

Type and size of return	2017 Percentage covered
United States, total	**0.5**
Taxable returns:	
▶ Individual income tax returns, total	0.6
▶ Returns with total positive income under $200,000 [7]:	
▶ Business returns without Earned Income Tax Credit:	
Nonfarm business returns by size of total gross receipts [10]:	
Under $25,000	0.9
$25,000 under $100,000	1.3
$100,000 under $200,000	2.1
$200,000 or more	1.9
▶ Small corporations	0.7
No balance sheet returns	0.6
Balance sheet returns by size of total assets:	
Under $250,000	0.5
$250,000 under $1,000,000	1.1
$1,000,000 under $5,000,000	0.9
$5,000,000 under $10,000,000	1.3
▶ Large corporations	7.9
Balance sheet returns by size of total assets:	
$10,000,000 under $50,000,000	4.0
$50,000,000 under $100,000,000	10.2
$100,000,000 under $250,000,000	9.9
$250,000,000 under $500,000,000	9.9
$500,000,000 under $1,000,000,000	11.2
$1,000,000,000 under $5,000,000,000	15.3
$5,000,000,000 under $20,000,000,000	26.8
$20,000,000,000 or more	58.4
▶ Partnership returns	0.4
▶ S corporation returns [20]	0.3

Pursuant to "Internal Revenue Service Data Book; Table 9. Examination Coverage."

Several conclusions can be drawn from these audit statistics. First, if your deductions go up by $5,000, $10,000, or more, you will not increase your chance of an audit. However, if your income suddenly skyrockets or triples, you might increase your chance of an audit. Second, your actual chance of an audit are about once every 30 years. The bottom line is to be as aggressive as possible.

Author's note: When I say that you should be aggressive, I do *not* mean cheat! An aggressive taxpayer is one who has a basis in tax law for the deductions that he or she takes and has the documentation to support those deductions. Also, you will notice that the chance of being audited while self-employed is roughly seven times that of being an employee. **Thus, it is CRITICAL that self-employed taxpayers have the proper documentation suggested in this book and keep a good tax tracker such as Taxbot for all expenses and mileage.**

Taxpayer Rights

You have significant rights as a taxpayer, and you need to be aware of those rights. As you may have seen in the Senate hearings, the IRS can exercise significant power.

A good example happened about 10 years ago. A couple ordered my Tax Strategy Program and Tax Organizer. About half an hour after my seminar was over and after they had gone home, they came back to the seminar to cancel their order. The wife was crying. What happened was that when they got home, they received a notice that the IRS had seized their bank accounts, and all their outstanding checks were bouncing. Now, without any funds left, they had to find an accountant to represent them. Good luck!

Because of problems such as this, Congress passed several laws that protect taxpayers. These laws provide for the following:

- If you get audited, or if the IRS wants any money out of you, you must receive a copy of all your appeal rights from the examination to the collection (IRS Publication 1, "Your Rights as a Taxpayer").
- You now have the right to be treated fairly, professionally, promptly, and courteously by IRS employees. This is why you may find a slightly "friendlier" IRS. However, don't be fooled by the friendly manner: The IRS still has just as much power as in the past.

You now can appeal to the Taxpayer Advocate Service (TAS). This is an independent oversight group that can overturn anything that the IRS does with a Taxpayer Assistance Order (TAO). The TAS can get back money taken, lift a lien, follow up on a refund claim, and much more. The phone number for your local TAS office must be published in the phone directory and is also usually found in both the White Pages and the Yellow Pages.

To apply to the TAS, you'll need to send a statement of the facts and problem with a special IRS form, "Application for Taxpayer Assistance Order." (You'll love the number of this "emergency" form: It's Form 911.)

To take advantage of a TAO, you must try to resolve your dispute with the IRS through normal channels first, or you must show that you will suffer a significant hardship if a TAO is not issued.[2] A significant hardship includes any of the following conditions:[3]

- There's an immediate threat of adverse action.
- There's been a delay of more than 30 days in resolving the problem.
- You'll be incurring significant costs and fees if relief isn't granted.
- If relief isn't granted, you'll suffer irreparable injury or a long-term impact.

What all this means is that you must try to deal with the IRS, but either the IRS isn't communicating with you or you're about to suffer a major irreparable injury such as loss of a business, inability to hire a professional to represent you because all funds are frozen, or a lien that's destroying your credit and drastically harming your ability to function in business or in life.

Author's note: All this sounds great, but the IRS and the Taxpayer Advocate Service have put into practice some strict policies before you can use the taxpayer advocate. First, you need to contact the IRS and try to get it to act appropriately if the agency is wrong. You generally must write to the IRS three times, and you can't have received within the last 30 days a notice that agents are working on your problem. Also, you should show that the IRS clearly acted improperly or that you have a very winnable case or that an irreparable injury will occur, as noted earlier. The following is an actual case.

Example: A couple called me who had sold their business to their ex-partner. Subsequently, the partner never paid the IRS any withholding taxes. The IRS seized the couple's bank accounts and garnished their wages, leaving them with $150 per week on which to live. They hired a lawyer who charged $5,000 and accomplished nothing. They then called me out of desperation. I recommended that they contact the Taxpayer Advocate Service with a cover letter noting that they had previously sold their business and include a copy of the sales agreement, garnishment notice, and bank seizure notice. Several months later, I received a bouquet of roses with a letter of thanks: They had got back all their money, and the seizure had been lifted. This whole unfortunate situation cost them $5,035—$5,000 for the lawyer, $10 for the Federal Express notice to the Taxpayer Advocate Service, and $25 for the roses to me. Had they known about the TAS, they would have saved a lot of money and suffered a lot less frustration and stress.

Here are some other rights in an audit:

- You have the right to have your personal and financial information kept confidential and the right to know why the IRS is asking for the information, how any information will be used, and what might happen if you don't provide the information.
- You clearly have the right to plan your business and personal finances in such a way that you will pay the least tax that is due under the law.[4] Thus the IRS states that you can plan your transactions to try to reduce your taxes. Tax planning is fully accepted by the IRS as long as you are using legitimate techniques.

- You also have the right to tape-record the audit. You must bring the tapes and give the IRS at least 10 days' notice of your desire to record the audit. The IRS can record you as well.

Author's note: I do not ordinarily recommend taping the audit. The reason is that audits are negotiating sessions, so taping makes the auditor nervous. The IRS is putting more auditors on cases that involved taped audits, and settlements tend to be fewer. I would, however, record an audit if you get a bad auditor, such as someone who appears to want to "nail" you or disallows a lot more in deductions than you think is warranted. You can stop the audit and request a postponement to get a recorder and some tapes, to obtain some representation, or to consult with an advisor.

- You can ask that the examination take place at a reasonable time and in a place that is convenient to both you and the IRS.
- You can request that the IRS not examine your return for the same items it examined in either of the two previous years if no change in your liability was proposed. Thus you can effectively end harassment on the same issue(s).
- You also can recover some litigation expenses (currently up to $150 per hour) if you substantially prevail in the dispute and the IRS does not show that its position was justified.[5]
- You have the right to enter into an installment agreement, which means paying your taxes over a period of months or years, if you don't have the money to pay the tax at present.
- You also have the right to claim Innocent Spouse Tax Relief if the IRS goes after you for something that arose from your ex-spouse if you filed a joint return. If you file jointly with your spouse, you are jointly and separately liable for the taxes due. Frequently, couples get divorced, yet the IRS goes after one ex-spouse for a tax problem resulting from the other. Now you can elect Innocent Spouse Tax Relief, which is your right to be taxed on your share of the income and deductions and not be taxed on your spouse's problems. You also can elect this relief if you can prove that you were an abused spouse and were forced into signing a joint return.

Author's note: This sounds great, but in practice there are some problems. You can't have known or should not have known about the potential problems of your spouse. The following examples will illustrate this point.

Example: Unknown to you, your spouse was a drug dealer. Despite having a nice state government job, you lived in a million-dollar home and drove a Mercedes. The IRS probably will hold that you should have known something was amiss and will not allow Innocent Spouse Tax Relief.

Example: You knew that your spouse had a part-time business that you were told made $10,000. However, your spouse really made $100,000 and placed the money into a separate account. You probably will be able to elect Innocent Spouse Tax Relief on all the earnings above the $10,000 that you knew about.

Nine Ways to Reduce Your Chances of an IRS Audit

Before I begin this discussion, you should know what happens to your tax return when you send it to the IRS. First, it goes to the local service center, where it's scanned and checked for math errors and with all Form 1099s to see if you underreported income. Your return is then sent to the Martinsburg, West Virginia, center, where it's given a score using a computer program known as the *Discriminant Function System* (DIF). The higher the score, the better is the chance that your return will be examined immediately for problems. However, if you've attached schedules and statements explaining the problem in more detail, the examiner may put your return back into the hopper, and you may totally avoid an audit. Although this program is the best-kept secret in government (better kept, in fact, than the making of the atomic bomb), there are some things that we know about this program that you can use to reduce the risk of an audit.

1. Mail your return either by registered mail, return receipt requested, Federal Express, or electronically. If the IRS regional service center fails to receive your tax return, your chances of being audited increase automatically. To make sure that you're not taking unnecessary chances, send your tax return by registered mail, return receipt requested, or by Federal Express Priority Overnight or Second Day service, DHL Same Day and Overnight Worldwide Express, Airborne Express (either overnight or next-day service), or by electronic filing.[6]

Author's note: Most returns are now filed electronically, but there are still some who use the paper version for their tax return. I would recommend electronic filing for everyone. It will assure that the correct social security number is used as well as assuring that the IRS will get your tax return since you will get an electronic receipt.

2. Send all changes of address to the IRS by filing Form 8822, "Change of Address," whenever you move. As reported in *USA Today* several years ago, the IRS wants to send out $78 million in refunds, but the people have moved, and it can't find them. (Maybe I'm crazy, but if the situation were reversed and the IRS wanted money from you, don't you think that it would find you?) The IRS likes to know where you are and appreciates being notified of any change of address. This certainly will benefit you if the IRS needs to notify you. If you move, you may be liable to the IRS without knowing it because you didn't provide a change of address. Its only responsibility is to send you all notices to your last known address.

3. Use the IRS's preaddressed label to speed up the processing of your tax return.

Author's note: There are rumors to the effect that the IRS label contains information that will be detrimental to you. To the best of my knowledge, this is not the case. This label is only used to expedite processing.

4. Make sure that your tax return is neat. I met a taxpayer who thought that if the IRS couldn't read the return, it wouldn't audit him. This is absolutely false! Although your tax return doesn't have to be typed, it must be neat and easy to read. Legible tax returns create an impression of attention to detail. In addition, you don't want your return to stand out in any way.

5. File all elections that you're entitled to. There are certain tax breaks and options that require the filing of an election, such as expensing equipment instead of depreciating equipment (as discussed in Chapter 6). Sometimes the filing can be done merely by picking a method of reporting. It's generally better to attach separate statements for all elections made in a tax return or to check all required boxes on the return. This further supports the impression of attention to detail and shows an understanding of the tax law.

Author's note: Again, the key is to have your return look professional and complete. You don't want it to stand out for any reason or have something clearly amiss that would cause increased IRS scrutiny.

6. Report all of your income. The IRS has implemented various audit programs for unreported income. Make sure that your tax return reports all income you earned and identifies the income by source. If you receive a Form 1099 for consulting services, for example, report the income on a supporting schedule, and include the taxpayer ID number from the Form 1099. Since the IRS already has the information from the 1099, you'll reduce your chances of being selected for an audit by enabling the IRS to match the Form 1099 information with your tax return.

Author's note: In addition, if you're incorporated, be sure that the Form 1099s match the entity that earns the income. Many people never notice that income earned by their corporation has their social security number on the Form 1099, and vice versa. If you receive an incorrect Form 1099, immediately notify the sender to give you an amended Form 1099. If you can't get this, attach a schedule explaining that there's a difference between what was reported and what is shown on the Form 1099.

7. Have your return prepared by a competent tax preparer. Most people are not aware that if they do their own returns, they increase their chances of an audit because the IRS perceives that they don't know as much as an accountant who prepares hundreds of returns. Moreover, accountants who prepare lots of returns use sophisticated software that ensures fewer errors. If you really want to save money on the cost of the preparation of your return, use Turbo Tax or some tax-preparation software, and then give your return to an accountant to get his or her name on it as the preparer. You may cut the costs of preparation—and the accountant may find things that you missed.

In addition, I would recommend a CPA, an enrolled agent, or an attorney prepare or review the return. This will help to minimize your chances of an audit examination.

8. Break your income and large expenses into small segments. Income reported to the IRS on Form 1099s should be separated from other income. The separation will help to determine that you've indeed reported all income earned. Also break down expenses as far as possible to explain to the IRS examiners exactly what was involved in the expenses. If, for example, you had promotional expenses of $10,000 and that's all that appeared on your tax return, your chances of audit would be significant. However, should your promotion be broken down into travel, advertising, and entertainment expenses, you may reduce your chances of audit. I should note that certain big-ticket items need not be broken down because the IRS understands that these particular items are inherently large. An example of this type of large item would be medical malpractice premiums for doctors.

9. Keep records of expert advice. If you relied on the advice of your accountant or lawyer, keep records as to the nature and date of the advice. There are cases in which penalties have been waived for a good-faith reliance on an independent expert.[7]

15 Steps for Preparing for an IRS Audit

Let's assume that you follow to the letter everything that is written in this book, but you still get a notice from the IRS that invites you down for a "chat." Don't panic or go on an extended vacation. Here are 15 steps that will help you greatly in the audit process.

1. Assume that you will be audited whenever you prepare your tax return. The time to get ready for an IRS audit is while you're preparing your tax return. This is the only time that you have all your tax information in front of you. Reference your support to the return so that you can find it later, if you should need it. Questionable items, if any, should be supported by tax memorandums or other information from your tax advisor.

2. Don't panic. An audit notice doesn't indicate that anything is wrong with your tax return. It's simply a request by the IRS to find out if your tax return was prepared properly and to determine the proper amount of tax—no more and no less. Generally, you'll be notified of the audit by mail, although you could be telephoned. If you're notified by mail, you'll be asked to telephone the examiner.

3. Try to limit the scope of the audit. There are a number of suggestions here. In an IRS office audit, the IRS tells you what's being examined and sets the scope of the audit. In addition, the IRS generally has three years from the date you file your return to audit it. Many times, an audit occurs in the last year allowed or the audit takes longer than usual, and the time limit may run out. In these cases, IRS agents usually ask taxpayers to extend the statute by a year so that it can continue the audit. Your first reaction may be to deny this request, but the IRS simply will disallow many deductions, and you'll be stuck in IRS appeals or, even worse, in court. The best thing that you can do is to negotiate an extension, but only regarding specific items on your return, such as for travel or for entertainment. The reason for limiting the scope of the extension is that if the IRS finds anything after the time limit for the audit expires, it can't assess anything against you except for those items that you agreed to extend.

4. Understand that the burden of proof is on you. Tax law requires you to prove that your deductions are valid and that you have paid the proper amount of tax. The IRS need prove nothing. When going through your records and getting ready for the audit, make sure that you keep in mind that the burden is on you. None of that "innocent until proven guilty" business applies to a tax audit, unless there's a potential criminal investigation.

5. Dress normally for the audit. Do not make a special trip to Goodwill Industries to buy clothes for your audit. Don't wear expensive clothes or jewelry such as Rolex watches. IRS examiners dislike people who look like they make more money than the examiners. Dress and act normally during the entire audit. Do not plead poverty or stupidity. Excuses don't work.

6. Be on time for the audit. Put an asterisk here, and burn this point into your head. IRS examiners are graded on efficiency. If you are late for your appointment and cause the auditor to be inefficient or to take a longer time on the audit than he or she should, you start the audit in an antagonistic environment. Moreover, IRS examiners start examining your return to see what the problems are about a half hour before the audit is scheduled to begin. If you're late for the appointment, you give the auditor extra time to scrutinize your records before the audit begins. Thus the bottom line is that if you're late, you irritate the auditor and allow more time to find problems. *The best bet: Be early.*

7. Bring organized information. Make sure that you're prepared to answer questions and deliver documents to the auditor. If you receive notification from the IRS about the documents that you need for the audit, make sure that they are organized so that you not only can answer the questions but also can deliver the supporting documents quickly. This helps the examiner to complete the audit more efficiently, get a better rating from his or her superiors, and bring the whole unpleasant task to a quick conclusion.

8. Don't volunteer information. Although I recommend that your accountant show up for the audit without you, sometimes your presence is necessary. If you attend the audit, there are only four statements that you should make. They are "Yes," "No," "I don't know," and finally, my favorite—"It's my accountant's fault." (Enron managers learned this technique very well.) Never say, "I've always done it that way." Don't elaborate; answer only questions asked. Be concise. If the question does not appear relevant, ask why it is being asked. Bring only the documents requested in the IRS's "invitation" letter. Do not volunteer any information during the audit process. Finally, be very careful what you say to an IRS agent. This information can be used in a criminal trial.[8]

9. Don't leave any ends dangling. I had a student who was being audited and found that she didn't have $500 worth of receipts for certain deductions. She asked me if she should point this out to the auditor before the audit begins. The answer? Absolutely not! If the examiner gets money out of you very easily, he or she may decide to dig deeper, and you'll end up losing your tail. Thus, if it's easy to find something wrong, the immediate conclusion is that there must be lots of other things wrong in your return.

10. Ask for tax law references. If you think that you're right, ask the auditor or agent for the legal references. Don't accept vague statements or interpretations of the law. Make your tax advisor the goat by saying, "My accountant told me that this deduction was proper. Can you give me something that shows he's wrong?"

11. Don't give in too quickly. Most people feel that if you give in quickly, the IRS audit will go faster, and the agent will like you. Nothing could be further from the truth. The IRS manual states, "Hasty agreement to adjustments and undue concern about immediate closing of the case may indicate that more thorough examination is needed." If you appear to be a soft touch, the IRS will look for larger contributions from you.

12. Never be alone with a Special Agent. Special Agents are not special. Their job is to investigate criminal actions. If there are ever two agents to see you, ask whether either of them is a Special Agent. If so, terminate the meeting, and seek out a good criminal tax lawyer.

Author's note: You've probably learned that "if you are nice to people, they are nice to you." This isn't true for Special Agents. They're promoted based on indictments. Thus, unlike with a regular IRS examiner, do not be nice or accommodating to Special Agents.

I also should note that there's no privilege protecting your communications with your accountant.[9] Accordingly, never hire an accountant to represent you in criminal matters. In addition, you should terminate your relationship with your accountant for a while because the IRS in a criminal investigation can obtain any communications to the accountant. If you need to deal and communicate with the accountant, have the attorney hire the accountant so that any future conversation is protected under the attorney-client privilege.

13. Don't *ever* tamper with the evidence. No backdating of documents or intimidating of witnesses should ever occur. More people get indicted for these items than for the original offense because they are easier to prove. To be safe, don't contact any witnesses for the government; let your lawyer do it.

14. Never, ever die. The IRS audits approximately 68 percent of all final returns. The only good thing about dying is that you may not have to show up at the audit.

15. Be careful of the "rat fee." The IRS pays a 10 percent commission for people to rat on you. If you want to make a living reporting tax cheats, get Publication 733, "Rewards for Information Given to the Internal Revenue Service."

Taxes Are Not Voluntary and Are Very Constitutional

In recent years, charlatans have gotten a lot of attention by claiming that taxes are unconstitutional and can be avoided with *pure trusts* or *foreign trusts*. You may have heard a well-dressed speaker declare that there have been many cases to this effect and that he or she has personally beaten the IRS in court on several occasions.

Who wouldn't want to avoid all federal and state taxes? However, before you invest your hard-earned money to create various recommended trusts, not to mention your life savings in a foreign or pure trust (otherwise known as a *constitutional trust*), *stop and reconsider!* Here's the real story. Here you'll find out what companies that promote these concepts are not telling you.

The only bit of truth to all these claims happened in the year 1895. In that year, the U.S. Supreme Court, in *Pollock v. Farmers' Loan & Trust Company*,[10] held that the Income Tax Act at the time was unconstitutional. However, what is not revealed by many seminar speakers on this subject is that in 1913 the country ratified the 16th Amendment to the Constitution to correct this problem and specifically overruled *Pollock*.[11] This amendment gave Congress the power "to lay and collect taxes on incomes, from whatever source derived" and allowed passage of the Income Tax Act of 1913, which was the predecessor to the current Internal Revenue Code.[12]

Since that time, there have been numerous attempts to get the courts to hold that the Internal Revenue Code is unconstitutional.[13] Some of the arguments have been that the 16th Amendment was ratified incorrectly.[14] Taxpayers even have tried to avoid paying tax on religious grounds.[15] What is important to know is that all taxpayer attempts have failed!

In fact, the courts are so tired of hearing these frivolous arguments that they are now assessing the government's legal fees against the taxpayers who claim this, as well as upholding the IRS's imposition of a special frivolous return penalty.[16] In fact, even the penalty for filing a frivolous return was held to be constitutional.[17] The bottom line is that the Income Tax Act and the Internal Revenue Code are quite constitutional, and Congress can enact almost any tax law as long as there's a rational basis.

The next major argument by many of these "tax protest" speakers is that you can avoid income tax by maintaining all assets and income in either a pure trust (otherwise known as a *family estate trust*) or a foreign trust. These types of trusts usually involve the transfer of your assets to a trust in a foreign jurisdiction with a corresponding assignment of lifetime services to the trust. These trusts usually pay fees and living expenses such as your rent and make other distributions of income.

Sadly, this has been at best a waste of thousands of dollars to set up and at worst a dangerous loss of all assets placed in trust. As many of these speakers note, these types of trusts are not subject to income tax. In fact, this is true! What they neglect to say is that all the income of the trust is taxed to the grantor (you) who set up the trust[18] if you meet any of the following conditions:

- You can revoke the trust.
- You can derive income from the trust.
- You can control the trust.

Thus, if you keep any control whatsoever, you are taxed on the income. In addition, even if you were willing to give up the requisite control, income from trusts reaches the higher tax brackets faster than individual income. You actually could be increasing your taxes. Moreover, if you place your assets out of the United States, you will not be subject to any U.S. legal protections if the assets are embezzled, which happens all too often.

The bottom line is simple: Whenever you hear someone tell you, "Psst! Taxes are unconstitutional and can be avoided with some trust," *run* away as fast as you can! Always remember that the difference between tax *avoidance* and tax *evasion* is five years!

Summary

- Be as aggressive with your deductions as possible.
- Understand and use your taxpayer rights when audited.
- Learn the nine ways to reduce your chances of being audited.
- Understand the 15 steps that you should apply if you get audited.
- Study IRS Publication 733 if you want to collect the "rat fee" from the IRS.
- Avoid all scam artists or tax protesters with various devices and claims that taxes need not be paid or that taxes are unconstitutional.

Notes

1. IRS Data Book "Examination Coverage."
2. Report on the IRS National Taxpayer Advocate's Fiscal Year 2001 Objectives.
3. Section 7811(a)(2) of the IRC.
4. IRS Publication 1.
5. Section 7430 of the IRC.
6. IRS Notice 2001-62, 2001-40 IRB 307.
7. *George S. Mauerman*, T.C. Memo 1993-23.
8. Section 7207 of the IRC and 18 U.S.C. 1001.
9. *Couch v. United States*, 409 U.S. 322 (1973).
10. *Pollock v. Farmers' Loan & Trust Company*, 157 U.S. 429 (S. Ct. 1895).
11. The Constitution of the United States: Analysis and Interpretation, S. Doc. No. 16, p. 1839 (1982).
12. *Brushaber v. Union Pacific Railroad*, 240 U.S. 1 (1915).
13. Ibid.
14. *United States v. Foster*, 789 F.2d 457 (7th Cir. 1986).
15. *Adams v. Commissioner*, 110 T.C. 137 (1998).
16. *Gerald Funk*, T.C. Memo 1981-506, *aff'd.*
17. *Heitman v. United States*, 753 F.2d 33 (6th Cir. 1984).
18. Sections 671-677 of the IRC. See also Revenue Ruling 75-257, 1975-2 CB 251.

8

How to Shield Yourself from the IRS Weapon of Classifying a Business as a Hobby

I have trouble reconciling my net income with my gross habits.

—Errol Flynn, actor

This is a crucial chapter. In fact, for many readers, this one chapter will pay for this book numerous times. The reason is that classifying an activity as a hobby instead of a business is the Internal Revenue Service's (IRS's) favorite weapon because it yields such nice results for the IRS. If you have a network marketing business or you are conducting a side business, you should read this chapter several times and apply every suggestion made.

Huge Benefits in Business Losses

Being in business is the last great tax-reduction opportunity. If your business produces a loss, you generally may deduct that loss against any form of income.[1] This loss can be used against your interest, dividends, rents, retirement income, and even your spouse's income if you file a joint return.

> **Chapter Overview**
> - Understand the huge benefits of business losses.
> - Learn why the favorite IRS weapon against taxpayers is to classify an activity as a hobby rather than a business.
> - Learn when the IRS is required to presume that you are in business.
> - Learn about the election that requires the IRS to postpone any determination.
> - Learn about the criteria to be deemed a business and not a hobby.
> - Learn how to bulletproof your activities from being classified as a hobby. (This one concept will pay for this book alone.)

Author's note: This should ensure that you never get divorced. However, what happens if your losses exceed your total family income for the year? Prior to 2018, if your losses exceeded your income for the year, you could carry back the losses two years[2] and receive a refund from the federal government and most state governments for the taxes paid in the last two years. If you wished, you could also carry forward all business losses over the next 20 years[3] and offset these losses over any income generated over the next 20 years into the future. As a result of the passage of the Tax Cuts and Jobs Act, the treatment of business losses has changed. You no longer can carry back any losses to prior years, which might hurt new business start-ups that need the cash. However, losses incurred by self-employed taxpayers or in S corporations with sufficient stock basis can be used against any form of income that you currently have in the year of loss. If the loss exceeds your income for the year, you can carry forward all unused losses indefinitely to the future and offset up to 80 percent of future taxable income until you have used up all the losses that were carried to the future. Thus you never lose a valid business deduction.

Example: David incurs a $10,000 loss from his business. If he earns $40,000 in wages from his full-time job, his taxable income would be $30,000. He thus would pay tax on only $30,000 of income.

The IRS Works to Treat Activities as Hobbies

This all assumes that the IRS treats your activities as a business. If, however, the IRS determines that you are not engaged in the activities to make a profit, then no deduction for losses is allowed.[4] Thus prior to 2018, deductions from the hobby were limited to the income from the hobby. In addition, no carryover of losses or carryback of losses from the hobby was allowed.[5] (OUCH!) Finally, if this isn't bad enough, we now maybe have inadvertently created even more of a problem for hobbyists. Prior to the new law, hobby deductions were only available as a miscellaneous itemized deductions. The new law eliminates all miscellaneous itemized deductions,[6] which could result in the loss of all of your deductions yet include any hobby earnings as taxable. OUCH!

Author's note: We can't be sure that this will be the result until the IRS rules on this topic. However, this result is a fair interpretation of the unintended consequences of the new law. It is thus absolutely crucial in my opinion that you run your business like a business. Meeting with your accountant yearly to help ensure this will be a very important thing to do, especially if your endeavor is an inherently suspicious activity that I have noted below. It will also be important for you to thoroughly understand what I have written in this chapter.

Example: Carrie has a side business in travel that she operates out of her home. She spends little time operating the business, and it generates little revenue. If the IRS classifies her activities as a hobby, all losses from that business are disallowed and potentially all of her deductions might be disallowed as well.

Presumption Based on Profit

There's a safe harbor where activities are presumed to be a business. Congress has given you a way to help solidify your business as a business so that the IRS doesn't treat it as a hobby. If your activity shows a profit for any three or more years in a period of five consecutive tax years, you are presumed to be engaged in a business.[7]

Author's note: If you're engaged in breeding, showing, training, or racing horses, this presumption test becomes a little bit better: two or more years in a period of seven consecutive tax years.[8] Even if you're not involved with horses, if you meet this presumption, you are usually home-free with the IRS.

Election to Postpone Any Determination

If the IRS comes after you to disallow your losses before the full five years (or seven years for a horse-related business), you may elect to postpone any determination of being a business or a hobby until there are five consecutive tax years from the time that you first engaged in the activity (seven years for a horse-related business, as noted earlier).[9] You generally must make this election within three years of the due date of your tax return for the year in which you first started your activity.[10] You can even make this election after the IRS notifies you about this problem, as long as it's within the three-year period and you make this election within 60 days of the IRS notice. If the IRS files a suit, no election is available under any circumstances.[11]

Example: If you started your business in June 2014, you must make the election by April 15, 2018 (within three years of the due date of your 2014 return). If, however, the IRS notifies you about this problem on June 1, 2014, you have to make this election by August 1, 2014 (within 60 days of the IRS notice).

Author's note: At first glance, you may think that this election is very useful and should be used. However, there are several problems with making this election to postpone any hobby determination. First, it calls unwanted attention to yourself. Second, it extends the statute of limitations for several years for the IRS to both catch you and go after you. In short, weigh the pros and cons before making this election.

Criteria for Being a Business, Not a Hobby

So you didn't have a profit three out of five years. In fact, you may have losses for many years in the future. All is not lost. If you follow the criteria that I outline below, you'll be much more bulletproof: The IRS won't be able to treat your activities as a hobby. A large number of my students have won with the IRS after using these time-tested strategies. If you are in network marketing, have a small business, or operate a home-based business on the side, take all these strategies to heart. You will thank me forever and save yourself an enormous amount of hassle and money.

There are numerous standards that the courts use in determining whether your activity constitutes a business or a hobby. Generally, the determination is based on the facts and circumstances of each case.[12] However, some planning certainly will help your facts enormously.

One important factor is that you must show that you entered into the activity with the objective of making a profit.[13] This is true even if the chance of making a profit is small.[14]

The majority of court decisions (as well as those of the IRS) indicate that you're required to have an honest profit objective when you undertake your venture. Thus, if you have a sincere purpose of eventually reaping an overall profit, you will be deemed to have a profit motive.[15]

Author's note: It is your motives at the time that you start your endeavor that determine whether you have business intent. This can change as time goes on, but the motive at the startup becomes crucial. If you're in network marketing or franchising, you should document this intent by sending a letter to your sponsor/company to express your reasons for entering this business, emphasizing your desire to make a long-term profit and career out of this activity. If you have a small business on the side, you should document your intent with studies that show why you started this business. This point will be discussed below.

The courts have looked at the following factors in deciding if an endeavor is a business or a hobby:

1. Business plan and projections and a budget. Most court decisions have looked favorably on taxpayers who prepare business plans showing projected estimated income and expenses of their endeavor.[16] In fact, this is such an important criterion that some cases have turned just on this factor alone. Thus, in one case,[17] a sailboat chartering business was held to be a business even with years of losses because the owners had 12 years of projections of anticipated revenues and expenses and projected an overall profit. They also showed a reasonable basis for the appreciation of the sailboat.

The *key* is to project an *overall* business profit. In addition, the projected numbers should have some reasonable basis in reality. You therefore should document how you estimated each of your figures and have projections for at least 5 years, with 10 years being even better. In addition, don't have your business plan showing only estimated loss with no eventual profit.[18]

It is also crucial that you prepare a budget that shows that you met with an accountant or some business expert and tried to cut expenses as much as possible in order to attempt to increase your profitability.[19]

Author's note: Despite the importance of these factors, most taxpayers who have lost in court did not have a business plan with projected revenues and expenses. This is especially true for people involved in network marketing. Thus, when preparing this plan, you should seek out an expert who has been successful in your business and have him or her help you with this plan. In network marketing, seek out the experience of a very successful person in your upline or, even better, in some other line, and document this help. If you have a small business, find an expert in the field to help you prepare this plan. There are always people who are "expert consultants" in just about any field of endeavor. Also, if your business involves inventories, you certainly should have enough inventory on hand to meet your goals.

2. Your own statements. Telling your friends that you're in business to make a profit usually is deemed too self-serving to be of any use in proving a business motive. However, if you make improper statements, the court may treat your activities as a hobby and kill your deductions. For example, one person who raised dogs argued at a local zoning hearing for his home that his dog-breeding activities constituted a hobby.[20] The IRS used these words against the taxpayer, and the court held that his dog-breeding activity was indeed a hobby. Thus don't ever say, "I'm in this only to save taxes" or "I'm in this only to get a discount and save costs." This may be partly true, but don't say it.

3. Conducting the activities in a business-like manner. This is probably the single most important factor that the IRS uses in judging a business intent. You must conduct your activity in a business-like manner and run it similarly to other businesses of the same size and type.[21] Thus you need to consult with experts about how similar businesses are run and follow their advice. It's also crucial to keep complete and accurate books and records and keep a good tax organizer or diary.[22]

Consulting with experts seems to be a crucial factor that the courts look at especially if you aren't making money. This involves not only consulting with experts about ways to increase sales but also meeting with your accountant to discuss expenses that can be cut back in order to achieve greater profitability.

It is crucial that you keep separate bank accounts and records for your business.[23] The key is not just to keep details of expenses and receipts but to have a "bookkeeping system ... that provides sufficient data for you to make informed business decisions."[24] These records must enable you to evaluate and improve your performance. What this means is that you should have the following:[25]

- A business plan showing at least 5 and preferably 10 years of projected income and expenses, showing an overall projected profit
- A marketing plan that is changed yearly to conform with what is happening
- A yearly income statement and balance sheet so that you can determine what is happening in your business and can make changes to improve profitability
- In addition, if you have losses, have your accountant review your financial statements yearly in order to suggest expenses that can be cut in order to try to produce a profit.[26]

If you're not making money, you should seek advice from people as to what changes you should make in your marketing and then follow through on the advice. Of course, you should document this advice. If you are in network marketing, don't just ask your upline people. Speak to different successful people to get different ideas. Don't follow the same advice from year to year if you aren't making money.[27] Businesses change the ways they market if they're not successful.

The following is a listing of activities, in addition to what was noted earlier, and the records that the courts found sufficient to enable a determination of being a business:

- *Horse breeding.* A registry of all horses bred or foaled, formal breeding, and complete breeding and medical records.[28]
- *Showing of horses.* Detailed notes on horses and horse show judges.[29]
- *Dog breeding.* Detailed records of the dogs, as required by the American Kennel Club, that allowed the taxpayer to determine the profitability of each dog.[30] This includes records of dogs bred and sold, the prices received for each dog, and the expenses incurred for each dog. Copies of advertisements showing an attempt to sell dogs and make money are also essential.

Author's note: Some cases have not mandated that you need these detailed records, but I would recommend them to be safe.

- *Charter boat operations.* An engine log, an expense log, and a revenue log indicating every financial and mechanical activity and all maintenance that the taxpayer conducted on the boat.[31] I would certainly keep a time log of business usage of the boat and a guest log.

Author's note: For network marketing,[32] in addition to keeping separate bank accounts, a tax diary, and profit and loss statements, I would keep all required receipts for travel and diary entries for appointments and meetings. I would note everyone to whom I gave marketing materials, such as tapes. If inventory is necessary, I certainly would keep some kind of inventory records and keep records that would show what was sold, given away, or used personally because personal consumption is not deductible. It is also imperative to have some form of budget, business plan, or breakeven analysis showing how much you need to sell in order to cover expenses and start showing a profit. If questioned, you should be able to explain in detail when your activity would become profitable.[33]

Author's note: Without question, network marketing has been held to be a business; however, there seems to be a higher burden with this business and with raising dogs and horses because of the popularity and social nature of these specific businesses. This may not be fair, but it's just the way it is. The key is to always try to make money and show the IRS that at least you're making a real effort, with daily activity, decent books and records, a business and marketing plan showing how much you need to sell or recruit to make money, and changes to your marketing, with the help of outside experts, if you have a loss.

4. Conducting the activities like a similar profitable business. It's essential that you show that you're carrying on your business like other similar businesses that are profitable.[34] Here is where the principle of duplication is critical. If you conduct your activity like other successful people in the same business, you have a very strong argument that you've conducted your activity like a business with the expectation of making a profit. In addition, if you follow the path of successful people, you also improve your chances of becoming successful. You actually might make a lot of money. You therefore want to adopt marketing efforts that are similar to those that are working for successful businesses.[35] Thus, you should do the following:

- Advertise your business in the Yellow Pages and the White Pages. Use the same ads in the same papers as other successful people have used. Get copies of their ads.
- Have business cards and stationery with your business name and address.
- Use a variety of marketing strategies used by successful people. Don't stick to the same thing year after year if it doesn't work.[36]

Author's note: This factor may seem similar to item 3, but there's a difference. You not only want to run your business in a business-like manner as noted in item 3, but you also want to run it the same way as people who've succeeded in similar ventures. The more you can show that you've copied the marketing and duties of successful people, the greater is your case for being deemed a business and not a hobby.

5. Prior business experiences. If you have prior business experience in this industry or with your product or service, this can make a big difference to the IRS. If you have no prior experience in this activity, your profit motive is more questionable.[37]

However, if you have no prior experience, don't be forlorn. You can overcome this deficiency with extensive study, listening to training tapes, taking seminars, and attending training meetings.

Some cases have looked favorably on taxpayers who take courses at the start of their business in order to get the training needed for success. "You can never get enough training" is an old adage to live by when you are trying to make profit.

Author's note: Document in your tax organizer any training that you attended or educational tapes that you heard. You can never get enough training! If you get help or suggestions from successful people or experts related to your field, document what was said and who helped you in your tax organizer or diary.

6. Advance research into the venture. If you were to buy a franchise or invest thousands in a business or investment, wouldn't you check it out first? Few good people start businesses without a good prior investigation of the business and any related companies. It's essential, therefore, that you investigate any business that you're considering before you get involved in it.[38]

Author's note: Many people ask me what should be done to conduct such an investigation. My suggestions depend on the type of business. If you're considering a franchise or network marketing distributorship, contact the Better Business Bureau in the area where the home company is located, and get a report in writing. Contact some franchisees/distributors and document what they tell you. Check out their products and see if you like them, see if they work, get copies of any reports on the products or any testing, etc. If you want to breed dogs, horses, or other animals, consult with experts in this area about how to run this type of business and what exactly you should be doing. The key is to consult with experts[39] consistently to keep improving your profitability and to follow what successful people are doing. The IRS doesn't care if you make money or not as long as you're trying to make a profit. Keep this in mind.

7. Devoting some time regularly to the activity. Although you certainly do not need to conduct your business full time, the more time and effort you put in, the better. Cases have shown that as little as one hour a day on average was sufficient to be deemed regular enough for a profit motive.[40] The more time that you devote to your endeavor, the better the chance that the endeavor will be classified as a business and not as a hobby.

Author's note: It seems that working one or two hours a day or more is much more important than doing nothing one week and working 20 to 30 hours the next week. Regularity seems to be important to both the IRS and tax court judges.

8. History of income/losses and measures to improve profits. Without question, your expenses certainly can exceed your income in a business. However, absent unforeseen circumstances,[41] such as theft, fire, flood, and sudden market changes, you should do everything reasonably possible to turn your losses into profits.[42] You should use common sense in running your business. For example, watch out for expenses that are unreasonably excessive in comparison with income. In one case, for example, a network marketing distributor's accounting fees alone exceeded his entire gross income. His travel also was 20 times his gross income. Other expenses also were very high.[43] In fact, the one taxpayer paid $2,300 in security expenses to cover $300 worth of inventory.[44] The bottom line is to use your common sense in how much you spend and on what.

Author's note: Based on my numerous discussions with various IRS personnel, it seems that this concept of using excessive, unreasonable expenses as a test for a "lack of business profit motive" has been applied to a variety of endeavors. For example, one who enters the travel business and tries to deduct all his or her "familiarization trips" (otherwise known as "fam" trips), despite earning very little gross income and making little attempt to sell vacation travel, would have a tough time establishing that these trips have a profit motive. This is especially true if the cost of each trip is greater than the gross income from the entire endeavor.

In addition, some recent IRS cases have noted that although you do *not* have to make a profit, you should have some gross income during the year. Judges and the IRS just don't believe that any business can have zero gross income if someone is truly try-ing to make a profit. Thus, if you have zero gross income, you may well be deemed a hobby despite all the preceding discussion.

9. Income from other sources. The amount of income from other sources is used to help determine your profit motive. Although it may not seem fair, the greater your income from other sources or other businesses or jobs, the less likely it is that your loss from your activity may be deemed a business loss.[45] Although this certainly is not a determinative factor, if you have substantial income from other activities, you need to more closely dot your *i*s and cross your *t*s. If you follow everything that I have discussed here, you can be a billionaire and still have your side venture be deemed a business.

10. Suspicious activities. Watch out for certain activities that the IRS considers inherently more suspect because they involve significant personal pleasure.[46] These include

- Antique collecting
- Stamp collecting
- Travel business
- Writing
- Ministerial duties
- Record recording
- Raising show horses
- Training and showing dogs
- Automobile racing
- Network marketing

Author's note: If you're engaged in one of these activities, you must pay careful attention to the other "business versus hobby" factors mentioned.

Author's note: I've had hundreds of students who were audited because of questions about their activities being a business and have prevailed, getting their losses allowed for years! If you follow everything that I've said in this chapter, you'll have the peace of mind of being bulletproof against one of the IRS's favorite weapons.

Summary

- Losses from businesses can be used against any income in current year, or carried forward indefinitely for up to 80 percent of future taxable income until all losses are used up. No deductions seem to be allowable for hobbies. This is why classifying an activity as a hobby is the IRS's favorite weapon.
- Try to have a profit in at least three of five consecutive years. This is not mandatory, but it's nice to have because it will provide evidence of your profit motive.
- An election is available to postpone a determination of the status of your activities as a business or as a hobby. Generally, don't bother making this election.
- Document business intent by sending a letter to your manager, sponsor, or franchising company to express your reasons for entering the business, emphasizing your desire to make a long-term profitable career out of this activity.
- Have a business plan showing at least 5 and preferably 10 years of projections for revenues and expenses.
- If your business involves inventory, always have enough on hand to justify your goals and the business plan.
- Don't make any improper statements such as, "I'm in this endeavor only to save taxes" or "… to cut costs" or "… to get my products at a discount."
- Keep accurate books and records, which should include a tax organizer or diary with your daily contacts and activities. Also have yearly balance sheet and income

statements prepared to help you improve your performance. Finally, keep separate bank accounts and inventory records of costs, sales, and products given away as samples or personally consumed, etc.

- At least yearly, consult with experts to find out what successful people are doing to make money in businesses similar to your own. Document who the expert was and what he or she said.
- Use advertising, telephone listings, business cards, and stationery with your business name, address, and telephone number.
- If you're not making money, change the way you market your business. It's essential that you try different documented approaches.
- Before entering your business, conduct an investigation of the industry and of any companies that you're thinking of associating with. At the least, you should get a Better Business Bureau report on any company that you're considering representing. Document your steps in this investigation.
- Keep getting trained and seeking tips on operating and improving your business. This shows that you're really interested in making a profit.
- It's much more important to work your business regularly, such as one or two hours a day, than once every two weeks for 20 hours. You should note all activities and appointments in your tax organizer or diary.
- If you have losses, meet with your accountant about costs that can be cut that won't negatively affect your business. Going over your financial statements becomes very important.
- Clearly document reasons for making any business trips.
- Try to have at least some gross income. You don't need to make money, but you should have some sales or commissions during the year.
- Be especially careful if you're engaged in one of the inherently suspicious activities.

Notes

1. Section 172 of the IRC and regulations thereunder.
2. Section 172(b)(1)(A)(i) of the IRC and see the Job Creation and Worker Assistance Act of 2002.
3. Section 172 (b)(1)(A)(ii) of the IRC.
4. Section 183(a) of the IRC and IRS Publication 535.
5. Section 183 of the IRC.
6. Section 67(g) of the IRC as amended by 2017 Tax Cuts and Jobs Act, Section 11045(a).
7. Section 183(d) of the IRC.
8. Ibid.
9. Section 183(e)(1) of the IRC.
10. Regulation Section 12.9(c) of the ITR.
11. Regulation Section 12.9 of the ITR.
12. Section 1.183-2(a) of the ITR.
13. Section 1.183-2 of the ITR. See also *Floyd Fisher*, T.C. Memo 1980-183.
14. Ibid.

15. *Dreicer v. Commissioner,* 78 TC 642; *aff'd.,* 702 F.2d 1205 (CA Dist. Ct. 1983).
16. Section 1.183-2(a) of the ITR and *Bryant v. Commissioner,* 928 F.2d 745 (6th Cir. 1991).
17. *Dennis Pryor,* T.C. Memo 1991-109. See also *Schwartz,* T.C. Memo 2003-86.
18. *Harry Van Scoyoc,* T.C. Memo 1988-520.
19. *David Williams, et al. v. Commissioner,* (2018) T.C. Memo 2018-48, 2018 RIA TC Memo ¶ 2018-48).
20. *Richard Glenn,* T.C. Memo 1995-399.
21. Section 1.183-2(c) of the ITR.
22. Section 1.183-2(b)(i) of the ITR.
23. *Frank Sutter,* T.C. Memo 1990-447; *Charles Givens,* T.C. Memo 1989-529; *Ransom v. Commissioner,* T.C. Memo 1990-381 (Amway distributor); *Frank Harris,* T.C. Memo 1992-638 (Mary Kay distributor).
24. *Thomas Burger,* T.C. Memo 1985-523, *aff'd.* 809 F.2d 355 (7th Cir. 1987).
25. *Kenneth J. Nissley,* T.C. Memo 2000-178 (Amway distributor); *Tony L. Zidar v. Commissioner,* T.C. Memo 2001-200.
26. *Smith v. Commissioner,* T.C. Memo 2007-154 (6/14/2007).
27. *Kenneth J. Nissley,* cited earlier.
28. *Lawrence Appley,* T.C. Memo 1979-433. Most subsequent cases were taken from the Research Institute of America's Federal Tax Coordinator (2002).
29. *George Doyle,* T.C. Memo 1982-537.
30. *Rufus Burleson,* T.C. Memo 1983-570.
31. *Patrick Edward McLarney,* T.C. Memo 1982-461.
32. *Peter Rubin,* T.C. Memo 1989-290.
33. *Theisen v. Commissioner,* T.C. Memo 1997-539; *Kenneth J. Nissley,* cited earlier.
34. Section 1.183-2(b)(i) of the ITR.
35. *C. Frank Fisher,* 50 T.C. 164 (1968) (acquiesced by the IRS).
36. *Sheldon Barr,* T.C. Memo 1989-69; *Kenneth J, Nissley,* cited earlier.
37. Section 1.183-2(b) of the ITR and *Ransom v. Commissioner,* T.C. Memo 1990-381.
38. *Wenzel Tirheimer,* T.C. Memo 1992-137.
39. *Sherman Sampson,* T.C. Memo 1982-276.
40. Ibid.
41. Section 1.183-2(b)(6) of the ITR.
42. Sections 1.183-2(b)(6) and 2(b)(7) of the ITR.
43. *Ransom v. Commissioner,* cited earlier, and *Abdolvahab Pirnia,* T.C. Memo 1992-137.
44. Ibid.
45. Section 1.183-2(b)(8) of the ITR.
46. Section 1.183-2(b)(9) of the ITR.

Part 2

How to Incorporate
to Shelter Your Wealth

9

Finding the Best Corporate Entity for Your Business

The beginning is the most important part of the work.

—**Plato,** *The Republic*

What was true for Plato 2,500 years ago still holds true today. What determines how much you can use in fringe benefits and losses, not to mention how much you can limit liabilities and how easily you can raise capital, is your business entity. It's thus crucial that you read over this chapter carefully and follow along on the flowchart (Figure 9-1). Moreover, even if an entity is great for you now, you may wish to change it as time goes by. For example, you may want to start off as a sole proprietor but later raise more capital and incorporate. Thus you will need to keep track of your "proper" business entity on a continuing basis if you want to make your life less taxing.

The flowchart in Figure 9-1 should help you to decide which form of business entity would be most appropriate for your business. If you are not a specified service business such as a law firm, accounting firm, real estate

---

Chapter Overview
- Learn why your initial choice of a business entity is so important.
- Use a great flowchart that will easily demonstrate which entity is best for you.
- Know the pros and cons of a sole proprietorship and why it's an ideal entity for network marketers.
- Learn about partnerships and why these generally should be avoided.
- Know the benefits of being an S corporation and how this one entity can eliminate up to 40 percent of your Social Security taxes.
- Learn why a limited-liability corporation is one of the most highly recommended entities for most business owners.
- Learn about when to form a regular corporation (C corporation) and, more important, when not to.
- Learn which entity is best if you have co-owners or partners and about the one document that's crucial to your long-term success.

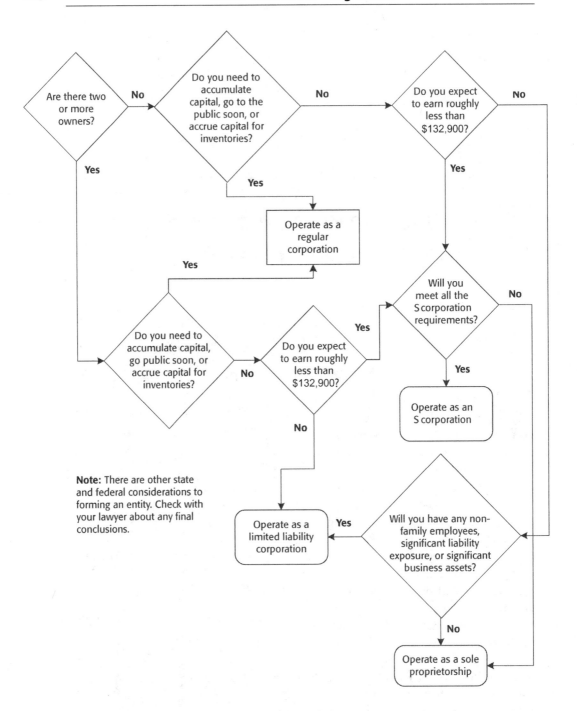

Figure 9-1. Entity selection flowchart.

management or brokerage firm, financial services firm, consulting firm, medical or health care or veterinary firm, athlete, or any business in which the principal asset of the business is the reputation or skill of one or more of its employees.

Let's begin by discussing the advantages and disadvantages of your entity options, with a recommendation on which types of business would be most or least appropriate for each option.

Sole Proprietorship

Sole proprietorships are great if you have no liability problems and no employees. Without question, the easiest, lowest-costing entity to run and manage is a sole proprietorship.

Advantages of a Sole Proprietorship

1. Simplicity. This is by far the least complicated form of business entity around. In fact, a sole proprietorship is defined by its lack of organization. There's only one owner. If you have no employees, there are no Internal Revenue Service (IRS) forms to file other than Schedule C with your federal Form 1040 tax return. You simply hang out a sign saying your business name, such as "Harriet Stowe, writer." Although it's highly recommended that you have separate bank accounts, you don't need to do so. You can have one account for you and your business. It doesn't get any easier than this!

2. Low startup costs. The startup costs are negligible. If you have no employees, there are no filings with the federal government, no organization documents, as with a corporation or a partnership, and no state filings unless you want to reserve a name or operate as an alias.

3. Simple control. You're in direct control all the time. There's no hassle with other owners or partners and only one layer of management—you.

4. Freely sellable. Sole proprietorships are easy to sell. There aren't a lot of hidden traps, as with corporations.

5. Great small-business tax benefits. As I've noted in prior chapters, you get lots of tax benefits being in business. However, there are limitations that apply to partnerships and S corporations that don't apply to sole proprietorships. For example, you can hire your spouse and deduct all your medical expenses with a self-insured medical reimbursement plan. (Do you remember this from Chapter 4?)

6. Carryover and carryback of losses. If you have a loss arising from your sole proprietorship, you can use that loss against any other type of income. In addition, any losses that exceed this year's income can be used against any earnings this year. If losses exceed your currently years earnings from any source, you can carry over those losses to future years forever against up to 80 percent of future taxable income. Not bad!

7. You are eligible for the 20 percent pass-through deduction that allows you to be taxed effectively on only 80 percent of your net income. See Chapter 20.

In short, this entity is cheap and simple.

Disadvantages of a Sole Proprietorship

1. Unlimited liability. Did you know that there are roughly 90 million lawsuits yearly?[1] This is certainly the $64,000 question to being a sole proprietorship. You have unlimited liability. Thus, if you are sued for any business problem or incur any debts, you're personally liable. To be sure, you can get insurance to help offset most of the potential problems, but there are a number of bankrupt people whose economic lives lie in ruin because of unlimited liability or because they didn't cover every eventuality.

If there's any chance that someone will sue your business, if you have any employees who are not immediate family, or if you have substantial assets (property) that you need to protect, you absolutely should not operate as a sole proprietorship. Pick either one of the corporate forms or become a limited-liability corporation (to be discussed below).

Author's note: If you have employees, you shouldn't be a sole proprietor. Employees who aren't your immediate family are walking lawsuits. The reason is that employers are liable for the acts of their employees. In addition, there are numerous lawsuits filed by employees over allegations of discrimination, violations of the Americans with Disabilities Act, the Occupational Safety and Health Act (OSHA), and so forth. Thus the bottom line is that if you have nonfamily employees, don't be a sole proprietor. Use another business entity.

Author's note: Whether you operate as a sole proprietorship or as a limited-liability coporation (LLC), get a liability umbrella policy for at least $2 million in addition to your regular business insurance. The cost is negligible, around $400 per year. I would recommend a liability umbrella of at least $5 million to be safe!

2. No checks and balances. Because a sole proprietorship has only one owner by definition, there is no board of directors or other partners who can oversee what the owner is doing. There's no one to say, "This is inappropriate or shouldn't be done."

3. Trouble raising capital. It's much tougher to raise capital as a sole proprietor. Basically, the assets of the owner are the primary collateral.

4. No continuity of life. If the owner dies, becomes disabled, or retires, there's usually no one who can take over the business. The business thus either dies or is sold for a very low price.

Author's note: Because of this problem, I strongly urge all sole proprietorships to have very good disability insurance and good life insurance. Thus, if the owner dies or becomes disabled, there's a continued cash flow.

Who Should Operate as a Sole Proprietorship?

Despite the wonderful simplicity of this entity, the unlimited liabilities involved should negate most reasons for operating as a sole proprietor. The only people who should consider operating under a sole proprietorship are those who have almost no chance of liability problems, *no* nonfamily employees, and little in the way of investments that need protection. Many home-based business people, especially network marketing home-based businesses, should consider this form of operation. If you're a freelance writer with no employees, this form of business also could be for you. However, if you feel or your lawyer feels that there is any significant liability exposure, take my advice: *Don't be a sole proprietor.*

Author's note: Real estate has large amounts of liability exposure. Thus, do NOT own investment real estate in your own name; use an LLC.

General Partnership

A partnership is essentially like a sole proprietorship but with two or more partners/ owners. However, there are some advantages and disadvantages to the partnership that a sole proprietorship doesn't offer. There are two kinds of partnerships: *general* and *limited*. Let's discuss the general partnership first.

Advantages of a General Partnership

1. Broader expertise. A sole proprietor is a one-man or one-woman shop. He or she must become a "jack of many trades"—good at management, marketing, accounting, liability protection, taxes, and much more—to become successful. With a partnership, several people can divide the work and share and develop expertise. Thus one partner can do the marketing, while another can manage the inside operation. This can result in more efficiency and can attract greater knowledge to the operation.

2. Easier to raise capital. With a partnership, you can bring in as many investor/ owner partners as you want: There's no legal limit. If you need to get a loan, you have more collateral at risk for a loan because more parties are involved. Thus a partnership can attract a lot more capital than a proprietorship.

3. Easy to form. Most partnerships are very easy to form. You just need to draft up a partnership agreement showing the rights and obligations of the partners. There are very few filings with either the IRS or the states unless you have employees, although it's more complicated than for a sole proprietorship—but then, every entity is more complicated than a sole proprietorship.

4. Low startup costs. As with proprietorships, the costs are low. Since there are few required filings with either the states or the federal government, formation costs are low. You will, however, need a partnership agreement, as noted earlier, which adds to your costs. In addition, a partnership needs to file a separate IRS form (Form 1065, U.S. Return of Partnership Income). Thus, the cost of filing a return is greater than for a sole proprietorship.

5. Partnerships are eligible for the new 20 percent pass-through deduction that potentially results in paying tax on up to 80 percent of your net income. See Chapter 20 for a full discussion on this.

6. No double taxation. All profits and losses flow through to the partners. There's no double tax, as there is with regular corporations. Any losses are limited to your partnership basis. However, that basis includes what you paid for your partnership interest, the basis of any other property contributed, plus your share of the liabilities.[2] Thus you should have sufficient basis for the losses.

Example: Sam contributes $10,000 in cash, plus stock worth $20,000 for which he paid $15,000, to get a 50 percent partnership interest. In addition, the partnership gets a bank loan for $40,000. Sam's basis in the partnership is $45,000:

Cash:	$10,000
Stock (basis):	$15,000
Prorated share of debt (50 percent):	$20,000
Total basis:	$45,000

Author's note: With partnerships, you always have to worry about your basis because losses are limited to the basis. With sole proprietorships, you don't have this problem.

With these increased benefits, you would think that everyone should run out, find some good partners, and form a partnership instead of being a sole proprietorship. However, there are some major drawbacks to partnerships.

Disadvantages of a General Partnership

1. Lack of continuity. Generally, partnerships terminate on the death, retirement, withdrawal, or resignation of a partner. The IRS notes[3] that if a 50 percent partner dies, retires, resigns, or withdraws; a partnership terminates for tax purposes regardless of what happens under state law.

Author's note: This one problem can be overcome easily with a well-drafted partnership agreement that notes, "The death, disability, resignation, or withdrawal of a partner will not terminate the partnership."

2. More management. With more owners comes more management, more layers of management. Partnerships thus can't respond as quickly to changes as a sole proprietorship.

3. Complaints about money and draws. There are usually major fights among partners about how much money should be distributed to each partner based on the production or efforts involved. More partnerships have terminated because of this one factor, in my opinion, than for any other reason. With a proprietorship, you don't have this problem—unless you like to fight with yourself.

4. Unlimited liability. This is probably the greatest drawback of all. Like sole proprietors, you're unlimitedly liable for all partnership debts unless they are specifically *nonrecourse debts* (which means that you have not guaranteed the debt personally). If this isn't bad enough, you're also unlimitedly liable for the actions of your partners. They can, in effect, bind you and make you liable for a host of obligations. Yuck!

5. Good luck finding the right partners. Having a separation of duties and finding people who specialize in different aspects of the business sounds wonderful in theory. In practice, however, it's very hard to do. Many partnerships break up because one partner isn't pulling his or her weight or is failing at some important designated task.

6. Fewer fringe benefits available. Partnerships have fewer fringe benefits than regular corporations. Moreover, the benefits derived from a self-insured medical plan are more limited for both partners and for owners of more than 2 percent of the stock of an S corporation. Partners and more than 2 percent stockholders of S corporations can set up a self-insured medical plan solely for routine physicals and laboratory testing.

Who Should Operate as a General Partnership?

Take my advice: Before you decide on being a partnership, take three aspirins and lie down until the desire passes. You should *never, ever* form a general partnership.

Why not?

From practical experience, I've seen too many partnerships break up because of fights among the partners about money, power, ego, who is failing to contribute, etc. It's just horrible. If you think that divorces aren't fun, you should see what happens in court with partnership splits. It's very nasty. In addition, being unlimitedly liable for the acts of your partners and for their malpractice could be a disaster, as will be shown with the Arthur Andersen Company. Take my advice: *Don't form a general partnership.*

Author's note: In the event that you don't listen to me, at least have a buy/sell agreement with any partners. This agreement provides that if there is a death, disability, or unsolvable disagreement among the partners, you have a way to buy out a partner using a fixed formula.

Partnership Startup Checklist

In addition to all the items just noted, if you have a partnership, you should have a good partnership agreement that notes the following:

- The term of the partnership
- How new partners may or may not be added
- Provisions in the event of the total disability, death, withdrawal, or retirement of a partner
- Provisions on the timing of any profit-sharing distributions and how they are to be determined
- Listing of the initial contributions of the partners and how any excess contribution is to be allocated
- List of all duties, work hours, and profit sharing
- Provisions for management and for handling disputes
- Provisions that no person can be a partner unless approved by a percentage of the remaining partners (to prevent creditors from being partners)

Limited Partnership

Because of all the partnership drawbacks, many people set up limited partnerships, which usually are formed for investments. These are formed with one or two limited partners and one general partner who is liable for all debts. This is not normally a problem because the general partner usually is a corporation with limited liability.

Advantages of a Limited Partnership

1. Limited liability. Unlike a general partnership, the limited partners are only responsible for their initial contributions, unless they personally guarantee any debts. They are thus insulated from all partnership liabilities, like a corporation. The general partner is unlimitedly liable, but since general partners usually are corporations, their liability is limited, too.

Author's note: The limited partners enjoy limited liability, but only if they do not in any way participate in management. If they're active in management, courts have held that they are the alter ego of the partnership, which causes the limited partners to be unlimitedly liable as a general partner. Thus, if you are a limited partner, you should only contribute capital and not in any way help out the partnership or make any management decisions other than voting for another general partner.

2. Great way to raise capital. Since there can be no limit to the number of limited partners, this form of entity can raise a lot of capital. This is one of the big reasons for using limited partnerships for investment.

3. Centralized management. By definition, limited partners only contribute capital and do not participate in management. There usually is a centralized management structure that handles all the business of the partnership.

4. Transferability. Although most partnership agreements require some sort of partnership consent before transferring any partnership interest, it's usually not a problem getting consent in the sale or transfer of a limited partnership interest.

5. Continuous life. Unlike general partnerships, most limited partnerships don't terminate on the death or disability of a limited partner. If the general partner becomes bankrupt, this could be a problem unless the partnership agreement allows the limited partners to get a new general partner.

6. Estate planning discounts. Because limited partnerships are not readily sellable and have very little voting power, their value is usually discounted for estate tax purposes.[4] This is the reason why many estate planners are recommending the use of family limited partnerships for estate planning purposes.

7. Flowthrough of income. Partnerships do not pay tax. All income and losses flow through to the partners, usually in accordance with their contributions. Family limited partnerships are great ways to shift income to family members.

Partnerships are eligible for the new 20 percent pass-through deduction that potentially results in paying tax on up to 80 percent of your net income. See Chapter 20 for a full discussion on this.

Disadvantages of a Limited Partnership

1. Limited transferability. There usually isn't a market for a partnership interest, so it's hard to sell. Moreover, the consent of the general partners usually is required for any sale.

2. Heavy costs. It's usually costly to set up a limited partnership because of the complexity of the partnership agreement needed and the requirement to file a Form 1065 plus K-1s for each partner at year end noting their share of partnership income and losses. In addition, since management is centralized, it must be paid, which raises the yearly costs considerably.

3. No control over the general partners. The general partner controls the day-to-day activities of the partnership. So who's overseeing the general partner? Who's on the alert for any embezzlement? Sadly, the answer is that you have an outside accountant doing the books (hopefully); however, there has been a lot of improper behavior by general partners who have taken more money than normally would have been allowed.

4. The limited partners may not participate in management. This has its good and bad points, but the limited partners must not participate in management or they'll lose their protected status as limited partners. If the general partner is running the business improperly (but not doing anything illegal), the limited partners will have very little say.

5. Passive loss problems. All limited partnerships are treated as passive activities.[5] This means that if there are losses, you can use them only to the extent that you have passive income. Passive income includes income that's not earned, such as rents, royalties, or other partnership income. Thus, if you want to use the losses, you must have some passive income for the losses to offset. If you don't have passive income, the losses get carried over to future years. Thus, as an investor, you should have some positive passive income.

Who Should Operate as a Limited Partnership?

As you can see, limited partnerships are very useful. They should be used mainly for investors who will not be active in the business. Real estate limited partnerships are an ideal example because all the depreciation and losses from the real estate pass through to the partners. In addition, family limited partnerships can be set up to shift income and to allow a big estate tax discount for the partnership interest. Consult a good estate planning attorney about this.

Corporations

The word *incorporate* means "to create a separate body." This is exactly what defines a corporation. It's a separate entity that, on its own behalf, can sue, borrow money, be responsible for its own debts, and run a business on its own behalf. Many entrepreneurs who are the sole owners of their corporations do not understand that they are not the business; the business is the corporation.

Advantages of a Regular Corporation (C Corporation)

1. Limited liability. Perhaps the greatest reason to set up a corporation is not taxes but liabilities. If a corporation is set up properly, and if the owners adhere to the corporate formalities, it can limit most liabilities to the assets of the corporation. The only exceptions are fraud, malpractice, and failure to adhere to the corporate formalities.

Author's note: Malpractice is a real problem for some small businesses today. The advantage of corporate status is that unlike in a general partnership, if a co-owner of a corporation commits malpractice, you would not be liable personally for it. Only the co-owner who committed the malpractice normally would become unlimitedly liable, and only the assets of the corporation are exposed.

Example: Doctors Alice, Bob, and Charley form a professional corporation. Alice commits malpractice. Alice is unlimitedly liable to the injured person, as is the corporation. However, Bob and Charley are not personally liable; the corporation has insulated them from liability.

2. Specialized management. Corporations can have as many officers as they can afford. Thus, unlike a sole proprietor, they can and usually do have different people handling different aspects of the business. In a sense, they get the same advantages in this way as a general partnership.

3. New 21 percent flat tax rate for regular corporations (C corporations).

4. Great tax advantages. Regular corporations (C corporations) and employees of S corporations who own less than 2 percent of the stock get the most fringe benefits among all the entities. Chapter 11 will cover this, but for now here are some examples:

- 100 percent deduction for health insurance premiums for the officers and their families—a benefit that is also available to sole proprietors and partners after the year 2002
- 100 percent deduction for disability insurance premiums
- 100 percent deduction for medical expenses that are not covered by insurance, using a self-insured medical reimbursement plan
- Qualified stock options that can give capital gains
- Tax-free life insurance—up to $50,000 of group term life
- A fully deductible athletic facility and athletic equipment, if on the premises of the business
- A cafeteria plan that can cover day care, unreimbursed medical expenses (with some limits), adoption assistance, and group legal service

Author's note: Cafeteria plans, which are special legal plans that let you choose your benefits, generally are not beneficial for small and home-based businesses because not more than 25 percent of the benefits can accrue to owner/employees,[6] and there are stiff, complicated nondiscrimination rules. Moreover, the plans apply only to employees. Self-employed people and partners are not deemed employees.[7] Thus we will not be discussing this benefit in this book.

- Tax-free supper money allowance
- Qualified pensions and profit sharing that allow borrowing

5. Accumulation of capital. Unlike other types of entities, corporations are subject to their own set of tax rates. For good reasons, corporations can accrue $50,000 of net earnings each year and get taxed only in the 15 percent tax bracket. Thus, if you need to accumulate capital for marketing, business expansion, or inventories, this can be a major benefit.

6. Transferability of ownership. Unlike with a partnership or even a limited partnership, you usually can transfer your stock holding without consent from the corporation or other stockholders if you have a buyer.

7. Great for a public offering. If you want to go public and raise capital, no entity is better than a regular corporation. We have exchanges that handle the raising of capital and the transferability of shares. There's rarely a problem with disposing of publicly traded stock.

8. Ordinary losses on sale of stock. Normally, when you sell a stock at a loss, your loss is limited to any capital gains; if it exceeds any gains, you may deduct up to $3,000 of the loss against other income. Losses in excess of this amount can be carried forward and used to reduce future capital gains, up to $3,000 per year.

Example: Wendy has a stock loss of $20,000. If she made $5,000 with some stock gains, she may use $5,000 of the loss against the gains and may use another $3,000 of the loss against her salary or other income. She carries over the remaining loss to future years to use in the same way.

If you plan correctly when the corporation is formed, when you sell corporate stock at a loss, it's an ordinary loss. This means that you would not be limited to offsetting any capital gains, and there wouldn't be a limit of $3,000 per year. In fact, the maximum amount of ordinary loss that you can take would be $50,000 if you are single[8] and up to a whopping $100,000 if you are married and file a joint return![9] *Yeah!* However, you must organize your corporation so that the stock you receive is deemed "Section 1244 stock."

9. Eliminate up to 100 percent of your gain when you sell your stock in your corporation. Yes, you read this correctly. If you are set up as a regular C corporation, you will probably qualify for a little-known but very available exemption allowed under the American Taxpayer Relief Law, the small-business stock.

Exemption. Thus, if you own a business and are selling your stock in that business, you might be able to avoid 100 percent on that gain if your stock qualifies as qualified small-business stock (QSBS). In order for you to qualify, you need to meet all of the following rules:

- You must be an individual who owns the stock. Thus, this benefit doesn't apply to corporate owners of stock.
- The stock was acquired after September 27, 2010, for cash, property, or services.
- You must have hold the stock for more than five years.
- As to the corporation, a qualified small business means any domestic sea corporation in which the aggregate gross assets of the corporation (or any predecessor of it) did not exceed $50,000,000:
  (a) after stock was issued
  (b) gain exclusion was capped at lower of $10,000,000 or ten times basis.[10]

  Note: This exclusion amount has changed over the years and there are other rules not mentioned. Thus, you need to check with a good tax professional about this.

10. Regularly corporations now pay a flat income tax of 21 percent. This is down from the prior maximum tax of $35 percent.

Disadvantages of a Regular Corporation

Despite all the wonderful benefits that are available to regular corporations, there are some major drawbacks.

Author's note: Don't you wish that there could be just one entity that has all positives and no negatives? Unfortunately, this doesn't exist. If you're considering forming a Nevada corporation, I recommend getting advice from Nevada Corporate Planners at www.nvinc.com.

1. Double taxation. Since regular corporations are treated as separate entities and have their own tax rates, you can have the possibility of double taxation: tax at the corporate level and tax for you at your rates if there's a dividend. As bad as this sounds—and it can be bad—most people who operate as regular corporations plan before year's end to pay enough in bonuses and salaries to eliminate most of the double-tax problem. However, it takes planning, and of course, this increases the cost involved.

Author's note: Before I became an S corporation, I would meet with my accountant before year's end and make projections of my yearly income and pay bonuses according to my projections.

2. Increased paperwork. Without question, operating a regular corporation is a "three-Tylenol" hassle. You *must* have yearly stockholder meetings to elect a board of directors, even if you're the only stockholder, and yearly board meetings to elect officers and approve major issues within the corporation. Also, you must keep corporate minutes. You need separate bank accounts and very good books and records. If you do not do this, your corporation will be deemed your "alter ego," and you may become liable for all corporate debts and obligations.

3. Added paperwork costs. Clearly, corporations are more expensive to operate than any other entity. You have to file a separate corporate tax return with schedules (Form 1120). In addition, you will be the employee of the corporation, so you must file with both the federal government and the state government for an Employer Identification Number (SS-4 and SS-5. Form SS-5 is Application for a Social Security Card), as well as for unemployment. Some states, such as California, have special corporate taxes that don't apply to proprietorships, which significantly increase the costs.

4. Losses don't flow through to you as stockholder. Unlike with partnerships and proprietorships, all losses in the corporation stay with the corporation. They don't flow through to you on your corporate tax return because corporations are separate entities. This disadvantage can be somewhat overcome, however, by electing S corporation status, which will be discussed below.

Author's note: The losses in a regular corporation get carried over to future years in the corporation and offset future corporate profits.

5. Lots of tax traps. Corporations have traps set up by the government to overcome perceived abuses, such as operating a corporation with a lot of unearned income (personal holding company) and accumulating too much in earnings (accumulated earnings tax).

6. Stockholder fights. Corporations are run and managed somewhat like a democracy. The ones who get the most votes (based on shares) elect the board of directors, which, in turn, elects the management. Sadly, many corporate owners end up fighting over management, trying to fire each other, trying to benefit one owner over the others, etc. It becomes just as bad as fights among partners. This is especially fierce if each owner owns 50 percent of the stock. It's vital to have in place some sort of buy/sell agreement that provides both a formula and a mechanism for buying out stockholders. A good lawyer can draft one, and, I promise, it will be one of the best things that you'll ever do. Don't pass up this precaution, as many have done, to their regret.

Author's note: Many years ago, I had a corporation with a 50 percent partner but didn't have a buy/sell agreement. It took hundreds of thousands of dollars in legal fees, not to mention a huge amount of hard feelings, to settle this situation.

Who Should Operate as a Regular Corporation and Who Shouldn't

Certainly because of the personal service corporation rules, people who render mostly services and who also perform the services should *not* be a regular corporation because they will pay the highest corporate rates on all earnings. Yuck! The people who should consider being a regular corporation are those who have some liability exposure that they want to protect themselves from *and* who are in any of the following situations:

- They have substantial inventories and need to accumulate capital for this purpose.
- They need to accumulate capital in the future for marketing and other projects.

- They expect to go public in the near future.
- They need all the fringe benefits such as health insurance.
- Those that are specific service businesses that don't qualify for the 20 percemt pass-through deduction due to having too much taxable income. See Chapter 20 for a thorough discussion about this.

Author's note: As I said before and want to restate because it's important, the main purpose of operating as any form of corporation is to limit liability exposure or perhaps to go public. If you don't have any significant liability exposure and don't plan on having a public offering in the near future, being a corporation—especially a regular corporation—is probably not advantageous.

Author's note: From my experience, I have found that most people, despite having the best of intentions, do not keep up with the corporate formalities, annual board meetings, minutes, etc. It just doesn't happen. If you're the kind of person who won't strictly adhere to these formalities every year, do not form a corporation. Did I say that clearly enough? Form one of the other entities, such as a limited-liability corporation, which will be discussed later on.

S Corporation

There are a lot of problems inherent to regular corporations. Congress allows taxpayers to avoid most of these without many negative side effects. You do this by electing S corporation status.

An S corporation *is* a corporation. To the surprise of many people, it has the exact same formalities as a regular corporation—stockholder meetings and board of directors meetings, etc. In addition, you must make an election by filing Form 2553 with the IRS within the first 75 days of the tax year if you want to operate as an S corporation for the year. An election is just that: It's a formal choice to become an S corporation. If you don't make this formal choice, you are treated as a regular corporation.

However, there are a number of advantages that an S corporation has over a regular corporation.

Advantages of an S Corporation

1. No double taxation.[12] With regular corporations, you would take the gross income of the corporation, subtract any business expenses, and pay tax at the corporate level on the net income.

With an S corporation, this is not the case. Unless you were a regular corporation and then elected to become an S corporation,[13] there's generally no double taxation because all the income and losses flow through to you as the stockholder. S corporations thus are treated like partnerships in this way. You actually would receive a form (K-1) noting your share of the net income. Thus you don't have to go through all the complicated year-end tax planning to eliminate the double-tax problem as with regular corporations.

2. Elimination of up to 50 percent of your Social Security and Medicare taxes.
As I mentioned, the main reason for setting up a corporation is to limit your liability
exposure. However, there's one major tax benefit to S corporations that can be so
great that many accountants have recommended setting up an S corporation solely
for this benefit: the substantial saving in Social Security and Medicare taxes with
the use of S corporation dividends.[14] This is especially true if you make under the
Social Security maximum ($128,400 in 2018). This benefit can be so substantial that
I devote Chapter 11 to discussing it.

3. Income splitting. As I pointed out in Chapter 4 on income shifting and income
splitting, you're better off having various family members being taxed on shares of your
income than one person—you—being taxed on the whole thing. This is so because
our tax system is a graduated rate system: The rates rise as income rises. By splitting
income among family members who don't have a lot of other income, the lower rates
allow you to save a bundle. The rich have known this for years and have planned
accordingly. An S corporation can allow you the same benefit. You can give some stock
to your children or grandchildren or to anyone in a lower tax bracket than you whom
you want to support. When the company earns money, they are taxed on their share
of the net income based on their stock ownership. Let me give you a true example that
happened to one of my friends.

Example: John and Martha have three children. They have a sole proprietorship
business that had net earnings of $112,850; they paid in federal income tax alone (not
counting Social Security) $24,265. I suggested that they form an S corporation and
give 15 percent of the stock to each of their three children, who were attending college. Each child then was taxed on 15 percent of the gain, and the parents paid tax on
55 percent of the gain. Each child paid $2,239 in taxes, and the parents paid $10,554.
The savings was $6,994 with this technique, computed as follows:

Tax payable by parents as sole proprietorship:	$24,265
Tax payable by all three children:	$ 6,717
Tax payable by parents using split technique:	$10,554
Total taxes paid by family:	$17,271
Net savings to the family using split technique:	$ 6,994

Author's note: No wonder the rich have used income splitting for years. Now that you
know about it, you can do the same thing. The rich, however, have paid a lot of money
in fees to find out about this; you have only paid for this book. What a deal!

4. Specialized management. Just like regular corporations, S corporations have
centralized management. You have a board of directors to help oversee what you're
doing and provide, in theory, some checks and balances.

5. Limited liability. S corporations limit liability to the same extent as regular corporations, no better and no worse.

6. Ordinary loss on the sale of stock. Just as with a regular corporation, you can have an ordinary loss on the sale of your stock, up to $50,000 if you're single and up to $100,000 if you're married. (See the earlier discussion dealing with regular corporations.[15])

7. Use of corporate losses. As I mentioned, an S corporation flows all income and losses to the owners. Thus, if you have a loss, the loss passes through to your individual tax return, just as with a sole proprietorship. However, there's an IRS "gotcha." The loss is limited to the basis in your stock.[16] That basis is what you paid for your stock in money plus the basis of any property contributed to the S corporation for the stock. It also includes any income that you were taxed on but didn't receive. You subtract what you received as a dividend. Thus, the formula for basis is:

> Cash paid for stock
> *plus*
> Basis (which is usually the cost) of property contributed for stock
> *plus*
> Income that was taxed to you in the past that you didn't receive
> *minus*
> Any dividends received or losses that were passed through to you.

Author's note: Limiting your losses to your stock basis is very different from the treatment of losses in sole proprietorships, in which you can take any losses on your individual tax return. This means that you must do some planning if you expect a loss in your S corporation to ensure that you have sufficient basis for the loss.

8. Limited benefits from self-insured medical plan. As I noted earlier, owners of more than 2 percent of the corporate stock and partners generally can't benefit from a self-insured medical plan except to cover routine physicals and laboratory testing.

   With all these wonderful benefits, you would think that an S corporation might be the way to go for most people. In fact, it's probably the preferred vehicle for most small businesses; however, there are some drawbacks to being an S corporation.

Author's elaboration: With an S corporation, a self-insured medical plan is limited to routine physicals and diagnostic testing for the owners, so you might want to consider an HSA, health savings account. (HSAs can be used only in conjunction with applicable high-deductible medical plans.)

9. 50 to 100 percent exclusion on gain from Qualified Small Business Stock (QSBS).[17] A big benefit to being incorporated is that noncorporate taxpayers can avoid between 50 to 100 percent of the gain from the sale of your stock depending on when you got your stock. Yes, you read this correctly. Generally QSBS held for more than five years can exclude:

- 100 percent of gross income from sale of the stock if the stock was acquired after September 27, 2010

Sadly, Congress can't make anything simple or straightforward. The gain may not exceed the greater of $10 million or 10 times your adjusted basis in the stock. To qualify for this special exclusion of gain, the underling company must be a "Qualified Small Business." This means that it will meet the following rules:

- At the date of issuance of the stock, it must be a domestic corporation whose assets did not exceed $50 million, and
- During substantially all of taxpayer's holding period, the corporation was a C corporation that conducted an active business and not just a holding company and not a DISC, a REIT, REMIC, or cooperative.

Check with your accountant or lawyer about meeting these rules when you start up your entity or to see if you qualify.

Disadvantages of an S Corporation

1. Severe limits on qualifying for S corporation status. There are several tests that you must meet to operate as a qualified S corporation:

- *You must have fewer than 100 stockholders.*[18] This is a strict limitation. If you exceed this number, you're disqualified. However, a husband and a wife count as one stockholder.[19] The limitation isn't too bad unless you have a large number of owners or investors. This one limitation is the reason why no public corporation is an S corporation.
- *The corporation must be a domestic corporation formed in the United States.*[20] It can't be a foreign corporation.
- *It can't be an ineligible corporation, such as a bank.*[21] For most small businesses, this is not a problem.
- *Only individuals, estates, and a certain type of limited trust can be stockholders.*[22] Another corporation, partnership, and most trusts can't own any stock in an S corporation. (Yuck!)
- *All stock must be owned by a U.S. citizen or a U.S. resident.*[23] Thus, if you have foreign investors, you can't be an S corporation. In addition, corporations, partnerships, and LLCs that are treated as partnerships can't own S corporation stock. This definitely does limit your options.
- *You can have only one class of stock.*[24] This has a number of drawbacks. First, this limits the estate planning benefits that you can do with multiple classes of stock because you can't have more than one class with an S corporation. Second, if you want to give out preferred stock that doesn't vote but is preferred in some way, you are prohibited from doing this.

Author's note: This limitation on shareholders and on not having different classes of stock provides less protection for the stock from creditors. Creditors can become stockholders with voting rights. LLCs have a real advantage here in that you can limit who becomes a member.

Author's note: You might be thinking that you would qualify for S corporation status and then, after you get qualified, violate the rules. This doesn't work. If you violate any of these six requirements, your S corporation status terminates on the first day of the violation.

2. Complete flowthrough of earnings. You can't accumulate capital at lower corporate rates as you can with a regular corporation because all income is taxed to you whether or not you receive it and it is taxed at your normal tax rates.

3. Limited ability to raise capital. Generally, because of the limits, the financing is done by the shareholders and is based on whatever assets they contribute.

4. Corporate debts don't increase your stock basis. With most partnerships, the partnership debt increases your basis. This is not true of an S corporation. If the corporation takes on any debt, this does not increase the basis of the stock for the stockholders. This one point makes S corporations very different from partnerships.

5. More limited fringe benefits than in regular corporations. S corporations allow fewer fringe benefits. For example, the owners don't get any major benefit from setting up a medical reimbursement plan such as a regular corporation can do and even a sole proprietorship can do by hiring a spouse. They get some fringe benefits, which will be discussed in Chapters 13 and 14, but fewer than with regular corporations.

Author's note: Starting in 2003, S corporations get the same benefit as regular corporations in deducting all health insurance premiums and most home healthcare premiums for officers and their families. In 2015 and thereafter, the deduction is 100 percent of the premium for medical insurance that is not subsidized by an employer. However, this is deducted above the line on personal returns for S corporations.

6. Same bookkeeping hassles of regular corporations. As I said, S corporations are corporations. The S status is only to elect to have all income and losses pass through to you as the owners/stockholders. Thus you must have yearly board of directors meetings, stockholder meetings, corporate minutes, and a separate corporate bank account.

Who Should Operate as an S Corporation?

An S corporation is ideal in the following situations:

- Officers/stockholders are earning less than $118,500 in 2015.
- There's no need for any capital accumulated for inventories or marketing.
- All financing will be shareholder financing.
- You meet all the rules.

Limited-Liability Corporation (LLC)

For many years, Europe and South America have allowed a type of hybrid entity, a limited-liability corporation (LLC). For you history buffs, the LLC started in this country in 1977 in Wyoming but has been accepted gradually by all the other states.

Essentially, an LLC is a cross between a limited partnership and a corporation. If there's only one owner, it's deemed a sole proprietorship for tax purposes, and you file the normal IRS Schedule C with your federal tax return. If there's more than one owner, you file for tax purposes as a partnership and file Form 1065, which is a bit more costly.

Regardless of how you file, LLC status protects you from liabilities in the same way as corporation status.

Advantages of an LLC

1. Limited liability. As with a corporation or a limited partnership, the LLC limits liability for debts and obligations. The only time you would be personally liable is if you personally guarantee the debt, the LLC commits fraud, or you commit malpractice. Also, as with a corporation, you're responsible for your own negligence and for the negligence of those whom you supervise directly, but not for the negligence of other LLC members.

Author's note: The bottom line is that the LLC is an easier way to get the same protection offered by a corporation without a lot of the legal formalities and administrative details of a corporation. Since your liability is limited to the amount of money or other capital you contribute to the LLC, you have the same protection against obligations and lawsuits as with regular corporations and S corporations.

2. None of the restrictions of an S corporation. You can have any number of members; they can be stockholders, whether corporate or otherwise; and you can have foreign investors. Thus the LLC gives tremendous flexibility while maintaining limited liability.

3. All losses and income pass through to stockholders. Since one-owner LLCs are treated as sole proprietorships and LLCs with two or more owners are treated as partnerships, all income and losses flow through to the members. There is no double tax. LLCs thus are beneficial for operating a business as well as for holding real estate. You also get the carryback and carryforward of net operating losses on your individual return as you would with a sole proprietorship as long as you are a one-owner LLC. Two or more owner LLCs come under the partnership rules unless you elected to be treated as a corporation, in which case the corporate rules would apply.

4. LLCs get higher basis with LLC debts. As with a partnership, if the LLC incurs any debt, the debt increases the basis of the members' portion of the LLC. Thus LLCs get the best of being a partnership without any of the drawbacks.

5. Much cheaper to operate and form than corporations. LLCs are inexpensive to form. You simply register your LLC articles with the state, and you're off and running. Moreover, unlike corporations, you don't have to have any formal meetings, minutes, or member meetings.

6. Asset protection. An LLC may protect assets better than all the entities. Yes, you read that correctly. An LLC may be better at asset protection than any other entity, even a corporation. If a partner or corporate stockholder gets sued for any reason, the creditor gets the stock or can become an unwanted partner. Partnerships and LLCs can prevent this possibility by providing in the orginal formation documents for the LLC that no new members of LLCs are allowed without the consent of the other members. This will keep creditors from becoming members.

A creditor can proceed against a member's interest in the LLC only by means of a *charging order*, which provides that any distribution made to the member who is a debtor would instead go to the creditor. This has a detrimental side effect for the creditor. If the LLC has undistributed income, the creditor would be taxed on the member's share of the undistributed income, just as the debtor-member, even though the creditor didn't receive the distribution! This makes most creditors leery about placing a charging order on the LLC member's interest.

Author's note: Think about this for a minute: What creditor would want to put a lien or charging order on a member's interest if he or she could be taxed on money that he or she never receives? This is why an LLC that's taxed as a partnership is very beneficial for asset protection. Single-owner LLCs are not as protected because a creditor may be able to take control of the LLC if there's only one owner.

As you can see, an LLC is a really great entity and, in my opinion, the entity of choice for most people. However, despite the attempts of most states to overcome most of the disadvantages of corporations and partnerships with an LLC, there still exist some disadvantages.

7. Same tax advantages as that of a sole proprietorship (if sole owned LLC or of a partnership if two or more owners of an LLC). Thus, you can uses losses from the LLC against your other earnings and can take advanatage of the 20 percent pass-through deductions to reduce the taxable income from net profits.

Disadvantages of an LLC

1. No saving on Social Security. With an S corporation, you can save Social Security and Medicare taxes by distributing dividends along with salaries. LLCs do not seem to have this advantage. All earnings are taxed like those of a sole propri-etorship or a partnership and are subject to Social Security.

Author's note: This isn't entirely clear. There's some argument that if you are an LLC member but have no management authority and do not actively participate in the day-to-day operations, you should be treated as a limited partner and not be subject to Social Security on your share of the earnings.[25]

2. More complicated paperwork. You have to file articles of organization for the LLC with the state in which it is formed. This certainly raises the costs. In addition, some states have a special tax on LLC income. You definitely should check with a good accountant about the state-law implications, which can result in some severe disadvantages for LLCs.

3. Lifetime limits. Some states mandate that LLCs terminate within 30 years or less. This is not true of Nevada, which is a good reason to form an LLC there (see Chapter 10). In addition, some states require dissolution of an LLC on the death or resignation of a member. This can be overcome by stating in the formation article that a termination won't occur on the death, disability, or resignation of a member.

4. May require two or more members. Some states require that an LLC have two members or more. In most states, however, this requirement is being changed to accommodate one-member LLCs. A problem arises if you form your LLC in a state that allows one-member LLCs but operate in states that don't. Your LLC in this situation may not protect you from liabilities! However, the LLC statutes in almost all states contain "nondiscriminatory provisions" that the laws of the state in which an LLC was formed govern its organization, its internal affairs, and the liability of its members.

Who Should Operate as an LLC?

An LLC is an appropriate entity for the following:

- Individuals who expect to earn more than the Social Security maximum
- Individuals who need liability protection but can't qualify as an S corporation
- Businesses that don't need to accumulate capital for inventories or for marketing
- Real estate businesses

Overall General Recommendations Based on the New Tax Law

Obviously, every situation and business is different, but I thought I would give some general rules based on an analysis of the new tax law, which will serve as some guidance, I would bet that few of you have gotten this information from your accountant.

1. If you expect losses when you first start your business or for a short period of time after you start up, you should operate as either a sole proprietorship or LLC. The reason is that if you have losses, you can use those losses on your personal tax return. If you were a corporation, these losses might be trapped in the corporation and only used by the corporation. Once losses are not a problem, you can always change to another entity.

Author's Note: If you have a business that has high liability exposure, you want to to the LLC route and NOT operate as a sole proprietorship because of the unlimited liability exposure of sole proprietors. If you are starting up a network marketing business, your liability exposure is small. Thus, starting off as a sole proprietorship is usually best.

2. If you want to accrue capital for future marketing, operate as a C corporation: The new law taxes corporations at a flat 21 percent rate. However, you will need a good business reason documented in your corporate minutes or you can be hit with an accumulated earnings penalty. See a good accountant or lawyer about this.

3. If you have several owners and want to distribute most or all profits annually, operate as an S Corporation. This usually results in the lowest overall tax because of the new 20 percent pass-through deduction.

4. If you expect to operate your business for at least 5+ years and then want to sell out, become a C corporation. C corporations, which qualify as small business corporations, can have a BIG benefit, When the stock is sold, the stockholders can avoid all tax up to $10 million in gain. Yes, they can sell their stock and avoid tax on the first $10 million of gain. However, you have to be in existence for at least five years and have assets of less than $50 million.

Also, you can't qualify for this benefit if you are:

- A service business in the fields of health, law, engineering, architecture, accounting, actuarial science, performing arts, consulting, athletics, financial services, or brokerage services
- A banking, insurance, financing, leasing, investing, or similar business
- A farming business
- A business involving the production of products for which percentage depletion can be claimed
- A business of operating a hotel, motel, restaurant, or similar business.

5. If you are a specified service business and make over $415,000 of taxable income (married) or are single and earn over $207,500, you should consider being a C corporation since you won't be eligible for the 20 percent pass-through deduction.

A specified service business is one that is:

- legal
- medical
- acturary
- accounting
- financial services
- consulting
- athletics
- performing arts
- any business whose reputation is the major asset in the business such as possibly realtors

6. If you are NOT operating a specified service business (such as a networking business or franchise), consider operating as either an S corporation or C corporation. This is especially true if you are married and earning over $415,000 or taxable income or over

$207,500 of taxable income and single since there are limitations to the 20 percent pass-through deduction based on wages. Being a corporation will allow you to avoid these limits with wages.

7. If you own investment real estate, consider establishing a sole-owner LLC for each property owned. First, this should make you eligible for the new 20 percent pass-through deductions. Second, it will allow for losses to pass through to your tax return if there are losses. Finally, real estate ownership carries high liability risks. The LLC wil potentially limit your liability.

Summary

- In choosing the best corporate entity to start your business, it's crucial to determine what fringe benefits you can obtain and whether business losses can pass through to you.
- You can always change entities as time and circumstances demand.
- A sole proprietorship is simple, simple, simple, but liability is unlimited.
- Don't operate as a sole proprietorship unless you are sure that you have the following:
    - No liability exposure
    - No significant business assets
    - No nonfamily employees
- If you even desire to form a general partnership, take three aspirin and lie down until the desire passes. In the event that your business is already a general partnership, get a buy/sell agreement immediately. "Don't pass go" until you do.
- Limited partnerships are great vehicles for obtaining investors without being subject to liability risks. They're great for investments such as real estate.
- Operate as a regular corporation only if
    - You intend to register on a national exchange soon (go public).
    - You need to accumulate capital for inventories or for mass marketing and can use the lower corporate tax rates to do so.
    - You will solemnly swear to adhere to all corporate formalities of corporate minutes, directors meetings, and stockholder meetings.
- If there are only a few corporate owners, get a buy/sell agreement as soon as possible. You'll thank me in the morning.
- Form an S corporation if you are NOT a specified service business and have taxable incomes over $315,000 married or $157,500 single.
- Form an S Corporation or even a regularly corporation if you are a specified service business and:
    - You make under $129,000 of net income *or*
    - You have some liability exposure or nonfamily employees.
    - You meet all the S corporation rules.

- To be a qualified S corporation:
  - You must have fewer than 100 stockholders.
  - It must be a domestic corporation only.
  - There must be only one class of stock.
  - There must be only individual owners and some limited trusts and estates.
  - All investors must be citizens or residents of the United States. No foreign investors allowed. Sorry!
- S corporations are corporations. You have the same formalities as a regular corporation. If you won't strictly adhere to them, don't operate as any form of corporation.
- When forming any corporation, make sure that you qualify for Section 1244, which enables you to take your stock losses as ordinary losses and not as capital losses on your tax return.
- When forming any corporation, don't forget that you may be able to avoid between 50 and 100 percent of the gain on the sale of your corporate stock if it's qualified small-business stock, depending on when you acquired your stock.
- Limited-liability corporations don't have formalities, and they protect against liabilities as well as corporations. Form an LLC when
  - You will have some liability exposure or have substantial assets in the business.
  - You can't qualify as an S corporation.
  - You don't need to accumulate capital for inventories.
- If you have a few owners in a corporation, partnership, or LLC, definitely have your lawyer draft a buy/sell agreement that outlines the formula and mechanism and establishes a price to buy out a partner/co-owner. This is crucial—and you will thank your lucky stars that this book prompted you to do so.

Notes

1. Information obtained from Nevada Corporate Planners and Nevada Corporate Headquarters.
2. Sections 722 and 742 of the IRC.
3. Section 708(b)(1)(B) of the IRC.
4. *Estate of Bischoff*, 69 TC 32 (1977); *Estate of James Barudin*, T.C. Memo 1996-395 et al.
5. Section 469 of the IRC.
6. Section 125 of the IRC.
7. IRC 1202(a)(4) as amended by 2015 PATH Act, Section 126(a)(1) Div Q.
8. Section 1244(b)(1) of the IRC.
9. Section 1244(b)(2) of the IRC.
10. IRC 1202(a)(4) as amended by 2015 PATH act, Section 126(a)(1) DivQ.
11. Sections 448 and 11(b)(2) of the IRC.
12. Sections 1361-1363 of the IRC.
13. Sections 1374 and 1375 of the IRC provide that there could be some tax at the 35 percent rate if you were previously a regular corporation with some prior accumulated earnings and profits. Check with your accountant if you are a regular corporation and want to convert to an S corporation.
14. Sections 61, 3121(a), 3306(b), Revenue Ruling 73-361, 1973-2 CB 331.
15. Section 1244 of the IRC.

16. Section 1366(d)(1)(A) of the IRC.
17. Section 1202 of the IRC.
18. Section 1361(b)(1)(A) of the IRC.
19. Section 1361(c)(1) of the IRC.
20. Section 1361(b)(1) of the IRC.
21. Section 1361(b)(2) of the IRC.
22. Section 1361(b)(1)(B) of the IRC.
23. Section 1361(b)(1)(C) of the IRC.
24. Section 1361(b)(1)(D) of the IRC.
25. Taxpayer Relief Act of 1997 (P.L. 105-34), Section 935 (8/5/97).

10

Forming a Nevada Corporation or a Limited-Liability Corporation in Nevada

The trick is to stop thinking of it as your money.
—**IRS auditor**

This chapter won't be long or complicated, but you'll find the information contained here to be very interesting and possibly vital to you. Perhaps this chapter really should be titled, "What the Rich Know That You Should Know." There are two major myths about incorporating in Nevada that I encounter all the time:

Myth 1: *Incorporating in Nevada will result in lower costs.* Nothing could be further from the truth. In fact, it's usually cheaper to incorporate in your home state. The reason is that Nevada has a number of fees that many states don't have, and although Nevada has no corporate income tax, you usually have to file a corporate tax return in the states where you're doing business as a nonresident. Thus you won't save money.

Myth 2: *Incorporating in Nevada will result in lower taxes.* This may be the most widespread myth of all. The truth is that incorporating in Nevada will *not* save any taxes whatsoever. You'll still have to file in many states as a nonresident.

> **Chapter Overview**
>
> Where do many movie stars form corporations? Where do most con artists form corporations? You may be surprised that these two questions have the same answer—Nevada. In fact, some of the infamous Enron partnerships were located in Nevada or in foreign jurisdictions. What these diverse groups know that you don't will be the subject of this chapter. We also will examine some of the benefits of incorporating in Nevada rather than in Delaware.

The reason that this myth is so pervasive is that some of the more unscrupulous incorporating companies emphasize the extreme privacy that Nevada provides (which will be discussed below) and, in effect, imply that no one will find out. This is not necessarily the case and is not legally correct either. Say it three times: "Incorporating in Nevada will *not* save you taxes!"

Thus, if it doesn't save taxes or costs, why do it? This is a good question. There are several good reasons to incorporate in Nevada instead of Delaware, which also has some good laws for business.

Why the Rich, the Famous, and the Crooked Incorporate in Nevada[1]

1. Greatest protection from liability. This is easily the number one reason for incorporating in Nevada.

There is a well-known legal concept called *piercing the corporate veil*. This is the process by which a court removes the protection provided to individual members of a corporation and holds these members responsible. Simply put, you'll become liable for corporate debts and obligations if the veil of your corporation can be pierced. Each state applies different tests for determining whether the court can pierce the corporate veil and hold the shareholders liable.

In many states, it's easier for this to happen than many people realize. In fact—and this may surprise you—here are the top states that allow this, in the order of occurrence:[2] California, Florida, Georgia, Louisiana, Texas, New York, and Pennsylvania. For example, many states require a lot of capitalization (or net assets) for a corporation to be respected and not pierced. In most states, the minimum capitalization is $1,000. In Nevada, it's $100. In addition, many states will hold you, as owner/officer, liable for corporate debts and obligations if you didn't adhere to the yearly formalities that I discussed in Chapter 9 concerning stockholder meetings, corporate minutes, and board of directors meetings. Nevada is much more liberal about this and usually won't pierce the veil and make the owners/officers liable for corporate debts if they haven't adhered to all the formalities.

In a famous Nevada case, *Rowland v. Lepire*,[3] the corporation committed many acts that in most states would have made the stockholders/officers liable for the corporate debts. There was minimal capitalization. There were no formal board of directors or stockholder meetings. No dividends were paid. Officers didn't receive salaries. No corporate minutes were kept nor was there any evidence that they were ever kept. However, the corporation had a checking account in the corporate name and licenses in the corporate name. The Nevada court held that the corporate veil could not be pierced unless fraud was shown.

Author's note: Despite this great case, I would follow the formalities that I mentioned in Chapter 9. However, the case shows how far Nevada will go to protect officers and stockholders of businesses incorporated there. The catch is that the courts won't allow this protection if it can be shown that the officers committed fraud or certain other special acts, such as malpractice.

Author's observation: Based on the information researched by one of the Nevada incorporating companies,[4] Nevada has allowed a piercing of the corporate veil, thus making the stockholders liable for corporate debts, only once in 23 years! If you think about it, this is amazing.

2. Higher degree of privacy. The shareholders' names are not part of the public record.[5] Many companies actually use nominees as directors so that it's difficult to find even the names of the directors. In addition, Nevada is less willing than many other states to share information about its corporations with other states and with the federal government. This also ensures a little more privacy. However, if you register in another state to do business, you may have to list the shareholders.

Author's note: Recently, I discussed this issue with various Nevada incorporators.[6] Their view is that Nevada may share information a little more freely than before owing to the terrorist activities occurring in this country. This would be especially true with the federal government. However, there's more privacy in Nevada than in other states.

3. No joint and several liability. In many states, if you are found jointly liable for a debt, you could be responsible for the entire debt if it can't be collected in whole or part from the other debtors. In Nevada, the courts must assign a percentage of responsibility. Every owner found liable is required to pay a share of the judgment no greater than his or her responsibility. Thus, if you and nine others owe $1 million, the courts would have to determine what percentage of the $1 million is your responsibility. You would not be held responsible for the others' shares if they weren't collectible.

Differences between Nevada and Delaware for Small Corporations

You might have heard that Delaware is also a great state for incorporating. Delaware protects stockholders, especially in public corporations, by giving them lots of rights and remedies. For example, Delaware corporate takeover laws are some of the most stringent in the country.

However, for small corporations, Nevada has some advantages over Delaware:

- Nevada protects officers from liability even if they didn't necessarily act "in good faith." Delaware has no such provision.
- Nevada provides greater protection for officers against monetary damages and other types of damages than does Delaware.
- Nevada protects a director even if there was a breach of his or her duty of loyalty to the corporation. No such protection exists in Delaware.
- Nevada does not require disclosure of the corporation's principal business. Delaware has no such privacy provision.

- Nevada does not require that a corporation disclose any locations or main offices located outside the state. This is not necessarily true in Delaware.
- Nevada has no corporate income tax. Delaware has an 8.7 percent corporate income tax.

The bottom line is that Nevada offers a slightly greater degree of privacy and confidentiality than provided by other states and, more important, offers some of the strongest protection possible from liabilities for stockholders, officers, and directors.

Avoidance of Sales Tax Problems and Other Liabilities

Some of the thorniest problems for small businesses are the filing of sales tax and income tax returns in many states. The problem is that many states require companies to file a sales tax return and, in many cases, an income tax return if they do any business in that state.

Most states have an allocation formula for determining how much income is taxed in the state. You're allowed to allocate your income to other states based on your assets in each state, the employees in each state, and the income earned in each state. For example, your corporation might earn $100,000 but do very little business in California and have no employees, no office, and no assets in California. Thus the actual tax owed might be only $100, or you might even have a corporate loss. Yet California, like a few other states, assesses a flat tax of $800 for companies that have a lower tax liability.

Even worse, if you had to file state sales tax returns in each state, you could be paying more in accounting fees than you would owe in taxes, fees that could add up to tens of thousands of dollars. For a small business with little capital, this cost could be catastrophic. Thus, owing to the cost involved, many small businesses "ignore" filing returns.

However, if these states find out that you failed to file the appropriate returns, you could be hit with huge penalties, plus interest, plus the taxes owed. Even worse, your home state usually enforces these obligations and may even prevent you from doing business until these obligations are paid. Thus what can small businesses do?

The answer that many of the top accounting firms are recommending is to set up a corporation or limited-liability corporation (LLC) just for the business conducted in the aggressive states, such as California. Then, if a state attacks this entity for not filing or for past-due taxes, all other entities are protected.

Author's note: If you are doing business in various states, I would strongly advise you to contact a major accounting firm that specializes in state tax issues. States have made deals to allow one filing to take care of many problems. Hopefully, the federal government eventually will step in and help to solve this problem for small businesses.

Author's note: You may have read about the many partnerships that Enron set up that led to its collapse. One of the reasons Enron did this was to insulate the liabilities for each entity so that if one entity had problems, they wouldn't affect the others. In addition, it ensures greater privacy: One entity may be uncovered, but not necessarily the other entities. This is one big reason why most Enron partnerships were formed outside the United States. Essentially, this technique is used for a wide variety of potential problems.

Summary

- Incorporating in Nevada will not be less costly or save you taxes.
- Incorporating in Nevada will provide some of the strongest liability protection of any of the states for officers and directors.
- Incorporating in Nevada will give you greater privacy than in most other states, unless you register in other states.
- In many cases, incorporating or forming an LLC in Nevada will avoid a lot of possible joint and several liability problems.
- As shown with Enron, forming separate entities such as corporations, limited partnerships, and limited-liability corporations will limit the liability problems to that entity and not taint other assets.[7]

Notes

1. Much of the information presented was provided by Scott Letourneau of Nevada Corporate Planners. If you need to consult with him about forming a Nevada corporation, you can reach the company at 888-627-7007 or www.nvinc.com.
2. *Cornell Law Review*, Vol. 76 (1991), p. 1050.
3. *Rowland v. Lepire*, 662 P.2d 1332 (1983).
4. Nevada Corporate Planners.
5. Nevada Secretary of State Web site at sos.state.nv.us/comm_rec/whyinc.htm.
6. Nevada Corporate Planners, Nevada Department of Revenue.
7. Nevada Corporate Planners.

11

How to Eliminate up to 40 Percent of Your Social Security and Medicare Tax with an S Corporation

It's a game. We [tax lawyers] teach the rich how to play it so they can stay rich——and the IRS keeps changing the rules so we can keep getting rich teaching them.

—**John Grisham, lawyer and author, *The Firm***

I should note that this chapter won't be long or complicated. In fact, it will probably be one of the shortest in the book. However, don't let the short length fool you. The tax benefits here alone could make you a millionaire, if you invest the tax savings yearly.

> **Chapter Overview**
>
> Have you ever heard that tax planning is beneficial only to the rich and not to Middle America? Well, this is a myth, as you now know from the previous chapters, which offered information applicable to everyone.
>
> However, this chapter is different. It primarily applies to Middle America and not the rich, since it works best for taxpayers who have a net income, after business deductions, of $118,500 or less per person. It is a proven loophole that accountants have been using for decades—using an S corporation to eliminate self-employment tax.

Overview of Taxation for S Corporations

Unless you converted from a regular corporation to an S corporation,[1] an S corporation is not subject to any tax.[2]

You would compute the corporation's gross income and subtract any business deductions to arrive at the net taxable income. You would then file an individual return on your pro-rata share of the corporation's net income or loss.[3] The S corporation would not pay any tax on the income.

Example: Mary is a 50 percent shareholder in an S corporation. The corporation had gross sales of $500,000 and deductions of $400,000, for a net income of $100,000. Since Mary owns 50 percent of the stock, she would pay tax on one half of the $100,000, which is $50,000.

Author's note: You pay tax on the net income of the corporation whether or not it's distributed to you. Thus, if all the income were left in the corporation for growth, Mary would still pay tax on $50,000. This undistributed amount would raise her stock basis, however, as if she had paid $50,000 more for stock. If she receives any dividends, this would reduce the basis.

Some income items and deductions get separately stated on your individual return as if you'd earned them.[4] Thus, such income items as tax-exempt income and capital gains and some deductions, such as charitable contributions, would be separately stated on your Form 1040 as if you'd earned these items.

The key to saving Social Security taxes is that with an S corporation you pay self-employment tax on wages, salaries, and bonuses but not on dividends.[5] Your share of undistributed earnings is deemed dividends and not wages and is treated as any actual dividend distribution. Let me repeat this again because it is worth repeating: *dividends and undistributed earnings are not subject to self-employment tax.*

Thus, the key is to pay yourself as little in salary as possible and as much in dividends as possible and wipe out most of your Social Security tax.

Example: John has a net income of $80,000 from his S corporation. If he receives this amount in the form of salary, all of it would be subject to self-employment tax at the 15.3 percent rate, so he would pay $12,240. If, however, John pays himself a reasonable salary of $40,000 and takes the other $40,000 as a dividend, he would save 15.3 percent on the dividend, a savings of $6,120 each year that he does this! Not bad, huh?

You may be thinking that this sounds fabulous. Why not pay zero salary and take all the earnings as dividends and completely eliminate all self-employment tax? Unfortunately, the IRS has thought of this.[6] The IRS requires you to pay yourself a "reasonable" salary. If you don't, the entire dividend and undistributed portion of the net income from the S corporation will be reclassified as wages, which are fully subject to self-employment tax. Yuck! In fact, all taxpayers who didn't understand this rule have ended up losing in court.

My favorite case involved an attorney named Joseph Radtke.[7] Radtke thought the same way. He formed an S corporation and paid himself no salary. He treated the entire net income as a dividend. The tax court rightly reclassified the dividend as wages, and poor Radtke had to pay self-employment tax on the entire amount. Thus, you must pay yourself some reasonable salary.

What Is a "Reasonable" Salary?

Good question! The IRS defines "reasonable compensation" as what would ordinarily be paid for like services, by like enterprises (similar in size and business to your own), under like circumstances.[8] This is generally interpreted to mean "what you would pay an outside agency or person to do the same duties."

There are a lot of factors that determine what is reasonable, such as:

- Actual services performed
- Responsibilities involved
- Time spent
- Size and complexity of the business
- Prevailing economic conditions
- Compensation paid by comparable firms for comparable services
- Salary paid to company officers in prior years

Sadly, as you can see, the factors are not very clear. I would highly recommend that you check with a good accountant or tax attorney when setting any salaries and bonuses for you. Get comparable salaries from government publications.

Author's note: Most people want a nice flat number or a flat percentage of income as the litmus test for reasonable compensation. Sadly, I can't give a number, because it varies from business to business and according to a number of factors. However, from the many cases that I have read, I have found that in most cases where salary paid was approximately between 40 percent and 60 percent of net income, this amount has been deemed reasonable.[9] Also, if there are unrelated minority stockholders, if they approve some compensation for the officers who are also majority stockholders, courts tend to give weight to this approval from the board of directors or stockholders, since the minority stockholders would then be receiving less in dividends.[10] The bottom line: check with a good accountant and tax lawyer about setting any salaries and bonuses in order to minimize your salary and minimize your self-employment tax. Here, an ounce of prevention is worth a bundle in wealth!

Note: Any net profits left in the S corporation that is NOT distributed as a salary will also qualify for the 20 percent pass-through deductions. See Chapter 20.

Summary

- This strategy is especially great for Middle America.
- S corporation salaries and bonuses are subject to self-employment tax.
- Dividends and undistributed earnings (which are treated as dividends) are not subject to self-employment tax.
- If you're an S corporation, pay yourself as little as possible in salary, as long as it's reasonable, and as much as possible in dividends.
- Use a good accountant and/or tax attorney to help you establish what a minimum reasonable salary should be. Failure to do this would be a hazard to your wealth.

Notes

1. Section 1374(a) of the IRC. This deals with built-in gains where you have accumulated earnings and profits for a regular corporation. If you started as an S corporation and never operated this entity as a regular corporation, this is not an issue.
2. Section 1363(a) of the IRC.
3. Section 1366 of the IRC.
4. Section 1366 of the IRC.
5. Section 1402(a) of the IRC.
6. Revenue Ruling 74-44, 1974-1 CB 287.
7. *Joseph Radtke v. United States*, 895 F.2d 1196 (7th Cir. 1990).
8. Section 1.162-7(b) of the ITR.
9. *Hamilton and Co.*, T.C. Memo 1959-153.
10. *Gilles Frozen Custard, Inc.*, T.C. Memo 1970-73; *William J. Hertz*, T.C. Memo 1998-210.

12

How to Get Assets and Money into a Corporation Tax-Free

Forming a corporation is similar to getting married. It is easy to get into but much harder to get out of.

—Sandy Botkin

Chapter Overview
- You'll learn about the requirements for transferring property tax-free to a corporation.
- You'll be aware of the congressional "gotchas" and how to avoid them.
- You'll understand why you should rarely own real estate in a corporate name, especially in a regular corporation.
- You'll understand the IRS filing requirements that will keep your transfers tax-free.

Many times people want to start their corporate business by transferring personal assets to their corporation. Let's face it—it's certainly a lot cheaper and easier to use assets that you already own than to purchase new assets.

You can transfer property to a corporation easily and tax-free if you know what you're doing. Generally, no gain or loss is recognized on the transfer of property to a corporation solely in exchange for stock in that corporation.[1]

Author's note: As noted, you can't take any loss on the transfer. Thus you generally should *not* transfer property that would result in a tax loss to you if you sold it. You're better off selling the property and taking the loss. You then can transfer the net cash received to the corporation.

To have no gain or loss apply, you must meet certain easy conditions:

1. You must transfer assets. It can be almost any property, such as other stock, real estate, cash, patents, copyrights, etc.[2] In fact, there's a lot of flexibility. However, and this is a *big however,* you cannot transfer services for stock tax-free. It doesn't matter

159

if the services have been rendered in the past or will be rendered in the future.[3] If you do, you will be taxed as ordinary income on the fair market value of what you receive.[4] If you both transfer property and render services for the stock, you will be taxed as compensation (ordinary income) on the portion of the stock received that applies only to the services.

Example: Ted and Carol form a corporation, and each receives 50 percent of the stock. Ted transfers $100,000 cash and Carol performs some legal services and incorporation services and transfers $50,000 cash. Since some of the stock that Carol received was for services, she would be taxed on the portion that relates to the services.

2. You must receive stock for your property.[5] This sounds very clear-cut, but there are a few issues that you should know about. First, *stock* means stock and not warrants, calls, puts, or any other options.[6] Second, it doesn't have to be solely for voting stock. It can even be preferred stock if you want some investors to get preferences as to dividends.

For those who don't know what preferred stock is, here's a great definition: *Preferred stock* is "stock that is limited and preferred as to dividends and does *not* participate in corporate growth to any significant extent."[7] Thus preferred stockholders would get a flat, fixed dividend, similar to a bond. They don't get to vote and don't benefit significantly from the growth or equity of the company. In addition, if the company makes a lot of money, the preferred stockholders don't get larger dividends. The use of preferred stock is normally to fix the value for estate planning and to bring in investors who want greater security in their dividends.

3. After the transfer, you must control at least 80 percent of the voting stock and at least 80 percent of all other shares of any other class of stock.[8] This simply means that you can have some stockholders getting voting stock and some getting other types of stock, such as nonvoting or preferred stock, as long as everyone together owns at least 80 percent of the voting stock and 80 percent of all the shares of the other stock.[9]

Author's note: If you and some others are organizing a newly formed corporation, you will, in all probability, receive over 80 percent control of all stock. Thus this third requirement is not normally a problem for new corporations. Also, and this is important, if you want to give away your stock (such as to your children or grandchildren) after the transfer, you may do so as long as you're not obligated to retransfer the stock. All stock should be issued to you first; then you can do with it as you please, as far as the Internal Revenue Service (IRS) is concerned.[10]

Traps in Transferring Property to a New Corporation

The bad news is that Congress created several traps that would result in tax to you on incorporating. The good news is that I'll show you how to avoid them easily.

Trap 1: Don't Place a Debt on Transferred Property Right before Forming the Corporation

As I said earlier, when you transfer property for stock in a corporation, you avoid all gains and losses. The corporation can even assume your indebtedness on the transferred property without any gain recognized by you or any other person who transfers property.[11] However, if it appears that the principal purpose of the assumption of debt was to avoid federal income tax on the exchange, then the debt will be treated as money received and taxed to you.[12] Yuck!

Author's note: Generally, if a debt has been on the property for a while, at least one year, you won't have a problem. If you place the debt on the property just within the last four to six months,[13] you'd better have a great reason for doing this. An example of a good reason actually given by the IRS would be to replace an existing debt on property.[14] Another good reason, in my opinion, would be to refinance an existing debt at a lower interest rate.

Example: Sue transfers for stock property worth $200,000, but with a debt of $50,000; the corporation assumes Sue's debt on the property. This would be a tax-free transfer.

Example: Assuming that Sue placed the debt on the property two months before transferring the property to the corporation, she probably would be taxed on the liability assumed by the corporation because the transfer was to avoid taxes.

Trap 2: Don't Receive Cash or Other Property Back from the Corporation

You must transfer property for stock. If you receive anything else besides stock, such as cash or other property, you will be taxed on the receipt of the cash or property received.[15]

Example: Mike and Gloria transfer property to form their corporation. Mike transfers $100,000 in cash, and Gloria transfers real estate worth $120,000 but gets the same amount of stock as Mike. If Gloria receives back $20,000 in order to equalize the transfer, she will be taxed on the $20,000 that she receives.

Trap 3: Don't Transfer Any Property That Has Debt Greater than Your Basis[16]

What does this mean? This is where you transfer property whose adjusted basis to you (cost plus improvements less depreciation taken) is less than the debt on the property. This can happen in a number of ways.

Example: You pay only $100,000 for some real estate that skyrockets to $600,000 in value. You then go to a bank and refinance the property and get a loan for 80 percent of the value, or $480,000. Your basis was $100,000, which is what you paid,[17] but your loan on the property is now $480,000, which is $380,000 more than your basis. If you transfer this property with this debt, you will pay tax on the $380,000! How's that for a congressional "gotcha"?

This also can happen if you take a lot of depreciation but your debt gets paid off over a longer period than the depreciation. Your property could be completely written off, but you still have some debt.

Author's note: There's a great way around this problem. In fact, if you ever have this problem, this book will pay for itself many times over.

Here's the IRS rule: You pay tax on the excess of your liabilities over your basis of the property transferred, but it's the sum of *all* the liabilities for each transferor over the sum of *all* the adjusted bases of the properties transferred by each transferor.[18] What this means to you is this: Transfer more property to the corporation so that the *total* basis of what you transfer exceeds the *total* debt on the transferred property.

Example: Calvin transfers some real estate to a corporation for stock. His real estate has a basis of $50,000, but there's a mortgage of $100,000 on the property. If Calvin transfers this property alone for stock, he would pay tax on $50,000. Thus he should either not transfer this property or add some other property so that the total basis equals or exceeds the total debt. Thus, if he also adds $50,000 in cash as part of the transfer, his total basis in the real estate and cash is $100,000, which equals the debt. Thus no tax! Pretty slick, isn't it?

If Possible, Don't Transfer Real Estate to a Regular Corporation

As my opening quote notes, it's hard to get property out of a corporation, especially a regular corporation. If you have real estate in the corporation that appreciates in value, which real estate tends to do, you may have to pay tax at the corporate level on the appreciation whenever you sell the property or liquidate the corporation[19] and probably pay tax at your individual level, too. That's double taxation! There are ways around it with reorganizations, etc., but it takes some knowledgeable tax planning.

The rich have known this for years. Thus what many top tax experts are recommending is to form an LLC or a limited partnership that would own the real estate and then lease it to the corporation. In this way, you don't have to worry about the real estate appreciation being "trapped" in the corporation, and you or your family members can receive the lease payments. Thus you can shift income to your family at lower tax brackets. Even better, you don't need to worry about the liability being over the basis because the property wasn't transferred to the corporation. Finally, you can take a deduction for the depreciation of the real estate on your individual tax return or the tax return of your family members if they're part owners. The real estate losses and depreciation won't be locked into the corporation because a flowthrough entity owns the real estate, so all losses flow through to you and your family or the owners of the flowthrough entity. What a great country this is!

Don't Forget to Attach the Required Schedules to Your Tax Return

There's a price for all these nice tax-free goodies: You get to somewhat enrich your accountant. The IRS requires a statement to your tax return noting a complete description of the property transferred, a complete description of what you received in exchange (including other property received), a complete description of the stock received, and a description of any liabilities that were assumed.[20] In addition, if this isn't bad enough, you need to attach a similar description to the corporate tax return.[21]

Summary

- To transfer property to a corporation tax-free, transfer it for the stock in the corporation.
- Do not receive warrants or options. This isn't deemed stock.
- The stock can be preferred stock as long as there's no mandatory buyback.
- Don't transfer property that would result in a loss if sold. You will lose the loss. It's better to sell the property and transfer the cash instead.
- Don't transfer services for stock, or you'll be taxed on the fair market value of the stock attributable for those services.
- All the transferors in total should own at least 80 percent of the voting stock and 80 percent of all shares of other stock issued.
- You can have the corporation assume any liabilities on the transferred property. Just don't place any liabilities on the property within one year (to be safe) before the transfer, unless you have one heck of a good corporate reason.
- Don't transfer property whose liabilities exceed your basis. If this is a problem, transfer other property so that the total basis of the properties transferred equals or exceeds the total of the liabilities assumed.
- Don't forget that if you receive anything other than stock from the transfer, you may pay tax on what you receive.
- Don't have a regular corporation own real estate. Do what the rich do: Form either an LLC or a limited partnership to own the real estate, and lease it to the corporation.

Notes

1. Section 351(a) of the IRC.
2. *George Holstein*, 23 T.C. 923 (1955); *DuPont de Nemours and Co. v. United States*, 471 F.2d 1211 (Ct. Cl.1973).
3. Section 1.351-1(a)(1)(i) of the ITR.
4. Section 351(d)(1) of the IRC and Section 1.351-1(a)(1) of the ITR.
5. Section 351(a) of the IRC.

6. Section 1.351-1(a)(1) of the ITR.

7. Section 351(g)(3)(A) of the IRC. I should note that when the preferred stock is sold, it could result in ordinary income and not capital gain under Section 306 of the IRC.

8. Sections 351 and 368(c) of the IRC.

9. *Marsan Realty Corp.*, T.C. Memo 1963-297; see also IRS Letter Ruling 8230028.

10. *Wilgard Realty Co., Inc. v. Commissioner*, 127 F.2d 514 (2nd Cir. 1942).

11. Section 357(a) of the IRC.

12. Section 357(b)(1)(A).

13. *W. H. B. Simpson v. Commissioner*, 43 T.C. 900 (1965); *W. H. Weaver v. Commissioner*, 32 T.C. 411 (1959); *Drybrough v. Commissioner*, 376 F.2d 350 (6th Cir. 1967).

14. Revenue Ruling 79-258 1979-2 CB 143.

15. Section 351(b)(1) of the IRC.

16. Section 357(c)(1) of the IRC.

17. For purposes of simplicity, I've ignored any depreciation that you may have taken. This would reduce your basis.

18. Revenue Ruling 66-142, 1966-1 CB 66.

19. Section 336(a) of the IRC.

20. Section 1.351-3(a) of the ITR.

21. Section 1.351-3(b) of the ITR.

Part 3

Every Fringe Benefit Available to Small and Home-Based Businesses as Amended by the New Tax Cuts and Jobs Act legislation

The following table summarizes the many deductions discussed in Chapters 13 and 14. (Legend: C = Corporations; P = Partnerships; SP = Sole Proprietorships)

Benefit	Available to	Discrimination Allowable?	Limitation on Benefits to Owners or Highly Compensated Employees?	Other Special Rules and Limitations
Working condition fringe benefit (tax-free use of equipment and services)	All entities, although proprietors deduct those as expenses	Yes	No limits	
No-additional-cost benefit	All	No	No limits	
Tax-free day care	All	No	Yes: no more than 25% of the benefits can go to 5% or more stockholders or owners	Limit: $5,000 per year and $2,500 for married filing separately
Adoption assistance	All with some limitations	No	No, but benefits phase out based on income	Limit: $13,840 per child in 2018 Benefit starts phasing out as modified adjusted gross income (AGI) goes over $207,850

Benefit	Available to	Discrimination Allowable?	Limitation on Benefits to Owners or Highly Compensated Employees?	Other Special Rules and Limitations
Health insurance	Fully deductible for all entities	No	No limits	
Self-insured medical reimbursement plan	C, SP (with hiring spouse)	No, but exceptions exist (under age 25, less than three years of service, works less than 25 hours per week)	No limits, other than that overall wages must be reasonable	
Disability insurance	All except owners of SP	Yes, apparently	No limits	
De minimis fringe benefits and occasional supper money	All except owners of SP	Yes	No limits	
Qualified employee discounts	Yes	Yes, but some limited exclusions allowed	No limits	Maximum discount allowed: for services, 20% of normal charge; for property, sale price less profit margin
Gym and athletic facilities	All	No	No limits	
Retirement advice	All	No	No limits	
No-interest or low-interest loans	All except owners of SPs	Yes for loans under $10,000 or less No for mortgage loans	No limits	Exceptions: 1. Loans under $10,000 2. Relocation mortgage loans 3. Bridge loans

Benefit	Available to	Discrimination Allowable?	Limitation on Benefits to Owners or Highly Compensated Employees?	Other Special Rules and Limitations
Educational assistance plans	All	No	Yes: no more than 5% of benefits to 5% or more stockholders or owners	Limit: $5,250 per employee per year
Reimbursed dues for country and health clubs	All	Yes	No limits	Either company gets deduction or employee gets business use tax-free—but not both!
Company-provided trips for employees and spouses	All	Yes	No limits	For tax-free reimbursement for spouse, spouse must be licensed in business, work for company, or provide convention duties
Company purchase of homes	All except the owner of a SP	Yes	No limits	Used only when house depreciates in value from cost
Reimbursements for moving and relocation expenses	All	Yes	No limits	
Tax-free transportation, limos, and chauffeurs	All except owners of SPs and those not paid overtime for overtime work, which is usually salaried people	Yes, but not available to people who are exempt from Fair Labor Standards Act	No limits	Nice, but limited benefit: can't be provided tax-free to the ones to whom most businesses want to provide it—the major officers—unless they get paid time-and-a-half for overtime work

Benefit	Available to	Discrimination Allowable?	Limitation on Benefits to Owners or Highly Compensated Employees?	Other Special Rules and Limitations
Vanpools, transit passes, and free parking	All except owners of SPs and 2% or more stockholders of S corporations	Yes	Yes: not available to owners of SPs and 2% or more stockholders in S corporations	Monthly limit on qualified parking: $260 per employee Monthly limit on transit passes and vanpools: $260 per employee. These are no longer deductible but can be reimbursed on a tax-free basis to employees.
Company-provided vehicles	All	Yes	No limits	The catch is how vehicles are taxed. Use cents per mile for vehicles that cost under $15,600 for passenger vehicles and $17,600 for trucks and vans, or use commuting method if available. If using annual lease value, company should pay for all insurance, repairs, and gas.
Cafeteria plan	All	No	Yes, strict (next column)	Limits on owners and officers: No more than 25% of the benefits can go to the group of officers or highly compensated individuals, or more than 5% stockholders.
Restricted stock	C	Yes	No limits	Taxation occurs at earlier of two dates: when stock is sold or when restrictions lapse. Company gets deduction when employee gets taxed.

Benefit	Available to	Discrimination Allowable?	Limitation on Benefits to Owners or Highly Compensated Employees?	Other Special Rules and Limitations
Phantom stock	C	Yes	No limits	
Qualified stock options	C	Yes	Yes: not available for 10% or more stockholders unless strike price is 110% of market value at time of grant and option is exercised within five years of grant	Limit: generally $100,000 per year of stock per employee. Employee can get long-term capital gains rates on stock sale. However, there are specific rules that both the corporation and the employee must follow or it becomes ordinary income to the employee.
Tax-free lodging	All except owners of SPs	Yes	No limits	
Tax-free meal	All except owners of SPs	No, with some exceptions for restaurant employees, emergency work, and lunch conferences	No limits*	Many ways: 1. Short business meal 2. Employees live on premises 3. Meals furnished for restaurant employees 4. Meals furnished if employees must be available during lunch for emergencies 5. If no nearby eating facilities 6. Meals provided to over 50% of staff 7. Staff lunch meetings and conferences

* The deductibility of meals for employees is generally limited to 50% under TCJA.

Benefit	Available to	Discrimination Allowable?	Limitation on Benefits to Owners or Highly Compensated Employees?	Other Special Rules and Limitations
Qualified pension and profit sharing	All	No, but some exceptions, such as three-year waiting period	No limits to certain people but overall contribution limits	Recommended plans: 1. Profit sharing: best for companies with varying incomes, limit: $55,000 for 2018. 2. SEPs: great especially if few employees, contribution limit: $55,000 for 2018. 3. SIMPLE IRAs: best for companies with many employees, limit: $12,500 in 2018 plus company contribution 4. Defined benefit: great for older employees, contribution limit: $220,000 for 2018 5. Roth 401(k) or regular 401(k) limit: $18,500 for 2018.

13

Fringe Benefits You Will Love, Part 1

*The proper avoidance of taxes is the only intel-
lectual pursuit that still carries any reward.*
**—John Maynard Keynes, economist,
Economic Consequences of the Peace (1920)**

One of the biggest questions that I get
at my seminars is, "How do I get
money tax-free out of my corporate
business?" The answer is to establish a load of
tax-free fringe benefits. In fact, this chapter
could be subtitled "Getting Money Out of a
Corporation Tax-Free."

If starting a successful small business is the
engine behind riches, then fringe benefits are
the wheels and the frame around this engine.

You've probably heard about how many of
the big, rich corporations are providing a host
of benefits to their employees. The interesting
fact is that most of these benefits can be provided by small businesses as well. It's just that
most small business owners never find out
about what choices are available to them.

Chapter Overview
- Learn about one of the fringe
  benefits that all corporations
  should have: tax-free use of
  property, equipment, and services,
  also known as *working-condition
  fringe benefits.*
- Understand the little-known way to
  get many fringe benefits with the
  no-extra-cost approach.
- Learn how to get day-care assistance
  for you and your employees on a
  tax-free basis.
- Understand the new and improved
  rules for company-provided adoption
  assistance.
- Learn why you should get your
  medical, dental, and nursing home
  insurance for yourself and your
  employees tax-free.
- Set up a self-insured medical
  reimbursement plan.

Author's note: The myth that "my accountant takes care of my taxes" has kept people ignorant about all the amazing fringe benefits that are available.

You will find some fabulous information in this chapter that, in many cases, isn't available elsewhere. It will give you a good overview of every available fringe benefit that I can suggest for small and midsized businesses. Use the various benefits as a checklist for your business.

Although time and space do not permit me to discuss every detail involved in all fringe benefits, and a whole book could be devoted to this subject alone, I give a good overview of what's required to establish each benefit and to bulletproof the benefit from the Internal Revenue Service (IRS). I also discuss any drawbacks to each benefit that you should be aware of, such as discrimination problems.

I should note that I discuss only benefits that would be available to small-business owners and not necessarily only to publicly traded corporations, although all the benefits mentioned here can and have been used by even the biggest companies.

Pay particular attention to which benefits can be offered to both owners and employees, which benefits can be offered only if you don't discriminate (which would be most of the benefits), and which benefits have limitations on what can be offered to owner/stockholders. In addition, although all these benefits assume that you're operating as a corporation, many also apply to other entities, such as limited-liability corporations (LLCs) and sole proprietorships. All in all, using the information in this chapter will result in huge tax savings that will pay for this book many times over.

Author's note: For a number of benefits, you cannot discriminate in favor of highly compensated individuals, stockholders, or owners of 5 percent or more of stock or profit interest. Highly compensated people for purposes of this book are people who make over $120,000 per year or who own 5 percent or more of the stock or who own

---

Chapter Overview (Cont.)

- Learn about providing tax-free disability insurance, and understand the one IRS loophole to obtaining the benefits tax-free.
- Understand the little-known de minimis fringe benefits.
- Learn when you can give property at a sizable discount to employees (qualified employee discounts).
- Learn how you can deduct your exercise equipment and set up a gym courtesy of the IRS.
- Have your company provide retirement advice tax-free.
- Learn how to get a low-interest or even no-interest loan from your company tax-free.
- Learn how you can get your company to pay for employee educational expenses and have them be tax-free to the recipient.
- Understand the rules for obtaining as much as $5,250 per year of educational assistance for employees' children for college costs tax-free.
- Learn when you can pay country club and health club dues and have the benefit be tax-free to the employee.
- Understand when company-provided trips to wonderful destinations can be tax-free.
- Learn about the benefit to your company of buying your home and getting all those closing costs tax-free.
- Learn why your company should provide tax-free moving expenses for you and your employees.
- Learn about when you can have employer-provided transportation, such as limos and chauffeurs, tax-free.

5 percent or more of the business. Thus, throughout Part 3 of this book, this is what I mean when I state that you can't discriminate in favor of highly compensated people.

Tax-Free Use of Property, Equipment, and Services

You're going to like this. This is one of the broadest ways to obtain tax-free fringe benefits. This benefit is also known as *working-condition fringe benefits*. These types of benefits are defined as "any property or services given to an employee by an employer that would have been deductible or depreciable by the employee as a business expense had the employee paid for the property or services."[1] It applies, however, only to employees and not to their dependents—sorry![2] Here are some examples:

- Most business publications
- Business-oriented books
- Use of employer-provided cars to the extent used for business
- Computers used for business
- Cell phones
- Fax machines
- Memberships in business-oriented associations
- Memberships to business-oriented Web sites
- Job-placement assistance if it results in some benefit to the employer, such as raising the morale of remaining workers, and the placement is in the same or similar trade or business

Example: Sam runs his insurance business as a corporation. He wants to receive memberships in the local Chamber of Commerce and life underwriters association. He also wants to receive various publications for insurance agents and various sales publications. His corporation may provide Sam with these memberships and subscriptions as tax-free working-condition fringe benefits because Sam could have deducted the cost of these publications and memberships had he spent the money himself.

Author's note: You may be wondering why a working-condition fringe benefit is such a good deal because the employee could have deducted the cost of such an item anyway. Good question! The reason is that when an employee takes a deduction for business-related expenses, it's as an itemized, nonbusiness deduction. These types of deductions have phaseouts and must exceed a threshold amount of 2 percent of your adjusted gross income (net income from a business plus wages, dividends, pensions, rents, etc.). However, if the employer provides these benefits, they are fully deductible by the corporation and tax-free to the employee. There are no phaseouts and no threshold amounts that they must exceed. Thus you get the full benefit of the deduction.

Example: Marjorie operates her network marketing business as an S corporation. She wants to subscribe to various home-based business publications and subscribe to special services for networkers, such as The Greatest Networker Web site maintained by the well-known John Milton Fogg George Madeau. If her corporation pays for these subscriptions, she may receive these benefits tax-free.

Discrimination Is Fully Allowable

This is one benefit in which Congress allows for any type of discrimination, even if the benefit is provided only to the officers or directors or other highly compensated employees of the company. You just can't discriminate when providing any product testing. Don't ask me why![3]

Example: Sock'em Corporation provides cell phones and computers only to its executive officers. These benefits are fully deductible by Sock'em and tax-free to the employees even though they're not provided to all employees.

What Is an Employee?

The working-condition fringe benefit applies to employees. Strangely, however, Congress allows many people to be treated as employees that you would never have thought would qualify for this one benefit. For example, for purposes of this rule, *employees* would include partners and members of the board of directors (although board members can't be used in any product testing).[4] In addition, independent contractors are allowed to be given working-condition fringe benefits on a tax-free basis as long as they don't involve parking or product testing.[5] Self-employed owners are not deemed employees under this rule; however, they can deduct these items anyway as business deductions without any limitation. Thus, in effect, they get the benefits too.

Author's note: I often wonder what Congress was thinking when it carved out such limited exceptions as product testing and parking for independent contractors. This simply adds needless complexity for some narrow exceptions.

Consumer Testing of Products by Employees

Your corporation can provide employees with products to test and evaluate that are manufactured by you for sale to customers. However, to avoid taxation of the employee on the receipt or use of these products, you must meet the following conditions:[6]

- It would be a normal expense of the employer (which is usually the case).
- Valid business reasons necessitate that the products be tested off the premises of the employer.
- The products are indeed furnished for testing and evaluation.
- The products are available to the employee for a period that isn't longer than needed for testing and evaluation.
- At the end of the testing period, the item is returned to the employer.
- The employee must submit detailed reports on his or her evaluation.
- The length of the testing and evaluation period is reasonable for the product.
- The employer imposes strict limits on personal use, such as a prohibition against nonemployees using the product.[7]
- The employer does not discriminate against highly compensated people in the testing unless it can show a good reason.

No-Additional-Cost Fringe Benefits

A company may provide services to employees on a tax-free basis and IRS bulletproof this benefit if it meets these conditions:

- The services are offered to customers in the ordinary course of business.
- The company doesn't incur substantial additional cost in providing these benefits.[8]

You could provide services at no additional cost, for example, when you have excess capacity.

Example: The Shipandstore Corporation provides air transit services and hotel rooms to customers. If there are some free spaces in the plane or some unoccupied hotel rooms, the corporation may provide these tax-free to its employees.

The key to this fringe benefit is that the services offered are in the same line of business as the employer and normally are offered to nonemployee customers.

Example: The Foolproof Bank offers car washes to nonemployees in order to raise funds for charity. This is not the business of the bank, and free car washes provided to employees would not qualify as no-additional-cost fringe benefits.

Author's note: Even if the employee agrees to reimburse the employer for the increased cost, this would not qualify as a tax-free fringe benefit. The following example illustrates this point.

Example: High-Cost Computer, Inc. (HCC), repairs computers. Jane is an employee with some big computer problems. HCC fixes her computer. The normal retail cost to fix it would have been $500 for labor and materials, but the actual out-of-pocket cost would have been only $100. Even if Jane reimburses HCC for the $100 cost, she would be taxed on the $400 of extra benefit. This is not a no-additional-cost benefit because HCC paid $100 to provide $500 worth of benefits. Jane's reimbursement does not alter this fact.

Discrimination Toward Owners or Highly Compensated People *Not* Allowed

Sadly, you can't discriminate in favor of highly compensated people or owners of the business who hold 5 percent or more of the stock.[9]

The Bottom Line

For this benefit to be tax-free, the employer must not incur any extra cost, and the benefit provided must be the same services as provided to customers in the employer's normal course of business.

Tax-Free Day-Care Assistance

You can provide day care tax-free to all employees[10] up to a maximum of $5,000 per year ($2,500 if married filing separately).[11] The self-employed are considered employees under this rule. Hooray! Even partnerships can offer this benefit to partners who are treated as employees.[12] Moreover, you can either pay for the employees' day care directly or reimburse the employees for the expenses.[13] How's that for flexibility? However, you *cannot* discriminate in favor of highly compensated people or owners or stockholders who have a 5 percent or more interest in stock or profits of the company, and there are limitations on the benefits that can accrue to the owners as well. This will be discussed below.

Requirements to Bulletproof Tax-Free Day Care from the IRS

In order to receive this benefit tax-free, you must meet all the following requirements:

- The plan must provide employees with dependent care to children who are under age 13 or to any other dependents who are either physically or mentally incapable of caring for themselves.
- You must have a separate, written plan. It doesn't have to be long and fancy, but you must have a plan in writing that shows who will get the benefits and what these benefits will be. You also have to notify the other employees of the availability of this benefit. You just can't keep it secret. Nice try!
- A company cannot discriminate in favor of highly compensated employees, more than 5 percent owners, or more than 5 percent stockholders. However, even if a company is found to be discriminating, those employees who are not highly compensated or do not own 5 percent or more of the stock or more than 5 percent of the business will have their benefits tax-free.
- The employee must provide some documentation to the employer, such as the name, address, and social security number or Taxpayer Identification Number of the provider. See your accountant about this.
- Even if you give this benefit to everyone, you can't have more than 25 percent of the total benefits go to any stockholder or business owner who owns more than 5 percent of the stock or the business.

Author's note: I personally find this extremely irritating, not to mention idiotic, that Congress would place a limit on the benefits available to owners even if they don't discriminate. This only complicates the tax law. Why place a limit on benefits to business owners if there's no discrimination? In addition, placing limits on benefits to owners hurts the small-business owner who may not have lots of employees, and in many cases, these people need the help the most.

I should note that you cannot have your child be the day-care provider if he or she is under age 19 by year's end or your dependent even if over age 19. Once your child hits age 19 and stops being your dependent, he or she can be a qualified provider for the other children.[14]

Author's note: The same rule would apply to any other relative, such as an employee's parents. If an employee pays one of his or her parents to take care of the employee's children, these payments would be tax-free if the parent was not a dependent of the employee. This might be a great way to get your parents some money and to take care of your child-care problems at the same time.

Company-Provided Adoption Assistance

There's a big demand from couples to adopt children. Because of this, Congress created a nice fringe benefit for adoption expenses. A company can set up a qualified plan and pay up to $13,840 in 2018 of adoption expenses per child[15] on a tax-free basis.[16]

Qualifications Needed to Bulletproof This Benefit from the IRS

In order for a company to provide these benefits tax-free, the adoption assistance must meet the following criteria:

- The plan must be in writing, and all eligible employees must be notified.
- The plan must be nondiscriminatory. However, unlike the day-care assistance benefit, there's no limit on how much goes to the owners or stockholders. The plan just can't discriminate in favor of highly compensated people, 5 percent or more stockholders, or 5 percent or more owners.

Unfortunately, what Congress gives, it also takes away. The tax credit for the benefits are expected to start phasing out as your adjusted gross income (AGI) exceeds $207,580 in 2018 and completely phases out if your AGI exceeds $247,580 in 2018.[17] As a reminder, your AGI generally means any net income from a business plus dividends, interest, rents, penalties, and wages, with a few further modifications. The following examples will illustrate how the phaseout works.

Example: John and Mary have an AGI of $227,580 in 2018. If they receive from Mary's employer $6,000 of expenses, only one-half, or $3,000, is tax-free. The other $3,000 is taxable. The reason is that they earn $20,000 more than the allowable $207,580, halfway to the $40,000 phaseout. If their AGI were $217,580, one-fourth through the $40,000 phaseout range, one-fourth ($1,500) would be taxable and three-fourths ($4,500) would be tax-free.

Author's note: Although this is not a tax policy book, think about what Congress has done. This program essentially subsidizes poor to middle-class taxpayers to adopt children and discourages wealthy people, who can best afford children. This also hasn't been affected by the Tax Cuts and Jobs Act (TCJA)

Also, if you operate as an S corporation and own more than 2 percent of the outstanding stock, any adoption assistance must be included in wages and also subject to FICA taxes. Of course, you can claim the adoption credit on your individual tax return subject to certain income limitations. However, you are generally better off paying for any adoption assistance individually and taking the credit on your tax return.

Tax-Free Health Insurance

One of the big disadvantages of being solely an employee (among the others mentioned in Chapter 1) is that you can deduct only medical insurance premiums and other medical expenses that exceed a very high threshold, 10 percent (or 7.5 percent if you are age 65 or older) of your AGI—your net income from a business plus wages, interest, dividends, pensions, and some other modifications.[18] Thus, unless you have a huge amount of medical and dental expenses, you likely won't get any deduction for these expenses.

However, if you have a side business, your business can provide you and your employees and their families with health insurance 100 percent tax-free starting in the year 2003 and thereafter.[19] Moreover, you just need to pay for the insurance premiums. No written plan is required, and the benefit is available to all forms of business, whether incorporated, partnerships, or even self-employed.[20]

In fact, health insurance almost always should be provided because of the tremendous flexibility of this benefit. For example, long-term care insurance is deemed to be health insurance,[21] as are Medicare supplement premiums.[22] Companies even can cover domestic partners, although for the payments to be tax-free for an employee, the domestic partner must qualify as a dependent of the employee.[23]

In addition, a company even can reimburse the employee for the insurance premiums paid under the following conditions:[24]

- The employer has a plan for health insurance coverage.
- The employer requires the employees to prove what actually was spent on health insurance.

Author's note: Being able to reimburse employees becomes essential, especially for small-business owners, whenever an employee would not be able to get coverage because of preexisting conditions.

Finally, and this is my favorite benefit of providing health insurance premiums, the health insurance can be provided on a discriminatory basis. You just can't discriminate based on health factors,[25] and it must seem to cover employees, not just stockholders or owners.[26]

Medical insurance must be nondiscriminatory but can have the same exceptions as that of the self-insured medical plans.

Example: Harry provides health insurance to all his full-time employees but charges a premium for those with prior health problems. This would be prohibited. However, if Harry provided health insurance to all the officers, regardless of health problems, and a lesser plan to other employees, this would be allowable.

The bottom line is that this is a great, flexible fringe benefit that most firms should provide regardless of size and regardless of entity. This deduction has not be affected by the TCJA.

Author's note: If you operate as an S corporation and own more than 2 percent of the stock, you need to go through a three-step process:

First, get your S corporation to pay all health premiums for you and your spouse and dependents.

Second, include these payments on your W-2 as income but are exempt from FICA taxes.

Third, deduct these premiums on your individual tax return (IRS Form 1040) under the line for a "self employed health insurance deduction," which is a deduction from adjusted gross income. Thus, you have no threshold that you must exceed.

Set Up a Self-Insured Medical Reimbursement Plan

This is a plan that covers all your medical expenses that are not covered by insurance, such as mileage to and from the doctor, deductibles, coinsurance, braces and other dental expenses, hearing aids, chiropractic therapy, over-the-counter medication that alleviates a medical condition, and much more. This is in addition to your health insurance. You're not dropping your health insurance coverage. However, this is much more limited for 2 percent or more owners of S corporations and partnerships. See the detailed discussion in Chapter 4 on this topic.

Provide for Disability Insurance

Disability insurance covers two situations: loss of income owing to being disabled from an accident or illness and payments for the loss of a bodily function, a limb, or an organ.

Loss of a Bodily Function, a Limb, or an Organ

Payments made for the loss of a bodily function or a limb are tax-deductible for your company and tax-free for the employee.[27]

Example: Juan works in a machine shop and loses an eye. The company provides disability benefits, paying $100,000 for the loss of a bodily function or an organ. The $100,000 that Juan receives is tax-free.

Disability Owing to Accident or Illness

Today, there's a much better chance of being injured by accident or suffering a long-term illness than dying. Sadly, when a catastrophe of this nature occurs, few would have the ability to continue their income if they could not work. This is the purpose of disability insurance.

Interestingly, companies have two options regarding disability premiums paid to an insurance company. The premiums can be either tax-free to the employee or taxable to the employee.[28] There's a drawback to each option. If they're tax-free to the employee, then the benefits would be taxable to the employee if he or she gets paid on the policy. However, if the employee gets taxed on the premiums or in fact pays the premiums, then the benefits are not taxable.[29]

Example: Wise Corp. provides disability insurance on all its employees tax-free. Joan, an employee, becomes seriously injured in a car accident that keeps her out of work for six months. All payments to her will be fully taxable because the premiums were tax-free.

IRS-Approved Tax-Planning Strategy

The IRS has ruled in a private ruling[30] that an employee who had paid the total premiums for disability coverage in the *policy year* in which he suffered a disability and received payments would not be liable for taxes on those payments, even though his employer had paid the premiums in previous years. In other words, all disability payments that the employee received would be allocable to his payments and would not be taxable.

Isn't this an amazing country?

What this means to you is simple. Have your company deduct all premiums and treat them as tax-free to all the employees. However, in the year of a disability, have the company treat the premiums as taxable to the disabled employee; thus it will make the benefits tax-free.

Example: Joan is permanently injured in a car accident. If in the year of the injury she were taxed on the premiums paid by her employer, the benefits would seem to be tax-free.

As a final note, self-employed taxpayers or S-corporation shareholders who own more than 2 percent of the stock or partners are *not* employees.[31] Thus a self-employed person cannot deduct disability insurance premiums. However, the benefits then would be tax-free.

The Bottom Line

All companies should provide for disability coverage and should both deduct the premiums and treat them as a tax-free benefit to the employee. If the benefit is for loss of a bodily function, the benefit is always tax-free. If the benefit is for loss of income owing to sickness or accident, treat the last year's payment as income, and the benefits should become tax-free as well, not withstanding what was done in the prior years.

Author's note: This benefit has not been affected by the TCJA.

If you operate as an S corporation and own more than 2 percent of the stock, you would include these payments as income on your W-2, but they are exempt from FICA taxes. This actually can be a benefit since if you collect disability payments from these policies, the payments are tax-free since you were taxed on the premiums.

De Minimis Fringe Benefits and Occasional Supper Money

Your company can provide any employee—even if it discriminates in favor of officers or highly compensated people[32]—property or services under both the following conditions:[33]

- The value of the property or services is so small or inconsequential as to not warrant an accounting.
- The property or services are not provided too frequently.

Thus, even if a fringe benefit were small in value but provided daily, it would *not* be deemed de minimis. It must be *both* infrequent and inconsequential to be a de minimis fringe benefit.

Example: Financial Destiny is a small corporation that provides income opportunities. If it provides a one-time payment of $1,000 to an employee, this would not be deemed inconsequential and would be fully taxable.

Example: Financial Destiny also provides bus fare for some employees daily. Even though the value of this benefit is inconsequential, it's provided too frequently, so the total value of the fares would not be considered inconsequential.

Author's note: Any use of an employer-provided car, constant use of a season tickets, or membership in a country club would not be a de minimis benefit. Such benefits may qualify as working-condition fringe benefits, however.

Examples of De Minimis Benefits

Now that you know what benefits are not de minimis, here are some de minimis benefits that can be provided:

- Occasional typing of a personal letter by a secretary
- Weekly coffee and donuts
- Holiday gifts of low value
- Holiday turkeys if the cost is usually less than $25
- Occasional theater and season tickets
- Free soft drinks
- Occasional use of the copy machine, fax machine, or other similar equipment if personal use is less than 15 percent[34]

Author's note: The IRS strangely has noted that monthly transit passes that cost no more than $21 would be deemed de minimis if paid to an employee.[35] But it doesn't treat the self-employed as employees. Sorry! Also, this benefit does not seem affected by any of the deduction cuts in the TCJA.

Author's note: If you operate as an S corporation and own more than 2 percent of the stock, there is no problem for you. This benefit is available for everyone and all entities.

Occasional Supper Money

The IRS allows the payment of occasional supper money under all three of the following conditions:[36]

- The supper money is provided occasionally and not regularly.
- The supper money allows an extension of the normal workday.
- The supper money enables the employee to work overtime.

Author's note: This benefit applies only to employees. Thus, if you're self-employed, you can't give yourself supper money. You can, however, give it to any employee of yours. In addition, if you incorporate your business, you then become an employee of that business and are eligible to receive supper money.

The key is that supper money can be provided to anyone or everyone if there's a need for emergency overtime. It can't be based on hours worked, such as $3 of supper money for each hour of overtime. Thus, if you have a business that requires some overtime owing to a time crunch or emergency, you can provide supper money.

Example: Footer Podiatry, Inc., has a crunch of business once or twice a month. If the employees work two extra hours of overtime, the company can provide tax-free supper money. If this happens every week, this probably would be deemed too frequent and would be taxable.

Author's note: I've spoken with the IRS ruling division about this. Their policy is to allow supper money if it isn't provided too frequently, such as two or three times a month. Thus, if you have overtime required of employees that does not exceed three days a month, you should be able to provide a reasonable amount of supper money tax-free. Limit the money to what it would cost one person to eat in a medium-priced restaurant. Paying $100 per day for supper money probably would not be reasonable.

The Bottom Line

I don't consider de minimis fringe benefits the top benefit in this chapter. They have a narrow application and, as the name indicates, can't be too beneficial. However, when you consider all the items that can be deemed de minimis, such as occasional supper money, these benefits can add up and not be de minimis to you or your company. Again, this doesn't seem to be affected by the TCJA.

Qualified Employee Discounts

How would you like to be able to provide your employees with tax-free discounts on a wide range of products and services? Well, you can, and it's easy to implement in any company of any size.

The term *qualified employee discounts* means giving your employees property or services that you normally provide to the public in your company's ordinary course of business but you provide them at a discounted price to your employees. If you provide qualified employee discounts, the employees receive the property or services tax-free.[37]

Example: Safecracking, Inc., runs a nationwide banking consulting service. If the company provides discounts on banking fees to its employees, this would be a qualified employee discount. However, if it purchases and distributes season's tickets for the Redskins football games, this would not be a qualified employee discount because the company is not in the business of selling season tickets.

A company can provide discounts on any product or service that it offers to the public—with the following exceptions:

- Stocks and bonds
- Commodities
- Real estate
- Money

Author's note: It's too bad that Congress passed these exceptions. I would have loved to work for a currency house or a bank and get discounts on money. Wouldn't you?

Limitations on Qualified Employee Discounts

Besides limiting discounts to qualified property, Congress has placed some limitations on the amount of the discount. As a result of some "tax simplification," the rules vary depending on whether you're providing services or property.

If you're providing a service, such as a flight or legal service, you can allow up to a 20 percent tax-free discount.[38]

Example: The law firm of Shaft and Shaft provides legal services to all its staff members at a discount. If the normal fees are $300 per hour, it can offer the legal services at a 20 percent discount, charging $240 per hour. If it offers these services for $100 per hour, the $140 "excess" discount would be taxable to the employee.[39]

If your firm provides discounts on property, the amount of the discount can't exceed the gross profit percentage.[40] You might be wondering what this means! The *gross profit percentage* is the sale price minus the cost of the property. Thus, in effect, you can offer the property at your company's cost.

Author's note: Why Congress couldn't use the term *cost* of the property instead of *gross profit percentage* is beyond me.

Example: HP offers computers to its employees at a discount. If the normal price of a computer to customers is $2,000 but the profit that HP makes on each computer is $500, the company can offer its computers to its employees at $1,500. Anything above this discount would be taxable to the employee.

Nondiscrimination Rules

In order to provide qualified employee discounts, you must offer them on a nondiscriminatory basis. You can't give the discounts just to the officers and other highly paid individuals. However, if you do discriminate, the discounts are still tax-free to employees who are not 5 percent owners of the stock or business or who make less than $120,000 for 2017 and 2018 and 2019.

There's a bit of sunshine here. There are some employees who can be deemed ineligible for the discounts:

- Employees who have less than one year of service with the company
- Employees who normally work less than 17.5 hours per week

- Seasonal employees who normally work less than six months per year
- Employees who are under age 21
- Employees who are subject to a collective-bargaining agreement (union contract)
- Employees who normally work less than 1,000 hours per year[41]

Author's note: As you can see from some of the fringe benefits, part-time workers need not be offered many benefits. Maybe this is the reason so many companies are hiring employees on a part-time or seasonal basis.

The Bottom Line

Qualified employee discounts can be a real benefit to companies and to their employees. They're available, however, only for products and services normally provided to the general public. Also, if they are services, the discount is limited to 20 percent. If the discounts are for property, they're generally limited to the gross profit percentage, which means that the employee can pay the cost of the property.

Author's note: This benefit is not affected by the TCJA.

Deducting Exercise Equipment and a Gym

As we've read in many news articles, exercise is being touted as a partial cure for many ailments. Wouldn't it be great if you could deduct the cost of exercise equipment, tennis courts, and even a gym and provide these items tax-free to your employees and, if incorporated, to yourself? The answer is that you can!

Requirements to Bulletproof Company-Provided Athletic Facilities from the IRS

In order to make this benefit tax-free, you must meet several well-defined tests:[42]

- The equipment or gym generally must be on the company premises or leased or owned by the employer. (Thus it doesn't have to be physically in the same building as all the employees.)
- The equipment or gym must be operated by the company.
- The equipment or gym must be used substantially by employees of the company, their spouses, and their dependent children.

There are a couple of implications that can be derived from these rules. First, you can't pay for a health or country club membership because these clubs would be used by the general public and not substantially by your employees.[43] Second, the facilities must be run or operated by the company. This means that you can't deduct the use of a resort with facilities such as tennis or a swimming pool, which would be part of the association dues.

In addition, the IRS has noted that *employees* can include partners and employees who are separated from the company (either through retirement or disability).

Example: Your company provides a gym in the office for your employees. The gym is staffed by personnel paid by the company. The gym would be fully deductible and tax-free to the employees. If the company paid for health club memberships, on the other hand, this would not be tax-free to the employees. In addition, the athletic facility must not be offered only to officers or highly paid employees. Most staff members should be allowed to use the facility.

Author's note: Self-employed individuals ordinarily cannot give themselves this fringe benefit because self-employed individuals are not considered to be employees. However, if you're self-employed and you hire your spouse and/or other family members, they become your employees. If you place a gym in the location where your family employees work, you may be able to deduct the cost of the gym and the equipment. It's vital, however, that only employees or their family members use this facility. Thus don't let your friends use the gym. Keep an exercise log for everyone using the facility.

What Types of Facilities Can Be Operated Under This Fringe Benefit?

Under this benefit, you can deduct and provide on a tax-free basis the following types of items:

- Gyms
- Exercise equipment
- Tennis courts
- Swimming pools
- Golf courses

Author's note: I really like the idea of being able to provide a golf course to my employees tax-free, but however, the cost would be prohibitive to small businesses. However, remember what I stated earlier: "Where there's a will, there's a lawyer." Check out the next exception.

In case you don't have the hundreds of thousands or, in the case of golf courses, millions necessary to provide this benefit to your employees, there's a great exception from having your company pay all the costs.[44] A company can have an agreement with other employers to operate the gym, golf course, or swimming pool. Thus, you find a company currently providing this benefit to its employees and cut a deal to pay rent or a fee so that your employees can use this facility. I should note that you must cut a deal with another company that provides this benefit solely to its employees. You can't go to a general health club or a country club and do the same thing.

Author's note: This is another idiotic rule passed by Congress. I can pay IBM to let my staff use a golf course that it owns and operates, along with employees of other companies that pay IBM for use of this course, but we can't pay a health club or a country club to do the same thing. Am I missing the point, or is this dumb?

Sandy's tax tip: Normally, self-employed individuals (otherwise known as sole proprietors) can't set up a deductible gym for themselves. However, if you were to hire your spouse and provide the gym in the location where your spouse works, such as your home, the gym should be deductible if used by you and your dependent children as well. This option, however, has not been tested yet.

The Bottom Line

This is a terrific and often overlooked benefit. Just have your company either operate the athletic facility or pay rent to another company that's operating a facility for its own employees.

Author's note: This benefit does not seem affected by the TCJA.

Retirement Advice

Congress has been concerned recently with the lack of retirement planning of most people. In fact, according to a Harvard University study, only 2 percent of the population can retire by age 65 on the same standard of living that they had before retirement. Thus, starting in 2002, companies now can provide qualified retirement services to their employees and their spouses.[45] However, the employer must have some kind of "qualified plan" in place, such as a pension, a profit-sharing plan, a simplified employee pension (SEP), or even a simple individual retirement account (IRA) (most of these plans will be discussed later in this chapter) so that the employees can see where this benefit fits in with all the other retirement planning.

Example: Stop the Clock, Inc., wants to provide retirement planning for its employees. It hires a financial planner to meet with each employee about his or her retirement and to set up individual retirement plans for each employee and his or her spouse. If the company pays a fee for these services, it can deduct the fee, and the benefit would be tax-free to each employee if there were no discrimination.

In addition, anyone, even highly compensated employees and officers, can have this tax-free benefit as long as it doesn't discriminate.[46] Thus provide it to all full-time people.

The Bottom Line

This is both a great benefit and a needed benefit. You'll have happy and economically healthier employees by providing this benefit. Remember, however, that this benefit must be nondiscriminatory.

Company-Provided Low- or No-Interest Loans to Employees

This has got to be one of the most used and yet misunderstood fringe benefits. Unfortunately, few companies are using this benefit correctly. However, you, my faithful reader, will not have this problem because you will learn exactly what you need to do to make these loans tax-free.

The rules provided by Congress are entitled "Treatment of Loans with Below-Market Interest Rates." These are defined as loans made to employees or even independent contractors at rates that are below the minimum rates allowed by the IRS, which are also known as the *applicable federal rates*. Thus, if you want to make the interest rates on these loans tax-free, there's a minimum rate that you must charge, or the employee is taxed on the forgone interest that he or she should have paid at the applicable federal rates.[47]

Example: Alice borrows $50,000 from her corporation for a 10-year period, interest-free. Because she didn't pay interest equal to the applicable federal rate, she would be taxed on the foregone interest using this rate each year. Yuck!

Applicable Federal Rates

The IRS publishes the applicable federal rates each month. They're available in your accountant's office, or you can call the IRS at 800-IRS-1040. (Isn't that a cute number?) There are three federal rates:

- *Short-term rates*—for loans of three years or less
- *Middle-term rates*—for loans over three years but not over nine years
- *Long-term rates*—for loans over nine years

Author's note: You would determine how long you want the loan and find out the latest applicable federal rate for the duration of the loan that you want. As long as you charge at least that rate, you can get these below-market loans tax-free. Also, as an estimate for you, the rate for long-term loans (over nine years) approximates the prime rate, whereas the rate for short-term loans is approximately one-half the prime rate. Thus the longer the duration, the more you must charge in interest.

Fabulous Exceptions to the Below-Market Loan Rules

1. $10,000 de minimis exception. The below-market loan rules do not apply to loans of $10,000 or less, which means that you can charge no or little interest.[48] However, if the amount is above $10,000, the rules apply even if you pay down the debt below $10,000.[49]

Example: You borrow $10,000 from your corporation, interest-free. This would be an exception to the rules, and you would not pay any tax on the foregone interest.

Example: You borrow $15,000 from your corporation, interest-free. This would not be an exception even if you pay the loan down below $10,000. You're taxed on each year's forgone interest.

2. Employee-relocation mortgage loans made in connection with a new place of work. One fabulous exception would be to provide mortgage loans to employees as part of a transfer to a new location.[50] Your new job location has to change, so you would qualify for the moving deduction. Generally, this means that your new job location should be on the other side of the city at least 50 miles away or, even better, in another city or another state. If you qualify, you can charge little or no interest.

The new workplace would have to be at such a distance from the employee's old residence as to require at least an additional 50 miles of commute. In other words, if the distance between the new site and the old residence is at least 50 miles greater than the distance between the old site and the old residence, the distance requirement is fulfilled.

Author's note: Hooray! Remember that I told you that we have good tax laws. You just have to know about them.

Requirements to Bulletproof Relocation Loans from the IRS

Nothing comes for free. To qualify, you must meet the following five easy tests:[51]

- The loan can't be for the purpose of avoiding taxes. This isn't usually a problem unless, for example, only the owner of the company gets it, and it isn't provided to other relocating employees.
- The benefits of this loan aren't transferable to a new buyer.
- The benefits of this loan are conditioned on continued future performance of substantial services by the employee. Thus the loan agreement could provide that "if the employee ceases working for the company, the applicable federal rate of interest will be charged the employee" or that "the loan will terminate and must be paid off within six months of termination."
- The employee must give a statement that the employee would itemize deductions on his or her tax return for each outstanding year. In other words, the employee would certify that he or she would be able to take a deduction for the interest on his or her federal tax return.
- The loan agreement provides that the mortgage money can be used only to buy a personal residence and not an investment property.[52] In short, you have to use the residence as your home and not rent it out.

Example: Karen works for the I've Been Moved Company (IBM). She is relocated from New York to California, and the company provides a no-interest mortgage for 15 years. As long as she uses the mortgage to buy a principal residence, is required to work for the company in order to keep receiving this benefit, and certifies that she will file an itemized return (Schedule A) with her federal tax return, the forgone interest would be tax-free.

Author's note: Any company of any size can offer this benefit to any employee of the company. Self-employed individuals are not employees, nor are independent contractors. This benefit is also very good for motivating and retaining an employee. What employees would want to leave a job if they were getting a tax-free mortgage that they would have to refinance at the going market interest rate if they quit?

I should note that this benefit is also available to corporate officers and to corporate owners as long as they are employees of the company.

3. Bridge loans. If you don't want to tie up your company's money in a mortgage, you can provide a no-interest or low-interest bridge loan to hold an employee until he or she is able to get a permanent mortgage on the real estate. To make this benefit tax-free, you must meet not only *all the criteria* for mortgage loans but also the following three criteria:[53]

- The loan agreement with the employee must provide that the employee must pay off the loan in full within 15 days of selling his or her principal residence.

- The total amount of all bridge loans must be less than the equity of the old house sold.

- The old house must be sold and not converted into investment property.

Author's note: As you can see, making a tax-free temporary loan (bridge loan) is more complicated than simply providing a mortgage. However, you may not want to tie up company funds in a long-term interest-free or low-interest commitment. Bridge loans are ideal in that they are short-term, temporary loans provided until the employee sells the former residence and has the funding to buy a new home. A corporation may provide bridge loans to the owners/stockholders. A sole proprietorship may provide them to employees—but not to the owner!

The Bottom Line

In order to provide tax-free below-market loans, either you must charge what the applicable federal rate would be for your loan's duration (which can be obtained from the IRS or your accountant) or you must meet one of the exceptions—loans of less than $10,000, relocation mortgage loans, or bridge loans. Make sure that you meet all the criteria noted in this book, and you will bulletproof this nice tax-free fringe benefit from the IRS. It also will provide for much more loyal employees because if they leave, this benefit can terminate.

Employer Educational Assistance and Other Tuition Plans

One big question that I get from most small-business owners is, "Can I provide my employees or my employed children with a tax-free tuition payment each year?"

There's good news and bad news here. The good news is that there are several possible ways to provide for tax-free tuition money: an educational assistance plan or tax-free use of property, equipment, or services, otherwise known as a *working-condition fringe benefit*. We'll discuss each of these in the order presented. The bad news is that for small businesses, most of these plans won't benefit the owner significantly but will benefit most of the employees of the business.

Generally, any educational expense paid for an employee or for a member of an employee's family is deductible by the company but taxable to the employee, unless you meet one of the exceptions noted below!

Educational Assistance Programs

You can set up an educational assistance program for your employees and pay up to $5,250 per year for tuition, fees, books, and supplies.[54] However, you cannot provide meals, lodging, transportation, or payments for sports, games, or hobbies unless they are part of a degree program.

Example: Jim is studying computers and takes some gym courses to keep in shape. His employer may not reimburse him for the gym courses. However, if Jim were studying exercise physiology and the gym courses were part of the curriculum, his employer could make such payments tax-free.

No discrimination is allowed in favor of business owners or highly compensated employees; however, employees of sole proprietorships can use this benefit. Now, for the bad news: No more than 5 percent of the total benefits can be paid to a stockholder who owns more than 5 percent of the stock or to an individual who owns 5 percent or more of the business even if you don't discriminate in any way. Yuck!

Author's note: If you have very few employees using this plan, you won't meet this requirement because more than 5 percent of the benefits will be benefiting the owner. Thus small-business owners get shafted because they can't avoid this 5 percent coverage, but larger businesses won't have a problem. You can, however, provide this assistance to your employees, such as your child, who do not have a 5 percent or more stock or business ownership interest.

Working-Condition Fringe Benefit

Although this was covered earlier, some special rules are applicable here. Even if you don't qualify for tax-free treatment as an educational assistance program, you may be able to deduct the courses and provide tax-free assistance as a working-condition fringe benefit if you meet certain criteria:[55]

- The educational expense would have been deductible by the employee if paid by the employee. This means that it doesn't qualify the employee for a new trade or business. (See author's note below for further explanation.)
- The courses taken are related to the duties performed by the employee on the job.[56]
- The employee submits receipts and an expense report for all educational reimbursements.[57]

Author's note: There's only one unclear issue here: When can an employee deduct the educational expenses? The answer is that the course must be to maintain or improve the skills needed by the employee for his or her current duties *and* cannot be part of a program of study to qualify the employee for a new trade or business. Thus college courses that lead to a basic college undergraduate degree would qualify for a new trade or business, as would law school and medical school courses. However, courses that would not qualify for a new trade or business, such as many postgraduate courses, would qualify as a working-condition fringe benefit. Let's take some examples to illustrate all this.

Example: Chan works for Hackers, Inc., a computer repair facility. He's studying computers at the local college. If the company pays for his tuition, without it qualifying as an education assistance program, it would be fully taxable to Chan because he's seeking an undergraduate degree, which is deemed to qualify most people for a new trade or business.

Example: Let's assume that Chan already has an undergraduate degree and is seeking a master's in computers. Now, Hackers, Inc., can pay for any computer courses because these courses would be related to his job duties and would not qualify him for a new trade or business.

Example: Marcia works for an accounting firm by day and goes to law school and takes some tax courses in the evening. If her firm reimbursed her for these courses, none of the reimbursement would qualify as a working-condition fringe benefit because Marcia cannot deduct law school courses that lead to a doctor of law degree. If she already had a law degree, however, and took some graduate law courses in taxation, she could receive reimbursement tax-free.

The Bottom Line

An educational assistance program is great, but you can't discriminate and can't have over 5 percent of the benefits go to the business owners or stockholders who own more than 5 percent of the stock. You also have a "fallback" position as a working-condition fringe benefit if the course is related to the employee's duties and the course doesn't qualify the employee for a new trade or business. Basic undergraduate courses, basic law courses that lead to the practice of law, and medical school courses that qualify a person to practice medicine would not qualify as a working-condition fringe benefit.

Reimbursed Country Club and Health Club Dues

Before 1987, country club dues were deductible to the extent used for business. Sadly, Congress did some "tax simplification"; thus, you know that you were shafted.

Today, there's generally no deduction for you or your company for country club or health club dues.[58] However, if an employee uses the club for business, any payments made for club dues would be deemed tax-free to the employee to the extent that the club is used for business under the working-condition fringe benefit rule, as discussed earlier.[59]

Author's note: Thus, if the club were used in part for business, some of the club dues would be tax-free to the employee using the club. The dues, however, would not be deductible by the company as a result of the "tax simplification" law.

Example: The Getwithit Corporation pays $2,000 a year to a health and golf club for use by its marketing employee. If the employee uses the club 40 percent for business, 40 percent of the $2,000, or $800, would be tax-free to the employee, who would be taxed on the remaining $1,200.[60] The employer would get no deduction for the dues.

However, if the company treated the club dues as fully taxable compensation, it could deduct the entire amount as compensation and not club dues, but the employee would be taxed on the full amount.[61]

Example: If, in the preceding example, Getwithit treated the $2,000 as additional compensation, it could deduct the entire amount as compensation, and the employee would get taxed on the full amount, even the portion that he or she used for business. So much for tax simplification!

Thus the bottom line is that either the employer gets a deduction and the employee gets taxed on all the dues or the employer gets no deduction for the dues and the employee pays taxes on some of the dues.[62]

Sandy's tax tip: The key is to have your company reimburse employees only for the business use of the club. Thus only the business portion would be disallowed as a deduction by the corporation, but the employee gets that portion tax-free. The corporation should treat the portion that's not used for business as "additional compensation" to the employee in order to take a deduction for this portion.

Author's note: An employee would establish business use by keeping some form of tax diary or tax organizer showing what business was discussed each day that he or she used the club for business and the name of the person with whom it was discussed. One final point: The disallowance of the club dues deduction by Congress does *not* apply to other types of expenses. Thus business meals at your club would be deductible.[63] The same reasoning would apply to golf caddie fees, green fees, tips, etc.

The bottom line is that health club, golf club, and country club dues are not deductible by a company unless it treats them as additional compensation to the employees who use the club. The company can forgo the deduction so that the employee could receive some of the benefits tax-free, but only to the extent that he or she used the club for business.

Company-Provided Trips for Employees and Spouses

Many companies provide their top salespeople with conventions in very desirable places as both a morale booster and, frankly, a reward for good performance.

Author's note: Unfortunately, as a speaker, I always seem to go to Arizona in the summer and Michigan in the winter. I'm definitely doing something wrong!

We discussed in great depth in Chapter 3 the rules for employees to deduct business trips. Generally, for a trip to be tax-free, the majority of the days must be for business. Training activities must predominate each day, other than weekend days that are sandwiched between business days. In addition, each day would be a business day if the employee attended at least four hours and one second of meetings or it were either a travel day or a sandwiched weekend day. See Chapter 3 for a more detailed analysis of this.

The key question that often arises is what happens if the spouse comes along? Congress actually has thought of this and provides that you can bring your spouse and either get a tax-free reimbursement or deduct the cost if you are not reimbursed—if you meet one of two tests:

- Your spouse is licensed in your business. (If you are an insurance agent, for example, your spouse would have to be licensed in insurance.)
- Your spouse can make money for you or the company at the convention! (You've got to like this one!) But what does this mean?

Author's note: Under the TCJA, travel costs incurred for attending business seminars are 50% deductible.

Requirements to Bulletproof Tax-Free Reimbursements for Your Spouse's Travel from the IRS

The IRS provides that if your spouse is not licensed in your occupation, the company may pay his or her travel and lodging expenses under all the following conditions:

- The spouse is there for a bona fide business reason and not just to keep you company.
- There is proper substantiation for the expenses that the spouse incurs, by keeping some form of expense log, tax diary, or tax organizer.[64]
- The spouse is an employee of the taxpayer.[65]

Author's note: The last requirement is waived if the spouse performs convention duties, such as registering guests and monitoring attendance at the meetings, etc.[66]

Example: Richard takes his wife to the company convention in Orlando. Her only duties are to accompany Richard and attend some seminars for spouses. The company could either deduct none of her expenses or deduct her expenses and treat them as taxable compensation for Richard.

Example: If, in the preceding example, Richard's wife also were an employee of the company, she could attend the convention and not be taxed on the reimbursed expenses if she either attends courses related to her duties or performs functions at the convention, such as registering guests.

Author's note: Self-employed taxpayers have the same rules for deductibility of their spouses' expenses on business trips.

The Bottom Line

The predominant reason for the trip must be business or training. Each day should consist of at least four hours and one second of training. For a spouse's expenses to be deductible and tax-free to the spouse or the employee, there must be a valid reason for the spouse to be there, such as convention duties, or the spouse must work for the company and attend meetings related to his or her own job duties.

Corporate Purchase of an Employee's Home That Has Declined in Value

I'm not sure that this is as much a fringe benefit as a tax loophole. But I should tell you about it.

If an employee sells a home to his or her corporate employer, it would be considered a sale as if the employee sold it to a stranger.[67] Thus there's little benefit to selling your principal residence to your corporation if it has appreciated in value.

However, if the home has declined in value, there's a possible benefit to the employee. If any employee, even an employee who owns 100 percent of the stock, sells his or her principal residence to the corporation at a loss, none of the loss would be deductible.[68]

Author's note: I find it interesting that if you have a gain on your home, you are taxed on the gain, but if you have a loss, the government wants no part of your loss! This is another example of the "golden rule": "He who has the gold makes the rule."

In addition, if there are sales expenses such as commissions, appraisal fees, and bank fees, the employee gets no benefit from these fees. It just accentuates the loss! Even worse, if your company reimburses an employee for the loss, the employee gets taxed on the reimbursement.[69] Yuck!

Sandy's tax tip: If an employee would have a loss on his or her residence, have the corporation purchase the house at the appraised fair market value, and then resell the house and pay all the selling expenses; although the employee would not be able to deduct the loss and also would not pay any tax because a loss would have resulted,[70] he or she won't incur additional nondeductible closing costs such as commissions. However, when the corporation incurs these expenses, it can deduct them as part of the resale of the house. Thus, in effect, the corporation is able to deduct the closing costs!

Example: Martha purchased a home for $300,000 several years ago. As a result of a bad real estate market, her home is now worth $250,000. If she sells it for the fair market value of $250,000, she cannot deduct the $50,000 loss (except to the extent that she may have claimed an office in the home). Even worse, if she were to incur $15,000 in real estate commissions and $5,000 in other closing costs, she couldn't deduct these either.

Example: Assume that Martha's company purchases the house from her for the fair market value of $250,000 and then resells the house for the same amount and, in addition, incurs the $20,000 of closing costs that Martha would have incurred. The corporation could deduct the $20,000 of costs as a loss. Everyone wins except the IRS.

Author's note: This will work for any corporation, whether a regular corporation or an S corporation. It also should work if you're running your business as a partnership or a multiple-owner limited-liability corporation. It will even work for a sole proprietorship, but only for the employees of the proprietorship, not the owner.

The Bottom Line

If you're incorporated or an employee in any business entity and you own a principal residence that has declined in value, let the corporation purchase the home at the fair market value and resell the home. The company then can deduct the closing costs incurred as a loss.

Reimbursement for Relocating Expenses for a Qualified Move

Prior to 2018, am employer could deduct the cost of reimbursing employees for their relocating expenses. This was deductible by the employer and tax free to the employee.

As a result of the new Tax Cuts and Jobs Act, no deduction is generally allowed for employer reimbursements for moving or relocation expenses. Even worse, other than for active duty military personnel, any reimbursement paid to or for relocation expenses of the employee are taxed to the employee. This applies to all payments made in 2018 until the end of 2015. However, IRS recently issued a gift to some people by noting that reimbursements for moves made in 2017 can be made tax free to the employee even if paid in 2018.

What Is a Qualified Move?

The IRS defines a *qualified move* this way (Publication 521): "Your move will meet the distance test if your new main job location is *at least 50 miles* farther from your former home than your old main job location was from your former home." It adds the following explanation: "The distance between a job location and your home is the shortest of the more commonly traveled routes between them. The distance test considers only the location of your former home. It does not take into account the location of your new home."

Author's note: Don't blame me if this sounds confusing. Blame your members of Congress. It's hard to believe that someone actually thinks of stuff like this.

In order to help you, I have illustrated this rule in Figure 13-1.

Example: Jan lives 20 miles away from her current office. She's transferred to a job location that's 60 miles away. If she moves, she does not qualify to deduct her relocation expenses because the distance between her old home and her new office isn't at least 50 miles more than her previous commute.

Discrimination Is Okay

As far as I can tell, you can discriminate in determining who gets relocation expenses covered and who doesn't. If your corporation reimburses you and your family for your moving expenses, this would be acceptable. I would, however, establish a class of people who would qualify, such as only officers or only senior officers. This would make it less likely that the IRS would challenge the reimbursement of relocation expenses as being only for the benefit of stockholders.

The change applies as of January 1, 2018. Under that effective date, it appears that any reimbursement in 2018 will be taxable even if it applies to a move that occurred in 2017. That seems unfair to individuals who may have incurred moving expenses in late 2017 and have not had time to process an employer reimbursement. But that seems to be the result unless later guidance provides a less onerous transition rule.

Company-Provided Transportation, Limos, and Chauffeurs

Generally, if your corporation provides you with free transportation to the job by taxi or limo, it's taxable. However, there's an exception that applies in some rare instances. This transportation can be provided at a phenomenally low cost to the employee of $1.50 each way,[72] regardless of cost, if you meet the following criteria:

- The transportation is provided because of unsafe conditions.
- There's a written policy that transportation is provided only for commuting and not for personal purposes.
- An unrelated third party provides the transportation. (Thus you shouldn't use your son or the owner's brother to drive the employees.)
- The person transported must be a qualified employee. (Here's the catch.)

Let's examine what all this means. *Unsafe conditions* means that "under the facts and circumstances, a reasonable person would consider it unsafe for the employee to walk or use public transportation at the time of the day the employee must commute."[73] Thus the employee would ordinarily have to have either walked to work or taken public transportation. If he or she had driven, this exception presumably wouldn't apply unless you could show that there was no safe parking near the job location or that walking to or from the parking lot would have been dangerous.

Author's note: If you're going to use this exception, you want to think like a prosecuting attorney. You want to show the history of crime in the area surrounding the employee's workplace *or* residence at the time of the day of the commute. Perhaps getting a police recommendation to take a cab to and from work because of the unsafe conditions would be very compelling to the IRS. After all, an IRS agent is a sort of police officer, so he or she should respect a police recommendation.

You can provide this benefit only to qualified employees. These are people who are not highly compensated and are not exempt from the Fair Labor Standards Act.[74] This simply means that if they put in overtime, they will be paid at least time-and-a-half.

Example: Perry Mason is a staff lawyer who works long hours for his firm. Even if Perry's commute, which ordinarily would have been by train, could be proven dangerous, he wouldn't normally be a qualified employee because most lawyers are not paid overtime. If he were paid overtime at overtime rates for work beyond the 40 hours, he would qualify.

Finally, self-employed people cannot qualify for this benefit unless they're incorporated. Bah, humbug! They can, however, provide this benefit for their employees.

Author's note: Company-provided taxis and chauffeurs may become fully deductible as a working-condition fringe benefit if these services are provided for deductible stops. For example, if you are meeting various clients, a taxi or chauffeur may be provided to drive you to each business stop.

However, any payments made for tax planning, tax preparation, or stock brokerage for an employee will be taxable to the employee.

The Bottom Line

Although this fringe benefit is interesting, it has a very limited use, and corporate owners and officers will not be able to use it unless they're not highly compensated. Moreover, any employee who wants to use this benefit must be subject to the Fair Labor Standards Act and be paid for overtime. Thus it would be available to traditional employees. The next fringe benefit, in Chapter 14, has some similarities but will be more widely useful.

Notes

1. Section 132(d) of the IRC.
2. Letter Ruling 199929043.
3. Section 1.131-5q of the ITR.
4. Letter Ruling 199929043 and Section 1.132-1(b) of the ITR.
5. Letter Ruling 199929043.
6. Section 1.132-5n of the ITR.
7. Ibid.
8. Section 132(d)(1) of the IRC.
9. Section 132(j)(1) of the IRC.
10. Section 129(a)(1) of the IRC.
11. Sections 129(a)(2) and 129(b)(1) of the IRC.
12. Sections 129 (e)(3) and 129(e)(4) of the IRC.
13. Section 129(a)(2) of the IRC.
14. Section 129(c) of the IRC.
15. Section 137(b)(1) of the IRC. See also American Taxpayer Relief Law.
16. Section 137(a) of the IRC. See also Rev. Proc. 2014-61.
17. Sections 137(b) and 137(c) of the IRC. See also Rev. Proc. 2013-15 IRB 444 and American Taxpayer Relief Law. See also Rev. Proc. 2015-53.
18. Sections 212 and 213 of the IRC.
19. Section 106(a) of the IRC. In 2002, the deduction for self-employed businesses and for partnerships was 70 percent of the premium.
20. Section 1.105-5(a) of the ITR.
21. Section 7702B(a)(1) of the IRC.
22. Revenue Ruling 67-360, 1967-2 CB 71.
23. Letter Rulings 9603011 and 9850011.

24. Revenue Ruling 61-146, 1961-2 CB 25.
25. Section 9802 of the IRS.
26. *Seidel v. Commissioner,* T.C. Memo 1971-238.
27. Sections 105(a) and 105(c) of the IRC.
28. Section 105 of the IRC.
29. Sections 105(a) of the IRC and 1.104-1(a) of the ITR.
30. Letter Rulings 8027088 and 9741035.
31. Sections 105(g), 105(b), and 137(a) of the IRC and Letter Ruling 9320004.
32. Section 1.132-6(f) of the ITR.
33. Section 132(e)(1) of the IRC.
34. Section 1.132-6(e) of the ITR.
35. Section 1.132-6(d)(1) of the ITR.
36. Section 1.132-6(d)(2) of the ITR.
37. Section 132(a)(2) of the IRC.
38. Sections 132(K) and 132(c)(1)(B) of the IRC.
39. Section 1.132-3(e) of the ITR.
40. Sections 132(c)(1) and 132(k) of the IRC.
41. Section 1.132-8T(b)(3) of the ITR.
42. Section 132(j)(4)(B) of the IRC.
43. Section 1.132-1(3) of the ITR.
44. Section 1.132-1(e)(4) of the ITR and Letter Ruling 9029026.
45. Section 132(a)(7) of the IRC.
46. Section 132(m)(2) of the IRC.
47. Section 7872(a)(1) of the IRC.
48. Section 7872(c)(3)(A) of the IRC.
49. Section 7872(f)(10) of the IRC.
50. Sections 1.7872-5T(a) and 1.7872-5T(b) of the ITR.
51. Ibid.
52. Section 1.7872-5T(c)(1)(i) of the ITR.
53. Section 1.7872-5T(c)(1) of the ITR.
54. Sections 127(a)(1) and 127(c) of the IRC.
55. Section 1.132-1(f) of the ITR.
56. Section 1.132-5(d)(2) of the ITR.
57. IRS Publication 508 (2000), p. 6.
58. Section 274(a)(3) of the IRC.
59. Section 1.132-5(s)(1) of the ITR.
60. Sections 1.132-5(s)(1) and 1.132-5(s)(3), ex 1 of the ITR.
61. Ibid.
62. Section 1.132-5(s)(3) of the ITR.
63. Revenue Ruling 63-144, Q&A 48, 1963-2 CB 129.
64. Section 1.132-5(t)(1) of the ITR.
65. Section 274(m)(3) of the IRC.
66. Payments for the spouse's expenses would be tax-free as a working-condition fringe benefit. See also Section 1.132-5T(1) of the ITR.
67. *Harris Bradley v. Commissioner,* 324 F.2d 610 (4th Cir. 1963).
68. Section 1.165-9(a) of the ITR.
69. See footnote 67 and Letter Ruling 9626026.
70. *Thomas L. Karston*, T.C. Memo 1975-2000.

71. Sections 132(a) and 217 of the IRC. See 2017 TCJA Section 11048.
72. Section 1.61-21(k) of the ITR.
73. Section 1.61-21(k)(5) of the ITR.
74. Section 1.61-21(k)(6) of the ITR.

14

Fringe Benefits You Will Love, Part 2

Corporate-Provided Transit Passes, Vanpools, and Parking

This fringe benefit really deals with three related benefits: corporate-provided vanpools, transit passes, and parking. Prior to the implementation of the Tax Cuts and Jobs Act, companies were allowed to deduct the cost of providing transit passes and parking. Employees could avoid taxation on these benefits up to $260 per month for transit passes and parking.[1]

However, as a result of the Tax Cuts and Jobs Act, the law repealed an employer's ability to deduct these costs after December 31, 2017[2]. However, Employers may still deduct expenses incurred that are necessary to ensure the safety of an employee (e.g., late-night transportation) and business travel expenses.

Author's note: Employees, on the other hand, still may elect a pretax salary deferral and/or exclude from income employer-provided transit passes, qualified parking, or transportation in a commuter highway vehicle.

> **Chapter Overview**
> - Understand how to get corporate-provided parking and transit passes, tax-free.
> - Learn how to get company-provided automobiles either tax-free or at a very low cost (such as $1.50 each way).
> - Learn why cafeteria plans can result in thousands of dollars of tax-free fringe benefits and give a host of wonderful benefits.
> - Learn how to get property such as stock tax-free for services rendered.
> - Learn about providing the same top benefit that CEOs of major companies get—incentive stock options.
> - Learn how to provide meals and eating facilities tax-free. Yum, yum.
> - Learn why every business should set up a qualified profit-sharing plan, a SEP, or a SIMPLE IRA and stash away a ton of money tax-free.

Qualified Transit Passes

Congress wanted to encourage workers to use mass transit. Accordingly, prior to the implementation of the TCJA, companies could provide transit passes or vouchers for mass transit tax-free to their employees, up to $260 per month for each employee who would use it. Again, this benefit was not available tax-free to self-employed individuals, independent contractors, or 2 percent or more stockholders in an S corporation; however, you could discriminate when providing these benefits. In addition, as with the other benefits noted earlier, self-employed owners and S corporations could provide this benefit to their employees, just not to the owners.

As noted above, however, companies can NOT deduct the cost of these transit passes after December 31, 2017.[3] Employees, however, can elect to receive up to $260 per month for transit passes and parking tax-free.[4] If, however, you are a 2 percent or greater stockholder of an S corporation, the value of the transit passes are fully taxable for both income tax and FICA taxes.[5]

Example: Big Bucks Corporation provides qualified transit passes of $260 per month to their employees. Big Bucks cannot deduct these costs, but the employees can elect to receive up to $260 per month tax-free.

Sandy's tax tip: Although owners of 2 percent or more of the stock of an S corporation can't receive the full transit pass benefit, they can receive up to $21 of transit pass benefits (by paying the difference, if any) as a de minimis fringe benefit. This may not seem like much, but it's an extra $21 per month that you can get tax-free.

Qualified Parking

In addition to qualified transit passes, corporations can provide qualified parking to any employee, as noted earlier subject to the same tax consequences as transit passes. As with transit passes, a company can provide qualified parking up to $260 per month on a tax-free basis if an election is made by the employee. However, no deduction will result to the company providing these passes.[6] Again, this can't be provided to self-employed people, independent contractors, or 2 percent or more stockholders in an S corporation. If, however, you are the sole owner of a regular (C) corporation, you can receive this benefit.

Author's note: As you can see, being a regular corporation gives some better fringe benefits to major stockholders and senior officers. However, this has to be compared with the potential savings in Social Security with an S corporation and the other drawbacks to being an S corporation. (See Chapters 9 and 11.)

The Bottom Line

Transit passes, and free parking are great fringe benefits but their benefit is reduced with the elimination of the deductions. Vanpools have some strict requirements on seating and use by employees.

All benefits noted here, however, don't apply to sole proprietors and 2 percent or more stockholders of S corporations; although the stockholders of an S corporation can have up to $21 of transit passes. C corporations, can have these benefits provided to even the owners and senior officers.

Company-Provided Vehicles

There seems to be a great misunderstanding about how company-provided vehicles are taxed. This section will clarify most questions that I have received over the years.

The general rule is that when a corporation provides a company vehicle, the employee is taxable on the personal use of the vehicle.[7]

Example: Financial Destiny is a corporation owned by Matt that conducts a multilevel business. The corporation provides Matt with a nice Mercedes and pays all the bills. Assuming that Matt uses the car 75 percent for business, he would be taxed on his personal use of 25 percent.

Author's note: I've emphasized throughout this book the importance of keeping a good tax diary or tax organizer or tax tracker. When company cars are provided, keeping a good tax organizer becomes twice as important because it will document how much of the car was used for business and how much was used personally, which is the taxable portion. It's critical, then, for every employee who receives a company vehicle to meticulously document business versus personal use.

This is the easy part of the discussion and the part that most people probably know best. But how do you compute what's taxable on personal use?

There are three methods of calculating the taxable portion of a vehicle based on personal use. These approaches provide very different results. Use the approach that provides the least amount of taxable income if—and this is a big *if*—you can use the approach.

Method One: Annual Lease Value Method

This is the general rule that the Internal Revenue Service (IRS) wants most companies and employees to use.[8] Since the IRS likes it, you probably can guess that it's the least beneficial to employees because it maximizes the amount of taxable income.

Author's note: In case I didn't make it clear, if one of the other methods is available to you or your employees, don't use this method! The table used in this method is found in Figure 14-1.

For an automobile with a fair market value greater than $59,999, the annual lease value is (25 percent × fair market value) + $500.

To use this table, find the fair market value of the vehicle provided, and then use the annual lease value that corresponds with the fair market value times the personal use. If

Automobile Market Value	Fair Annual Lease Value	Automobile Market Value	Fair Annual Lease Value
$0-$999	$600	22,000-22,999	6,100
1,000-1,999	850	23,000-23,999	6,350
2,000-2,999	1,100	24,000-24,999	6,600
3,000-3,999	1,350	25,000-25,999	6,850
4,000-4,999	1,600	26,000-27,999	7,250
5,000-5,999	1,850	28,000-29,999	7,750
6,000-6,999	2,100	30,000-31,999	8,250
7,000-7,999	2,350	32,000-33,999	8,750
8,000-8,999	2,600	34,000-35,999	9,250
9,000-9,999	2,850	36,000-37,999	9,750
10,000-10,999	3,100	38,000-39,999	10,250
11,000-11,999	3,350	40,000-41,999	10,750
12,000-12,999	3,600	42,000-43,999	11,250
13,000-13,999	3,850	44,000-45,999	11,750
14,000-14,999	4,100	46,000-47,999	12,250
15,000-15,999	4,350	48,000-49,999	12,750
16,000-16,999	4,600	50,000-51,999	13,250
17,000-17,999	4,850	52,000-53,999	13,750
18,000-18,999	5,100	54,000-55,999	14,250
19,000-19,999	5,350	56,000-57,999	14,750
20,000-20,999	5,600	58,000-59,999	15,250
21,000-21,999	5,850		

Figure 14-1. Table for calculating fair annual lease value from IRS Regulation 1.61-21(d)(iii).

the vehicle is owned, that value is normally the cost of the vehicle plus any taxes.[9] The following example will illustrate this.

Example: If Matt's corporation purchases a BMW for $38,000 (which includes all applicable taxes), the annual lease value would be $10,250. If his personal use were 25 percent, he would record as additional compensation $2,562.50 (25 percent of $10,250).

The annual lease method includes insurance and repairs and doesn't get reduced if the employee pays any part of the insurance or repairs. Thus, if you're using the annual lease method, *don't* have the employee pay the insurance or repairs. Have the corporation pay these.

Strangely, however, the annual lease approach does not include gas. If the employer provides the gas, the receiving employee is taxed at 5.5 cents per mile,[10] which is a very good deal. However, if the employer reimburses an employee for the gas, then the employee is taxed on the full reimbursement.

Example: Matt's corporation pays for the gas on his BMW. Matt normally gets 15 miles to the gallon and pays $4.00 per gallon. If he's taxed using the annual lease method, he would pay tax at only 5.5 cents per mile (or 82.5 cents per gallon) driven in the U.S. The remaining cost of $3.175 per gallon would not be taxable. Not a bad deal! If, however, Matt gets reimbursed for the gasoline, he would pay tax at the full $4.00 per gallon on any personal mileage.

Author's note: If you're subject to the annual lease method, have your corporation provide the gas by obtaining a corporate credit or gas card.

Method Two: The Cents-per-Mile Method

The good news is that this second method results in less tax than the annual lease method. The bad news is that it's limited to inexpensive cars.

To use this method, you must meet the following three criteria:[11]

- The cost of the vehicle must be no more than $15,600 for passenger automobiles and $17,600 for trucks or vans.
- The company reasonably expects that the vehicle will be driven regularly for its business by the employee, which means that generally more than 50 percent of the mileage must be for business,[12] or that it will be used as a commuter highway vehicle, or that the employee will put on at least 10,000 miles and use it for commuting.
- If the car is provided for less than a year, then all mileage requirements are prorated.[13]

Example: Lori Ann owns a corporation that she uses for her consulting business. If the corporation provides her with a car for only half the year, all mileage requirements are prorated. Thus, under the usage test, she needs to put on only 5,000 miles.

Example: Lori Ann buys a used car for $12,000. As long as she either uses it more than 50 percent for business or regularly commutes in the car and drives it at least 10,000 miles per year, she can use the cents-per-mile method.

Author's note: I don't know what the members of Congress were thinking when they placed a $15,600/$17,600 cost limit on the cents-per-mile method. I guess this method is ideal for cheap cars, such as Daewoo, Kia, or Suzuki, or used cars. In addition, keeping a good tax organizer or diary will establish your 50 percent business usage or that you drove over 10,000 miles.

If this isn't a good enough deal, the cents-per-mile method *includes* insurance plus repairs and company-provided fuel. Thus anyone who uses this method should not be paying for any of this. Let the corporation pay for all these items.

Method Three: The Commuting Value Method

This may be the best and cheapest method to be taxed on a company car; since Congress makes the rules, this method is the most limited for owners and officers. The main benefit is that you're taxed only at a ridiculously cheap flat rate of $1.50 each way for commuting.

To use this method, however, you must meet the following four criteria:[14]

- The company must own the vehicle, not lease it.
- The employee must use the vehicle for commuting to work.
- The company must provide in writing that any employee must use it for business and cannot use the vehicle for personal use. (This part is easy.)
- Except for de minimis use, the employee in fact doesn't use the car for personal purposes.

Here's the final catch: The employee cannot be a director or officer who earns at least $110,000 for 2018, any employee who earns at least $220,000 for 2018, or a 1 percent or more stockholder. In addition, this method is available only to company-owned cars. Thus, sole proprietorships can't use this method for the owner but can use it for an employee of the proprietorship.

Example: Fred owns a corporation that sells products. If he provides himself with a car, he cannot use the commuting method because he owns more than 1 percent of the stock or more than 1 percent of the ownership of the business.

Author's note: The restriction that's applicable to 1 percent owners applies to any type of entity, even regular corporations, which is very unusual.

The Bottom Line

- If your corporation provides you or an employee with a vehicle, it's vital to maintain a good tax diary showing business usage. This will drastically cut back on what's taxable to you or the employee.
- Anyone who receives a corporate-owned or leased car is taxed on the fair market value of the personal use. Business usage is not taxable.
- The annual lease method is the general way that you would compute the taxable portion of the personal use—and the most expensive method. If you use it, don't pay for repairs or insurance because they're included in what is being taxed to you.
- The cents-per-mile method is great, but it's available only for cheap cars that cost $15,600 or less or trucks and vans that cost under $17,600. I wonder what most members of Congress are driving these days?
- The $1.50-per-commute approach is fabulous, but it doesn't apply to directors, officers who make at least $110,000, employees who make at least $220,000 for 2016, or 1 percent or more stockholders. Thus, you the owner of a self-employed business can't use this method.
- A car can be provided on a discriminatory basis.

A Cafeteria Plan Can Provide Thousands of Dollars of Tax-Free Benefits

How would you like to get a host of fringe benefits for yourself and your employees tax-free by implementing one benefit? You can with what's known as a *cafeteria plan*. A cafeteria plan, as its name suggests, allows employees to pick and choose among benefit options. In fact, there must be at least two options to choose from.[15] Each employee then chooses specific benefits that he or she wishes to have. There are lots of potential choices; in fact, cafeteria plans can provide the following benefits as choices in the plan:

- Medical insurance
- Long-term care insurance
- Disability insurance
- Group term life insurance
- Dependent-care assistance
- Qualified pension or profit-sharing plan
- Adoption assistance[16]
- Qualified group legal services (Although this isn't clear, it seems to be allowed in a cafeteria plan. Outside of one, however, these benefits would not be tax-free.)
- Credits for additional paid vacation weeks

Example: You make $50,000 per year from your corporation and have $2,000 in unused credits. If you wish, you can take $1,000 of the credits in cash and an extra week of vacation in addition to the normal two weeks provided by the company. This would result in taxable income of $51,000 and three weeks vacation.

Author's note: Cafeteria plans are almost the ideal benefit. By implementing one benefit, you can offer your employees many benefits that I've discussed; thus you will save a lot of time, legal and accounting fees, and money. The only problem, which will be discussed below, is that Congress stupidly limited the cafeteria plan from helping most owners and officers of a business. Because a cafeteria plan generally is available for nonowner employees, many small businesses have not implemented cafeteria plans. I guess the thinking of small-business owners is that "if I can't benefit, I won't use it for my employees either."

In 2018, the maximum deferral for employee contributions is $2,650. However, up to $500 of unused funds can be carried over to next year's use. This is different from the older rules for cafeteria plans, which didn't allow for any carryover of unused funds.

Criteria for Bulletproofing This Benefit from the IRS[17]

- It generally must be provided to all employees on a nondiscriminatory basis, although you can have a waiting period for eligibility of up to three years.[18]

Author's note: Actually, there's a limited amount of discrimination allowed. You can worry yourself and your accountant about this to see if you meet the various percentage tests. I suggest, however, that you simply cover everyone equally who has at least three years of service and let your accountant live longer.

- The participants must choose from two or more options.
- The participants must make a specific election of the benefits they're choosing and make this election at the beginning of the year or when they start work, whichever comes first.
- No employee is required to complete more than three years of employment.
- The cafeteria plan must be in writing and contain specific information about the plan. In other words, you have to notify your employees about all the choices and what they have to do in order to elect various options. You just can't keep it quiet and hope that they choose nothing. Sorry, that won't work.
- The plan cannot discriminate in the benefits provided.
- Over 25 percent of the total of the nontaxable benefits cannot go to "key employees." This is a group that comprises:
  - Highly compensated employees (who generally make over $120,000)
  - Officers
  - Individuals who own more than 5 percent of the stock
  - Spouses and dependents of anyone noted above

Author's note: Thus, it's difficult, but not impossible, to benefit the owners of the business with a cafeteria plan, even if it doesn't discriminate, unless you earn less than $120,000 in taxable compensation.

Example: Happysue Corporation, a corporation formed for the practice of law, provides all employees with credits of up to $10,000. They can use these credits as they like to obtain various benefits, such as medical insurance, pensions, and vacations. If Happysue doesn't discriminate on the eligibility for this benefit and the owners/key employees receive less than 25 percent of all the actual benefits used, this plan will meet the IRS requirements.

The Bottom Line

A cafeteria plan is a fabulous plan for rank-and-file employees and even for owners if the corporation doesn't discriminate and doesn't provide more than 25 percent of the benefits to the owners or certain key or highly compensated employees.

Receipt of Restricted Property and Restricted Stock Tax-Free for Services Rendered

Most small businesses are not publicly traded; thus they do not normally provide stock, especially with the securities rules requiring lots of legal work in order to provide stock legally. This would be especially true if one or two people own all the stock because there would be no incentive to giving the owners more stock. However, there are occasions when a company agrees to provide stock or other property to an employee for future services.

Generally, employees are taxed when they receive the stock or other property unless there's a "substantial risk of forfeiture."[19] What this means is that an employee who receives restricted stock is not taxed on it if he or she has to perform future service in order to sell the stock or benefit from it. Taxation ordinarily would occur at the *earlier* of two dates: when the employee sells the stock or when the risk of forfeiture ends. The employee is taxed at ordinary income rates on the fair market value of the stock at this time. Any appreciation thereafter would be a capital gain.

Example: Anita is a staff member of a small advertising consulting corporation, Better Sales or Else, Inc. (otherwise known as BESI). If she receives 100 shares of stock worth $10,000 today but she must work for two years in order to be able to sell it or pledge it for a loan, she's not taxed on the stock because there's a substantial risk of forfeiture. She may not work another two years for BESI. If in two years, when the risk of forfeiture ceases, the stock is now worth double, she would be taxed on the whole $20,000 as ordinary income.

Author's note: When you receive restricted stock with a risk of forfeiture, you have the option of paying tax on the stock now. If you do this, you then would report any appreciation in the future as capital gain and not as ordinary income.[20] This can be a two-edged knife because the stock might depreciate after you paid tax on a higher value. Even worse, you must make this election within 30 days of the date of the transfer of restricted stock. Thus make this election only with a lot of care.

Phantom Stock

Many small businesses want to make employees feel that they own "a piece of the rock." However, if they give the employees stock, there are all sorts of legal security problems that require heavy legal fees in order to comply with. However, some great tax attorney came up with the concept of phantom stock in order to avoid all these security and legal issues.

Phantom stock is simply a promise of a bonus equivalent to either the value of company shares or the increase in that value over a period of time. Phantom stock is treated as if the employees received actual shares in the company. If the stock appreciates in the future, the employees will be paid that appreciation. They might even be eligible to receive dividends. Thus it's like owning the stock without getting any actual shares. Phantom stock allows employees to participate in the appreciation of their employer's stock. Phantom stock is taxed much like any other cash bonus, as ordinary income at the time it's received.

Criteria for Bulletproofing This Benefit from the IRS

The IRS has stated that employees are not taxed on any phantom stock or appreciation until they actually receive payment, under two conditions:

- The employer owns and is the beneficiary of any assets or stock that this benefit is based on.
- The stock or assets are subject to the employer's general creditors.[21]

In other words, the corporation keeps any stock in treasury and doesn't issue it to the employees.

Example: I will use my company as an example. The Tax Reduction Institute (TRI) of Germantown, Maryland, wanted to give our staff the feeling that they participate in the growth and benefits of our company. Thus I provided some employees with phantom stock. If there is any sale of the company, or if we go public, any price received above what it would be worth at the time of the grant would go to them. When they receive this benefit, they will pay tax, and TRI will get the deduction.

Author's note: There are two observations about both phantom and restricted stock. First, the stock can be given to anyone, even if the benefit discriminates in favor of officers and highly compensated employees. Second, no deduction accrues to the employer until payment is made on the phantom stock or until the employee is taxed on the restricted stock.

The Bottom Line

Phantom stock is a greatly underused fringe benefit. It usually makes employees feel as if they are owners (which, in essence, they are) yet doesn't involve any significant legal fees to provide as with regular stock. It also can be combined with a restriction that the employees must work a certain number of years, thus tying the employee to the company and increasing retention.

Qualified Stock Options

How would you like to provide your employees with the same incentives as receiving phantom or restricted stock but with the employees taxed only at capital gains rates? This is the major benefit of providing qualified stock options, the most significant benefit that public companies are using for their top management.

What Are Stock Options (Calls)?

The stock options that we are discussing are not stock. They give the employee the right to purchase the stock at a fixed price over some period of time.

Example: Mary has the right for two years to buy company stock for $100 per share. Assuming that the stock goes to $150 per share, Mary has the right to purchase this stock for only $100 per share. This is called *exercising the option*. The price that she gets to pay ($100) is called the *strike price*. The option will benefit Mary if the stock appreciates in value. If it decreases in value below the strike price, she won't exercise the option. Who would pay more for a stock than it's worth?

Tax Consequences

The employer gets no deduction on the grant or exercise of these options by the employee.[22]

Author's note: Since the corporation gets no deduction on either the grant or the exercise of these options, this is not my favorite benefit for corporations. However, for employees, this is a terrific benefit.

When the employee sells the option, as long as he or she has held it for a certain period, to be discussed below, all gain is long-term capital gain.[23]

You may have read about companies that have overstated their earnings in order to boost their stock values. The use of qualified stock options may have been a major factor in this overstatement of earnings because qualified stock options aren't deductible by the corporation either on grant of the option or on the exercise of the option. Depending on the size of the options, this can cause a substantial overstatement of earnings.

Criteria for Bulletproofing This Benefit from the IRS

Since there are such great benefits to employees, you probably can guess that Congress has lots of requirements in order to obtain these nice benefits. If you thought this, you made a good assumption. If you don't do it right, these benefits will be treated as the receipt of any other stock or option and will be taxable to the employee as ordinary income. Thus you must follow everything said in this book to the letter!

The following requirements are necessary to obtain all the wonderful tax benefits promised above:[24]

- There must be a written plan to offer the option with an option price and a set period of time during which the employee can buy the stock. The plan should show the total number of shares that will be issued and which employees are eligible to receive the options.
- It must be stock of the employer, the employer's parent, or a subsidiary of the employer.
- There must be a formal stockholder approval of the plan, even if all the stock is owned by one person or family within 12 months before or after the plan is adopted.
- The option must be granted within 10 years of the *earlier* of two dates—the date the corporation adopts the incentive stock options plan or the date that the shareholders approve the plan.

Author's note: I usually recommend that the option be granted within nine years of the earlier of the two dates in order to avoid any potential problem. Thus, there should never be a mistake.

- The written plan must provide that the employee must exercise the option within 10 years of the grant of the option.

Example: Amy receives an option on December 31, 2018. She must exercise the option by December 30, 2028.

- The option price must be at the fair market value of the stock at the time of the grant using any reasonable valuation method.[25]

Example: Thus, if the stock in a corporation is worth $100 per share based on an appraisal, the employee must pay the strike price of at least $100 per share in order for the options to be deemed qualified stock options.

- The option can be exercised only by the employee who was given the option. If the recipient dies before exercising the option, his or her estate or the beneficiary named in his or her will can exercise the option.

Author's note: Thus this option cannot be transferred.

- The employee can't have owned 10 percent or more of the voting power of the stock at the time the option was granted.[26] Thus incentive stock options won't benefit many small corporate owners. It's for the employees who either don't already own stock or own less than 10 percent of the stock.

Author's note: Just like most things in life, there are exceptions. A 10 percent or more stockholder can get incentive stock options if the strike price is 110 percent of the fair market value *and* the option can't be exercised more than five years from the date of the grant.[27]

- The total value of optioned stock can't exceed $100,000 per calendar year.

Example: Sonia has the right to exercise 1,000 shares at $100 per share. This would fall within the $100,000 limit. If she had the right to exercise 2,000 shares, only 1,000 shares would qualify as incentive stock options.

In addition, you have two holding periods to worry about.

- You must *not sell* stock for at least two years after the option is granted.
- You must hold the stock for at least one year after you actually receive the stock.

Sandy's warning: If you don't hold the stock long enough, you'll be taxed on the gain as ordinary income when you sell it. Yuck! Take my warning to heart.

Author's note: Whew! I told you that there were all kinds of strict congressional requirements. However, if both the corporation and the employees meet the rules, then the employee really comes out ahead. But if the employee doesn't hold the stock long enough and therefore makes a sale that disqualifies the option, the proceeds from the sale are considered as ordinary income, and the corporation obtains a deduction. I can almost hear most corporate owners wishing for their employees to make a mistake on the holding period when they sell the stock, so the corporation can obtain a deduction.

The Bottom Line

Incentive stock options are fabulous for employees in that income from selling them is taxed at the long-term capital gains rate, which is currently only 20 percent, rather than at regular tax rates, which go up to 39.6 percent plus a Medicare surcharge.

New Rule for Restricted Stock: Under the new TCJA, employees may elect[28] to defer inclusion of income from restricted stock to a leter year. The year that they report income can be deferred to the earliest of:

1. The first date that the qualified stock becomes transferable, or
2. The date that the employee becomes an excluded employee (a 1 percent stock-holder or has been the corporation's chief executive officer or who bears a family relationship to one of these, or was one of the four highest compensated officers of the corporation), or
3. The first date on which any stock of the corporation that issued the qualified stock becomes readily tradable on an established securities market), or
4. The date that's five years after the first date the employee's rights in the stock are transferable or aren't subject to a substantial risk of forfeiture, whichever occurs earlier, or
5. The date on which the employee revokes (at the time and in the manner that IRS provides) the Code Sec. 83(i) election with respect to the stock

Author's note: This extension to a potential five-year deferral of income is based on an election by the employee. This, however, is based on the fact that she or he doesn't meet one of the exceptions noted above.

Tax-Free Lodging

Under limited conditions, a company can provide tax-free housing to its employees. This is a great benefit if it's available to your business.

Criteria for Bulletproofing This Benefit from the IRS

You can provide lodging and meals to any employee if you meet the following conditions:[29]

- The lodging is for the convenience of the employer.
- The lodging and/or food is provided on the business premises of the company.
- The lodging must be accepted by the employee as a condition of employment.

One of the big issues is, "What does *convenience of the employer* mean?" This can be proven in a variety of ways. If the employee is on 24-hour call and must be available for duty, this would qualify, or if the employee can't perform the services unless the lodging is furnished, this would qualify.[30]

Example: A prison guard is required to live on the premises in accommodations supplied by the government. The guard must be available if there's a prison riot or break. The lodging can be provided tax-free.

Example: James and Sheila accept a position as managers of a bed-and-breakfast facility. Their job is to manage the facility, supervise the housekeeping to ensure clean rooms, and provide breakfast for guests. They're required to stay in the facility and handle emergencies. Their lodging and food would be tax-free.

Author's note: In order to have the meals and/or lodging tax-free, the employer must pay for them and provide them directly.[31] Do not have the company reimburse for any meals or lodging.

Exclusion for Meals

As you might expect, the exclusion for meals alone is a bit easier; meals only have to be provided for the convenience of the employer and furnished for a noncompensatory business reason.[32] There are a number of situations where employers can provide tax-free meals. In fact, most small businesses will be able to use this benefit very much.

The following are some illustrative examples of situations in which your company can provide tax-free meals to employees:

Short business meal during working hours.[33] A corporation can provide meals to employees during working hours if there's a required short lunch period, which is usually less than 45 minutes. However, there's a catch: The employees cannot eat elsewhere in the short time allowed for lunch.

Example: Many times my staff is required to break for lunch no longer than 30 minutes because of the number of customers calling at lunchtime. We normally could furnish meals tax-free to my staff even though there's a Burger King near us. (Who doesn't have a Burger King or McDonald's near them?) The reason is that there's little chance that my staff would be able to stand in line, get their meals, and then eat within the short break. Thus we could furnish employees lunch on these crunch days tax-free.

Example: Alice, John, and Mary work for a Sockittotheirs, Inc. The office is located on the East Coast. During lunch, usually around 12 p.m., many customers from the West Coast call up the company. Because there's a great deal of work during the lunch periods every day, the company can provide free meals.

Meals furnished for employees who are required to live on premises. If an employee can be provided tax-free lodging, as discussed earlier, because he or she is required to live on the company premises as a condition of the job, the company also can provide tax-free meals as part of the deal.[34]

Meals furnished to restaurant employees are almost always tax-free, whether furnished before, during, or after their shift.[35]

Author's note: It amazes me that more restaurants aren't using this benefit more often. It would be a great tax-free fringe benefit and a great way to retain employees.

Meals can be furnished tax-free if the employee is available for emergency calls during his or her lunch period. Thus, if the company provides an employee with meals at his or her desk in order to field calls that come in during lunch, these meals are tax-free.[36] To receive this tax-free benefit, the employee can't perform personal errands during the lunch period.

Example: A medical corporation provides lunch for all staff members and the doctors because emergencies occur during the day, and the corporation wants the staff available for these problems. Lunch can be provided tax-free.

Meals can be furnished if there are insufficient eating facilities near the workplace.[37] If employees have few or no facilities for lunch within a reasonable distance of work, the company can provide meals. It certainly will be important to show that you've checked the Yellow Pages for eating facilities in the area and made estimates on how long it would take to get to and from any facility and to eat lunch there.

Meals furnished to over 50 percent of all employees will be tax-free. This is a great way for any company to provide meals tax-free. As long as the company furnishes the meals on the premises to over 50 percent of all employees, the meals are tax-free.[38]

Example: A hospital provides 210 staff members out of the total 230 staff members and doctors with free meals. Supposedly it's to keep them available for emergencies, but these emergencies rarely occur. However, because the hospital provides free meals to more than half the employees, all meals provided are tax-free to the staff.[39]

Example: We at the Tax Reduction Institute provide a free lunch once a month and discuss business over lunch. Since we provide lunch to more than half the employees, all meals are tax-free, even to me.

Lunch conferences are deductible, even outside the company premises and even if only to senior officers.[40] There is one important case that you'll like. A company provided daily lunches for its officers where attendance was compulsory. The lunches were in a hotel conference room rented by the corporation. The officers discussed daily events and any upcoming activities necessary for the day and shared their experiences. The tax court allowed the corporation to provide tax-free meals even though it was done off the company premises and was done daily.

Author's note: You should notice that meals, especially for good business reasons, can be furnished to officers and directors on a discriminatory basis.

Other Interesting Exceptions for Meals

There was an interesting case that may provide a lot of small-business owners with tax-free meals and company provided housing, *F. R. McDowell*.[41] It involved a husband and a wife who were the sole owners of a large farm, which was leased to a corporation owned by McDowell's children. Thus the only business that the McDowells' corporation had was to lease out the land. The tenant, the children's corporation, was engaged in ranching operations and was required to keep the buildings and other improvements in good condition. McDowell retained the right to inspect the property. McDowell actually lived on the land through most of the year and made daily inspections of the leased land. The tax court held that the meals and lodging furnished by the corporation to the McDowells were tax-free.

What does this mean to you? This case has many implications. Here are some examples of how you may use this case to your advantage.

Example: Tiffany is an antique dealer. She runs her business out of her home using a corporation. She's required to work out of her home and to provide security for the antiques. She receives phone calls at home from potential customers and past customers. Tiffany may have her corporation provide housing and meals for her business.

Author's note: Although there is no case on this, I wonder what would happen in this hypothetical situation. A network marketing professional runs her network marketing business out of her home using a corporation. At her home she gets calls daily from distributors and from customers. She meets with her distributors at least weekly and stores inventory and marketing materials in her home. Her corporation provides that she must be available to handle all calls on a 24-hour basis. It would appear that, based on the *McDowell* case, she might be able to receive corporate meals and lodging tax-free. Let me warn you, however, that there is no case on this. Thus this benefit may need to be tested in the courts.

Author's note: This would work only for network marketers and other home-based business owners who are incorporated. It will not work for the owners of a sole proprietorship.

Finally, meal expenses incurred for the convenience of the employer are normally 50 percent deductible under the new TCJA.

Qualified Pension and Profit-Sharing Plans

Without question, this may be the most important fringe benefit that you can provide. It not only allows a large deduction but also can provide a great deal of legal protection against lawsuits because some qualified plans are exempt from creditors.

Author's note: Everyone should be stashing away at least 10 percent of what they make for retirement. Having a qualified plan is a great way for most people to achieve their retirement goals. There are wide varieties of plans; in fact, I could also write a book on just this one topic. However, to keep this topic manageable, I want to discuss the most popular and most recommended plans among small businesses today.

Profit-Sharing Plan

This plan allows you to put away in any business for any employee up to 25 percent of his or her wages or, if you're self-employed, up to 25 percent of the net income of the company. There's a maximum contribution of $55,000 for 2018 per employee.[42]

What's great about a profit-sharing plan is its flexibility: The amount of an employee's wages that you can contribute can vary from year to year. Thus, if you want to contribute 25 percent of all wages to the plan in one year but only 10 percent in a less profitable year, you can do so. Thus flexibility is the name of the game with profit-sharing plans.

I would unqualifiedly recommend this plan to all business owners. However, there are some drawbacks to this plan. First, it's nondiscriminatory. You generally must cover all full-time employees. You can have a three-year waiting period before coverage, but all employees must be covered under the plan. Second, as with most qualified plans, these are expensive to set up and require filing expensive forms with the IRS, thus enriching your accountant.

Author's note: Despite the disadvantages of a profit-sharing plan, I like them a lot, especially because of their tremendous flexibility. This is one plan that you should consider.

Simplified Employee Pension (SEP) Plan

In many ways, this plan is similar to a profit-sharing plan. It allows you to contribute up to 25 percent of your net income if you're self-employed or 25 percent of an employee's wages. Again, this plan has a maximum contribution limit of $55,000 for 2018.[43]

As with a profit-sharing plan, a company can vary its contribution from year to year. Thus a company can contribute up to 25 percent of wages this year and much less or even nothing next year. It thus has the same flexibility as profit-sharing plans. However, a SEP has some benefits over a profit-sharing plan. First, SEPs are inexpensive to set up. You simply fill out IRS Form 5305-SEP, but you don't file it with the IRS; you keep the form with the company records. Second, there are no complex annual filings as with other qualified plans, so administrative expenses are very low.

A SEP plan, however, has the same drawbacks as a profit-sharing plan in that it is nondiscriminatory.

Author's note: I love SEPs. If you have few or no employees, a simplified employee pension is the way to go. This also can be used by sole proprietorships.

Defined-Benefit Plan

This is a very different type of qualified plan. Most plans require you to contribute a set percentage of wages. A defined-benefit plan uses an actuary to compute how much you or your employees may contribute in order to get a set retirement income. Thus you figure out how much you need at retirement and, in effect, work backwards. Because of this, a defined-benefit plan normally allows you to contribute much more than other plans, especially if the worker is 50 years of age or older. Since the older the worker, the less time there is available to build up to the desired goal, older workers can contribute much more than younger workers. The maximum yearly contribution to the defined-benefit plan is a whopping $220,000 in 2018.[44]

With this wonderfully high contribution limit, you would think that I would be wholeheartedly recommending this plan. However, this is not the case because this plan has two major drawbacks. First, a defined-benefit plan is the most administratively expensive plan available. You need not only a good accountant to file some complicated forms but also a yearly actuary to design contributions each year. Second, if this isn't bad enough, there's very little flexibility to this plan. You must contribute a set amount each year, as determined by the actuary, regardless of profitability. Given their lack of flexibility, I normally don't recommend defined-benefit plans.

Author's note: A defined-benefit plan is ideal for older owners who are 50 years of age or older and for firms that have net incomes that don't decrease significantly from year to year.

SIMPLE IRAs

In many ways, this is my favorite plan, especially if you have employees. This also works for all sole proprietorships and even for the owner of the proprietorship. A Savings Incentive Match Plan for Employees (SIMPLE) IRA is like a traditional IRA, except that with an IRA, you can contribute up to 100 percent of your wages, with a maximum contribution of $12,500 in 2018. If you are 50 or over, you get to contribute an extra $3,000 catch-up contribution. What is so different and beneficial about a SIMPLE IRA is that the employee, and not the employer, makes most of the contributions. The employer need only match an employee contribution if the employee makes a contribution for the year.

A SIMPLE IRA allows an employee to contribute up to $12,500 in 2018. In addition, the employer need only match the employee's contribution, if any, up to 3 percent of their wages, up to a maximum of $275,000 for 2018.[45] This means that the maximum employer contribution would be $7,950 in 2018.

Example: Stitchem, a medical corporation, provides a SIMPLE IRA for all its employees and doctors. If the doctors contribute the maximum amount of $12,500 in 2018, Stitchem may contribute up to 3 percent of the doctors' wages, up to another $7,950, for a total contribution of $20,450. Not a bad deal! The doctors get $20,450 put away for them because they contribute $12,500, and the corporation contributes $7,950 (3 percent up to $275,000 in earnings).

Example: Sarah is a receptionist for Stitchem and earns $25,000. If Sarah makes no contributions to the SIMPLE IRA, Stitchem need not make any contributions on behalf of Sarah.

Example: Let's assume that Sarah contributes $2,000 to the SIMPLE IRA. Stitchem would have to match Sarah's contribution, but only up to 3 percent of her wages. Thus, since she earns $25,000, Stitchem would contribute only $750 for Sarah.

Author's note: Many medical and legal firms set up SEPs or profit-sharing plans because they allow a much greater contribution, $55,000 in 2018. However, if there are other employees, this can be very expensive. If there are several employees, I recommend considering setting up a SIMPLE IRA. The overall contribution by the owner may be less than with a SEP, but the benefit of not contributing as much for employees may greatly offset this. If, however, a company wants to contribute as much as possible on behalf of employees, a SEP may be the better choice.

Notes

1. Section 132(f)(2) of the IRC. See also Rev. Proc. 2015-53. See IR 2014-99. See IRS Publication 15B.
2. Section 274 (a)(4) of the IRC as amended by 2017 Tax Cuts and Jobs Act Section 13304 (c)(1)(B)
3. Ibid.
4. Notice 94-3, Q-3a, 1994-1 CB 327; see also Section 132(f)(2) of the IRC, 2015-53. See also Rev. Proc. 2016-14, Section 3.02, 2016-09 IRB. Section 132 of the IRC.

5. IRS Pub 15-B, Employer's Tax Guide to Fringe Benefits (2018)
6. Rev. Proc. 2007-66, 2007-45 IRB 970. See also Rev. Proc. 2008-66.
7. Section 1.61-21(a) of the ITR.
8. Section 1.61-21(d)(2)(iii) of the ITR.
9. Section 1.61-2(d)(5) of the ITR. See also Notice 2007-87, 2007-45 IRB 966 (2008 limits on highly compensated employees).
10. Section 1.61-2(d)(3)(ii)(c) of the ITR.
11. Rev. Proc. 2010-10, 2010-3 IRB.
12. Section 1.61-2(e)(1)(4) of the ITR.
13. See note 12.
14. Section 1.61-21(f) of the ITR. See Notice 2007-87 found in footnote 9. See also IR 211-103, 10/20/11.
15. Section 125(d)(1) of the IRC and Section 1.125-1 Q&A 8.
16. Notice 97-9, Section II, 1997-1 IRB 365.
17. Section 125(d) of the IRC.
18. Section 125(g)(3) of the IRC.
19. Section 1.83-1(a) of the ITR.
20. Section 83 of the IRC and Section 1.83-2(a) of the ITR.
21. Revenue Ruling 72-25, 1972-1 CB 127.
22. Section 421(a)(2) of the IRC.
23. Section 14a-422(a)(1), Q&A 1 of the ITR.
24. Section 422(b) of the IRC.
25. Section 422(c)(1) of the IRC and Section 1.421-7(e) of the ITR.
26. Section 422(b)(6) of the IRC and Letter Ruling 8238113.
27. Section 422(c)(5) of the IRC.
28. Section 83(i) as amended by the 2017 Tax Cuts and Jobs Act, Section 13603(a).
29. Section 119(a) of the IRC.
30. Letter Ruling 8002003.
31. Section 119(b) of the ITC.
32. Section 1.119-1 of the ITR.
33. Section 1.119-1(a) of the ITR.
34. Section 1.119-1(a)(2) of the ITR.
35. Ibid.
36. Section 1.119-1(a)(2) of the ITR and Revenue Ruling 71-411, 1971-2 CB 103.
37. Section 1.119-1(a)(2)(ii)(C) of the ITR.
38. Section 119(b)(4) of the IRC.
39. Section 1.119-1(f), Example 9 of the ITR.
40. *Mabley v. Commissioner*, T.C. Memo 1965-323.
41. *F. R. McDowell*, T.C. Memo 33 CCH TCM 372 (1974).
42. Sections 404(a)(3)(a), 404(a)(8)(D), and 415(c)(1) of the IRC. See also IR notice 2017-64.
43. Ibid.
44. Ibid.
45. Ibid.

Part 4

Miscellaneous Tax Strategies

15

The Four Most Overlooked Real Estate Tax Deductions in America

Unquestionably, there is progress. The average American now pays out almost as much in taxes as he formerly got in wages.

—H. L. Mencken

What's the Point of Mortgage Points?

Buying homes in America is as American as apple pie. Everyone seems to be getting into the act. In fact, in June 2002, President Bush even proposed broad incentives that would enable more Americans than ever before to purchase their own homes.[1]

Although everyone dreams of owning his or her own personal "piece of the rock" to call home, there are some stiff expenses involved in buying a home. One big, misunderstood, and often overlooked expense deals with points.

Points, otherwise known as *loan origination fees* or *loan processing fees*, are normally incurred when you obtain a loan at

> **Chapter Overview**
> - Learn about when you should deduct all mortgage points paid to banks.
> - Understand a real estate deduction most often overlooked: unamortized points.
> - Learn why making repairs in investment property is much better than making improvements.
> - Learn why making improvements on a principal residence is much more important than making repairs.
> - Learn how to IRS-bulletproof your designation of repairs or improvements.
> - Understand the new universal exclusion that allows you to avoid up to $500,000 of gain.
> - Learn about new untapped markets where you should be buying because of the universal exclusion. (This is a killer.)

a set interest rate. Many times, paying more in the form of "upfront" points results in a lower interest rate than if no points are paid.

Chapter Overview (Cont.)
• Learn why it's a tragic tax mistake to purchase the family's home as part of a divorce (which, sadly, is done all the time).

Author's note: You can tell how many points you paid by looking at your settlement statement. It will note exactly how much your points are. In general, points are a percentage of your loan. Thus, if you have a $100,000 loan and pay two points, you would pay 2 percent of the loan in points, which would be $2,000.

Rules for IRS-Bulletproofing Deduction of Your Points

The good news is that you may fully deduct all points paid in the year that you pay them, even if they are paid out of the loan proceeds and even if they are VA or FHA points, provided you meet five conditions:[2]

- You use them to either purchase or improve your principal residence; thus, you can't fully deduct points incurred for a second home, a rental property, or refinancing a home. (We'll discuss this below.)
- Your down payment exceeds the charge for the points.
- Your principal home fully secures your loan. In other words, your home is collateral for the loan.
- Charging points is a normal, established practice in your area.
- The points charged are not excessive. This means that they do not exceed the usual charge for points in your area.

Example: John and Mary purchase their main home for $250,000. They make a down payment of $50,000. In order to get their 6 percent loan, they have to pay two points, $5,000. They may deduct the full $5,000 on their tax return as interest. It would be reported on Schedule A, Itemized Deductions.

Author's note: Many people overlook this deduction because the bank doesn't send any information forms. You just have to recognize it on your settlement statement and know that these points are deductible. If you've purchased a home within the last three years, check out your settlement statement. If you didn't deduct the points, you can file both federal and amended returns for up to three open tax years.

Moreover, the IRS used to require that people pay the points separately, using a separate check, in order to deduct the points. Recently, the IRS yielded on this requirement and now allows you to deduct points even if you did not pay the points in cash or use a separate check. In fact, you can have the points paid from the loan proceeds.[3] However, and this is the catch, you can claim the deduction only if the money that you bring to the settlement (down payment, recording fees, etc.) exceeds the charge for points.

Example: Jack and Jill incur $5,000 in points to purchase their lovely house on the hill. These points are to be paid from the loan. If Jack and Jill want to deduct the $5,000, they must make a down payment of at least $5,000 at the closing. If they pay only $3,000 down, then only $3,000 of the points would be immediately deductible.

Author's note: I wonder if the people at the IRS are actually developing a heart.... Nah!

Points Paid by the Seller

Sometimes a seller agrees to pay points. This often happens when the contract provides that the loan points be split between buyer and seller. The tax consequences are great. The seller treats these payments as selling expenses and you, the buyer, get to deduct the points paid by both you and the seller as interest, as long as you reduce your purchase basis by the seller's payment of the points.[4] Isn't this a great country?

Example: Bob purchases a home with a $100,000 loan. Bob has to pay two points ($2,000) for this loan. The real estate contract provides that Bob and the seller will split the points. Even though Bob pays only $1,000 in points himself, he may deduct the entire $2,000 of points paid. He must, however, reduce his basis in his home by the $1,000 paid by the seller.

Amortize All Other Points Paid

As I noted above, you can deduct the points paid only if you meet certain specific conditions, such as incurring them for the purchase of a principal residence. If you don't meet these specific conditions, you can't immediately deduct all the points. This can occur in many situations. You can incur points to buy investment property or a second home or to refinance a loan rather than using the loan proceeds to purchase or improve the home. In these cases, you cannot deduct the points immediately; you must amortize the points over the life of the loan. This means, in plain English, that you must deduct the points ratably over the number of months of the loan. The following example will explain this.

Example: Howard refinances his home and pays $3,600 for a 15-year loan (180 months). Since this loan is not used to purchase or improve his principal residence, he may not immediately deduct all the points. He must write them off over the life of the loan. Thus, the loan is for 180 months, he would deduct $20 per month or $240 per year.

The main question, which applies to almost everyone, is what happens if you don't hold the house for the full loan term or keep the loan for the full term of the loan? The answer is that you get to deduct all unamortized points in the year that you either sell your home or refinance the loan that you incurred points on.

Example: Let's assume that, in the above example, after you deduct only $240 of the $3,600 of points paid, you refinance your loan. You would deduct the remaining, undeducted portion of the points—$3,360 in unamortized points!

Author's note: From my many years of experience in taxes, I've found that almost everyone fails to notice this major deduction and, of course, to take it on their tax returns. Why? Most people don't know about it and their banks don't send them any notice about this. Also, it requires that you or your accountant check the settlement statement that you received when you purchased the property or incurred the loan to find the amount of the points, which most people forget about because of the time that's passed since the closing. If you've sold your home or refinanced a loan within the last three years, check whether you have any unamortized points. If so, you can file an amended tax return (Form 1040X) for up to the last three years and claim the deduction. Even better, many states allow you to claim this deduction in computing state taxes, too.

Repairs vs. Improvements: Which Is Better?

The second most overlooked real estate deduction deals with the difference between improvements and repairs. When should you try to make an improvement and when should you try to make repairs? At first, they seem similar, but learning to classify and structure them correctly can result in thousands of dollars of extra benefits to you. Much of the answer is a question of facts; however, how you present and structure the facts can result in two entirely separate tax results.

I should note that this issue is even tough for the IRS; the agency's internal manual states that "it is a difficult issue requiring maximum use of judgment."[5]

The key is that, with rental and commercial properties, you always prefer to have fix-ups classified as repairs *and not as* improvements. The reason is that repairs are deductible now, while improvements on rental property are capital items that must be depreciated over a recovery period of 27.5 years for residential rental property and 39 years for commercial property.[6] What would you rather have, a deduction now or over many years?

Example: Dan spends $10,000 fixing up his residential rental property. He can deduct the $10,000 now as a repair or take deductions of $364 per year for 27.5 years if he classifies it as an improvement. But the $364 per year is not really $364 in today's dollars. We must consider the time value of money. If the time value of money is 6 percent, the $364 per year improvement deductions for 27.5 years are worth $4,840 in today's dollars, compared with the $10,000 repair deduction. To put it another way, a repair deduction is twice as valuable as an improvement.

With your residence homes, in contrast with rental or commercial properties, you have a different attitude. Any repair made to a residence is completely nondeductible. You don't get to add it to your basis and you don't get a deduction—nothing, nada, zip! Improvements, on the other hand, get added to the basis of the home and help reduce the gain, if any, when you sell the home. So, with a residence, you want improvements and not repairs.

When is a fix-up a repair and when is it an improvement? That's the big question.

To repair means to restore to a sound state or to mend. You make a repair to keep the property in ordinary, efficient operating condition. It does not add to the value of the property or appreciably prolong its life.[7] Repairs merely keep the property usable and operating over its probable life.[8]

Improvements make the property better in some way. You make improvements when you do one or more of the following:

- You increase the value of the property.[9]
- You make the property last much longer.[10]
- You adapt the property to a new or different use.

Author's note: When does fixing up a roof cease to be a repair and become a partial replacement (improvement)? In situations of this sort, careful tax planning, careful understanding of what's in this book, and complete records can yield big tax savings.

Fortunately, there is a great but little known case that will show you what to do in order to get the right classification for your property.[11]

Roger Jacobson bought a four-unit apartment for $30,000. It had one tenant, but the building was in poor shape. Jacobson spent $6,247 to have a contractor do the following:

- Remove tree limbs that were rubbing on the roof
- Repair water damage
- Clean the carpet, floors, and exterior
- Repair the cracked front porch
- Install new cabinet doors
- Install new countertops

Although the IRS tried to classify all the work as improvements, the tax court allowed $5,000 as a repair deduction. The only improvements were the new cabinet doors and new countertops. In siding with Jacobson, the court noted that:

- There was a tenant in residence, whose presence meant that the property was commercially active.
- $6,247 in total and the $5,000 allowed were not material based on the $30,000 building price.
- Most items were fixed using the same or similar materials.

Author's note: The word "new" signals improvements and not replacement or repair.[12]

Eight Great Strategies to Ensure Repairs

Based on the Jacobson case, here are eight great strategies that could ensure that you get the classification that you want.

1. Segregate repairs from improvements. If you're going to renovate the place, but also make certain repairs, you must segregate the repairs from the improvements to deduct the repairs.[13] In fact, the IRS says in its audit manual that fix-ups that would be a repair when made separately would be an improvement when made as part of a general overhaul of the building.[14]

Example: Karen wants to fix up her rental property. Unfortunately she both needs a new roof, which would be an improvement, and needs to clean out and fix the clogged gutters, which are repairs. If she does it all in one job and gets one combined bill, the entire project would be considered an improvement that would be depreciable over 27.5 years. She should get an itemized bill for the roof and a separate bill for the gutter work. The gutter work would be deductible as a repair.

Author's note: Make sure repairs are not part of an overall plan and, if possible, have repairs done by a different contractor. Certainly, you should get a separate bill for the repair work.

2. Fix a minor portion only. If you're replacing an entire wall, roof, or floor, you're often making an improvement.[15] If you repair only part of a wall, roof, or floor, you're generally making repairs.[16]

3. Use similar, comparable, or less expensive materials. If your purpose is to mend and restore to a sound state, you should use comparable materials.[17] If your purpose is to improve, you use better-quality or improved materials.[18]

Example: If, in the above example, Karen fixed her ducts with much better materials, she would have an improvement rather than a repair.

4. Fix damaged areas only. If you repair, you replace or restore worn-out, broken, or deteriorated areas of the property.[19] When you expand your repair to areas of the property that are not worn out, broken, or deteriorated, you make an improvement.

Example: Mark has an air conditioner that suddenly stops working. If he fixes only the compressor, it's a repair. If he puts in a whole new unit, it's an improvement.

Example: Marcia has a leak in her roof. If she needs to replace only half the roof to fix the repair and she uses similar materials, this would be a repair. If she puts on a whole new roof or uses better materials, such as slate instead of shingles, this would be an improvement.

5. Repair after an event. Generally, you think out an improvement in advance.[20] With a repair, something happens that calls your attention to the need for the fix-up.[21] A broken water pipe requires repair. Wear and tear produces a need to repaint. Events made it necessary to repair the pipe and paint the building.

Example: Your floor is damaged. If you resurface it, it would be a repair.

Example: Your building is sinking because of the subsoil. If you shore up the building and replace a good portion of the floor because of this problem, you would probably have a repair. If you put in more than is required, such as a new wood floor to replace linoleum, you would have an improvement.

Author's note: With rental properties, many times repairs occur as a result of calls by tenants. You should document that a tenant called you in order to fix a problem. You can put your tax diary or organizer to good use here.

6. Repair during occupancy or between tenants. The IRS audit manual says that people may buy a property, renovate it, and then try to expense the cost instead of treating these expenses as rightful improvements.[22] The IRS tells its agents to watch for such situations and propose adjustments. You avoid a lot of scrutiny when you own the property for a time before making repairs. Also, you have a much stronger argument for repairs when you have tenants in place when you make the repairs.

7. Classify the fix-up as a repair (or improvement) on your books. The bean counters should put the beans in the right spot. If you classify them as improvements on your books, the IRS will use this against you.

8. Try to replace less than half of any wall, ceiling, or floor. If you put in a whole new wall, this would be an improvement; however, if you fix part of the wall, this would probably be deemed a repair.

Author's note: Your best proof may be a photograph. Take pictures before and after. If they look alike, that suggests a repair. Make sure you get the photo processed with a date stamp on the prints. Many digital cameras will date-stamp the photos too.

The bottom line: A combination of good planning and good records of proof—such as tenants calls, photos, separate bills for repairs and improvements—is critical toward getting the repair deductions that you want. If you want your fix-ups to be deemed improvements, as with your residence, you would do the opposite of what's recommended here. Remember: for rental properties, repairs are best, because they give a deduction now. For your home, you want improvements, because they're added to your basis. Repairs give you nothing.

As you can see, there are a number of factors that must be considered as to whether a fix-up can be a deductible repair or capitalized as an improvement. The IRS has recently come to the rescue with a safe harbor approach. If you don't get audited financial statements, you can treat a fix-up as a repair if the total invoice does not exceed $2,500. If you do get audited financial statements, this safe harbor amount increases to $5,000 per invoice. If the invoices are over these numbers, you are subject to considering the criteria noted above in this book. To take advantage of the safe harbor, there is an easy election that you will need to make on your tax return. See your tax professional about this.[23]

The Universal Appeal of the Universal Exclusion

Prior to 1997, you were able to exclude up to $125,000 of gain on the sale of your principal residence if you were 55 or older. However, this discriminated against most of the population and it involved some complex requirements to obtain this exclusion. Many people felt this was unfair. To simplify the law dealing with residences, Congress passed a terrific law in 1997.[24]

Requirements Needed to Audit-Proof the Universal Exclusion

The general rule is that you may exclude up to $250,000 of gain from the sale of your principal residence ($500,000 if married filing jointly, which will be discussed below) if you meet the following requirements:[25]

- You owned the residence for any two of the last five years.
- You occupied your residence for any two of the last five years.
- You haven't used the exclusion within the last two years.

Author's note: As you can see, you can't have used the exclusion within the last two years. However, this also means that you can use the exclusion every two years!

Example: Tony sells his home for a $200,000 gain and uses the exclusion. He then moves into his summer home in Hyannis and lives there for two years. After the two years, he sells his second home. He may use the exclusion again.

Author's note: You can use the exclusion with every home that you own, by simply moving into it and making the home your new principal residence. You would live in it for two years and then sell the home and take the exclusion. Thus, you can avoid all or most of your gains on every home that you own. Isn't life great?

If you're married and filing a joint return, you may exclude up to $500,000 of gain if you meet these three requirements:[26]

- You *or* your spouse have owned the residence for at least two out of the last five years.
- *Both* you and your spouse have used the house as your principal residence for two out of the last five years.
- Neither spouse is ineligible because of using the exclusion within the last two years.

Ownership vs. Residence Test

The two-years-out-of-five requirement is applied strictly, with some exceptions, to be discussed below. To use the $250,000/$500,000 exclusion, either you or your spouse must have owned the residence and used it as your principal residence for any two out of the last five years.[27] The key, however, is that the ownership period may differ from your use period, as long as you satisfy both tests within the previous five-year window. Like the prior law, the two years need not be consecutive.[28] You can even count short absences for vacations as periods of use even if you rent out the home.[29]

Example: Matt and Lisa rent and live in a home in year 1. In year 2, they purchase the home and live in it until the end of the year. In year 3, they move out and rent the home to Smith until the end of year 5, when they sell the home. They have owned the home for two out of five years (years 2, 3, and 4) and used it as their principal residence for two out of the last five years (years 1 and 2), so they qualify for the exclusion.

Even if you are living apart from your spouse and file jointly, each of you can claim the $250,000 exclusion for your individual residences if you meet the ownership and use rules.[30]

Example: Bill and Hillary file jointly, but live in different homes. They have each met the two-year ownership and use requirements for their respective homes. Each may avoid up to $250,000 of gain on the sale of each of their homes.

The general rule is that you can use the exclusion once every two years. Thus, if you use the exclusion less than two years ago, you must wait until the two-year period has passed.[31] However, remember my favorite saying: "Where there's a will, there's a lawyer." There are several exceptions to both the two-year ownership rule and the use rule.

If you or someone in your family becomes physically or mentally incapable of self-care,[32] you are deemed to meet both the ownership and use requirements if you've owned and used the home for only one year out of the last five years.

Example: Myra has been diagnosed with Alzheimer's disease. She lived in her home for one and a half years before she needed to be put into a nursing home for proper care. Despite the fact that she owned and used her residence for less than two years, she will be deemed to meet the ownership and use requirements for the full $250,000 exclusion if her home is sold.

You can even be exempt from all of the two-year rules.[33] Congress specifically allows some leeway to use the exclusion even if you fail the two-year ownership requirement or the two-year use requirement or you've used the exclusion within the last two years.

To avoid all these rules, your sale or exchange must be for one of the following reasons:

- Change in place of employment
- Health
- Other unforeseen circumstances as provided by the IRS.

Example: Warren was told by his doctor to move to a warm climate because of his asthma. If he moves to Arizona after living in his principal residence for only one year, he may still use part of the exclusion. The two-year ownership and use requirements are waived.

Example: Karen had lived in her home for just one year when her firm transferred her to another city. She moves because of this job change. Despite living in the home for only one year, she may still use part of the exclusion.

As found in much of the recent tax legislation, what Congress giveth, it taketh away. If any of the two-year requirements are waived due to hardship, but you still don't quite meet one or both of the other requirements, the amount of the exclusion is calculated according to percentage of the months out of 24 that you met the rules. Let's take an example to explain this.

Example: Sarah sells her home because she gets a new job in another town. She has not used the exclusion in the last two years and has lived in the home for only six months. If she had both owned and occupied the home for the full two years, she would be able to exclude up to $250,000 of gain. However, since she lived in the house for only six months out of the required 24, by reason of her change in employment, she can exclude only 25 percent of the potential $250,000, so she pays taxes on $187,500 of gain.

Author's note: If she didn't meet the hardship exception, she would have to pay tax on the whole gain. Even though she doesn't get to use the whole $250,000 exclusion, she still avoids taxes on $62,500 of the gain.

IRS "Gotchas" with Prior Depreciation

As I've noted, you can rent out your home or conduct business in part of the home and still qualify for the exclusion. However, there's something that you should know about depreciation taken on your home.

If you've taken any depreciation on your home after May 6, 1997, any gain up to that amount of depreciation will be taxable at your normal rates, up to a maximum of a special long-term capital gain rate of 25 percent, as long as you have owned the property for at least one year.[34]

Example: Samantha sells her home in 2008 for a $200,000 gain. She used her home as a home office and claimed depreciation on part of her home. If the depreciation taken after May 6, 1997 was $5,000, Samantha must pay tax on the $5,000 at the rate of 25 percent. If Samantha had held the property for less than 12 months, the tax rate on this depreciation would be at her ordinary income tax rates.

Author's note: Frankly, I don't consider this payback of the allowable depreciation to be a problem. If you were in the 36 percent tax bracket when you took the depreciation, but you have to pay back the depreciation at only the 25 percent maximum rate, you're still coming out way ahead by taking any allowable depreciation.

New Tax Laws Effective 2009

OLD Law: Prior to January 1, 2009, you could move into either your second home or vacation home or rental property, live in it for two years, and avoid up to $500,000/ $250,000 of gain.

NEW Law: For sales after 2008, the home sale exclusion will be reduced proportionately for the period of time that the home wasn't used as a principal residence.

Example: In 2008–2009, Sam had a second home in Florida. If Sam were to sell his principal residence in January 2011 and move into the second home for two years before selling the second home, 50 percent of the gain qualifies for the exclusion.

Author's note: The period of time that the home was used as a second home (after 2008) precludes the universal exclusion from applying to those years (see exception 4 below).

Exceptions to New Law

1. *No retroactivity.* No improper use prior to 2009 exists. Thus, if you use your second home as a vacation or rental property prior to 2009, it won't count against you.
2. *Temporary absences don't count against you.* If you are away for a temporary absence, not to exceed two years, due to health, employment changes, or certain unforeseen circumstances, those years will still qualify.
3. *Qualified military.* Ten years of absence for a qualifying member of the military (and certain government employees) won't result in disqualifying use.
4. *Disqualifying use after your home was a principal residence.* You might wonder, "What if I have a hard time selling my home and need to rent it out? Will that result in disqualifying use?" The answer is that Congress is giving you a break.

You can rent out the house that was your principal residence first and not result in disqualifying use if it occurs:

a. Within the last five years preceding the sale, AND
b. You permanently stop using the house as your main home.

Example: In 2009, Alice rents out her principal residence for two years. If she sells the home afterwards, she would meet the requirements and the full gain would be allowed toward the exclusion.

Author's note: If spouses who file jointly move into the rental property, they can exclude up to $500,000 of gain.

Transfers of Property as Part of a Divorce

One of the most overlooked real estate tax traps affects millions of Americans yearly as a result of divorces. If you sell your home to your ex-spouse as part of the divorce, his or her basis in the home is equal to the old joint basis and any gain or loss is measured against this old basis. Any payments your ex-spouse makes do *not* increase that basis.[35] The following example will illustrate this disastrous problem.

Example: Marc sells his share of his home to his ex-wife for $300,000 as part of the divorce. *If* they paid $40,000 for the house 10 years ago, her basis for gain or loss remains at $40,000. She gets no benefit from the $300,000 payment. Thus, if she sells the home for $600,000, she would have to pay tax on the entire $560,000 gain (less the $250,000 universal exclusion). Thus, she gets hit twice: when she pays $300,000 to buy her ex-husband's share of the house and the second time when she sells the house and must pay tax on all the gain above the original basis. Yuck!

Author's note: In a divorce situation, neither spouse should purchase the house. Instead, the home should be sold to a third person. Each spouse can then buy a new home with his or her share of the tax-free money!

Author's note: As a result of the Tax Cuts and Jobs Act, payments pursuant to a divorce agreement incurred in 2019 are no longer deductible. However, this carryover basis trap seems to be intact.

For more tax planning involving real estate, see Sandy's newest book, *Real Estate Tax Secrets of the Rich.*

Summary

- Deduct all points incurred in purchasing and improving your principal residence.
- If you're going to finance the points, make sure that your down payment at least equals the amount of the points.
- If you pay points for any purposes other than to purchase and improve your home (such as to refinance a loan or to purchase a second home), amortize the points over the life of the loan.

- Any points paid by the seller are deductible by the buyer!
- Deduct all unamortized points when the loan is refinanced or when the property is sold.
- Try to structure all fix-up expenses on rental property as repairs rather than improvements.
- Try to structure all fix-up expenses on residences as improvements rather than repairs.
- To qualify for a repair, do the following:
  - Segregate repairs from improvements in the bill.
  - Fix minor areas only. Don't replace a whole wall or roof.
  - Use similar, comparable, or less expensive materials.
  - Fix damaged areas only.
  - Repair after an event or after a tenant complains about a problem.
  - Make repairs during occupancy or in between tenants.
  - Classify the fix-up as a repair (or improvement) on your books.
  - Try to replace less than half of any wall, ceiling, or floor.
- Take advantage of the safe harbor election to be able to expense fix-ups under $2,500 per invoice or the much higher $5,000 per invoice (if you receive audited financial statements), which I don't think would apply to most of you reading this.
- Take advantage of the universal exclusion when selling your principal residence. Follow these three rules for the exclusion:
  - Own your residence for any two of the last five years.
  - Use your home as your principal residence for any two of the last five years.
  - Wait at least two years before you use the exclusion again. (Note: if you're married filing jointly, both you and your spouse must use the house as a principal residence for two out of the last five years.)
- The two years of ownership and the two years of usage don't have to be the same two out of five years.
- There's a partial exclusion from the rules if you sell your home as a result of a change in employment, health, or other unforeseen situation.
- Consider buying fixer-uppers and living in them for two years in order to use the exclusion.
- Consider moving into your rental houses for two years before selling them. You would avoid most of the gain.
- If you divorce, don't buy a home from your ex-spouse as part of the divorce. Instead sell the home to a third party and use the tax-free money to purchase a new home. You can even buy the home back as long as it isn't part of a prearranged plan.

Notes

1. Dana Milbank, "Bush Calls for Increasing Minority Home Ownership," *Washington Post*, June 18, 2002, p. A2.
2. Section 461(g)(2) of the IRC; see also Revenue Procedure 92-12A, 1992-1 CB 664.

3. Revenue Procedure 92-12, 1992-1 CB 663.
4. Revenue Procedure 94-27, 1994-1 CB 613.
5. *Internal Revenue Manual*, Section 4843.22.
6. Section 168(c) of the IRC.
7. Section 1.162-4 of the ITR.
8. *Illinois Merchants Trust Company v. Commissioner*, 4 BTA 103 (1926).
9. Section 1.263(a)-1(a)(1) of the ITR.
10. Section 1.263(a)-1(b) of the ITR.
11. *Jacobson v. Commissioner*, 47 TCM 499 (1983).
12. Ibid.
13. *Allen v. Commissioner*, 15 TCM 464 (1956).
14. *Internal Revenue Manual 4232.7, Techniques Handbook for Specialized Industries: Construction*, Subsection 72(18).
15. Section 1.164-4 of the ITR; see also *Ritter v. Commissioner*, 47-2 USTC ı 9378 (6th Cir. 1947) (new roof).
16. *Kingsley v. Commissioner*, 11 BTA 296 (1928), *acq.* VII-2 CB 22.
17. *Illinois Merchants Trust Company v. Commissioner*, 4 BTA 103 (1926).
18. *Abbot Worsted Mills, Inc. v. Commissioner*, 42-2 USTC ı 9694 (NH Dist. 1942).
19. *Sanford Cotton Mills v. Commissioner*, 14 BTA 1210 (1929).
20. E.g., *Jones v. Commissioner*, 24 TC 563 (1955).
21. *J.F. Wilcox and Sons v. Commissioner*, 28 BTA 878 (1933) (broken glass replaced).
22. *Internal Revenue Manual 4232.7, Techniques Handbook for Specialized Industries: Construction*, Subsection 72(18), Expensing of Capital Items.
23. IR 2015-82. See also IRS Regulation 1.263-1(f)(1)(i).
24. H.R. 2014, Congressional Committee Report Accompanying Taxpayer Relief Act of 1997, Section 312.
25. Section 121(a) of the IRC.
26. Section 121(b)(2) of the IRC.
27. Section 121(b) of the IRC.
28. Section 121(b)(1) of the IRC.
29. Section 121(d)(6) of the IRC. By mandating depreciation recapture, Congress allows the home to be used in part as a business or as a rental.
30. See footnote 24, noted above.
31. Section 121(b)(3) of the IRC.
32. Section 121(d)(7)(A) of the IRC.
33. Section 121(c)(2) of the IRC.
34. Sections 1250 and 1(h)(1)(D) of the IRC.
35. Section 1041 of the IRC.

16

Making Colleges Less Expensive with Tax Planning

Binghamton University Motto,
"We're only 207 road miles from Yale."
—Tony Kornheiser, *Washington Post*

Chapter Overview
- Understand why most people should set up qualified tuition plans for their kids' future education.
- Learn the great benefits of both the Lifetime Learning Credit and the Hope Tax Credit.
- Understand the rules of deducting student loan interest.
- Learn how to deduct up to $4,000 of college expenses.

Toward the end of her junior year, we were investigating colleges for my daughter. When I heard about the current tuition and fee rates, I was having an "out-of-body experience." Most private schools charged between $24,000 to $38,000 per year for tuition alone! When you filter in the outrageous fees that colleges are now surreptitiously adding plus the high cost of room and board and books, the cost can easily equal or exceed $50,000 per year. Imagine having to buy a BMW every year, which is what paying for college is akin to.

Although the public schools were a lot less expensive, they too have been increasing their tuition rates from 6 percent to 10 percent per year, with many experiencing double-digit increases in tuition.[1]

In fact, over the last 30 years, college tuition costs for both public and private schools have risen far more than our cost of living. College costs today are much less affordable to the average American than they were for our parents.

The good news is that Congress added some great tax benefits to help reduce the sting of high tuition and fees. These benefits provide tax-free savings accounts for colleges, otherwise known as Qualified Tuition Plans, and tax credits, which reduce your taxes on a dollar-for-dollar basis. In addition, you may now be able to deduct some student loan interest if you meet the rules and may even deduct some of the college tuition costs. Yes, you read this correctly. Thus, if you have dependents going to college, or are in college now, or even if you are considering attending college, this chapter could be a goldmine for your bank account.

Deductibility of Educational Expenses

I get asked many times, "Can I deduct the cost of college, or the cost of taking a course, or of going for a graduate degree?"

General Rule

For courses to be deductible they must either maintain or improve skills required by your present job, trade, or business; or must meet the express requirements of your employer; or must be required in order to retain your salary, status, or rate of compensation.[2] If you meet these tests, you can deduct your tuition, fees, books, and certain travel and transportation expenses.[3]

Example: Sally takes some courses in order to maintain or improve her job skills as an accountant. She may deduct not only the tuition and fees and books but also her round-trip transportation to the school.

Example: Gina is a teacher who is taking a college course related to teaching English as required by her school. She may deduct all the costs related to this course.

Exceptions to the general rule

Although the above-noted general rule sounds easy to understand and apply, it is a bit misleading. Congress and the courts have carved out some exceptions to this rule. The main exception is that despite meeting the requirements of the general rule, the education isn't deductible if it either meets the minimum educational requirements for qualification in your current trade or business (or job) or is part of a program of study that would qualify you for a new trade or business.[4] The question thus becomes, "whether the course or program of study qualifies you for a completely different task than you were previously qualified to perform."[5] Let me give you some examples of those courses and programs that would be deductible and also those that wouldn't be deductible. This will give you a feel for what you can and cannot write off.

Courses and programs that were held to be deductible

- A night manager for a store could deduct a food market management program.[6]
- An aeronautical engineer was allowed to deduct the cost of a graduate degree in business management and administration since he also performed some administrative and management duties in his job.[7]

- Even obtaining a master of business administration (MBA) was held to be deductible if you have a current job that involves skills and tasks related to the MBA, such as cost analysis, marketing, advertising, managing, etc.

Note: However, a new case notes that you had to have worked at your current occupation more than a few months to be considered to have a trade or business or occupation. As a recent case notes, if you work at a job for only two months before getting fired, you may not be able to deduct the tuition for attaining an MBA.

Caution: The costs associated with obtaining an MBA wouldn't seem to be deductible if you didn't have a current job that involved duties and skills related to the MBA.

- Costs involved in becoming a specialist in your profession would also be deductible.[8] Thus, a lawyer who pursues a master in taxation law could deduct the costs if that lawyer is currently employed as a lawyer or accountant.
- Other examples would be an elementary teacher studying to teach secondary school, a math teacher studying to teach science, or a classroom teacher studying to be a guidance counselor.

Examples of courses that would not be deductible because they qualify for a new trade or business

- Obtaining a law degree or taking a bar review course.[9]
- Taking a CPA review course.[10]
- The costs associated with obtaining an undergraduate degree are not normally deductible because they are deemed to qualify you for a new trade or business.[11]

The Bottom Line

If your program of study simply maintains or improves your current job skills, the program would be deductible *unless* such a program qualifies you for a new trade or business.

Qualified Tuition Programs (QTPs) and Prepaid Tuition

Wouldn't it be great if you could set up a special savings account that would earn tax-free interest and tax-free gains and could be used for most college expenses? The answer is that you can with a Qualified Tuition Program (QTP).

There are essentially two types of these programs. The first is a prepaid tuition program that is used mostly for state universities. Here you would prepay a set amount that covers all tuition. The second is a form of investment fund that can be used for all qualified higher education expenses and for any school, whether it is publicly supported or privately supported.

Tax consequences of QTPs

QTPs are *not* tax deductible;[12] however, the benefits are tax-free to the extent that they are used for qualified higher education expenses.[13]

Example: Juan prepays $25,000 to the University of Maryland. Six years later when this money is used to pay for the tuition of his daughter, the proceeds are all tax-free.

Author's elaboration: Prepaid tuition programs, unlike that of other QTPs, are only usable to prepay tuition and not room and board. They usually cover all four years regardless of the cost of living increases. Some of them, such as the one set up in Maryland, can even be used for other non-Maryland state schools. The state of Maryland will pay what would have been the highest in-state tuition for a Maryland state university. Thus, if your state has a program akin to that of Maryland, they can use the money for any school. However, you really need to check out what happens if your kids don't attend your state university. Not all states have such a consumer-friendly program.

Also, transfers to the QTP qualify for the annual gift tax exclusion, which is $14,000 per year per beneficiary if you are single and $24,000 per year per beneficiary if you are married.[14] Thus, there is no gift tax if you limit the per-person contribution to less than or equal to these amounts.

Qualified Savings Plan

This is another type of Qualified Tuition Plan for higher educational expenses. It differs from a prepaid tuition plan in that it can be used for both graduate and undergraduate studies. Also, it can be used for a lot more than just tuition and required fees. See the following paragraph for the allowable Qualified Higher Educational Expenses that can be covered using this type of savings plan.

What are qualified higher education expenses?

This is the great part that you are going to like. Qualified higher education expenses consist of tuition and required fees, books, required supplies, and required equipment.[15]
It also includes room and board for eligible students who attend at least half-time.

Example: Rich has a daughter attending college and covered by a QTP. Her tuition, room, board, and books total $32,000. The QTP distribution can cover all of the $32,000 on a tax-free basis.

New tax law change: Under the Economic Stimulus Law, you can now also pay your child, from the qualified tuition plan, for a computer and for Internet access charges.

Author's hot tip: No income limitations for QTPs: Unlike that of other educational benefits and credits, there are no income limitations for using QTPs. In addition, the kiddie tax rules, discussed in Chapter 4, don't apply to earnings in QTPs. Thus, you could be making millions of dollars annually and still be eligible to set up and fund a QTP. With the kiddie tax age increased to 18, use of a QTP is even more important now than ever.

QTPs can also be used to pay expenses of special needs beneficiaries for any expenses involved in either enrollment or in attendance at the school.[16]

Author's elaboration: If you have children who are handicapped and need special services such as wheelchairs, readers for exams, etc., QTPs could presumably be used to pay for these services.

Contributions to QTPs

All contributions must be made in cash or by check or by credit card. Thus, you can't contribute your stock portfolio to the QTP.

Caution: In addition, there are few limitations noted on the QTP. The IRS, however, is a bit of a killjoy here. They have published some private letter rulings noting that either the QTP has to pay for the anticipated qualified higher education expenses for each dependent, which should presumably include a cost of living increase,[17] or, alternatively, up to five times the cost of tuition at eligible colleges.[18] Thus, this area is in flux, and you need to see a good financial professional in order to determine what maximum amount of contribution you are allowed for each dependent. In fact, you should see a good financial planning professional about setting up a QTP plan, other than that of a prepaid tuition plan, which is usually covered by your state.

Many types of qualified beneficiaries can be covered

What is so great about a QTP is that you can cover just about any person. In fact, if the person covered decides not to use the plan, you can transfer the proceeds on a tax-free basis to any other qualified beneficiaries. This is a huge list of people:

- Spouse
- Any descendant of you or of your spouse
- Stepson or stepdaughter
- Stepfather or stepmother
- Any in-law such as daughter-in-law or son-in-law; even a brother-in-law or sister-in-law qualifies
- Spouses of any of the above-named people

Author's elaboration: As you can see, you have a host of people that you can cover with a QTP. However, you should also take note that your cousin is not a qualified beneficiary.

Author's hot tip: *You can use American Opportunity Credit on QTP expenses:* Later on, you will learn that many middle-class taxpayers can claim a American Opportunity Tax Credit on the first two years of college tuition expenses.

Tuition and medical exceptions: As noted above, you can give each person up to $15,000 in 2018 with no gift tax. However, there are some exceptions in which you can give an almost unlimited amount in one year without a gift tax.

Big exception: The first exception is tuition.[19] Any tuition that you provide for your family that is paid directly to a college or university for education and training are exempt from the gift tax and are thus not subject to the $15,000 limits in 2018.

Example: Donald, a famous real estate investor, pays $100,000 in tuition to Bentley College, which should cover four years of tuition and required fees for his grandchild. This amount is not subject to any gift tax.

The second exception from the gift tax involves payment of medical expenses. If Donald, noted above, pays for the medical expenses of his grandchild, these would not be subject to any gift tax.

Author's note: As a result of the new Tax Cuts and Jobs Act, everyone gets roughly an $11 million lifetime exemption from estate and gift taxes in addition to the yearly $15,000 exclusion. A married couple get a bit over a $22 million lifetime exemption.

Series EE and Series I Government Bonds

This is a great way for lower and middle income parents to save for college costs for their dependents. The interest from these bonds is normally taxable for federal income tax but usually exempt from state income tax. However, if the bonds are used to pay for qualified tuition and fees for higher education for you, your spouse, or your dependents, the interest could be tax-free.[20]

Qualification for tax-free status

There are certain qualifications that must be met to make the interest on series EE and series I bonds tax-free:

a. **It can only be used for higher education expense:** Higher education expenses are tuition and required fees only. The costs of room, board, and books don't qualify, unlike that of other tax credits and QTPs. Why Congress didn't allow for room and board here, as it does for other tax provisions, is a mystery. This is just another example of "tax simplification."

b. **It must be purchased for the education of the taxpayer, his spouse, or his dependent:** If you use the bonds for your education, your spouse's, or for your dependent children's, you would qualify for the tax-exempt status of the interest, assuming that you meet the other tests. However, if the bonds were purchased by a grandfather for his grandkids, the interest would be fully taxable unless the grandkids qualified as his dependents.

c. **You must be on the cash basis:** With series EE bonds, you have a choice of being taxed each year on the interest, which is known as being on the accrual basis, or you can wait until you cash in the bonds and become taxed on all previous interest at the date that you received the cash for the bonds, which is considered the cash basis. You can't have made an election to be taxed on each year's interest, which is the accrual basis.

d. **You must be at least age 24 when you purchase the bonds**

e. **You must not earn too much money:** This is Congress's gotcha! To have all the interest tax-free for educational expenses, you can't earn too much money.[21] The benefits of receiving tax-free interest from saving bonds used for education phase out are as follows for 2018:

- For single filers and heads of households: $79,550–$84,559
- For married filing jointly: $119,300–$149,300
- For married filing separately, there is no exclusion. Yuck!

Author's elaboration: What these phaseouts mean is that if you are a single taxpayer or head of household and earn over $84,559 of modified adjusted gross income or if you are a married taxpayer who files a joint return and has a modified adjusted gross income of over $149,300, you won't get any tax-free benefit from the savings bonds even if you meet the other qualifications. If you make less than these amounts, you will get a benefit. If you feel that you meet these rules, you should definitely see your accountant in order to see if you qualify. Getting tax-free interest from federal savings bonds can be a great way to save for college.

Wonderful Tax Credits for Education

Congress gives you two terrific tax credits for college tuition. As a reminder, a tax credit is better than a deduction because it results in a dollar-for-dollar reduction in your taxes.

American Opportunity Credit[22]

This provides you with a tax credit for the first four years of undergraduate college. The credit is 100 percent of your college tuition up to $2,000 plus 25 percent of the next $2,000 for 2018 and thereafter. Thus, the total credit for each of the first four years would be $2,500 per year.

This credit is available for you, your spouse, and for each of your dependents. Especially nice is the fact that you can claim this credit for each eligible dependent. Thus the $2,500 maximum credit is per individual and not per tax return.

Example: John has three kids in college. (I definitely feel sorry for John.) He pays tuition of $5,000 for Jeremy, $18,000 for Matthew, and $34,000 for Allison. He may claim the maximum $2,500 credit for each kid, which totals $7,500 for each of the first four years of college.

Caution: Phaseout of benefits: Sadly, Congress can't make anything simple. The benefits of this credit start phasing out for married taxpayers filing joint returns if your modified adjusted gross income (MAGI) exceeds $160,000 in 2018. It is eliminated completely if your MAGI equals or exceeds $180,000 in 2018. For single taxpayers, the phaseout limits are between $80,000–$90,000 in 2018; so much for tax simplification!

Author's hot tip: *Don't claim your kids as dependents and give them the tax credit:* If your income exceeds the phaseout amount so that you can't get the credit, don't be forlorn. Remember, where there is a will … there is a lawyer. If you don't claim them as dependents, they should be able to get the credit for themselves. This will reduce the taxes that they would pay on earnings from jobs or on investment earnings. I should note that they can't claim this credit if you claim them as dependents.[23] Thus, you would need to not claim the child or relative who is taking the credit as a dependent on your tax return.[24]

Author's elaboration: Because this provision excludes a student enrolled in a secondary school from the definition of an eligible student, it appears that the credit is not available for the expenses of a high school student taking courses at a college or university.[25]

Caution: *Convicted drug felons:* The American Opportunity Credit is not allowed for any student who has been convicted of a federal or state felony drug offense.[26] Presumably, if your kids were convicted of treason, murder, rape, or robbery, they would still be eligible for the American Opportunity Tax Credit. How stupid can Congress be?! However, this limitation for drug felonies does not apply for the Lifetime Learning Credit. Thus, if your kid was convicted of a drug felony, he or she is still eligible for the Lifetime Learning Credit.

The Bottom Line

This is a nice benefit that Congress gave to middle-income taxpayers. It's too bad that they didn't give it to everyone.

Lifetime Learning Credit

This is the second tax credit for tuition and related expenses such as tuition, books, supplies, and required equipment. The amount of the credit is 20 percent of tuition and related expenses up to $10,000 per year. Thus, the maximum yearly credit is $2,000.[27]

Difference between Lifetime Learning Credit and American Opportunity Credit

Since you can only use either the Lifetime Learning Credit or the American Opportunity Credit for a specific dependent per year,[28] you need to know the differences between the two credits.

1. **Different credit amounts:** The American Opportunity Credit gives you 100 percent credit for the first $2,000 of tuition and 25 percent for the next $2,000 for a total credit of $2,500 per student per year. The Lifetime Learning Credit gives you a 20 percent credit for tuition and related expenses, which includes fees, supplies, and required equipment up to $10,000, for a total maximum credit of $2,000 per year.

2. **One credit is per student, and one is per year:** You can take an American Opportunity Credit for each student's tuition for postsecondary education. Thus, if you have triplets in college, during their first four years of college, you can get three Opportunity Credits each year. The Lifetime Learning Credit is one credit per year per tax return. Thus, your maximum credit is $2,000 regardless of the number of kids in college.

Example: Kevin takes the American Opportunity Credit for the first four years of college for his daughter Karen. For the remaining years of Karen's education, Kevin can claim the Lifetime Learning Credit.

3. **American Opportunity Credits are only for the first four years of college:** The American Opportunity Credits are only for the first four years of postsecondary education. The Lifetime Learning Credit can be used for any year of postsecondary education and even for graduate school.

Author's elaboration: Previously the American Opportunity Credit could be used only for the first two years of college tuition. Under the Economic Stimulus Law, you can now use the credit for the first four years of tuition. Thus, if your kid is taking longer than four years to graduate, you get the credit only on four of those years. The credit also has been increased to a maximum yearly amount of up to $2,500 per child. In 2009, the name of the credit changed from the "Hope Tax Credit" to the "American Opportunity Credit." You have to love the names that Congress gives to its legislation.

4. **Unlike that of the American Opportunity Credit, there is no half-time requirement for education with the Lifetime Learning Credit:** The American Opportunity Credit requires that students spend at least half-time pursuing a degree. This means that they must take enough credits to equal one-half of a full-time workload for at least one academic period.[29] There is no similar requirement for the Lifetime Learning Credit. The Lifetime Learning Credit can be used for any course or program of study that either leads to a degree by an accredited college or can be used for any course(s) that helps the student acquire or improve job skills.[30] It can actually be used to take as few as one job-related course.

Lifetime Learning Credit is available for convicted drug felons: Unlike the American Opportunity Credit, the Lifetime Learning Credit is available to convicted drug felons.

Example: Christy, a professional photographer, enrolls in an advanced photography course at a local community college. Although the course is not part of a degree program, Christy enrolls in the course to improve her job skills. The course fee paid by Christy is a qualified tuition and related expense for purposes of the Lifetime Learning Credit.[31]

Author's hot tip: In the same taxable year, a taxpayer may claim an American Opportunity Credit for each eligible student's qualified tuition and related expenses and a Lifetime Learning Credit for one or more other students' qualified tuition and related expenses. However, a taxpayer may not claim both an Opportunity credit and a Lifetime credit with respect to the same student in the same taxable year.[32]

Example: In 2018, Dan has two daughters in college. His daughter Allison is a first year, full-time student. His daughter Karen is a graduate student. Dan may claim the American Opportunity Credit for Allison and the Lifetime Learning Credit for Karen.

Phaseouts for Lifetime Learning Credit: Congress can't do anything in a simplified way. The Lifetime Learning Credit has a different phaseout than that of the American Opportunity Credit. For single taxpayers the credit starts phasing out at modified adjusted gross income of $57,000 and completely phases out at $67,000. For married filing jointly, the phaseout begins at $114,000 and completely phases out at $134,000.

The Bottom Line

Take the credit that gives you the best results.

5. **Deducting student loan interest:** With ever-escalating college costs, many kids are saddled with a lot of debt as a result of their educational expenses. Congress came to the rescue in the past few years by allowing up to $2,500 in interest on qualified student loan debt to be deductible per year. Sadly, this deduction starts phasing out for single taxpayers whose modified adjusted gross income exceeds $65,000 in 2016 and is completely phased out for modified adjusted gross incomes of $80,000 in 2018. For married taxpayers filing joint returns the phaseout limits are between $135,000 and $165,000 in 2018.[33]

Author's hot tip: Moreover, you used to be able to deduct interest on debt on up to $100,000 of home equity debt. Starting in 2018, home equity interest is no longer deductible.

Author's hot tip: If your modified adjusted gross income prevents you from claiming the student loan interest as a deduction, consider having your kids pay off the loan. If you don't claim them as dependents and they are jointly liable on the loan, they should be able to take a deduction for the interest as an adjustment from gross income.

Author's observation: I find it extraordinarily idiotic that Congress has different phaseout amounts in order to determine eligibility for the tax credits, for tax-free series EE bond interest, and for deducting student loan interest. In addition, Congress based the eligibility on modified adjusted gross income instead of simply using adjusted gross income, which you can easily determine from your tax return. I truly believe that something negative happens to the common sense of Congressmen and Senators when they are in office too long.

Higher education expense deduction: In case things aren't complicated enough, in 2018 and thereafter, Congress gives you an additional choice regarding educational tuition for colleges. You can claim the tax credits, such as the American Opportunity or Lifetime Learning Credit, or you can take a deduction for 100 percent of your tuition and required fees up to $4,000 per year as long as your adjusted gross income (AGI) is less than $65,000 if you are single, or less than $130,000 if you are married filing jointly. If you are single and earn between $65,001 and $80,000 of AGI, you can deduct up to $2,000 per year per person. For married taxpayers who file joint returns, you can deduct up to $2,000 of college tuition if you earn between $131,001 and $160,000 of AGI. If you earn over the upper limits of these phaseout numbers, you get no deduction even if it is only $1 more. Also, the deduction for Qualified Higher Education Expenses applies to graduate school and professional school tuition.

Author's elaboration: With the new, higher American Opportunity Credit that gives a whopping $2,500 credit, you are usually better off using that credit unless you don't qualify because of the income phaseout. Even the Lifetime Learning Credit is usually the better choice.

The Bottom Line

There are certainly a number of good tax credits and benefits for middle-class taxpayers that help ease the sting of high college costs. In addition, using Series EE bonds and especially Qualified Tuition Programs are great ways to save for your dependents' college expenses. It certainly is better to use a QTP than trying to save up for college paying tax on the earnings.

Summary

- You can deduct all the ordinary and necessary educational expenses that maintain or improve either your trade or business or job performance. They are not deductible, however, if they either meet the minimum educational requirements of your current trade or business or are part of a program of study that qualifies you for a new trade or business.
- Qualified Tuition Programs (QTPs) are used to pay for postsecondary educational expenses. They are tax-free to the extent used for qualified expenses such as tuition, required fees, supplies, required books, and required equipment. There is no income limit for QTPs; thus, they are available to everyone.
- Prepaid tuition plans are a form of QTP. They are normally used to prepay state tuition and usually cover four years of tuition.
- QTPs are portable. Their benefits can be transferred to most lineal descendants, ancestors, or spouses of descendants or ancestors.
- American Opportunity Credits can be used on educational expenses paid with QTP funds.
- The American Opportunity Credit can save you $2,500 in taxes per student, applies to you, your spouse, and your dependents. However, this is available only for middle-income taxpayers. Thus, you must be aware of the phaseout of these benefits as your modified adjusted gross income increases.
- The American Opportunity Credit, is now available for four years of postsecondary school education but only if the student attends school at least one-half of what a full-time schedule would be. Thus, if a full-time schedule would be at least 12 credits, students would have to take at least 6 credits to qualify.

- The Lifetime Learning Credit gives up to $2,000 per tax return and not per student. It is available for students for any courses that improve their job performance or qualify them for a new trade or business. This credit has the same phaseout limit as that of the American Opportunity Credit.
- If you can't qualify for either credit because of the income phaseouts, consider not claiming your kids as dependents and have them get the credit on their tax returns.
- Series EE and Series I bonds are great ways to save for tuition and required fees for you, your spouse, and your dependents. Be aware, however, of the phaseouts of this benefit if you make too much money.
- Don't forget to deduct student loan interest of up to $2,500 per year. You can only do this if your modified adjusted gross income does not exceed the phaseout limits. If you can't qualify for the deduction because of your earnings, consider not claiming your kids as dependents and have them pay the loan interest; at least, this would be a deduction for them on their tax returns.
- In lieu of taking a tax credit for tuition, you can elect to deduct up to $4,000 of the tuition.

Notes

1. *Chronicle of Higher Education.*
2. Section 1.162-5 of the Regulations.
3. Ibid.
4. Section 1.162-5(b)(3) of the Regs.
5. *Diaz v. Commissioner,* 70 T.C. 1067 (1978), *Aff'd* 607 F. 2d 995 (2nd. Cir. 1979).
6. *Granger v. Commissioner,* T.C. Memo 1980-60.
7. *Beatty v. Commissioner,* T.C. Memo 1980-196.
8. Section 1.162-5(c)(1) of the Regs.
9. Section 1.162-5(b)(3)(ii) of the Regs. See also *Sharon v. Commissioner,* 591 F. 2d 1273 (9th. Cir. 1978).
10. *Cooper v. Commissioner,* T.C. Memo 1979-241.
11. *Garwood v. Commissioner,* 62 T.C. 699 (1974).
12. Section 529(c)(3)(B) of the IRC.
13. Ibid.
14. Section 529(c)(2)(A) of the IRC.
15. Section 529 (e)(5) of the IRC.
16. Section 529 (e)(3)(A) of the IRC.
17. PLR 200030030.
18. PLR 200024055.
19. Section 2503(e)(1) of the IRC.
20. Section 135(a) and section 135 (c)(2)(A) of the IRC.
21. Section 132(b)(2)(A) of the IRC. See also Rev. Proc. 2018-18, Section 3.18, 2018-10 IRB 392.
22. H.R. Report #220, 105th. Congress, 1st. Session (1997). See also Notice 97-60, Section 2, Q&A 6, 1997-46, I.R.B. 8. See also Section 25A(a)(1) of the IRC.
23. Section 25A(g)(3)(A) of the IRC. See also Rev. Proc. 2009-21, Sec. 4, 2009-16 IRB.

24. Section 1.25A-1(f)(1) of the Regs.

25. Kleinrock's Analysis and Explanations, Section 31.2 (2006).

26. Section 25A(b)(2)(D) of the IRC.

27. Section 25A(c)(1) of the IRC.

28. Section 25A(c)(2)(A) of the IRC.

29. Section 25A(b)(2)(B) of the IRC.

30. Section 25A(c)(2)(B) of the IRC.

31. Kleinrock's Analysis and Explanation, Section 31.2(b) (Hope Scholarship and Lifetime Learning Credits, Example 1.)

32. Section 1.25A-1(b)(1) of the Regs. See also footnote 24, noted above.

33. Section 221(b)(2) of the IRC and Rev. Proc. 2007-66, 2007-45 IRB 970. See also Rev. Proc. 2017-58. 2017 IRB 45.

17

Tax Planning for Stock and Bond Investments

Taxation with representation ain't so hot either.
—Gerald Barzan, humorist

The affects of the federal tax system vary as to how investments are taxed. It does depend on your tax bracket and the type of investment you have. Having an understanding of the tax implications of your investments can make a big difference to your return on investment (ROI) as well as the type of investments that would be most suitable to you.

There are several types of tax implications that can occur. You can either have:

- *Completely tax exempt.* This means that it is exempt from tax completely for both federal and state taxes. Municipal bonds issued by the state where you live would be an example of this.
- *Partially tax exempt.* This means that the investment will be free of tax for either the state or federal government

but not both. Treasury bonds are taxable for federal tax purposes but exempt from state taxation.

- *Tax deferred.* This means that you pay taxes on the investments down the road. However, they aren't immediately taxable. Monies put into tax-advantaged accounts such as IRAs or tax-deferred annuities are examples of this.
- *Ordinary income or fully taxable.* This means that you would pay both federal and state taxes at your ordinary tax rates as if you earned the money as salary. Corporate bond interest is fully taxable as ordinary income.
- *Capital gains.* Here you would pay tax at your normal rates up to a set capital gains rate, which, as of the writing of this book, has a maximum capital gains rate of 20 percent plus a potential 3.8 percent surcharge. Thus, depending on income, the maximum federal long-term capital gains rate can be as high as 23.8 percent in addition to any state rate. Sale of stocks, bonds, and mutual fund shares can produce long-term capital gains. In addition, collectibles have a special capital gains tax of 28 percent.

Investment Taxes

Table 17-1 is a great chart that you can use to summarize most of the tax consequences. It should be able to answer just about any investment tax question for you. Although I did try to simplify the chart, don't blame me for its complexity, however. You can thank your trusty Congress for "tax simplification." Please study it because we will be using it in our discussion.

How the Tax Law Works with Capital Gains and Losses

As you can see from Table 17-1, interest can be either tax exempt or fully or partially taxable depending on the type of bond that you purchased. Capital gains and losses can also vary depending on the asset as well. For example, collectibles such as antiques, coins, and stamps are taxed at the higher capital gains rate of 28 percent.

Stocks and bonds also have a bit of a cumbersome calculation. In order for you to fully understand some of the strategies that I will present, I want to give you the steps necessary when you have short- and long-term capital gains. You don't need to be an

Table 17-1. Tax Liability by Income Type

Types of Income	Federal Income Tax Treatment
Corporate bond interest[1]	Ordinary income
Municipal and state bond interest	Usually tax-free[2] for federal, and tax-free for state if you buy your own state bonds
Federal government bonds	Fully taxable for federal tax but exempt from any state tax
Qualified dividends (which includes corporate earnings and profits)	Long-term capital gains are taxed at a maximum rate of:[3] 0 percent for taxpayers who are in the 10–12 percent tax brackets, which includes the gain. Dividends are taxed at a meximum rate of 15 percent for those who earn up to $425,800 single and up to $479,000 married. It you earn over these amounts, Qualified Dividends are taxed at a maximum rate of 20% over these amounts. Note, you can also be subject to a 3.8 percent medicare surcharge too.
Dividends (that are not out of company earnings)	Nontaxable up to when you recoup your investment (basis) back[4]
Capital gains for securities estate	Short-term gains for assets held for less than one year, are taxed at ordinary income tax rates. Long-term capital gains are taxed at: 0 percent for taxpayers in the 10–15% tax brackets, 15% for taxpayers in the 25–35% tax brackets, and 20% for taxpayers who are in the 39.6% tax bracket in 2016
Assets held for less than year	Long-term capital gains rates are taxed as dividends. See above[5]
Assets held for more than a year	Long-term capital gains are taxed at a maximum rate of:[6] 0 percent for taxpayers in the 10–12% tax bracket (which includes the gain)
Special tax on real estate depreciation when property is sold	25% of the gain up to any depreciation taken on property[7]
Sale of collectibles	Ordinary income up to 28% rate[8]
Capital gains distributions from mutual funds	Same as capital gains; depends on holding period of mutual fund[9]
Capital gains for folks in 10%–12% tax bracket*	For 2018: zero, zilch, nada, nothing![10]
Capital losses for individuals[11]	Deductible against capital gains. Moreover, $3,000 of any excess capital loss can be used against any other income that you have. All the remaining part of any capital loss can be carried over to future years forever.
Corporate capital losses	Can only be used against corporate capital gains and *not* against other income. Any excess can be carried back up to three years and used to offset any capital gains or can be carried forward five years.

*Capital gains, interest, dividends, and rents could be subject to a 3.8% Medicare surcharge in 2016 and thereafter. The amount subject to this surcharge is the lesser of your investment earnings (noted above) or the amount that exceeds a threshold amount. The threshold amount is $200,000 of modified adjusted gross income for single taxpayers, and $250,000 for married filing jointly.

accountant to understand this, and understanding the process can be very helpful. Here are the steps:

1. You would separate all bond and stock gains and losses into two categories: short term and long term. This means that anything held for over one year (such as a year and a day) would be considered long term. Anything held for less than that would be considered short term.[12]

2. You would separately compute your *net* short-term gains for all stocks and bonds that would be considered short term.[13] Thus you would combine all short-term gains with short-term losses.

Example: Laurel has $10,000 of short-term gains from mutual funds but has a short-term loss from some stock sales of $4,000. Her net short-term gain would be $6,000.

3. You would also separately net out your long-term gains and losses.[14] This would result in a net long-term gain or net long-term loss.

4. If one of these computations is a gain and one is a loss, you would net them out.

Example: Assume that Carol and Nick have a net long-term loss of $10,000 but have a net short-term gain of $4,000. By netting these out, you would have a net capital loss of $6,000, which would be considered long term in this example. This leads to the following strategy:

Strategy 1: Offset all capital gains with capital losses. Thus, if at year's end, you have some capital gains, consider selling some stock or bonds that generate a loss. This way, you can offset any gains with the losses. In fact, you can even buy back your loss stocks if you wait at least 31 days after their sale.

Caution: Beware of Wash-Sale Rule: This almost sounds like you are putting your stocks in your washing machine. In a sense that is what is going on. Taxpayers would sell their loss stocks on December 30, buy them back on January 2, and keep the same positions. In essence, they "washed" their gains away, if you will pardon my bad pun.

In order to stop this, Congress enacted the Wash-Sale Rule.[15] This rule says that you can't take a loss on any security, such as stock or bond or mutual fund, if you acquire, or enter into an option to acquire, substantially identical securities within 30 days either before or after the date of sale of the security. Whew, it is hard to believe that Congress actually has folks thinking about this.

Author's elaboration: If you read what I said very carefully, you will see that losses on your stocks and other securities are disallowed if you buy identical stocks or securities within 30 days either before or after the sale of the stock loss. Thus, if you bought the same stock within 30 days before you took the loss, those losses would be disallowed. Moreover, for those quick-thinking taxpayers among you, the IRS also said that your spouse or corporation can't buy identical stock in order to avoid this rule from applying to you.[16] Thus, the strategy would be as follows.

Strategy 2: Wait at least 31 days either before or after the sale of any stock or securities at a loss before you purchase back the same stock or securities in order to be able to use the loss.

I should also note that you can't buy back identical securities. Thus, if you took a loss on Exxon stock, you can't buy it back within 30 days. In fact, even convertible preferred stock from the same company is considered by the IRS substantially identical to common stock of the company.[17] However, stock from one corporation isn't generally considered identical to stock from another corporation.[18]

Strategy 3: Consider buying stock in a different corporation within 30 days in order to avoid the application of the Wash-Sale Rule.

1. If both the short-term and long-term netted figures result in losses, you would then offset up to $3,000 of your other income.[19] I should note that if you are married filing separately, you each can offset up to $1,500 of other income with capital losses. You would then carry all the losses forward to future years, and they keep the same status in future years. This means that they remain as either long-term or short-term losses.
2. If, however, both computations produce gains (thus, you have net short-term gains and net long-term gains), you would treat these net gains separately. The short-term gains are taxed as ordinary income, and the long-term gains, plus qualified dividends, are taxed at a maximum tax rate of 15 percent.

Author's elaboration: As you can see from Table 17-1, if you are in the 15 percent or less tax bracket, your capital gains tax for federal tax purposes is zero!

Corporate Capital Gains and Losses

Corporations have a different treatment for capital gains and losses. First, corporations don't get any special tax break for capital gains. It is all ordinary income. Second, if a corporation has a capital loss, that loss can be used only against the capital gains of the corporation.[20] Finally, unlike individuals who can carry over all capital losses indefinitely, corporations can either carry back capital losses three years or carry over capital losses five years and offset capital gains in either the past or the future.[21]

Example: Tim has a regular corporation that has a $10,000 capital loss. If he has no capital gains that year, he can either carry back the loss for the prior three years or carry forward the loss five years and offset any capital gains. He cannot use the loss to offset income other than capital gains.

Special rule for S corporations: S corporations are special, which might be why we call them "S corporations." These corporations pass through all capital gains and losses to the stockholders. Thus the stockholders treat these capital gains or losses as earnings on their individual returns. This means that capital gains from S corporations can get the same 15 percent maximum tax benefit and capital losses can be used against capital gains plus you can get an extra $3,000 of unused losses against any other type of income. Nice!

Investment Tax Mistakes Made by Taxpayers

Over the years, I have noticed a number of mistakes made by individuals regarding their investments. I would bet that at some time in your life, you make one or more of these errors. If you want to significantly increase your rate of return on all investments, not to mention avoid these mistakes, read the following very carefully.

Strategy 1: Hold stocks and bonds for more than one year in order to obtain long-term gain. This is very important. You have to hold any capital asset for *more than one year* in order to obtain the benefit of reduced capital gains tax rates. Numerous folks, who missed this deadline by even one day, were subject to ordinary tax rates on their gains. The IRS isn't a very forgiving agency in case you didn't guess this.

FIFO and LIFO aren't names of dogs. Here is the problem: You bought shares in a mutual fund or stock in a corporation at different times and at different prices. Now you want to sell some of these shares. They have different basis and different holding periods because you bought them at different times. How do you calculate the cost basis of the shares you want to sell?

The answer to this problem is that unless you adequately identified exactly which shares were sold, the IRS takes the position that you sold the oldest shares that you bought or were given to you as a gift, as determined by the date of the gift.[22] This is known as "first-in-first-out" or, using the nice cuddly acronym, "FIFO."

Example: In 2005 Rachel bought some mutual fund shares as follows:

> January 2005, purchased 300 shares @ $30 per share = $9,000
>
> March 2005, purchased 300 shares @ $40 per share = $12,000

If in 2014 Rachel sells 200 shares for $50 a share, unless otherwise specifically identified, she will be viewed to have sold the original shares, and she will pay tax on $20 ($50 sale – $30 basis) per share. This leads us to our next strategy.

Strategy 2: Identify the shares sold and pay less tax.[23] You are allowed to specifically identify which shares were sold and change your tax effects. In the example above with Rachel, had she told her broker to sell the shares that she bought in March, she would have had to pay tax on only the $10 per share gain. Not specifically giving the broker instructions to sell the later-purchased shares doubled Rachel's tax bill! The same can be said for shares sold at a loss. You want to sell the shares with the highest basis in order to get the bigger loss. Thus the rules are as follows:

- If you have a gain, sell the shares that give you long-term gain. If all shares qualify, sell the shares that have the highest basis. This will reduce the taxable gain to you.
- If you have a loss, sell the shares with the highest basis in order to maximize the loss.

Author's elaboration: You might wonder why the government institutes FIFO as the default. The reason, which actually was to benefit stockholders, was that using FIFO usually meant that stock gains would be from the oldest purchased shares. This would normally result in long-term capital gain. However, as you can see, this isn't always the best alternative. In order to avoid the FIFO rule, you need to adequately identify which shares are to be sold. You could do this by either specifically requesting shares be sold using the document number of the shares or by specifying to the broker (assuming that the broker has custody of the shares) exactly which shares are to be sold[24] and getting a confirmation within a reasonable time of what was sold. *Always* keep copies of any e-mails or correspondence with the broker in case the IRS wants to ensure that you gave the correct instructions to your broker; otherwise, FIFO will be applied to you automatically.

Strategy 3: Keep good records on your mutual funds. Mutual funds are a big problem for many people. You have to keep track of your basis in order to minimize your gain. The higher your basis, the lower your gain, and the less tax you pay.

Basis for mutual funds starts off with what you paid. This is the same for stocks. Moreover, like stocks, mutual funds send you a statement of dividends and stock gains and dividends received. You are taxed on the gains and on dividends received. Many people reinvest these dividends, which creates a paperwork nightmare in trying to figure out your basis.

Two Methods for Mutual Fund Basis Calculations

Because mutual funds create basis headaches with numerous purchases, dividend reinvestments, and distributions over a period of years, the IRS gives you two ways to calculate your basis. Both methods have their pros and cons, and you should pick the one that you personally like the most, or feel is the least hassle. I should also note that you can use different methods for different funds or even for different families of funds within the same mutual fund. However, once a method is elected, you are bound by it unless the IRS gives you permission to change.[25]

1. Double-Category Method.[26] In this method, you would divide all mutual fund purchases and share reinvestments between those shares that you owned for over a year (long term) and those that you owned for one year or less (which would be deemed short term). You would keep track of all the purchases and of all taxable dividends for each category and divide the total purchases and taxable dividends in each category by the number of shares in that category. Whew, that was a mouthful. Let's use an example (see Table 17-2) to explain this method.

Thus, from the example given in Table 17-2, you would have 410 shares deemed long term (this includes the original 400 shares purchased plus the 10 shares that were reinvested with dividends) with a total basis of $12,400. This provides a basis per share of $30.24 per share. The basis for the 315 shares (300 purchased and 15 purchased with the reinvested dividend) is $6,200, which gives a basis of $19.68 per share.

Table 17-2. Example of Tracking Shares for the Double-Category Method

	Long-Term Ownership	Short-Term Ownership
January 2006, bought 400 shares @ $30 per share	$12,000	
July 2009, bought 300 shares at $20 per share		$6,000
Dividend reinvestment in 2006–2008 for 10 shares	$400	
Dividend reinvestment in 2009 for 15 shares		$200
Total long-term basis	$12,400	
Total short-term basis		$6,200

Author's elaboration: If you were to sell 200 shares, without identifying which shares are sold, for $50 per share, you will be deemed to have sold the older shares first, giving you a profit of $3,952, which is computed by taking the sales price of $10,000 and subtracting the basis of the shares ($6,048), which is computed by multiplying the sold 200 shares by $30.24 per share. You would also reduce the gain by having to pay any commissions incurred in the sale.

2. Single-Category Method.[27] If the double-category method is too complicated, you can elect to use the single-category method. This method requires you to take the total basis of all shares you hold in the mutual fund, including those that were gotten through dividends and dividend reinvestments, and divide by the number of total shares regardless of the holding period.[28]

Example: Assume that you contributed $100 per month for 36 months to a mutual fund and reinvested $120 of dividends. Your total basis would be $3,720. If you owned a total of 120 shares, your basis per share would be $31. If you withdraw $500 from the fund, this would result in a sale of 16.13 shares.

Thus, the average basis of your remaining shares, which in the example was $31 per share, stays the same until you purchase new shares. Your new remaining basis would be $3,220.

Author's elaboration: This might not be easy, but it is easier than trying to determine the accuracy of what shares you sold, when you withdrew the $500, and trying to figure out the basis of these shares. In addition, you are deemed to have sold the older shares first, known as FIFO, unless you have specifically identified the shares to be sold.

Making the election: In order to use one of the averaging methods, you need to make an election on your tax return for the first year in which you want the election to apply.[29] The election should say that you are using the single-category or double-category averaging method for determining both gain and loss for shares of [insert name of mutual fund]. It is a really easy election.

You also should maintain good records of all calculations used in computing the averaging method. You should have a spreadsheet for *each* fund family. Table 17-3 provides an example of what you would put down for a purchase or reinvestment of shares.

If this was all that occurred during the year, your year-end spreadsheet would look like the one shown in Table 17-4.

Strategy 4: Don't fail to use tax efficient funds. Most investors hold their mutual funds for the long term. Thus they are quite surprised to find that they get a bill for short-term gains realized by the fund. The reason is that mutual funds are *not* investments to the surprise of many. They are simply vehicles that hold assets such as

Table 17-3. Record Share Transactions

XYZ FUND					
Buy Date	**Purchase Price**	**Number of Shares**	**Cost per Share**	**Holding**	**Comments**
3/20/09	$4,020	100.0	$40.20	Short term	Purchase
7/1/09	$54	1.2	$45.00	Short term	Reinvested dividends

Table 17-4. Annual Share Transaction Statement

XYZ FUND					
Buy Date	**Purchase Price**	**Number of Shares**	**Cost per Share**	**Holding**	**Comments**
3/20/09	$4,020	100.0	$40.20	Short term	Purchase
7/1/09	$54	1.2	$45.00	Short term	Reinvested dividends
Year-End Subtotal	$4,074	101.2			
Average Cost Basis			$40.26		

stocks, bonds, and real estate. Thus they can sell some of their assets at a short-term gain if they didn't hold the stock over one year. These gains and losses incurred by the funds are passed through to the shareholders.

However, as of late, some mutual funds try to become more tax efficient. These funds not only try to buy shares in quality companies, but they also minimize the tax burden on shareholders by holding their underlying stocks or bonds for over a year. Thus gains would usually be long-term gains that would pass through to the shareholders of the fund as long-term gains instead of short-term gains.

Investing in tax-efficient funds can certainly increase your rate of return, but they can also result in fewer tax headaches. There are a number of tax-efficient or tax-managed funds available that you can find with a Google search.

Strategy 5: Put the right investments in the right accounts. One big question that I get a lot is, What are the best investments for my retirement accounts? Should I use stocks and real estate in my IRAs and own bonds individually? The answer to these questions will probably surprise you.

In effect, there are two types of investment accounts. The first is a tax-advantaged account such as 401(k), IRA, simplified employee pension, and profit-sharing plan. The other plans are your normal or traditional investment accounts that you own in your name or own in joint names. Placing the wrong investments into the wrong account can literally cost you thousands of dollars each year! Here is the rule:

> Place investments that produce ordinary income into tax-advantaged accounts, and place investments that produce little tax or are taxed at long-term capital gains rates in traditional accounts.

The reasoning for this is that monies that are distributed from tax-advantaged accounts are taxed at ordinary income rates. If you put stocks or other investments that normally produce long-term capital gains and dividends that are taxed at a 15 percent maximum tax rate into a tax-advantaged account, you have converted what would be a 15 percent rate into ordinary income, which can result in a federal tax rate as high as 35 percent. Yuck!

Thus the best investments for tax-advantaged accounts are those that produce ordinary income such as corporate and Treasury bonds, mortgages, and stocks held for short-term gains. Stocks with long-term gain potential or those that pay high dividends are best owned individually.

Author's elaboration: If you don't have a lot of money to invest in traditional accounts, you might need to place some stocks in your investment accounts since that is all that you have for retirement.

Strategy 6: Do *not* place real estate or tax-exempt bonds or even annuities in tax-advantaged accounts.

As I noted above, all funds that come out of the tax-advantaged account, such as a traditional 401(k) and IRA, are taxed at ordinary income rates. Placing tax-exempt bonds into these accounts would convert tax-free interest into fully taxable interest.

Moreover, real estate would also be a poor investment for tax-advantaged accounts despite what many of the promoters of real estate will tell you. Why? There are several big tax benefits of investment in real estate: it produces long-term capital gains on sale, if there is a gain, and ordinary losses if there is a loss. It allows for a lot of leverage since you can borrow most of the purchase price from a lender or from the seller. Finally, it also produces a lot of depreciation throughout the time you own the property, which you can use against the rent and maybe even your earned income. However, when you use a tax-advantaged account to own real estate, you have done away with all these real estate benefits. First, all distributions from the plan, including the real estate, will be ordinary income to you. Second, there will be no losses allowed on the sale of the real estate by the plan. Third, you can't use borrowed money to buy real estate in a tax-advantaged plan. Thus you don't get the benefit of leverage. Last but not least, you won't get any depreciation deductions. The plan gets the depreciation, which is worthless to it since tax-advantaged plans don't generally pay tax.

However, as I am fond of saying, where there is a will, there's a lawyer. If you want your plan to own some real estate for diversification, you should seriously consider owning some REIT stocks. These are real estate investment trust shares that are readily marketable like those of any stock. The distributions don't qualify for the special 15 percent tax rate on dividends, and they don't spin off any depreciation anyway. Thus you can get the benefit of owning real estate without the hassles. REITs are, in fact, ideal for tax-advantaged investments.

Moreover, don't own annuities in tax-advantaged investments. The reason is that annuities are tax deferred anyway, just like tax-advantaged investments. You won't need to have them in tax-advantaged investments.

Finally, as with real estate, don't buy assets in your tax-advantaged investments that produce a lot of depreciation. I have seen people purchase vending machines and other equipment used for investment in their pension plans and, thus, lose all the depreciation from that equipment because it was in the plan.

Summary

- There are a number of tax implications from being totally tax-exempt to being fully taxable, when you sell stocks or receive interest and dividends.
- Use Table 17-1 to address most of these implications.
- You always net out your capital gains against capital losses.
- If you have either capital gains or losses, sell other stock that has the opposite effect in order to either wipe out your gains or use your losses.
- Hold your stocks for more than one year in order to obtain long-term capital gains. This will result in a maximum tax to you of only 15–20 percent plus the state rate. However, there is an additional 3.8 percent Medicare surcharge on capital gains and rents, and taxable interest if you earn over $250,000 of adjusted gross income (AGI) and married; $200,000 of AGI if single; or over $125,000 of AGI if married filing separately.

- If you have a loss on the sale of stocks, bonds, or mutual funds, don't buy the same security within 30 days of the sale of the bonds, stocks, or mutual funds. This is known as the Wash-Sale Rule.
- Shares of one corporation are not deemed identical to shares of another corporation.
- It is usually better to specifically identify the shares sold by your broker in order to minimize your taxes. Otherwise, the FIFO (first-in-first-out) rule applies.
- If you have a gain, sell the shares that give you long-term gain. If all shares qualify, sell the shares that have the highest basis. This will reduce the taxable gain to you.
- If you have a loss, sell the shares with the highest basis in order to maximize the loss.
- Keep good records of any purchases made for your stock and mutual fund investments. This should also include any reinvestment made with dividends. These records should include any copies of broker's statements plus a spreadsheet for each mutual fund or stock showing purchase date, amount spent on the purchase (which includes any commissions), the number of shares, the cost per share, and whether it was a purchase of shares or a reinvestment of dividends.
- There are two alternative methods for keeping track of your basis in a mutual fund. The first is the double-category method and the second is the single-category method. They both take the total amount invested by you or invested with dividends and divide by your total number of shares. However, the double-category method breaks it down further between those shares owned for more than one year and those owned for less than one year.
- Consider using tax-efficient mutual funds that generally hold stocks over a year so that you can get long-term gains on their stock sales.
- Place investments that produce ordinary income into tax-advantaged accounts, and place investments that produce little tax or are taxed at long-term capital gains rates in traditional accounts.
- Do *not* place real estate or tax-exempt bonds, depreciable equipment, or even annuities in tax-advantaged accounts.

Notes

1. Section 61 of the IRC.
2. See Section 103 of the IRC. Note that State Private activity bonds aren't necessarily tax free.
3. 15 percent for taxpayers in the 25–35 percent brackets, and 20 percent for anyone in the 39.6 percent bracket. This is all in addition to state tax rates.
4. Section 301(c)(2) of the IRC.
5. Section 61 of the IRC.
6. 15 percent for taxpayers in the 25–35 percent brackets, and 20 percent for anyone in the 39.6 percent bracket. This is all in addition to state tax rates.
7. Although this chapter doesn't apply to real estate, I thought I would mention the tax consequences of taking depreciation when you sell your rental property at a gain. If there is a gain, you are taxed at a 25 percent rate for all gain up to the amount of depreciation you have taken. See Section 1(h) of the IRC.

8. Section 1(h)(1) of the IRC.

9. Section 1(h) of the IRC and Notice 97-64, Section 4, 1997-2 CB 323.

10. This applies in 2018 to single people who earn less than $38,700 and to married people filing joint returns whose taxable income is under $77,400.

11. Section 1211(b) of the IRC.

12. Sections 1222(3) and 1222(4) of the IRC.

13. Section 1222(5) of the IRC.

14. Section 1222(7) of the IRC.

15. Section 1091(a) of the IRC.

16. IRS Pub Number 550 (2007), p. 55.

17. Rev. Rul. 77-201, 1977-1 CB 250.

18. IRS Pub. Number 550 (2007), p. 55.

19. Section 1211(b) of the IRC.

20. Section 1211(a) of the IRC.

21. Section 1212(a)1 of the IRC.

22. Section 1.1012-1(c)(1) of the Regulations.

23. Ibid.

24. Section 1.1012-1(c)(3) of the Regulations.

25. Section 1.1012-1(e) of the Regulations.

26. Section 1.1012-1(e) of the Regulations.

27. Section 1.1012-1(e) of the Regulations.

28. Section 1.1012-1(e)(4) of the Regulations.

29. Section 1.1012-1(e)(6) of the Regulations.

18

Trader versus Investor: The Best-Kept Secret Around

Most people don't realize that being in business is the last great tax reduction opportunity left. In fact, as noted in our tax strategies system, we actually have two tax systems. One is for employees, and one is for business. If you are an employee, you can deduct your home interest, property taxes, charitable contributions, and IRAs or 401(k) contributions—that is until some sort of flat tax or consumption tax is passed. However, if you are in business, you get all the deductions that employees get *plus* you can deduct part of your house, vacations, education for kids (if done correctly), and some automobile expenses. And you can set up a pension plan that makes any government pension seem paltry by comparison—and much more.

> **Chapter Overview**
> By reading this chapter, you will learn the following:
> - Advantages and disadvantages of being a dealer
> - Advantages and disadvantages of being an investor
> - Advantages and disadvantages of making the election to include capital gains as investment income
> - Advantages of being a trader
> - An understanding of the factors used by courts in determining trader status

Wouldn't it be great if you could take advantage of all the business deductions that traditional and home-based business owners get by simply trading in stock and securities for your own account? You can, if you are deemed a "trader."

Entities

When buying stocks and bonds, you are considered to be one of three types of entities: a dealer, an investor, or a trader. We discuss all the pros and cons of each category. However, being a trader has a lot of the advantages of the other two categories with few of the disadvantages. All gains and losses from securities result in a capital gain/loss. Moreover, all investment-related expenses are business expenses, which are deductible on Schedule C as is the case with all other types of business expenses noted in our Tax Strategy program. Moreover, traders can claim deductions available to most home-based businesses if the trading occurs out of the home. Thus this is one circumstance where "you can have your cake and eat it too."

Who Is a Dealer?

A dealer is someone who has an established place of business and regularly purchases securities for resale to customers.[1] In addition, the courts generally note that to be a securities dealer, you must be licensed in securities and have an office that sells stocks and bonds.[2]

Observation: The IRS will rarely even consider you to be a dealer if you are not licensed in securities and work for or own a securities brokerage. Even if this is the case, it is still rare to be treated as a dealer in your own portfolio. Thus most people will not be considered dealers.

Advantages of Dealer Status

If you are a dealer, you can declare all investment expenses as a business deduction. In fact, even expenses normally not deductible for investors (such as convention and seminar expenses) would be deductible for dealers.[3] Dealers can, therefore, set up qualified pension/profit-sharing plans and even claim home office expenses if the business is operated out of their homes. Moreover, if there is a loss from their activity, the loss may be used against any form of income (such as wages, interest, dividends, and pensions).[4] Any loss that exceeds your yearly income may either be carried back 2 years or carried forward 20 years and may offset future income from any source.[5] Finally, unlike investors, dealers may sell securities at a loss and buy them back shortly thereafter and still claim the loss. Investors and traders must wait at least 30 days after the sale to buy back the securities to keep the loss.[6]

Disadvantages of Being a Dealer

The one significant disadvantage of being a dealer is that all income is ordinary income, and thus you can rarely take advantage of long-term capital gains rates that can be as low as 10 percent. In addition, dealers pay Social Security on all income including stock sales.[7] Dealers must also recognize gains and losses on all inventory on hand as if they sold it on December 31. This is called mark-to-market.[8] All gains recognized are considered ordinary income, and all losses result in ordinary losses, not capital losses.[9]

Observation: Unless you own a stock brokerage company, don't worry about being classified as a dealer. You will probably be either an investor or a trader.

What Is an Investor?

For the most part, court decisions have treated taxpayers as investors. In fact, it is very difficult not to be classified as such. The following are factors that the courts examine in order for someone to be classified as an investor:

- A major source of income is dividends or interest.[10]
- Generally he or she holds for securities long term or at least six months.[11]
- He or she doesn't usually have very frequent trades (usually less than 200 per year).[12]

Example: Mary buys and sells stocks and options for her own investment account. She usually holds stocks for at least one year or more and conducts about 50 trades a year. She makes substantial income from dividends from her stocks. Her status would be deemed to be an investor.

Author's elaboration: The courts are real sticklers for trying to classify taxpayers as investors. If you want to obtain trader status, you really need to watch all the criteria noted above for investors. If you meet any of these, you will probably be deemed an investor and not a trader.

Advantages of Being an Investor

Without question, the single biggest advantage of being an investor is that most gains constitute long-term capital gains. The rules for long-term gains have been greatly complicated by the Taxpayer Relief Act of 1997. Who says tax relief and simplification go hand in hand, because they don't! The capital gains rate is dependent on the length of the holding period and your current tax rate. Table 18-1 summarizes these rates.

Table 18-1. Capital Gains Rates

Holding Period	Capital Gain Rate[13]	Other Requirements
Less than 12 months and a day	Normal tax rate is (0%–37% plus a potential 3.8% Medicare Surcharge)	None
At least 12 months and a day	Maximum rate is (0%–23.8%) plus state rate	None

Disadvantages of Being an Investor

Congress is very good at giving benefits and taking some back. It is Congress's way of increasing taxes without anyone knowing. This may be a major reason so many congressmen and congresswomen and senators get reelected. Investors have some serious disadvantages. They cannot deduct any expenses of attending a convention or seminar on investing. This disallowance applies to food, lodging, and transportation as well as the cost of the actual seminar.[14] Yuck! Moreover, investors are also subject to some of their investment interest being disallowed. Investment interest (such as margin interest) is limited to investment income. However, you may carry over any excess unused margin interest and use it against investment income in the future.[15]

In addition, you would think that capital gains count as investment income. Think again. In an effort to raise taxes without anyone knowing, Congress noted that capital gains don't count as investment income for purposes of offsetting investment interest.[16] However, in order to avoid too much criticism, Congress allows investors to elect to have all capital gains treated as investment income. But before you run to make this election, you should be aware that any election to treat capital gains as investment income will prevent you from using the much lower long-term capital gains rates for that year.[17]

Example: John has $5,000 of margin interest (investment interest). If he has $2,000 of dividends and $10,000 of capital gains resulting from the sale of stock, he may use only $2,000 of investment interest. The remainder gets carried forward. However, if John elects to treat his capital gains as investment income, he may use the full $5,000 of investment interest to offset his gain.

Making the election: You may make the election by filing IRS form 4952. This form must be filed by the due date for your tax return (including any extensions).

Observation: It usually is *not* advisable to make this election if you have substantial long-term capital gains. However, if most of your gain is short term or if you have a lot of investment interest with little investment income (i.e., dividends and interest), you may want to make this election.

Problem for Investors

Investment expenses such as newsletter subscriptions, seminars, computer charges and accountin fees are no longer deductible by investors as a result of the new tax law.[18] There is some good news though. Itemized deductions used to phase out under what was called the peace limitation. Thus, if you made over a certain income, you would lose 3% of your itemized deductions as your income exceeded a threshold amount. The good news is that there is no longer any phase out of itemized deduductions. Thus, the peace limitation was eliminated by the new tax Cuts and Jobs Act.[19]

Author's observation: Welcome to the beginning of flat and consumption taxes. You are taxed on your income but get to deduct very little in the way of expenses against it. As you can see, this is a big disadvantage for investors and for the public at large. The main hidden goal of most of these tax reform proposals is to *raise taxes*.

Second Major Problem for Investors

Investors' capital losses have some significant limitations.[20] You need to first understand how capitals gains are computed. Investors take all their short-term gains and net these out with short-term losses. They then take any long-term gains and net these out with long-term losses. Net short-term gains are taxed at your normal tax rate. However, long-term gains, which are gains from sales of bonds, stocks, and mutual funds held over one year, get a special 0–20 percent plus a potential extra 3.8 percent surcharge on long-term gains for a total maximum tax rate of 23.8 percent. This is great for gains. However, losses are treated a bit differently.

If you have a net capital loss, you can use that loss only against capital gains. However, despite this, you are allowed an extra $3,000 of capital losses against any other form of income; the remaining losses getting carried over to future years.

Example: Lynn and Joe have net capital gains from some stock sales of $10,000. However, they also have some capital losses of $30,000 resulting from the stock market decline. They may offset $10,000 of these losses with the capital gains and then take an extra $3,000 against their earned income. The remaining unused $17,000 of losses gets an unlimited carryover to future years and is treated as if these losses were incurred in those years.

Trader Overview

As you can see, being an investor has some big advantages (capital gains on security sales) and some big offsetting disadvantages (either no deduction for expenses or phaseouts of those deductions that would be allowed and capital loss limitations). There is a third category available to you. This category is called a trader. Amazingly, many people are not aware of this status and are also not aware of how beneficial this status can be. Traders get many of the advantages of being a dealer with the ability to get capital gains on stock, bond, and option sales. In addition, traders can deduct investment expenses with no phaseouts or thresholds! Thus it achieves the best of all worlds yet eliminates most of the negatives.

Trader Advantages

There are a number of advantages to being considered a trader. First, all gains from the sale of stock, bonds, and options are treated the same way as they are with investors; they result in capital gains and capital losses.[21] However, as you will learn, most of the gains and losses must be short term in duration.

Second, and most important, traders may treat all investment expenses as business expenses and not as itemized deductions.[22] Traders are deemed to be in business.

This means that, as a trader, you can deduct all convention and seminar expenses that are directly related to your trading business (unlike an investor), and all investment expenses are deductible with no thresholds (as with a dealer). Moreover, you can deduct all other reasonable business expenses since a trading business is considered to be a business just like any other type of business. In fact, the expenses are reported on IRS Schedule C. Investers, as a result of the new Tax Cuts and Jobs Act, can no longer deduct investment expenses such as publications as itemized deductions.

Example: Susan has $20,000 of gains as a trader and has incurred $4,000 of investment expenses such as stock advisory fees, safe deposit fees, accounting fees, and management fees. The $20,000 is capital gain (probably short term), and the fees are completely deductible dollar for dollar on Schedule C.

In addition, traders are exempt from the investment interest limitations just as dealers are because traders are deemed to be in a business.[23] Traders may also use the mark-to-market rules (discussed below for commodity traders) like dealers and recognize gain and loss on all securities held on December 31.[24] Last, but not least, a trading business is *not* subject to Social Security taxes unlike most traditional businesses.[25]

Mark-to-Market Election

Mark-to-market election is a special rule that applies to all traders, but it is especially valuable to commodities traders. This election allows traders to recognize all gains and losses at year end as if the stock or commodity were sold on December 31. For stock traders, this isn't a good deal since they would have to recognize gain even though the stock or bond wasn't sold. However, for commodity traders, this could be a good deal because by making this election, you can recognize 60 percent of your gain as long-term capital gains! The catch, of course, is that you have to recognize your gains even though you may not have closed out the position. However, you would also recognize loss positions, which would help offset some of these gains.

Author's elaboration: As you can see, being a trader is almost too good to be true. You get all the positives of being a dealer with none of the negatives. However, since it is so good, the IRS, being the grouchy organization that it is, makes it tough to classify yourself as a trader. It is doable, but you must meet all the rules noted here.

What Is a Trader?

Amazingly, there is no Internal Revenue Code section defining "trader status." However, there are literally dozens of cases dealing with the subject. Thus the concept of being in the business of trading your own securities is well established in tax law. The cases note that being a trader lies somewhere between being a dealer and being an investor. Although "trader status" is a factual issue, there are a number of factors that the courts examine in order to determine whether you meet this status:

1. Traders trade securities on a frequent and regular basis in order to catch the short-term market swings.[26] This frequency must be regular. Simply working hard at managing your portfolio is not enough if your trading is not frequent and regular.[27] Thus, in one case Mr. Boatner was held to be an investor and not a trader even though he worked 40–60 hours a week in managing his portfolio because he had only 5–12 days of trading per year. Moreover, the tax court has held that 29 purchases and 22 sales in a year was not deemed frequent enough.[28] Likewise, only 75 transactions per year wasn't held to be frequent and regular enough.[29] In one case, however, 332 transactions worth a total of $3.2 million qualified the taxpayer as a trader.[30] Here the taxpayer not only put in a substantial amount of time in managing his portfolio but also talked to officers of companies. He also attended numerous lectures on security and investment topics and on trading.

Observation: As noted in Chapter 8, you can never get enough training. You should document any training that you attended and any other day-to-day activities involved in managing your portfolio. A good diary works wonders here. You can get a tax diary from our offices at Tax Reduction Institute. See www.taxreductioninstitute.com.

2. The transactions should be throughout the year and not solely over a short period. In fact, even large numbers of transactions are not enough if they're carried out in a short period of time. Thus, in one case, a taxpayer had 326 substantial transactions in a year. Normally, this would be enough to constitute being a trader. However, 40 percent of all transactions occurred in a one-month period.[31]

Observation: Being in business is a year-round occupation. The courts have not allowed trader status for people who don't have numerous transactions all year round. The key is to trade at least four days a week (and preferably five days a week) and at least ten days a month for most of the months throughout the year.

3. Traders do not have a substantial amount of dividends, interest, and long-term capital gains. Regardless of the frequency of transactions, if a substantial part of your income is from dividends, interest, or long-term capital gains, you will be deemed an investor and not a trader. This point cannot be overemphasized. A great illustration of this is found in two cases. Mr. Moeller[32] had over 1,000 transactions throughout the year. He was not held to be a trader because most of his income was composed of interest and dividends. A great but gross example of this point occurred in a little publicized case called *Ropfogel*.[33] Here the taxpayer had over 12,000 transactions. You certainly can't beat this for frequency and regularity. However, because most of the profit came from dividends and long-term capital gains and not short-term gains, he was held to be an investor. Likewise, having a thousand or more transactions during the year is immaterial regardless of how hard you work or how much time you put in if most of your gain is long-term gain.[34]

Observation: There are numerous other cases involving this issue. The bottom line is that traders hold securities, for the most part, for a short period of time (usually less than

30 days and preferably a shorter period of time). This results in most gains being short term and very few dividends accruing.

4. Most of the gain should be short-term gain from securities held less than 30 days. As noted, the type of income that you generate is very important. Traders trade for short-term market swings. They usually do not hold stock for long-term gains like investors. This is a vital distinction. Mr. Mayer was a good illustration of this point.[35] He worked full time managing his portfolio. He had so many transactions that a brokerage firm provided him with an office. He had over 1,000 purchases and sales during the year totaling over 1 million shares. However, only 6 percent of these shares were held less than 30 days. Most were held long enough to obtain long-term capital gains (at that time there was a six-month holding period for long-term gain). The court held that Mr. Mayer was not a trader but was an investor. Interestingly, Mr. Mayer was so upset with this decision that he fought the IRS twice on this issue in two different courts by altering some minor facts. I guess some people can't take a hint.

Observation: Traders can have some long-term gain. If you feel that you have a winner, you surely can hold on to it for a long period of time. Although there is no hard-and-fast rule as to how much of your gain must be short term, a good rule of thumb should be that approximately 80 to 90 percent or more of all securities purchased should not be held for more than 30 days.

Author's hot tip: Since traders must hold most securities under 30 days, if you want to hold some securities over a longer term, put the title to these securities in a different name. You could title the securities in the name of your kids, or spouse, or even set up a separate corporation for your investments.

You can even run your trading business out of a subchapter S corporation (since all income and losses flow through to you as a stockholder) and keep your investments in your personal name. (See Chapter 9, dealing with finding the best entity for your business.)

5. Traders control all purchases and sales of securities and do not use money managers except as advisors. As in any business, you must materially participate in order to deduct business expenses above business income.[36] This means that you must be involved in your business regularly and continuously. This generally means working at least 100 hours per year more than anyone else or working at least 500 hours per year.[37] Likewise, you should be making all purchase and sales decisions. If you are delegating this responsibility to money managers, you may well be treated as an investor and not as a trader.[38] A good rule of thumb is as follows: the more involvement by you and less by others, the better.

6. The greater the volume, the better. There are certainly no numbers set in stone as to what amount of funds should be at stake to be a trader or what number of shares should be traded.[39] Most cases leaning toward trader status usually involved hundreds of thousands of shares per year. Note: You do not need this amount per transaction. It is a per-year figure. You may not need to trade this many shares yearly. Probably the cases that have appeared in the courts with these high numbers have been there because of the vast amount of money involved. You may very well be deemed a trader with as few as a couple of hundred shares traded weekly. To be safe, however, the higher the volume traded per week, the better.

7. Treat your trading business as a trading business for IRS purposes. This simply means that you should put the beans in the right jar. If you are a trader, file Schedule C for your expenses and document your business expenses as noted in our tax advantage system.[40]

In short, if you read our analysis of what constitutes a trader, you will get a good "feel" for what criteria are important in being considered a trader. This should provide a strong framework for you to plan your business.

What Expenses Are Deductible for a Trader?

As noted above, being a trader means that you are in business. You can, therefore, take all the ordinary and necessary business deductions that most other "traditional" businesses get. In addition, there generally are no limits, phaseouts, or thresholds to exceed for these expenses. Many of the business expenses that are available are found throughout this book and in my home study course, Tax Strategies for Business Professionals. However, the following is an overview of some of the more usual trader's expenses:

- Safe deposit box rentals
- Accounting and bookkeeping fees
- A portion of your home expenses (see Chapter 6)
- Car expenses allocated to your business (see Chapter 5)
- Subscription for investment publications, periodicals, and stock investment newsletters
- Books on investing, trading, and security analysis
- Seminars on investing, trading, and security analysis
- Video and audio tapes on investing and on security analysis
- Tax advice such as this book or our Tax Strategies for Business Professionals series
- Equipment depreciation for business (computers, calculators, cell phones)
- Any investment reporting service
- Salaries of assistants and helpers
- Brokerage fees (which may be added to basis or subtracted from sales price)
- Meals and entertainment of analysts, brokers, and other related people (see Chapter 2)
- Season tickets, golf, movies, and plays (see Chapter 2)
- Qualified plans and IRAs
- Travel to caretake investments or meet with money managers or corporate officers (see Chapter 3)
- Deductions for the equivalent of your children's education and weddings by hiring them (see Chapter 4)

Table 18-2. Tax Treatment Summary for Dealers, Traders, and Investors

	Type of Investment	Character of Gain or Loss	Investment/ Business Expenses	Interest Expenses
Dealer	Stocks or bonds	Normal tax rates for gains and losses	Business expense	Business expense
Dealer	Stock options	Ordinary	Business expense	Business expense
Investor	Stocks or bonds	Capital gain/ loss	Investment expense no deduction	Investment interest limits
Investor	Options	Capital gain/loss	Investment expense limits	Investment interest limits
Trader	Stocks or bonds	Capital gain/ loss	Business expense	Business interest
Trader	Options	Capital gain/ loss	Business expense	Business interest

Summary

- There are three possible classifications for those who buy and sell stocks: dealer, investor, or trader.
- A dealer is someone who has a fixed place of business and regularly purchases securities for sale to customers.
- Dealers have ordinary income and can deduct all their ordinary and necessary business expenses. You probably won't be classified as a dealer.
- As a rule, most taxpayers are treated as investors when buying and selling stocks. You get the advantage of capital gains and can get long-term gains.
- If you own stocks, bonds, and mutual funds over a year, you can get long-term capital gains, which provide a maximum tax rate of 20% plus a 3.8 percent Medicare surcharge plus state taxes. However, taxpayers who are in the 10–15 percent tax bracket anyway have a reduced long-term capital gains rate of *zero*!
- Investors can no longer deduct investment expenses because Congress eliminated all miscellaneous itemized deductions. Stock traders, on the other hand, can deduct investment expenses.

- Investors also have their capital losses limited to their capital gains; however, they can get to use up to $3,000 of these losses against any other form of income. Any unused losses get carried over to future years forever and are used as if these losses were earned in those years.
- Traders are investors who meet certain criteria. They have the advantage of getting capital gains, like investors (although the gain is generally short term), and, unlike investors, they can deduct investment expenses and investment seminars with no threshold.
- Commodity and currency traders can make mark-to-market elections and have 60 percent of their gains treated as long-term capital gains.
- Being classified as a trader is tough to do. According to a number of court decisions, you must meet all the following criteria:
  - Traders trade securities on a frequent and regular basis in order to catch the short-term market swings. This means that you should have at least 300 or more trades per year. In fact, the greater the number of the trades, the better.
  - Transactions should be conducted throughout the year and not solely over a short period. You should be conducting your trading activities at least 4–5 days per week and at least 11 days per month throughout most of the year.
  - Traders do not have a substantial amount of dividends, interest, and long-term capital gains. At least 80 percent of your income should *not* be from interest and dividends.
  - Most of the gain should be short term from securities held less than 30 days. In fact, it would be even better if most of your trades were closed within one week.
  - Traders control all purchases and sales of securities and do not use money managers except as advisors.
  - Treat your trading business as a trading business for IRS purposes.

Notes

1. Section 1.475-5 of the ITR.
2. *Pan-Am Bank and Trust v. Comm.*, 5 BTA 839(1927); *Pacific Securities v. Comm.*, 63 TCM 2060(1992); *Furer v. Comm.*, 65 TCM 2420(1993).
3. Section 162 of the IRC.
4. Section 172 of the IRC.
5. Section 172(b)(1)(A) of the IRC.
6. Sections 1091 and 1091(a) of the IRC (except as it relates to dealers).
7. Sections 1401(b) and 1402(a,b,c) of the IRC and Section 1.1401-1(c) of the regulations.
8. Section 495(a) of the IRC.
9. Section 475(d)(3)(A)(I) of the IRC.
10. *Ralph Purvis v. Comm.*, 530 F.2d 1332 (9th Cir. 1976); *John Klawa v. Comm.*, T.C. Memo 1968–1985.
11. *Hsiao Liang Chajang*, 23 TC 1040(1955).
12. *Frank Mayer*, 1994-209 TC Memo.

13. If you are in the 15 percent tax bracket or lower, your long-term capital gains rate is zero! See our Chapter 17, "Tax Planning for Stock and Bond Investors." See Section 1(b) of the IRC.

14. Section 212 of the IRC.

15. Sections 163(d)(1) and (2) of the IRC.

16. Section 163(d)(4) of the IRC.

17. Section 163(d)(4)(B)(ii) and (iii) of the IRC.

18. Code section 67(g) as amended by the 2017 Tax Cuts and Jobs Act , Sec. 11045.

19. IRC Sec. 68(f) as amended by 2017 Tax Cuts and Jobs Act, Section 11046(a).

20. Section 1211 (b)(1) of the IRC.

21. *Frank Lester*, T.C. Memo 1995-317; *Anthony Reinachus v. Comm.*, 373 F.2d 900 (2nd Cir. 1967); *Crow v. Comm.*, 79 TC 541(1982).

22. *Norbert Wiesler*, 6 TC 1148(1946).

23. Section 163 of the IRC.

24. General Explanation of Taxpayer Relief Act of 1997(JCS-23-97), 12/1/97, p. 181.

25. Section 1402(a)(3)(A) of the IRC and Section 1.1402(a)-6(a)(1) of the ITR.

26. *John Moller v. United States*, 721 F.2d 8106 (DC Cir. 1983); *King v. Comm.*, 89 TC 445 (1987); *Groetzinger v. Comm.*, 771 F.2d 269 (7th Cir.1984).

27. *Nathan Boatner*, T.C. Memo 1997-379 (1997).

28. *Asch v. Comm.*, T.C. Memo 1986-236.

29. *Rudolph Staffler*, T.C. Memo 1995-271.

30. *Levin v. United States*, 597 F.2d 760 (Ct. Cl. 1979).

31. *Stephen Paoli*, T.C. Memo 1991-351.

32. *Moeller v. United States, supra.*

33. *Ropfogel v. United States*, U.S. Dist. Lexis 9697(DC KS 1991).

34. *Estate of Louis Yaeger v. Comm.*, T.C. Memo 1988-264, *Aff'd*, 889 F.2d 29 (2nd Cir.1989); *Liang v. Comm.*, 23 TC 1040 (1955); *Purvis v. Comm., supra.*

35. *Mayer v. Comm.*, T.C. Memo 1992-769; see also *Mayer v. Comm.*, 32 Fd. Cl. 149 (1994).

36. Section 469(c)(1)(B) of the IRC.

37. Section 469 of the IRC.

38. *Ralph Purvis v. Comm.*, 530 F.2d 1332 (9th Cir. 1976); *Kales v. Comm.*, 101 F.2d 35 (6th Cir. 1939).

39. *Groetzinger v. Comm.*, 771 F.2d 269(7th Cir. 1985).

40. *Mayer v. Comm., supra.*

19

Tax Scams and Other Shams

The money is the same, whether you earn it or scam it.

—Bobby Heenan

Who said crime doesn't pay? Look at how much Madoff made.

—Anonymous

You are attending a seminar in a nice room with plenty of expensive audio-visual equipment. Many of the seats are filled with folks who are well-dressed and quite courteous. Out comes a speaker who is well-dressed and polished and seems to be very competent. He informs members of the group that they can eliminate paying taxes based on a number of legal arguments. He cites numerous cases that have supposedly supported his arguments.

Stop! Before you blow your hard-earned cash on his training materials and documents, take a deep breath and read this chapter.

There are a number of tax scams, not to mention other types of fraud, which are being

Chapter Overview

This chapter covers the following:
1. Tax scams such as:
   a. Phishing scams
   b. Economic stimulus scams
   c. Frivolous tax arguments
   d. Fuel credit scams
   e. Hiding income offshore
   f. Abusive retirement scams
   g. Claiming zero wages
   h. Filing false claims for refunds
   i. Return-preparer tax fraud
   j. Disguised corporate ownership
   k. Misuse of trusts
   l. Abuse of charitable contributions and organizations
   m. Slavery tax credits
2. Investment scams
   a. Ponzi schemes
   b. Trading software scams
   c. High-priced training scams
3. Inheritance scams

perpetrated upon the American public. It has become such a widespread phenomenon that many of the enforcement agencies are overwhelmed. My purpose is to protect you, dear reader, from being another victim of the newest types of thefts:

Chapter Overview (Cont.)

4. Pyramid scams
5. Advertised products scams, especially on infomercials
6. Jobs scams
7. Fabulous offer scams
8. Free vacation for attending a seminar scams
9. Telephone scams
10. Seminar and investment scams
11. Book scams
12. Identity theft and what to do if you are a victim

1. Tax scams. There are an ever-increasing number of scams being investigated by the IRS. Some of these scams are so devious and clever that even the smartest of folks can be fooled. Every year the IRS publishes a list of the "dirty dozen" tax scams. Here are some of the latest scams being investigated by the IRS.

a. Phishing scams. Folks are receiving letters or e-mails with the IRS/Treasury department logo informing them that they may be owed a refund or to inform them that they may owe a lot of taxes unless they clear up a possible error in identity. In order to obtain this refund, or to clear up the error, they have to prove that they are the right person by confirming certain personal information such as social security number, mother's maiden name, address, and so on. To date, the IRS has identified as many as 1,500 different phishing scams.

Author's elaboration: The IRS will never call you or write you asking for this type of personal information. You should never provide it to anyone by phone, letter, or e-mail. If you get an e-mail requesting this type of information allegedly from the IRS, forward the e-mail to phishing@irs.gov.

b. Economic stimulus scams. Some scam artists are trying to trick individuals into revealing personal financial information that can be used to access their financial accounts by making promises relating to the economic stimulus payment, often called a "rebate." To obtain the payment, eligible individuals in most cases will not have to do anything more than file a federal tax return. But some criminals posing as IRS representatives are trying to trick taxpayers into revealing their personal financial information by falsely telling them that they must provide information to get a payment. Sometimes, these criminals might ask for bank account information for the IRS to directly deposit the rebates, which then results in the thieves cleaning out the bank account.

Author's elaboration: The IRS will *never* ask for this type of information regarding your social security number or bank account information.

c. Frivolous tax arguments. There are a host of frivolous arguments being made by promoters of scams that purport to reduce or even eliminate most tax liability. Some of the many fallacious arguments are:

- Taxes are unconstitutional or not properly codified by Congress.
- Folks are promised a nonexistent mariner's tax deduction.

- Tax filing is "voluntary," and thus you don't have to pay anything.
- Taxes are required only for federal employees.
- There is no statute that properly codifies the tax code.
- Wages, tips, and other service income are not taxable.

You can get a complete list of these frivolous arguments by going to www.irs .gov/pub/irs-utl/friv_tax.pdf.

Author's elaboration: None of these frivolous arguments has won in court. In fact, the judges are so tired of hearing them that they are assessing the government's legal fees against those who make these arguments in court.

d. Fuel credit scam. Sometimes there is some truth behind the scam. Farmers are allowed a fuel tax credit for off-highway business purposes. However, some individuals are claiming the tax credit for nontaxable uses of fuel when their occupation or income level makes the claim unreasonable. Fraud involving the fuel tax credit was recently added to the list of frivolous tax claims, potentially subjecting those who improperly claim the credit to a $5,000 penalty.

e. Hiding income offshore. To my knowledge this scam has been around for years but is now being aggressively investigated by the IRS. Promoters are promising that by placing assets offshore in foreign banks or tax havens, taxpayers would avoid all taxes and, at the least, not have their income discoverable by the IRS on these accounts. Interestingly, some Swiss banks helped promote this scam to the detriment of those involved. As an offshoot of this, some promoters set up foreign credit cards and promised that all income earned is paid to the credit card. This way, they promote that there will be no tax and that the IRS will never find out.

Author's elaboration: U.S. citizens are taxed on their worldwide income. Setting up foreign bank accounts will *not* shield them from taxation. Even worse, on the federal tax return, there is a question about foreign bank accounts. Now a taxpayer may have foreign accounts for many reasons; however, if a taxpayer doesn't disclose these accounts, he or she is subject to criminal fraud penalties. Moreover, the IRS is aggressively investigating these accounts and has cut deals with most foreign jurisdictions.

f. Abusive retirement scams. The IRS continues to uncover abuses in retirement plan arrangements, including Roth Individual Retirement Accounts (IRAs). The IRS is looking for transactions that taxpayers are using to avoid the limitations on contributions to Roth IRAs. Taxpayers should be wary of advisors who encourage them to shift appreciated assets into Roth IRAs or companies owned by their Roth IRAs at less than fair market value. In one variation of the scheme, a promoter has the taxpayer move a highly appreciated asset into a Roth IRA at cost value, which is below annual contribution limits even though the fair market value far exceeds the amount allowed.

Author's elaboration: Contributions to retirement plans must be made in cash and *not* with appreciated assets. Also there are limitations to yearly contributions, which must not be exceeded.

g. Claiming zero wages. Some taxpayers try to file phony wage- or income-related information such as Form 4852 which is a substituted W-2 or amended Form 1099 (for income, dividends, and royalties) in order to improperly reduce their taxes to zero. This type of behavior is being tracked by the IRS and is aggressively being prosecuted. Don't get fooled into thinking that this scam will work.

h. Filing false claims for refunds. Usually taxpayers file Form 843 to abate previously assessed taxes giving some fictitious argument. Even worse, many individuals who have tried this haven't even previously filed a federal tax return.

i. Return-preparer tax fraud. Perhaps this has been an ongoing problem for years. However, I have seen a dramatic increase in enforcement by the IRS against fraudulent tax preparers. Thirty years ago, it was rare if more than 2 or 3 tax preparers per week were barred from preparing taxes or representing taxpayers. Today, I have seen as many as 30 tax preparers per week barred from preparing taxes.

The range of what these accountants are doing varies quite a lot. Some fraudulently puffed up their credentials claiming that they were CPAs or lawyers, which wasn't the case. Some improperly gave the fuel tax credit noted above. Many inflated deductions for taxpayers that the taxpayers never paid for. As an example, there was one accountant who claimed for his clients thousands more in charitable deductions than the clients made.

Author's elaboration: The IRS investigates these fraudulent accountants and audits all their clients. You should certainly look for an aggressive accountant but also one who is honest.

j. Disguised corporate ownership. Some folks are forming entities in some states in order to hide the owners who are conducting a wide variety of illegal activities such as hiding income, money laundering, and so on. The IRS is working with state authorities to investigate these activities.

Author's elaboration: No entity can guarantee complete shielding from the IRS. If the IRS wants to investigate an entity, it can get the names of the owners, officers, and any other pertinent information. There are some states that do promise increased privacy, such as Nevada. However, even a Nevada corporation can easily be investigated by the IRS. Don't be fooled into thinking that any entity can be used to hide income from the IRS.

k. Misuse of trusts. Many promoters have promised taxpayers that certain trusts can be set up to minimize taxes by deducting a wide array of personal expenses or avoiding estate taxes. While there is a kernel of truth to this, especially regarding estate taxes, these trusts must be set up correctly. Moreover, they usually do not allow for deduction of personal expenses. It is vital to seek a good, qualified tax attorney to verify that these trusts do accomplish what was promised and are set up correctly. Finally, putting property in trust where you can control the assets or receive distributions can result in you, the grantor, being taxed on all the trust income.

l. Abuse of charitable contributions and organizations. Many promoters promise to maintain control over donated property while taking a deduction. Examples of phony charitable deductions involve taxpayers who claim tuition payments as charitable contributions. Also, if you own property for over a year, you can donate property and get a deduction for the fair market value. However, promoters have set up scams in which they sell paintings, antiques, closely held stock, and so on to taxpayers on the promise that they will get these taxpayers an appraised value of many times the cost in a year for charitable deduction purposes. These overvaluation scams are fairly rampant.

m. Slavery tax credit. Although this isn't on this year's "dirty dozen" tax scams per se, the IRS has noticed that this is fairly widespread as a "frivolous argument." Promoters promise African Americans a special tax credit as reparation for slavery and oppressive treatment. This is absolutely false, and no one should be fooled by this.

n. Filing for false refunds. According to a recent article, identity thieves are using fraudulently gotten social security numbers to get false refunds from the IRS. This is a HUGE problem. IRS estimates that as much as $6 billion in false refunds were issued in 2013 alone! Scammers get social security numbers from hospitals, nursing homes, and even from lists of the dead. It is thus VITAL that you place a fraud alert every 90 days on one of the main three credit bureaus such as TransUnion, Experan, or Equifax. I think TransUnion will do this for you for free. Also, file your tax returns as early as possible. This will alert the IRS if someone files a new "false" return after you.

Author's note: Each year, the IRS publishes a new list of their "dirty dozen" tax scams. You should be aware of these widespread scams. They can cost you large penalties, and you may even be subject to criminal penalties if you follow the advice of the scammers. Avoiding these scams and running from people who promote them will make your life less taxing.

2. Investment scams. These comprise a wide array of activities, some of which follow:

a. Ponzi scams. Many of us are aware of the Ponzi scheme perpetrated by Bernard Madoff. This is where new investors' money is used to pay other investors "profits." There is very little investment or profit made. However, not only has this scheme been around a long time, but, sadly, it seems to be very pervasive.

Author's elaboration: Many folks have asked, "How can I avoid being a victim of these Ponzi schemes?" The answer involves several steps. First, always check out the money manager or promoter of the investment. This includes going to the BBB (Better Business Bureau). In addition, you should carefully read over their prospectus and see if you spot any glaring problems. For example, if there is a major down market, you probably should not be making money absent some very unusual conditions.

Finally, and this is important, you should *never* have most of your money with any one money manager. You should diversify the management of your money. This includes not putting all your money in one hedge fund, one mutual fund, and so on. Since you are insured by the government for fraud for $500,000, you might consider putting no more than $500,000 with any one firm or person. Obviously, if you are worth hundreds of millions, this can be unwieldy. Thus, as a rule of thumb, you might want to limit your investment with any one manager or firm to no more than 10 percent of your total investible assets.

b. **Trading software scams.** You attend a big seminar where you weren't charged much money to attend (this should clue you in that you are going to be hard sold a product or service). There is a lot of excitement in the room generated by loud motivational music, famous speakers, high energy, lots of comments about avoiding procrastination, and so on. Suddenly a good-looking speaker gets up and promotes the fabulous value of his stock, commodities, or Forex trading software or training program. He cites wonderful glowing testimonials. He cites how much money you can make. He shows you actual profitable trades made by people, although these trades might not be a result of using the trading software. He shows you pictures of his big house and fancy car. He then guarantees you a refund of your several thousand dollar fee if you don't like their training by the end of the first day. He notes that his training class has a limited number of seats. Suddenly, you see hundreds of folks running to the back of the room to take advantage of this "wonderful" limited time offer. Before you become another sucker, take a moment to breathe and thank me for warning you about this.

Ask yourself a question: If you had a gold mine that simply needed a shovel to scoop up the gold, would you tell anyone about it let alone sell entry to the mine? The answer, if you are smart, is no way. Look at Warren Buffett as an example. He has made billions investing in companies. Despite this, you don't see him publishing his formulas or his secrets for evaluating companies.

Even if you had developed some fabulous software that continuously makes money as a trader by finding bargains or uncovering market trends, couldn't you sell it to a major investment house for billions? Not only could you sell it for billions, but you would get capital gains on the sale, which means very little tax compared to the ordinary income that you would realize selling the software at seminars. In fact, the interest alone on the cash sale to the investment company would provide more money than you would make hawking the software at seminars.

Moreover—and this is a seminar inside secret—the promoter of the seminar gets a huge piece of the profit for getting you in the room, not to mention that the salespeople get well paid too. Thus, why sell the software or training program at the seminar? *The answer, if it didn't occur to you, is that the software either doesn't really work or doesn't work better than other less expensive software on the market.*

c. **High-priced training scams.** Even worse, when you get to their "training" program, usually on the second day of training, which is after your refund period has run out, some of these organizations notify you that you really can't use the best of their Web site or training materials unless you upgrade for a whopping extra $10,000 to $25,000 or more! Hey, you were a sucker once; why not try another pitch on you!

If all this doesn't alarm you enough, you should note that studies have shown that traders rarely make money long term anyway even with good trading software. I can honestly say that I know many traders, and very, very few have made money long term.

Author's rules for avoiding this scam:

Rule 1: *Never* buy software programs at seminars that cost more than $2,000.

Rule 2: Rarely buy training programs that cost more than $2,000 at a seminar *unless* you really know what will be presented at these programs. Go to the seminar's or sponsor's Web site and see who is speaking at the program. It would be best if you can do a Google search for all speakers or for their companies and see what others have said about their products and services. Checking out the products in advance can really make a big difference between knowing what you should invest in and what you should avoid.

Author's elaboration: Let me be clear about this. There are some good-quality training programs, and some of these good programs are expensive. You really need to understand what you are buying, what will be presented, and what specific benefits will accrue to you from the training.

Rule 3: Don't buy their product or enroll in their seminar unless you get two pieces of information (from the speaker) that will either make a big change in your life or put money in your pocket! Speakers tend to overpromise and underdeliver. I ignore the hype of promising to make me rich and famous and allow me to acquire huge houses, fancy cars, etc. I look for content present in the sales presentation. My test is that I simply look for two items of information given by the speaker that will either significantly impact my life *or* put money in my pocket. If you can't find two new ideas that will meet my test, then the speaker probably has little content to offer, and I would stay away from buying anything from that speaker. *Note:* I am not that demanding; however, you will find this to be a great test.

3. Inheritance scams. There seem to be a number of inheritance scams, otherwise known as Nigerian scams since they usually involve some Nigerian who wants you to provide a few dollars in order to get a clearance certificate from the U.S. The scam notes that they have over $15 million awaiting them, but they can't get it into this country because of legal hassles and IRS clearance. They usually cite famous folks who can vouch for them. If you would provide American bank account information for them, they will transfer the full $15 million to you. All they want is for you to pay them 90 percent of the proceeds, keeping 10 percent for yourself.

Author's elaboration: I actually got a letter like this and laughed at its obvious fraudulent content. However, it seems that many suckers . . . er . . . wronged victims fell prey to this façade and had their bank accounts cleaned out by the scammers. Never fall victim to this type of hoax. Never, ever give out your bank account information and bank routing number. Remember, if it sounds too good to be true, it probably is.

4. Pyramid scams. These fall into two categories. The first involves a clearly illegal scam involving chain letters. There are a number of names on the letter that you should send a copy to in addition to a check for money. If each of the people on the list does the same, you will supposedly make a lot of money. The catch is that it rarely happens that way, and it is plainly illegal to participate in this. Don't do it.

The second type of scam is the illegal pyramids that are structured as multilevel marketing (MLM) companies.

Author's elaboration: Let me be clear about this. Not all network marketing companies are illegal. In fact, the vast majorities of them are quite legal, provide a very viable opportunity, and are quite good at providing good marketing and business training. I have personally met some folks in these businesses who have earned over $100,000 per month! No, I am not kidding about this. You can check out an article on evaluating a network marketing opportunity found in the articles section of my Web site at www.taxreductioninstitute.com.

A legal MLM should encourage retailing of products in addition to recruiting. If the only way you can make money is to recruit other people to be distributors and if products cannot be purchased without being a distributor, it is probably an illegal pyramid. Most court cases require a certain amount of retailing of the MLM products to nondistributors for the MLM to be a legal operation.

5. Advertised products scams. I know you are thinking, "Wait, Sandy. Advertising is perfectly legal as long as the company doing the advertising lives up to its promises." You are correct in thinking this. However, did you ever ask yourself, "Who pays for the ads?" The answer is that you do! Everyone who buys a product as a result of expensive television ads pays a lot more for that product than they would if they bought from a company that doesn't advertise as much. This is particularly true if a well-known celebrity is pitching the product, which geometrically increases the cost of the advertisement.

Check out the cash value of whole life products and term costs of companies that advertise a lot on television, and compare that to companies that don't advertise as much. I learned about this the hard way.

I had a radio show where we had advertisers. On my show I thought I was doing a service to my listeners telling them about companies that provide the most competitive rates. Thus I mentioned companies that had the lowest mortgage interest, companies that had the lowest stock commissions on the purchase and sale of shares, and so on. I even noted those insurance companies that had the best life insurance based on cash values. I then compared them to the companies that had the highest rates or highest prices for the same products or services. Interestingly, my advertising base slowly disappeared, and I eventually was removed from the show. Little did I realize that firms that were giving the best deals weren't those that advertised! It was those that gave the worst deals or prices that did the most advertising. You will see a lot of companies suddenly hawking products on infomercials and TV. You should always carefully evaluate your potential purchase of these products. More often than not, I have found them to be of inferior quality and found that they don't live up to the advertisement.

Bottom line: Before you buy into that highly promoted toothpaste, razor, gold buying service, or wonderful new infomercial-promoted gadget, shop around for a better deal.

6. Job scams. Today, if you haven't been right-sized or capsized, you are probably worried about being right-sized, capsized, or just laid off. Sadly, there are a number of scams being perpetrated on people who have experienced this. The scams vary from requiring payment for jobs to advertised jobs whose sole intent is to get money from the victim for some home-based business.

Author's elaboration: You should *never* have to pay money in order to get a job unless the job offer actually comes through. Most legitimate employment agencies work this way. Moreover, advertising jobs that are really a home-based business scheme is just plain wrong and probably illegal.

One exception to this might be newsletters. There are some employment newsletters that list jobs for a specific category such as federal job openings. Frankly, with some research, you could probably get this information for free. However, these occupational newsletters do perform a service and aren't all scams. Just make sure that the jobs offered are real jobs and involve real, current openings. I have found that many jobs in the newsletter are closed to applications by the time you receive the newsletter.

7. Fabulous offer scams. You suddenly get a letter in the mail or by e-mail that you have won a big prize or can get a product at a fantastic discount. Sometimes, you are asked for a wire fee to cover the cost of the wire transfer. Don't pay the fee.

Author's elaboration: It is illegal for a company to charge a fee to give a prize.

8. Free vacation for attending seminar scams. You get a letter promising you free airfare for two and maybe even a free hotel stay for several days if you will attend a wonderful seminar that deals with vacation discounts. I attended three of these in order to check them out. I got vouchers that took over three months to arrive after a lot of complaining. In addition, the vouchers had so many restrictions that they were worthless. Moreover, the seminars were simply high-pressure sales tactics used to lure folks to purchase their overpriced vacation packages. Stay away from these.

9. Telephone scams. These come in many varieties. For example, you get a call from the "phone company" asking you to test your phone. In order to do that, they ask you to use *90 or #09. These scamsters can now make long-distance calls and charge it to your phone number. Never use *90 or #09.

The second version of these types of scams has you dialing an 809 area code. You might get a message on your answering machine that your parent has died and to call a specific phone number or that you need to call a specific number to claim a prize. You are probably told to call an 809 number that will result in charges of $1,000 per minute and up. Sadly, these numbers are in locations that can't be regulated by U.S. authorities.

10. Seminar and investment scams. There was an old joke that noted, "The most expensive thing in the world was a lady who was free for the evening." Today, this has changed to "The most expensive thing in the world can be a free or almost free seminar." *No one offers seminars for free or at a very low cost without trying to sell you something!* I hope that putting this in italics will indelibly make you remember this. I was reading about two retirees who attended an investment seminar run by an accountant who promised at least 8 percent return on their investments. Needless to say it was a Ponzi scheme, and they lost all of their money. Sadly, most folks trust people, and that is exactly what you should *not* do.

Author's elaboration: Before you attend these free or significantly discounted seminars, always check them out on the Web. See what they are selling. Check out the organizations that are selling products. You will find, more often than not, that many of these products or services are just bad deals and way overpriced for what you are getting. Think about it: Both the seminar provider and salesperson has to be very well paid. Who do you think is paying for this? Answer: the suckers.

Thus, the easiest way to avoid these types of fraud, according to Joseph Borg of the Alabama Securities Commission,[1] is to ignore the pitches; hang up on the telemarketers; reject invitations to free seminars, especially free lunch or dinner seminars; and toss out mail with promises of surefire investments and cheap or free travel.

I would follow the advice of the Kiplinger's Retirement letter:[2] Do *not* give any cold caller or visitor money, whether by wiring money or sending money orders or personal checks. If you suspect telemarketing fraud, call your state attorney general's office or the National Consumer League's Fraud Information Center at 202-835-3323 or go to www.fraud.org. Also *never* let someone push you into an immediate decision. Finally, never give out social security or bank account information to unsolicited callers or to someone you don't implicitly trust. When in doubt, always, always check them out on the Web and with the Better Business Bureau before making a purchase.

11. Book scams. I was recently contacted by a well-known individual who wanted me to promote his book on my database. The e-mail promised to pay me for each person who bought his book as a result of my contact. He promised me leads and promised to pay me for other affiliates who have large databases. However, nowhere in the letter was there any discussion about what was in the book or why it would be a good book to read. He was solely interested in selling lots of copies during a one-week period in order to get on the bestseller list, and he assumed that I couldn't care less about the quality of his work! Yes, this happens a lot too. Moreover, I have read other books by this person and found them to be very thin in both content and style. However, this person is a great marketer.

Always be wary of folks who suddenly promote someone else's book when it is first published. Don't assume that because a book made some bestseller list, it is necessarily a good book. In fact, I know authors who have purchased enough books by themselves, supplemented by hiring folks to buy enough books, so that they can make a bestseller list.

12. Identity theft. In our era of electronic purchasing of products through the Internet and wire transfers and credit cards, identity theft is becoming the biggest type of fraud worldwide. Here is what the Department of Justice says about it:

> Identity theft and identity fraud are terms used to refer to all types of crime in which someone wrongfully obtains and uses another person's personal data in some way that involves fraud or deception, typically for economic gain. These Web pages are intended to explain why you need to take precautions to protect yourself from identity theft. Unlike your fingerprints, which are unique to you and cannot be given to someone else for their use, your personal data—especially your social security number, your bank account or credit card number, your telephone calling card number, and other valuable identifying data—can be used, if they fall into the wrong hands, to personally profit at your expense. In the U.S. and Canada, for example, many people have reported that unauthorized persons have taken funds out of their bank or financial accounts, or, in the worst cases, taken over their identities altogether, running up vast debts and committing crimes while using the victims' names. In many cases, a victim's losses may include not only out-of-pocket financial losses, but substantial additional financial costs associated with trying to restore his reputation in the community and correcting erroneous information for which the criminal is responsible.
>
> In one notorious case of identity theft, the criminal, a convicted felon, not only incurred more than $100,000 of credit card debt, obtained a federal home loan, and bought homes, motorcycles, and handguns in the victim's name, but called his victim to taunt him—saying that he could continue to pose as the victim for as long as he wanted because identity theft was not a federal crime at that time—before filing for bankruptcy, also in the victim's name. While the victim and his wife spent more than four years and more than $15,000 of their own money to restore their credit and reputation, the criminal served a brief sentence for making a false statement to procure a firearm, but made no restitution to his victim for any of the harm he had caused. This case, and others like it, prompted Congress in 1998 to create a new federal offense of identity theft.

What are the most common ways for criminals to steal your identity?

According to the Department of Justice,[3] "Many people do not realize how easily criminals can obtain our personal data without having to break into our homes.

In public places, for example, criminals may engage in "shoulder surfing"—watching you from a nearby location as you punch in your telephone calling card number or credit card number—or listen in on your conversation if you give your credit card number over the telephone to a hotel or rental car company.

Even the area near your home or office may not be secure. Some criminals engage in "dumpster diving"—going through your garbage cans or a communal dumpster or trash bin—to obtain copies of your checks, credit card or bank statements, or other records that typically bear your name, address, and even your telephone number. These types of records make it easier for criminals to get control over accounts in your name and assume your identity.

If you receive applications for "preapproved" credit cards in the mail, but discard them without tearing up the enclosed materials, criminals may retrieve them and try to activate the cards for their use without your knowledge. (Some credit card companies, when sending credit cards, have adopted security measures that allow a card recipient to activate the card only from his or her home telephone number but this is not yet a universal practice.) Also, if your mail is delivered to a place where others have ready access to it, criminals may simply intercept and redirect your mail to another location.

In recent years, the Internet has become an appealing place for criminals to obtain identifying data, such as passwords or even banking information. In their haste to explore the exciting features of the Internet, many people respond to "spam"—unsolicited e-mail—that promises them some benefit but requests identifying data, without realizing that in many cases, the requester has no intention of keeping his promise. In some cases, criminals reportedly have used computer technology to obtain large amounts of personal data.

With enough identifying information about an individual, a criminal can take over that individual's identity to conduct a wide range of crimes: for example, false applications for loans and credit cards, fraudulent withdrawals from bank accounts, fraudulent use of telephone calling cards, or obtaining other goods or privileges which the criminal might be denied if he were to use his real name. If the criminal takes steps to ensure that bills for the falsely obtained credit cards, or bank statements showing the unauthorized withdrawals, are sent to an address other than the victim's, the victim may not become aware of what is happening until the criminal has already inflicted substantial damage on the victim's assets, credit, and reputation.

Author's elaboration: This happened to me. I had an insect control guy in my home. He found a credit card slip on the kitchen counter of my home. Within a month, I had several thousand dollars of unauthorized charges on my credit card. I had the Secret Service in my home conducting an investigation. It was very unpleasant.

Identity theft has become such a big problem, that it's worth further discussion.

What Can You Do to Avoid Identity Theft?

Over 16.7 million people were victims of identity theft or fraud in 2009 for an astounding $16.8 billion. The following will help you protect yourself and your investments from this kind of crime.

1. Rarely give out any personal data or even credit card information to anyone unless you have a very good reason to trust that person.
2. Never give out information that the company should already know. Thus, if you have a password for your online banking or you need a pet's name, the bank employee shouldn't be asking you for these personal items. This should be in the bank's database. Likewise, you should almost never give out your social security number to anyone.

Author's elaboration: Many doctors routinely ask for your social security number. I think they do this in order to track you down if you don't pay the bill. I *never* give out my social security number. I only give my health insurance group number.

3. According to the Department of Justice, if someone you don't know calls you and offers you a prize or credit card and wants personal information such as a social security number, ask to be sent a written application. Moreover, check with the company that called you in order to verify that it really is offering you what it purportedly says it does. Double-check that the application is going to the organization that called you.
4. When you give someone a credit card number while you're traveling, such as a hotel clerk, make sure that no one is looking over your shoulder. Also, don't give credit card information or personal information over any phone while you're in a public spot such as an airport. I have heard folks doing this. I could have easily written down their credit card number while they were talking.
5. Check your credit information monthly. I subscribe to a credit information reporting service and monitor my credit. This service also looks for new accounts that might be established in my name. Although I use MYfico.com, there are other services such as freecreditreport.com and even Lifelock that place a fraud alert on your credit report every 90 days. Since I am not familiar with Lifelock or freecreditreport.com, I can't specifically endorse them. You would have to check them out for yourself.
6. Read over your credit card statements carefully. Too many of us do not read these statements as carefully as we should. Always look for unauthorized transactions. Some crooks charge only one or two minor things each month in the hope of not being noticed.
7. If someone has managed to make unauthorized charges on your credit card or has taken money from your bank, you need to contact the credit card company or financial institution where you bank immediately and report the transaction. You would then place a fraud alert with your bank and all credit reporting agencies and cancel any credit cards that have been compromised.

If you are a victim of credit card or identity theft, here is a checklist provided by the California Public Research Group (CALPIRG) of what to do. First contact the Federal Trade Commission (FTC) to report the situation. You can do this online or

- To report identity theft go to: www.identitytheft.gov and fill out the form. You will be given some easy to follow prompts.

In addition, the Department of Justice notes that you should call the fraud units of the three principal credit reporting companies.

For Equifax:

1. To report fraud, call (800) 525-6285 or write to P.O. Box 740241, Atlanta, GA 30374-0250.
2. To order a copy of your credit report ($8 in most states), write to P.O. Box 740241, Atlanta, GA 30374-0241, or call (800) 685-1111.
3. To dispute information in your credit report, call the phone number provided on your credit report.
4. To opt out of preapproved offers of credit and marketing lists, call (888) 567-8688 or write to Equifax Options, P.O. Box 740123, Atlanta GA 30374-0123.

For Experian (formerly TRW):

1. To report fraud, call (888) EXPERIAN or (888) 397-3742, fax to (800) 301-7196, or write to P.O. Box 2104, Allen, TX 75013.
2. To order a copy of your credit report ($8 in most states), write to P.O. Box 2104, Allen TX 75013, or call (888) EXPERIAN.
3. To dispute information in your credit report, call the phone number provided on your credit report.
4. To opt out of preapproved offers of credit and marketing lists, call (800) 353-0809 or (888) 5OPTOUT or write to P.O. Box 919, Allen, TX 75013.

For TransUnion:

1. To report fraud, call (800) 680-7289 or write to P.O. Box 6790, Fullerton CA 92634-6790 for ordering credit report.
2. To order a copy of your credit report ($8 in most states), write to P.O. Box 390, Springfield, PA 19064 or call: (800) 888-4213.
3. To dispute information in your credit report, call the phone number provided on your credit report.
4. To opt out of preapproved offers of credit and marketing lists, call (800) 680-7293 or (888) 5OPTOUT or write to P.O Box 97328, Jackson, MS 39238.

Contact all creditors with whom your name or identifying data have been fraudulently used. For example, you may need to contact your long-distance telephone company if your long-distance calling card has been stolen or you find fraudulent charges on your bill.

Contact all financial institutions where you have accounts that an identity thief has taken over or financial institutions that have been created in your name but without your knowledge. You may need to cancel those accounts, place stop-payment orders on any outstanding checks that may not have cleared, and change your automated teller machine (ATM) card, account, and personal identification number (PIN).

Contact the major check verification companies (listed in the CALPIRG Privacy Rights Clearinghouse checklist) if you have had checks stolen or bank accounts set up by an identity thief. In particular, if you know that a particular merchant has received a check stolen from you, contact the verification company that the merchant uses:

1. CheckRite—(800) 766-2748
2. ChexSystems—(800) 428-9623 (closed checking accounts)
3. CrossCheck—(800) 552-1900
4. Equifax—(800) 437-5120
5. National Processing Co. (NPC)—(800) 526-5380
6. SCAN—(800) 262-7771
7. TeleCheck—(800) 710-9898

Author's elaboration: Some insurance companies for a small fee will provide identity theft protection. They not only will insure you for damage, but they will provide a person to handle your case and perform on your behalf many of the steps that I noted above.

Identity theft, as well as all other scams, can be avoided by paying attention to your surroundings, using common sense, and doing your research on the individual and/or company before you make a purchase or investment. Hopefully this information will prevent you from becoming another statistic and should make your life less taxing.

Notes

1. Kiplinger's Retirement Report, volume 16, p. 4 (2009).
2. Ibid.
3. www.usdoj.gov/criminal/fraud/websites/idtheft.html.

20

Highlights of the New Tax Cuts and Jobs Act Legislation

People who struggle with their taxes fall into two categories: men and women.

Introduction

U nless you have been living in a remote cave, you are probably aware that Congress has passed one of the biggest tax law changes in decades based solely on party lines. This means that this was a Republican bill. By time of the publication of this book, it has been signed by President Trump and is now law.

The Senate initially passed it like a thief in the night … literally at 2 a.m. The legislation was so rushed that there were no real debates and no public hearings, which is NEVER a good thing. Legislation such as this should be transparent and should, at the very least, involve public hearings from experts. As a result, there will be unintended and mostly undesirable consequences, some of which will be discussed here.

Chapter Overview

If you listen to the Democrats, you will think that this legislation is a terrible tax scam on the American public. The Republicans would like you to think that this is fabulous legislation that will turbocharge America and create a huge amount of jobs. Both interpretations are wrong in my opinion, which will be discussed below.

My main problem with this legislation, and yes, I have a lot of problems with it, is the deficit that it creates. Here is an analogy:

> Let's say that I was to wave a magic wand and reduce your taxes between a few hundred dollars per year to up to tens of thousands of dollars based on income, would you be happy?

I will be focusing on changes that apply to individuals and especially to small businesses. Thus, I won't be discussing all changes such as those that apply to life insurance companies, etc. In addition to the changes discussed, I will also give you my opinion of the changes.

Tax Changes for Individuals Found in the Tax Cuts and Jobs Act Legislation

Tax Rate

When I compared the tax rates under the Tax Cuts and Jobs Act legislation to that of the current tax rates, everyone gets a slight cut in rates. In fact, when I ran the numbers, most people will reduce their tax burden, apart from those who are in the middle class earning less than about $250,000, or are in high-income tax states and who pay a lot of property tax. These people are the losers in this legislation and will probably pay more in federal and possibly state taxes since they will lose all deductions for state and local taxes that exceed $10,000. This will probably result in their *not* itemizing their deductions, which means that they won't even get the benefit of the allowable $10,000 state and local tax deduction cap.

> **Chapter Overview (Cont.)**
>
> Yes, you would probably enjoy the extra money. Moreover, if I were to do this for four years or more, would you be very happy?
>
> HOWEVER, if I were to say in four years that you owe me all the tax savings back plus interest, many people would be aghast and might have to declare bankruptcy. This is essentially the main problem with this legislation. The government incurs a $1.5 trillion debt to provide these tax savings. This is completely unacceptable to me as it should be to you. It is basically "smoke and mirrors." This is probably the worst part of this legislation in my opinion. Also, there are numerous badly written and confusing provisions that will take years for the IRS to clarify. In the meantime, there will be many mistakes made by taxpayers and even tax preparers. Think about all of this as you read about these changes.

The ones who get the most benefits, however, are those in the 35 percent tax bracket and above, which means those whose taxable incomes are over $400,000 married filing jointly or over $200,000 and are single. Please see Appendix A for the new tax rates for 2018.

Doubling of Standard Deduction but Elimination of Exemptions[1]

Under the prior law, you could deduct up to $4,100 per person as an exemption and would have gotten a standard deduction of $6,350 for single people and $12,700 for married filing jointly.

Under the new Tax Cuts law, the standard deduction is almost doubled to be $12,000 for single people and $24,000 for married filing joint returns. This sounds wonderful EXCEPT that all exemptions for the family (with the exception for those who are blind and over age 65) are eliminated.

Example: John and Mary have two kids. They live in a state that has moderately high income taxes and pay out $12,000 in property taxes. Under the prior law, they would get $12,700 in a standard deduction, $16,400 in exemptions, and probably could deduct part of their state and local taxes as an itemized deduction. Under the new Tax Cuts law, they get no exemptions, they get $24,000 of a standard deduction and probably won't be able to itemize since their standard deduction will exceed their allowable itemized deductions because of the disallowance of state and local taxes.

Sandy's hot tip: One of the best tax strategies mentioned in this book is to hire children in your business. This strategy becomes even better under the new Tax Cuts law since their standard deduction that can be used against wages increases from $6,350 to $12,000. Thus, you can pay your kids up to $12,000 tax free if these wages are reasonable for what they do.

Increase in Child Tax Credit[2]

To help offset the loss of itemized deductions, Congress has increased the child-care credit from the current $1,000 to $2,000 per qualifying child under age 17. In addition, a $500 credit is provided for certain non-child dependents.

Even better, up to $1,400 of this credit is refundable for each qualifying child. This means that if you didn't owe enough taxes, you can get this excess back as a refund! This is designed to especially help poorer people.

What Congress gives it tends to take back. This credit phases out for single taxpayers earning over $200,000 and for married filing joint taxpayers who earn over $400,000.

Sandy's opinion: I never thought it was good tax policy to simply give credits to people to have more children. This doesn't create jobs or improve the economy. This is an example of a political move that doesn't have much economic sense. It was put in, however, to help ameliorate the detrimental effects on the middle class of eliminating exemptions and itemized deductions.

Elimination of State and Local Taxes above $10,000[3]

All state and local taxes above $10,000 are eliminated under the new Tax Cuts law. This applies to all state and local taxes such as state income tax, property tax, and sales tax.

Sandy's elaboration: Frankly, this $10,000 allowance is illusory for most people since they probably won't itemize deductions because of the doubling of the standard deduction. Remember, you can only take itemized deductions that exceed the standard deduction.

Moreover, Congress thought of the tax planning tip of prepaying your state income taxes and property taxes. Under the reconciliation, this won't be deductible for taxes prepaid for next year. In other words, a taxpayer who in 2017 pays an income tax that is imposed for a tax year after 2017, can't claim an itemized deduction in 2017 for that prepaid income tax.

Sandy's hot tip: While the state sales tax is eliminated, it is only eliminated for personal property not used in a trade or business. If the property such as a car or desk is used in a trade or business, you can deduct the sales tax as a business expense to the extent the property is used for business. Also, state property taxes, even above $10,000, would be partly deductible on your Schedule C if you claim a valid home office deduction as a self-employed business owner or as an independent contractor.

New Measure in Computing Inflation[4]

There are many subtle changes in the new Tax Cuts law. One change involves reducing the way inflation is computed. While I won't get into the technical details of this, what it means to you is that it reduces what is known as "tax bracket creep." This means that as people earn more money, they tend to eventually reach higher tax brackets unless the brackets are adjusted for inflation. Thus, reducing the inflation effect on tax brackets will result in more people at the lower end of the income scale having to pay more in taxes in the future instead of less. Think tanks have estimated that by 2027, if no changes occur, everyone earning under $75,000 will pay more.

Kiddie Tax Modified[5]

In most areas of tax law, people are taxed on their earnings. Thus, if I earn $5,000, I am taxed on the earnings. The kiddie tax was a major and, in my opinion, stupid departure from this principle.

Children who are under age 24, who are full-time students and unmarried, can only earn roughly $2,100 of unearned income taxed at their tax bracket. Anything above that was taxed at the highest bracket of their parents. If the children were not full-time students or got married, then the kiddie tax only applied if they were under age 18.

The new Tax Cuts law makes it clear that earned income is taxed to the child at the single taxpayer rates. However, unearned income, which includes interest, dividends, rents, and capital gains are taxed at the highest rates in the Internal Revenue Code (IRC), which is the trust tax rate (found above).

Sandy's hot tip: If you have kids subject to the kiddie tax, you want to keep their unearned income at no more than $2,550 to take advantage of the trust tax rate of 10 percent. Also, the kiddie tax will not apply to earned income at all.

Casualty Losses Eliminated Except for Federally Declared Disaster Areas[6]

If you have an uncompensated losses arising from fire, storm, shipwreck, weather (such as a hurricane or tornado), earthquake, theft, etc., you could deduct this loss as an itemized deduction.

Under the new Tax Cuts law, casualty losses incurred before January 1, 2026, are no longer deductible UNLESS they arise in a federally declared disaster area.

Sandy's elaboration: Thus, unless you are in a federally declared disaster area, you will no longer be able to deduct damage from fire, theft, tornadoes, hurricanes, or earthquakes. I STRONGLY recommend that you reevaluate your property insurance coverage on everything that you own to be sure you are covered as much as possible. To maximize reimbursements from your insurance carrier, be sure to video record all your items in your home and those used for business too. If it involves electronic equipment or furniture, be sure to dictate any serial numbers into the recording. Thus, if your house or business is burglarized, you can trace your equipment.

Gambling Losses and Expense Limits Are Modified[7]

Do you like to gamble? The current rule for 2017 is that gambling losses are deductible as itemized deductions up to gambling winnings, which is like hobby losses. If you have other gambling expenses such as lodging, transportation and admission fees, you could deduct them as itemized deductions regardless of winnings.

The new Tax Cuts law provides that *all* deductions for expenses incurred in carrying out wagering transactions, and not just gambling losses, are limited to the extent of gambling winnings.

Modification of Home Mortgage and Home Equity Interest Deduction[8]

Prior to the Tax Cuts law, you could deduct home mortgage interest on up to $1 million of debt if used for either the acquisition or improvement of your principal or secondary residence. In addition, you could claim an interest deduction on up to another $100,000 of home equity debt.

For years beginning after December 31, 2017, and continuing to January 1, 2026, the deduction for home equity indebtedness is suspended. In addition, the deduction for home mortgage interest is allowed up to $750,000 of debt. However, a taxpayer who has entered into a binding written contract before December 15, 2017, to close on the purchase of a principal residence before January 1, 2018, and who purchases such residence before April 1, 2018, shall be considered to incur acquisition indebtedness prior to December 15, 2017.

Sandy's hot tip: If you are eligible for a valid home office deduction, you could deduct a portion of the interest as a business expenses. Your deduction for interest on debt might NOT be limited to $750,000 of debt to the extent that the home is used for business.

Example: Let's assume that you bought a castle for $48 million, paying $8 million as a down payment and borrowed the rest of the $40 million. If you use your home 25 percent for business, you should be able to deduct the interest on 25 percent of the debt, which is the interest on $10 million, regardless of the debt limitation.

Medical Expense Deduction Threshold Temporarily Reduced[9]

Normally, you can claim medical expenses if they exceed 10 percent of your adjusted gross income (AGI). This was raised due to Obamacare changes from 7.5 percent of AGI.

The new Tax Cuts law brings back the 7.5 percent limitation, but only until January 1, 2019. In addition, the alternative minimum tax (AMT) used the 10 percent threshold that was now changed to the same 7.5 percent threshold used for income tax calculations.[10]

Sandy's hot tip: I never recommended that small business taxpayers, such as self-employed people or regular corporations, deduct medical expenses as medical expenses. I always recommended that they set up a Health Reimbursement Arrangement (HRA) and deduct their family's unreimbursed medical expenses as a business expense under Section 105 of the Internal Revenue Code (IRC) by hiring their spouse. More information on this will be found in this book. I should note that the HRA is still available despite the changes made by the Tax Cuts and Jobs Act legislation.

Charitable Contributions Deduction Limitation Increased[11]

Prior to the Tax Cuts law, you were only able to get a deduction for cash contributions if the amount contributed was less than 50 percent for public charities and 20 to 30 percent for private charities. In addition, for contributions of $250 or more you needed to get an acknowledgment from the charity to substantiate the contribution.

Under the new Tax Cuts law, cash contributions made before January 1, 2026, are now subject to 60 percent of your adjusted gross income (AGI). This also applies to certain private foundations.

No Deduction for Amounts Paid for College Sports Tickets[12]

Prior to the Tax Cuts law, some colleges required a "contribution" to the university to be able to buy sports tickets. The payor could claim, under some circumstances, 80 percent of the payment as a charitable contribution. The new Tax Cuts law eliminates this deduction as a charitable contribution if it was made after December 31, 2017, if the payor receives any right to purchase tickets or seating at an athletic event.

Alimony Deduction Eliminated and No Income Inclusion by Payee[13]

Prior to the Tax Cuts law, you could deduct payments that qualified as alimony to your spouse. The spouse would have to pick up these payments as income.

Under the new Tax Cuts law, for any divorce or separation agreement executed after December 31, 2018, or executed before that date, but modified after it, alimony will no longer be deductible by the payor spouse. Also, alimony will *not* be includible in income of the recipient spouse.

Sandy's hot tip: You can still deduct alimony if you meet the rules for alimony for divorces in 2018.

Elimination of Miscellaneous Itemized Deductions

Prior to the Tax Cuts law, you could deduct certain nonbusiness deductions as miscellaneous itemized deductions that were subject to a threshold of 2 percent of your adjusted gross income (AGI). You were able to deduct things like tax preparation fees, safety deposit boxes, investment journals, and employee business expenses. The new Tax Cuts law suspends all miscellaneous itemized deductions until January 1, 2026.

Sandy's elaboration: Since this tax bill has been ushered through Congress like a thief in the night, with no public hearings or discussion, there will be unintended consequences. Accountants will be finding unintended problems for years.

Hobbies

There is one detrimental, but unexpected, effect of the new Tax Cuts law that might not have been considered: hobbies. If you start a business and it generates a loss, you could use that loss against any current earnings. Any excess loss could then be carried forward for an indefinite carryforward up to 80 percent of any future taxable income. If, however, the endeavor doesn't rise to the level of a business and is considered a hobby (which people won't know until they get audited), the deductions are probably now disallowed since miscellaneous itemized deductions are eliminated. Thus, the big change that can result from eliminating miscellaneous itemized deductions is that all deductions from hobbies would seem to be eliminated but the income would seem to be fully taxed. The same can be said about gambling expenses and losses.

Example: I start up a company to make money raising dogs or horses or a network marketing company. I gross $3,000 in the first year but have $6,000 in deductions. If my company doesn't rise to the level of a business but is deemed to be a hobby, the result is that I will be taxed on the full $3,000 of gross income and get no deductions at all. This could stifle people from trying to start businesses. At least if they didn't do it correctly, they could have taken deductions in the past up to their income from the endeavor, which results in "no gain and no foul." This is an example of what happens when there are no hearings and no discussion on legislation. Hopefully, this will either be clarified by the IRS or Congress will enact some fixes to this legislation.

Qualified Bicycle Commuting Exclusion Suspended[14]

Prior the passage of the new Tax Cuts law, an employee could exclude up to $20 per month in qualified bicycle commuting reimbursements. Starting after December 31, 2017, and continuing until January 1, 2026, this exclusion is suspended.

Sandy's hot tip: Despite the elimination of this exclusion, bicycles used in a trade or business are depreciable. Thus, if you have a newspaper route and are treated as an independent contractor, you can depreciate the bicycle to the extent it is used for business.

Exclusion for Moving Expense Reimbursement Suspended[15]

Prior to the passage of the new Tax Cuts law, employees could exclude qualified moving expenses reimbursements from their gross income and from their wages. Beginning on January 1, 2018, and ending before January 1, 2026, the exclusion for qualified moving expenses reimbursements is suspended, with an exception for members of the Armed Forces on active duty and for their spouses and dependents who move pursuant to a military order and incident to a permanent change of station.

Moving Expense Deduction Suspended[16]

Prior to the passage of the new Tax Cuts law, employees could claim a deduction for moving expenses incurred in connection with starting a new job if they met certain distance requirements. Beginning after December 31, 2017, and ending before January 1, 2026, the deduction for moving expenses incurred in connection with starting a new job is suspended, with an exception for members of the Armed Forces on active duty.

Sandy's elaboration: I think it is sad that Congress would get rid of the small bicycle deduction used for commuting and the moving expense deduction to give people who earn over $400,000 a tax break.

Repeal of Obamacare Individual Mandate[17]

Under the law before the passage of the Tax Cuts and Jobs Act legislation, the Affordable Care Act (ACA) required individuals who were not covered by a health plan that provided at least minimum essential coverage to pay a penalty when filing their federal tax returns. Starting after December 31, 2018, the penalty is reduced to zero, and this repeal of part of the ACA is made permanent.

Sandy's elaboration: The point of this is that with fewer people not being required to obtain coverage, this would mean that more people would *not* meet the rules to obtain subsidized coverage since they would either drop out or obtain disqualifying coverage that doesn't meet the minimum standards for the subsidy. The new Tax Cuts law does keep the 3.8 percent surcharge on net investment income for high-income individuals and the 0.9 percent additional Medicare tax, both enacted by Obamacare.

In addition, the thinking is that the people who drop out of coverage will be the younger, healthier people who don't think they need to keep this expensive coverage, which could significantly raise premiums much higher than they are now. Thus, if you think your medical premiums are high now, wait a few years and see what happens when the healthier people drop out of Obamacare. As Randy Bachman said, "You Ain't Seen Nothing Yet."

Alternative Minimum Tax (AMT) Retained with Higher Exemptions[18]

The Alternative Minimum Tax (AMT) is a tax system that is separate from the regular tax system. The AMT is intended to prevent higher-income taxpayers from avoiding *all* tax liability by using various deductions, exclusions, and credits.

The exemption amounts for individuals prior to passage of the new Tax Cuts law:

  i. For married filing joint taxpayers, $86,200
 ii. For single individuals, $55,400
iii. For married filing separately, $43,100

The exemption amounts for individuals following passage of the new Tax Cuts law, beginning on January 1, 2018, and ending before January 1, 2026, increase.

The exemption amounts for individuals are:

  i. For joint returns and surviving spouses, $109,400
 ii. For single taxpayers, $70,300
iii. For married filing separately, $54,700.

Also, the above exclusions are reduced by 25 percent over the following phased-in amounts:

  i. For joint returns and surviving spouses, $1 million
 ii. For all other taxpayers, other than for estates and trusts, $500,000

Sandy's elaboration: I like this change. The AMT hits people without their knowledge until they file their tax return. Frankly, though, eliminating the AMT altogether would have made filing a tax return simpler.

ABLE Account Changes[19]

ABLE accounts are little-known accounts that are used to fund tax-preferred savings accounts to pay for the support, education, and maintenance of individuals with severe disabilities and their families. Prior to the new Tax Cuts law, the annual contribution limitation was the amount of the annual gift tax exemption, which in 2018 was $15,000.

Effective for tax years beginning after the enactment date of the Tax Cuts and Jobs Act legislation and before January 1, 2026, the limit on the annual contribution has been increased. Once the annual exclusion has been reached, the ABLE account's designated beneficiary can contribute an additional amount, up to the lesser of (a) the federal poverty line for a one-person household, or (b) the individual's compensation for the tax year.

Expanded Use of Section 529 Plan Funds for Private School tuition[20]

Prior to the Tax Cuts and Jobs Act legislation, funds in a Section 529 plan account could only be used for qualified higher-education expenses. These included college and graduate school costs for tuition, fees, books, supplies, and required equipment, as well as reasonable room and board if the student was enrolled at least half time. Eligible schools included colleges and universities, vocational schools, or other post-secondary schools eligible to participate in a student-aid program of the Department of Education. For distributions made after December 31, 2017, the new law includes up to $10,000 of tuition at an elementary or secondary public, private, or religious school.

Sandy's note: Thus, if you want to send your kids to a great private school or want to send them to a religious-oriented school, you can do so and use up to $10,000 of Section 529 fund money each year to do so.

Student Loan Discharged on Death or Disability[21]

Gross income generally includes any discharge from indebtedness of a taxpayer. An exception to this rule is that gross income does not include any amount from the forgiveness of certain student loans if the forgiveness is contingent on the student's working for a certain period in certain professions. Starting after December 31, 2017, and extending until before January 1, 2026, certain student loans that are discharged because death or total and permanent disability of the student are also excluded from gross income.

Sandy's elaboration: It's nice of Congress to care about dead or severely disabled kids. It's too bad that they don't care as much while these kids are alive.

Estate and Gift Changes[22]

Prior to the Tax Cuts and Jobs Act law, the first $5 million adjusted for inflation was exempt from estate and gift tax. For decedents dying and gifts made after December 31, 2017, and before January 1, 2026, the new Tax Cuts law doubles the base estate and gift tax exemption from $5 million to $10 million, which is indexed for inflation occurring after 2011. Thus, it is expected to be around $11.2 million by 2018.

Sandy's elaboration: Each spouse gets his or her own exemption. Thus, the exemption for a couple should be about $22.4 million in 2018.

Small Business Tax Changes Found in the Tax Cuts and Jobs Act Legislation

Corporate Tax Rates Reduced[23]

Prior to the Tax Cuts and Jobs Act law, corporations were subject to graduated tax rates from 15 percent on the first $50,000 to a maximum rate of 35 percent on taxable incomes over $10 million. Personal service corporations paid a flat 35 percent tax on all their income.

The new Tax Cuts law, beginning after December 31, 2017, reduces the corporate tax rates to a flat 21 percent.

Sandy's elaboration: This is the only thing that I actually like in the new tax law. Corporations have been leaving the U.S. to go elsewhere and avoid all tax on foreign income. A favorite place where they tend to relocate to is Ireland, which has a corporate tax rate of 12.5 percent. Thus, reducing the corporate rates might make companies reconsider leaving the U.S. and provide more dividends to stockholders and higher earnings, which is why we are seeing so much gain in the stock market. Frankly, I wish Congress lowered the tax rates even lower to compete more successfully with places like Ireland and not increase the child credit.

However, I do NOT agree with the Republican argument that lowering corporate taxes will improve hiring. In fact, most CEOs questioned said they will use the newly found money from the tax savings to buy back stock.

Sandy's elaboration: The Tax Cuts law really gives bigger benefits to operating as a regular corporation. In addition, the pass-through tax deduction that applies to S corporations, sole proprietors, and partnerships doesn't really match the beneficial tax rates of being a regular corporation. I will be discussing the pass-through tax deduction below.

Pass-Through Tax Deduction for Small Business[24]

Prior to the passage of the Tax Cuts and Jobs Act, small businesses, such as self-employed taxpayers, partnerships, and S corporations, paid tax on their net income from the business as a pass through. They used the normal tax rates like the ones posted above.

Because of the new Tax Cuts law, small business taxpayers, which include independent contractors, will be able to reduce their net income by 20 percent. This won't apply to any capital gains earned by the business, but does include Real Estate Investment Trust (REIT) dividends. This discount applies to their Qualified Business Income (QBI). QBI is defined to be from items of income, gains, deductions, and losses related to any qualified trade or business that is effectively connected to a trade or business conducted in the U.S., plus certain REIT dividends less any capital gains or other investment income, such as interest. (See IRC Section 199A.)

Sandy's note: Effectively, the 20 percent pass-through deduction allows small businesses who operate as a pass-through entity to only be taxed on 80 percent of their net business income (not counting investment income). Moreover, the 20 percent deduction specifically doesn't reduce your adjusted gross income (AGI). Instead it is used in computing taxable income. Congress did this so that small business taxpayers would pay the full amount of Social Security and Medicare tax without taking this deduction into account.

Sandy's note: What Congress gives, it tends to take back. As noted above, this nice 20 percent deduction for Qualified Business Income (QBI) becomes limited if your qualified business income is *more* than $315,000 (married filing joint filers) and $157,500 for everyone else. Here are the limitations:

The first limitation applies if you're single and earn more than $157,500 or you're married and earn more than $315,000. In this case, you can't deduct more than the greater value of *either* 50 percent of your W-2 wages *or* the sum of 25 percent of your wages plus 2.5 percent of your depreciable property. By the way, this wages-based limitation will mean that high-income sole proprietors, partnerships, and real estate investors without W-2 employees will miss out on the deduction unless they form an S corporation. (Again, this logic sort of matches the old IRC Section 199A deduction just mentioned.)

Example: Say you have $1 million of qualified business income and you're potentially entitled to a $200,000 deduction. If your business's wages equal $300,000 and you hold no depreciable property, you can only deduct $150,000 because 50 percent of $300,000 equals $150,000.

The second limitation is that this 20 percent deduction is phased out based on income for specified service businesses or where the principal asset of the business is the reputation or skill of one or more of its employees (whatever this means). Thus, the 20 percent pass through deduction may not apply to financial service companies, law firms, medical firms, dental firms, athletes, consulting firms, actuarial firms, and those in the performing arts. For some reason, engineering firms and architectural firms are not subject to this limitation.

This is important since the deduction for service businesses completely phases out if their taxable income is $50,000 over that of a threshold amount for single taxpayers and $100,000 for taxpayers who file joint returns. The threshold amount is $315,000 for joint filers and $157,500 for everyone else. Thus, if you file jointly and have a taxable income over $415,000, or if you are single and have a taxable income over $207,500, and you are one of the specified service businesses, you don't get this 20 percent deduction. If you earn between $315,000 and $415,000 (married filing jointly) or between $157,500 and $207,500 (and single), you get part of the deduction. If you earn less than the threshold amounts, you get the full 20 percent deduction on taxable income not counting capital gains or reasonable salaries.

Sandy's note: IRS has recently stated that realtors are not considered brokers within the definition of specified service businesses. Thus, realtor firms do not have to worry about the problems arising from being a specified service business. Insurance professionals would likewise not be deemed to be conducting a specified service business regarding insurance sales other than sales of securities.

Sandy's elaboration: What this means in plain English is that for businesses other than specified service businesses, the deduction will be capped at 50 percent of wages or 25 percent of wages, plus a bit extra if you have a lot of equipment and/or furniture in your business, whichever is higher. This benefits manufacturers and hotel owners and others who use a lot of tangible property over that of service businesses such as doctors and lawyers. People like President Trump and Senator Corker make out well here. Who would have known that becoming president could save you a bundle in taxes?

If your business is a "specified service business," this limitation will potentially eliminate the deduction for you if you earn $50,000 more than the $157,500 threshold for all individual taxpayers who do not file joint returns or $100,000 more than the $315,000 threshold (for married filing joint taxpayers). Finally, if your taxable earnings are less than these threshold amounts (you earn less than $315,000 of taxable income and are married or you earn less than $157,800 of taxable income and are single), you are eligible for the full 20 percent pass-through deduction, *regardless of your type of business*. Thus, the limitations don't apply if your taxable income (not counting this deduction) is less than these shold amounts.

Sandy's note: This tax deduction will certainly encourage more people to become business owners. I can see many people trying to "game" the system by being treated either as an independent contractor or by forming their own corporation. While I do appreciate the attempt by Congress to benefit small businesses, I see a lot of problems with having two different tax rate systems: one for small businesses and one for employees.

In addition, the way this is determined is complicated and adds a great deal of complications to the tax return. If a small business didn't need an accountant before, it will surely need one now. I can assure you that if you have any business or real estate investment ownership, you won't be filing your tax return on a postcard-sized form. There is a lot of complexity to this new law. My final problem with all this is that I can see a LOT of people gaming the system and trying to classify themselves as independent contractors, thus increasing the deficit way beyond projections.

Figure 20-1 is a summary of this provision in the form of a flowchart that should help you understand this provision:

The Dividends Received Deduction Percentage Reduced[25]

Prior to the passage of the Tax Cuts and Jobs Act legislation, corporations that received dividends from other corporations were entitled to a deduction for dividends received. If the receiving corporation owned at least 20 to 80 percent of the dividend-paying corporation, an 80 percent dividends received deduction was allowed. Otherwise, the dividends received deduction was 70 percent for ownership interests of less than 20 percent. For tax years beginning after December 31, 2017, the 80 percent dividends received deduction is reduced to 65 percent, and the 70 percent dividends received deduction is reduced to 50 percent because of the lower corporate rates.

Alternative Minimum Tax Repealed for Corporations[26]

Prior to the passage of the Tax Cuts and Jobs Act legislation, corporations were subject to an alternative minimum tax (AMT) of 20 percent with a $40,000 exemption. Under the new Tax Cuts law, beginning after December 31, 2017, the corporate AMT is repealed permanently.

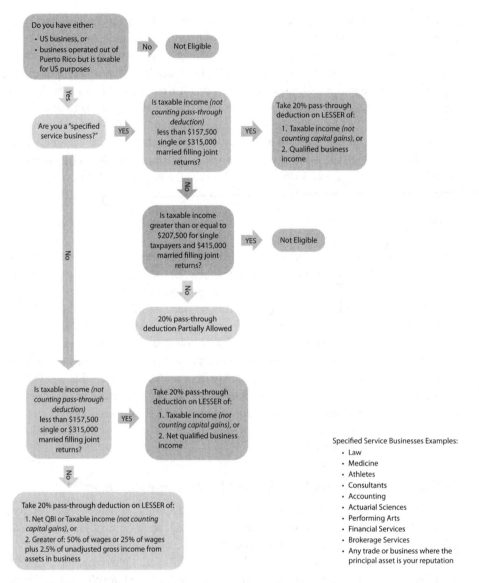

Figure 20-1. 20 Percent Pass-Through Deduction Flowchart.

Increase in Expense Deduction[27]

A taxpayer can either depreciate equipment used in a trade or business or elect to write it off in one year. In 2017, the amount that could be expensed was $500,000.

Under the Tax Cuts and Jobs Act law, for property placed in service after December 31, 2017, the maximum amount that taxpayers can expense has been increased to $1 million and phases out if equipment purchases exceed $2.5 million. In addition, the items that can be expensed has been expanded to include depreciable tangible personal property used primarily to furnish lodging and certain improvements in nonresidential real property, such as roofs, heating, ventilation, and air conditioning property, fire protection and alarm systems.

Sandy's elaboration: The benefits of being able to use the expense deduction on certain tangible property that provides lodging and for nonresidential real property will be a big boon to investors in commercial real estate and even for investors in residential property. It certainly will help President Trump with his hotels.

Luxury Automobile Depreciation Limits Substantially Increased[28]

Prior to the passage of the Tax Cuts and Jobs Act legislation, cars had some limits on yearly depreciation. The following is the maximum amount that a passenger automobile that isn't a qualified SUV or truck could be depreciated:

Year 1	$11,160
Year 2	$ 5,100
Year 3	$ 3,050
Years 4, and thereafter	$ 1,875

Under the new Tax Cuts law, these numbers, other than for year one, have been substantially increased as follows:

Year 1	$10,000, which is a slight decrease
Year 2	$16,000
Year 3	$ 9,600
Years 4, and thereafter	$ 5,760

Sandy's elaboration: This is one of the better changes in the tax law. It substantially increases the yearly vehicle depreciation for vehicles used in business. To give you an illustration of how good this new law is for vehicles, if you purchased a $50,000 luxury car such as a BMW, it would have taken you about 18 years to write it off. However, under the new law, the same $50,000 car would take about 5.2 years!! I can just see the luxury car dealers advertising, "buy a BMW, Mercedes, or Cadillac and eliminate your taxes."

Sandy's tip: You can take bonus depreciation up to $8,000 on new and used passenger cars, thus making the maximum first-year depreciation up to $18,000. HOWEVER, there is an unforeseen tax trap in doing this. You won't get any depreciation until year 7, in which you can write off the rest of the business usage. I, therefore, don't recommend that you take bonus depreciation on passenger automobiles. Only use it on equipment, qualified SUVs, and vans.

Computers and Peripheral Equipment Not Listed Property[29]

Listed property is a special classification for assets that lend themselves to both personal and business use. It involves things like computers, peripherals, and cars. It requires more strict depreciation than if it weren't listed property and it can't be expensed unless business use exceeds 50 percent.

Under the new Tax Cuts law, computers and peripherals are removed from the definition of listed property, which is good news. What this means to you is that you don't need to use computers more than 50 percent for business to qualify for accelerated depreciation or even to expense the business portion of the computer.

Example: I use my newly purchased home computer 40 percent for business. I can thus either elect to write off 40 percent of the cost in one year or take accelerated depreciation on 40 percent of the cost. In addition, there is less-restrictive record keeping for computers too. See your accountant about this.

Temporary 100 Percent Cost Recovery for Certain Qualifying Business Property[30]

Prior to the passage of the Tax Cuts and Jobs Act legislation, taxpayers were allowed an additional bonus depreciation of 50 percent of the property's adjusted basis if it was new to the taxpayer and had its original use by the taxpayer, which means it wasn't purchased as a used item.

The new Tax Cuts law allows for 100 percent bonus depreciation for the adjusted basis of the property if it was placed in service after September 27, 2017, and before January 1, 2024. There is a phasedown of the bonus depreciation starting in 2023 to 80 percent. In 2024, the bonus depreciation will be 60 percent. In 2025, the bonus depreciation drops to 40 percent, and in 2026 it drops to 20 percent.

Sandy's elaboration: A big winner will be qualified new sports utility vehicles (SUVs). Normally, these can only be written off up to $25,000 of the business use. However, using 100 percent bonus depreciation allows a complete write-off of the business use of a new SUV. This becomes just as good as a new qualified truck, which is also 100 percent deductible.

Modification of Net Operating Loss Deduction

If you have a non-corporate business that generates a loss, prior to passage of the Tax Cuts legislation you could use any business loss against any form of income including wages, rents, pensions, and a spouse's earnings. If the loss exceeded this year's income, you would get to carry it back up to two years and offset that last two years of taxes. This allowed businesses which had losses to be able to get cash for their losses and use this cash immediately when they needed it. If the losses exceeded the last two years of income, you could carry the loss forward up to 20 years.

The new Tax Cuts law somewhat changes this. Taxpayers can still use losses from a business against any other form of income. However, if the losses exceed the other income for the year, you no longer get to carry back losses except for losses incurred in the trade of business of farming. Losses not used in the year of the loss against other income and incurred after December 31, 2017, get an unlimited carryforward but can only be used up to 80 percent of taxable future yearly income.

Example: Kim operates a network marketing business that generates a $10,000 loss. if she has $50,000 of earned income from a job, she can offset that income by the $10,000 loss and only pay tax on $40,000. If , however, she had no income this year to offset, she can carry the loss forward forever using it against up to 80 percent of yearly income until the loss is used up.

Like-Kind Exchanges Limited to Investment Real Estate

Prior to passage of the Tax Cuts legislation, a non-taxable like-kind exchange was available for real estate and for tangible personal property. Therefore, there was no gain or loss when you traded in your car, since it is treated as a like-kind exchange.

Under the new Tax Cuts law, for transfers made after December 31, 2017, like-kind exchange treatment is only available for real property that is not held primarily for sale. Tangible personal property no longer qualifies as like-kind property.[31]

Sandy's elaboration: This change has some major implications. For example, if you trade in a vehicle that you use for business, some gain or loss might be recognized upon the exchange.

Employer's Deductions for Meals and Entertainment Limited

Prior to passage of the new Tax Cuts legislation, taxpayers were able to take clients out to a business lunch and deduct 50 percent of the cost of the meal. This also applied to fun types of entertainment such as golf, movies, plays, and sporting events. In addition, companies could provide employee outings and parties and write off 100 percent of the cost for the parties if they only invited employees and/or members of their families. Under the new Tax Cuts law, amounts paid or incurred after December 31, 2017, for the above-noted types of entertainment are disallowed other than for some meals.

Sandy's elaboration: This is a very big deal that has escaped the notice of most media. Small businesses normally don't market on major events such as the Olympics or the World Series. They don't even usually market on television. They market using "belly-to-belly" marketing. Thus eliminating the deductions for entertainment, such as golf, is a major deal for small businesses. They probably will still incur this type of expense, but they won't be able to deduct it. However, the deduction for business meals, such as at a restaurant with a prospect, is allowable pursuant to a recent IRS notice. Thus, if you discuss business at a restaurant and document this discussion correctly in Taxbot®, you should be able to get a 50 percent deduction for meals.[32] Also, meet with your tax professional before you take the position about deducting meals.

In addition, there are other types of meal deductions seems to be still allowed. Here is a list of what I think will be available to businesses:

- Business gifts: Business gifts would still be deductible up to $25 per person, per year. Gifts to organizations in which there is no named person to use the gift would also be 100 percent deductible as it is currently. Employee achievement awards would be disallowed under the new Tax Cuts legislation. I should note that IRS has said that gifts of meals are NOT deductible unless the business owner or a business employee is present when the gift is made. Thus, mailing a year end candy basket to clients won't be deductible. If however, you were present and had a business discussion at the same time that you gave your prospect or client the candy basket, it would seem to be deductible up to $25.

- Business meals with clients or prospects are 50 percent deductible if they are ordinary and necessary to your business, and are not lavish and you or an employee of your company are present during the business discussion in which the meal occurred. You also need to document this correctly in a good Tracker as noted in chapter 2.
- All food and prizes for open houses would still be 100 percent deductible.
- All food served at a business seminar would be 100 percent deductible by the seminar promoter.
- All food served at a sales presentation, such as an opportunity meeting, should still be 100 percent deductible.
- Any food served on the premises of an employer through an eating facility that meets the requirements for de minimis fringes would be 50 percent deductible.
- Meals furnished by the employer to keep employees on premises for emergencies or because there are no nearby restaurants in which the employee can get lunch and get back on time should be 50 percent deductible.
- Meals bought while on business travel can be reimbursed by the employer.
- Meals treated as compensation to employees are deductible.
- Meals served to employees and stockholders at business meetings seem to be 50 percent deductible.
- Meals and other expenses directly related and necessary to the attendance of business meetings of certain charitable organizations, such as business leagues, chambers of commerce, real estate boards, and boards of trade, seem to be 50 percent deductible.
- Expenses of goods and services made available to the general public, such as food served in an open house or at an opportunity meeting, are 100 percent deductible.
- Expenses for goods or services sold in a bona fide transaction for full consideration in money or money's worth would be 100 percent deductible.

No Deduction for Amounts Paid for Sexual Harassment Subject to Nondisclosure Agreement[33]

No deduction is allowed for any settlement, payout, or even attorney fees related to sexual harassment or sexual abuse if such payments are subject to a nondisclosure agreement.

New Credit for Employer-Paid Family and Medical Leave

For wages paid in tax years beginning after December 31, 2017, but not beginning after December 31, 2019, the new Tax Cuts and Jobs Act law allows businesses to claim a general business credit equal to 12.5 percent of the amount of wages paid to qualifying employees during any period in which such employees are on family and medical leave (FMLA) if the rate of payment is 50 percent of the wages normally paid to an employee.

The credit is increased by 0.25 percentage points (but not above 25 percent) for each percentage point by which the rate of payment exceeds 50 percent. All qualifying full-time employees must be given at least two weeks of annual paid family and medical leave (all less-than-full-time qualifying employees must be given a commensurate amount of leave on a pro rata basis). (See Code Sec. 45S, as amended by Act Sec. 13403.)

Cash Method of Accounting

Prior to passage of the new Tax Cuts legislation, businesses that were required to use inventory or were corporations could only use the cash method of accounting (treats income when received and gets deductions when paid) if their gross income was under $5 million (if inventories were involved, the gross receipts test was under $1 million), otherwise the accrual method of accounting was mandated. This required all businesses to report income when it was earned (such as when you sent out your bill) and they could only take deductions when all events were fixed and clear as to what they must pay. Under the new Tax Cuts law, businesses that have gross receipts under $25 million can use the cash method of accounting.[34]

Sandy's elaboration: Frankly, the accrual method was a real pain since you might have to claim as income items those owed to you even if you didn't get the cash yet.

Final Evaluation: So, what do I think of this new Tax Cuts and Jobs Act law? There are both good and bad parts. I LIKE the reduction in corporate rates to stem the tide of corporations leaving the U.S. This was a long time coming and should have happened long ago. I like the newly increased depreciation rules for vehicles and for allowing more cars and equipment to be eligible for bonus depreciation. I also somewhat like the idea of giving small businesses a special tax break to encourage people to start up small businesses, but I'm worried that many people will try to take advantage of this by gaming the system.

I especially HATE that there will be a $1.5 trillion deficit or even higher amount to pay for these tax cuts. I also disagree with any elimination of a deduction that hurts small businesses, such as making hobby expenses possibly nondeductible, or eliminating entertainment expenses, or eliminating the carryback for business losses. I am also unhappy with getting rid of a few fringe benefits, such as free parking, which were designed to reduce street congestion and encourage greater savings on energy. I also don't like the increased deduction for simply having children. It doesn't make any economic sense to do this.

However, you are the judges. There should be enough information here for you to form your own opinion.

Tax Planning

As many tax professionals become increasingly familiar with this new law, there will be a lot of tax planning opportunities. Here are just a few:

1. *Use a corporation as a tax shelter.* Corporations are taxed at a flat rate of 21 percent. This is a far cry from the top individual rate of 37 percent. Reclassifying yourself as a corporation and having your "client(s)" pay the corporation can save a bundle.

Also, although the corporation can subject you to double tax: tax at the corporate level and tax to you as a dividend, this can be avoided with good planning. Even if there is double tax, the sum of the corporate tax plus the tax on dividends is still less than the top tax rate for individuals.

Finally, you can keep the money in the corporation and wait until you die. Obviously, this isn't my favorite technique. However, upon death, your heirs get a step up in basis for the corporate stock and can liquidate the corporation and receive the proceeds tax free.

2. *Reclassifying as a contractor.* Instead of being a highly paid employee, simply quit and get treated as a contractor. There are some legal hoops to go through, but this could be possible. This will allow you to use the 20 percent pass-through deduction.

3. *Fire all employees and hire robots.* I am not kidding here. President Trump promised to create more jobs. However, he didn't finish the sentence. The full promise under this law is to, "create more jobs for robots." Robots are considered tangible business property if used in the business, and 2.5 percent of their cost counts in increasing the limitation for the 20 percent pass through deduction. Also, you don't need to pay them salary or benefits. This will be a big boon to manufacturing firms such as automakers.

4. *Incorporate your business if you would be deemed a "specified service business."* If you are earning more than $415,000 and are married filing joint returns or earning more than $207,500 and you are a single or head of household taxpayer, you won't get any benefit from the 20 percent pass-through deduction. Thus, you might want to incorporate and get taxed at the 21 percent rate for any monies left in the corporation. In addition, you avoid Medicare taxes on monies left in the corporation and not paid out in salaries.

5. *Max out your deductions with a good tracker.* Because of passage of this new Tax Cuts and Jobs Act legislation, most people will see an increase in their state taxes because the deductions in most states are similar to what the federal deductions were. Thus, people will have fewer deductions for state taxes, but the state rates will be the same. Thus, you have a wider base for taxation without a drop in the rates. Maximizing your deductions becomes even more important. Moreover, you might also want to keep track of nondeductible expenses too. This will help prove that you are operating your business like a business and not like a hobby. Hobbies will get no deductions under the new Tax Cuts law but will be taxed on the income. Ouch! Many famous and rich taxpayers like Henry Flagler, who was the partner of John D. Rockefeller in Standard Oil, kept track of all his expenses, even those that were nondeductible expenses, in order to track his money and control his spending.

6. *Consider giving appreciated property to your parents.* Right now, if you own property such as a principal home, you can get a $250,000 exclusion from gain if single or $500,000 of gain if married. However, to get this benefit, you must live in and occupy the residence for at least 2 out of the last 5 years.. If you don't meet these rules, you generally must pay tax on all gain unless you can show a hardship such as job change, mandatory sale, etc. Vacation home sales are fully taxable as are investment property sales. However, if you were to transfer real estate or even stocks to parents who die, your basis, as a result of inheritance, is the full fair market value upon their death! Thus, you get a big step up in basis. Even better, with the substantial increase in the estate tax exemption to 11.2 million dollars per person, you can do this with a lot of property, with no estate or gift tax. However, while this has some amazing estate and

income tax implications, it can pose some problems from an elder law perspective. For example, you would have to be sure that you get the property back from your parents in their will or trust and that any siblings will agree to this. Also, if your parents get sued or need nursing home care, any assets in their name can be attached. Thus, you need to see a good elder law or tax law professional before you implement this strategy.

Notes

1. IRC Section 63(c) (7), as modified by Act Section 11041(a).
2. IRC Section 24(h)(7), as added by Act Section 11022(a).
3. IRC Section 164(b)(6), as amended by Act Section 11042.
4. IRC Section 1(f), as amended by Act Section 11002(a), which is a permanent change.
5. IRC 1(j)(4), as amended by Act Section 11001(a).
6. IRC Section 165(H)(7), as amended by Act Section 11044.
7. IRC Section 165(D), as amended by Act Section 11050.
8. IRC Section 163(h)(3)(F), as amended by Act Section 11043(a).
9. IRC Section 213(f), as amended by Act Section 11027(a).
10. IRC Section 56(b)(1)(B), as amended by Act Section 11027(b).
11. IRC Section 170(b)(1)(g), as added by Act Section 11023.
12. IRC Section 170(l), as amended by Act Section 13704.
13. Act Section 11051 eliminates Code Sections 215, 61(a)(8) and Section 71.
14. IRC Section 132(f)(8), as added by Act Section 11047.
15. IRC 132(g), as amended by Section 11048.
16. IRC 217(K), as amended by Act Section 11049(a).
17. IRC Section 5000©, as amended by Act Section 11081. The repeal is permanent.
18. IRC Section 55(d)(4), as amended by Act Section 12003(a).
19. IRC Sections 529A(b), 25B(d)(1), 529A(b)(2), and 529(c)(3), as amended by Act Sections 11024(a), 11024(b), and 11025.
20. IRC Section 529©(7), as amended by Act Section 11032(a).
21. IRC Section 108(f), as amended by Act Section 11031.
22. IRC Section 2010©(3), as amended by Act Section 11061(a).
23. IRC Section 11(b), as amended by Act Section 13001.
24. IRC Section 199A.
25. IRC Section 243, as amended by Act Section 12002.
26. IRC Section 53, as amended by Act Section 12002.
27. ITC Section 179, as amended by Act Section 13101.
28. IRC Section 280F, as amended by Act Section 13202.
29. IRC Section 280F IBID.
30. Internal Revenue Code Section 168(k) as amended by the 2017 Tax Cuts and Jobs Act Sections 13201(a) and 13201(e).
31. IRC Section 1031, as amended by Act Section 13303.
32. The new law eliminates the deduction for entertainment except for meals incurred in operating a trade or business. It is uncertain whether meals served in a restaurant are deductible, even if they are incurred primarily for business. We think they are, but this area may need a ruling from the IRS. See your tax professional about this. IRS Notice 2018-76.
33. IRC Section 162, as amended by Act Section 13310.
34. IRC Sections 448 and 471, as amended by Act Section 1310.

21

The Top 10 Tax Questions

The questions answered in this chapter have universal appeal, have been asked numerous times at my seminars, or are very interesting. I hope you enjoy reading them as much as I've enjoyed answering them.

Question Number 10

"I have heard that the penalties for not having medical insurance or for not having "minimum essential coverage has been repealed. Do I need to pay any penalty if I didn't have insurance?"

Sandy's Answer: Due to the new tax reform law, there will no longer be a penalty for being without minimum essential health insurance coverage starting in 2019. Just because the penalty has been removed beginning in 2019 does not mean taxpayers will get a pass on being medically uninsured in 2017 or 2018.

Taxpayers who did not have insurance for all of 2017 may still face a penalty if they do not qualify for an exemption. Likewise, those who do not have insurance for 2018 could face a penalty when they file their 2018 return next year.

If you didn't have the minimum essential coverage for all of 2017, a tax professional can help you identify if you qualify for any number of exemptions. You will also want to see if you qualify for a special enrollment period for 2018 to avoid the same penalties.

Question Number 9

"I have been told that I can deduct up to $25,000 of rental property losses that might exceed rental property income and use those losses against any other form of income, such as my wages. Is this true? Also, I am a part-time property manager (working about 300 hours per year). I heard that being in real estate or property management can allow me to take all the rental loss deductions without limit and regardless of income. Is this true?"

Sandy's Answer

You're asking a very good question that affects a lot of people. For many years, real estate investors were allowed to deduct all rental property losses against any form of income. Real estate was the best legal tax shelter available. Starting in 1987, Congress limited rental property losses to rental property income and other passive income. However, there are two little known exceptions.

The first exception, which you noted in your question, applies to real estate professionals. If you're in the business of real property development, construction, acquisition, management, leasing, or sales and you meet two tests, there are no limits to being able to use rental property losses. In fact, if you're in any of the occupations listed, your real estate losses are deductible against any other form of income, with no limitation. However, to meet this exception, your real estate business must meet either of the following two tests:

- You perform more than half your business working hours in the real estate business.
- You perform more than 750 hours of this type of work during the year.

Since it seems that you do not meet either of these tests, you do not qualify for the real estate professional exception.

However, you may qualify for the second exception. If you actively manage your real estate investments—such as making the management decisions of approving tenants, deciding on rental terms, and approving repairs and improvement expenditures—and your income is under a certain ceiling (this is the congressional "gotcha"), you can deduct up to $25,000 of rental property losses against any other form of income.

The ceiling for that maximum loss allowance is an adjusted gross income (AGI) of $100,000 for either single or joint filers or $50,000 for married filing separately. If your AGI is over $100,000, the maximum gets phased out by $1 for every $2 that you earn over $100,000. But you can carry over to future years any remaining unused losses; the same limits apply. You also can use the losses against any gains from the sale of rental property.

Let's take some examples.

Example: David and Kari earn $120,000 AGI together. They have substantial rental losses that exceed their rental income. Since they earn over $120,000 AGI, they may only use $15,000 of the losses against their wages (the $25,000 maximum less 50 percent of the $20,000 excess AGI over $100,000). They can carry over the remaining unused losses, subject to the same limits.

Example: Deb and Donald earn $180,000 AGI and also have the same amount of rental property losses. They may not use any of the rental losses above their rental income because their AGI exceeds $150,000, which is the top for the phaseout ($25,000 less 50 percent of the $80,000 excess AGI over $100,000).

Question Number 8

Here is a vital question dealing with pension distributions. If you terminate your relationship with your company and you get your vested pension in cash, this question and answer will save you a bundle!

"I got a pension distribution made to me when my job got terminated. If I want to avoid any gains, I was told that I would have to roll over the contribution to my IRA within 60 days of receipt of the distribution to avoid all gains. The problem is that my company took out 20 percent of the distribution as a withholding for the IRS pursuant to IRS requirements. What do I do now? I can't roll over the withheld amount."

Sandy's Answer

You're right in noting that you have to pay tax on all pension, 401(k), and IRA distributions (other than the new Roth IRA) if you don't roll over the distribution within 60 days to another qualified plan or IRA. If this isn't painful enough, you also could be hit with a 10 percent penalty if you're younger than 59½.

Because the distribution was sent to you, the prior plan trustee *must* withhold 20 percent of the distribution. Your only choice is to contribute other money to the IRA to make up for the withholding. You would therefore not be taxed on any of the distribution and will get a refund of all withholding.

The better solution, which is too late for you, would have been to require the plan trustee to directly roll over the funds to your IRA and not to distribute the money to you. In this way, you would have avoided withholding.

Question Number 7

This question does not have universal appeal. However, as you'll see, I had fun with the answer.

"I have begun a photo enhancement/alteration service in which I can turn any 'would have been a good shot if only...' photo into something worth displaying. My biggest target markets are the consumers and business providers of the equestrian (horse) industry. Currently, I have a display at the public stable where my horse resides. If I display it on my horse's stall door, can I deduct my monthly board that I pay to keep the horse there? I view this as being similar to taking a home office deduction for displaying products and services in a home office."

Sandy's Answer

This is a great question. I met a couple on my travels who were "equine expression specialists." I wonder if that was you and your wife.

As for your question, the home office rules are very specific. They apply only to a residence that you live in. Thus, unless you live with your horse—and I doubt that your horse is cute enough to warrant this—the home office rules are not applicable.

Having a display at a public stable probably wouldn't alone allow for a deduction of the boarding fee of the horse; you probably could get a display posted even if your horse weren't there. You may, however, be able to deduct the stable fee if you run your horse business like a business and not just "horsing around" like a hobby.

The following are some factors that the IRS would look for:

- Do you race or breed your horse?
- Are you making money?
- If you're not making money, what steps are you taking to make money?
- What consultants or specialists have you used?
- What training have you attended?

If you're considered to be running your horse business as a business, this could be a "horse of a different color" as far as the IRS is concerned. See pages 145 to 149 of the workbook in my *Tax Strategies for Business Professionals* series.

Question Number 6

If you own some investment property, such as rental property, you'll find this question and answer very useful.

"I currently own some houses that I rent out. I want to sell the houses but don't want to pay tax on the sale. I guess I want to have my cake and eat it too. Any suggestions, Sandy?"

Sandy's Answer

You can indeed avoid all capital gains on your real estate by structuring a *like-kind exchange*. This is where you trade one investment property for another. You may trade an apartment building for land or a commercial building for residential rentals, etc. The exchange must, however, be investment property for investment or commercial property. You can't have a like-kind exchange for your residence. Moreover, you cannot receive anything in exchange, such as cash or other property, or you may have to recognize gain to the extent of the other property received.

In addition, you don't even have to know which property you want to receive in the exchange. You can have a deferred exchange, where you would identify the property that you want within 45 days of the contract and then acquire the replacement property within 180 days of the contract. Check with your accountant and a good realtor who specializes in this type of transaction.

Note: Under the new tax law (Tax Cuts and Jobs Act), only the real estate qualifies for a like-kind exchange. Personal property located in real estate do not qualify.

Question Number 5

This question is for you "party animals." It involves entertainment and alcohol.

"I am having a business party in my home. I will be following your advice about sending out an announcement that I am celebrating 10 years in business and will have displays of what I do. I intend to serve alcohol, and in my state, there is a special alcohol tax like a sales tax. Can I deduct the cost of the alcohol just like deducting food, and can I deduct the tax?"

Sandy's Answer

Alcohol is treated like any other beverage. It would be as deductible as food. The tax on the alcohol also would be deductible, as would any tax on food. However, under the new law, entertainment deductions are eliminated. However, there is an old saying, "Where there is a will, there is a lawyer." Make sure that your food and drink are served as part of a sales presentation to customers. If so, you could potentially deduct up to 100 percent of all food and drink. Cha, cha cha.

Question Number 4

This question will have universal appeal. It deals with the issue of when you can start taking business deductions. This is a vital issue for all new businesspeople.

"I just bought some investment real estate. It's in bad shape and needs some work. When can I start deducting the depreciation and maintenance on the property? Also, my wife is opening up a restaurant. When can she start deducting expenses related to the restaurant?"

Sandy's Answer

These are good questions that apply to many small businesses. You're deemed to be in business and therefore able to deduct business expenses when you're open for business. Thus you must be able to sell services or products or take customers. It's at this point that any reasonable business expenses that you incur become deductible.

In your real estate investment business, you would reach this point when your property becomes habitable, and you start advertising for a tenant. In your wife's restaurant, she would reach this point when she is able to accept customers.

Some businesses, however, incur some expenses before they open the business, such as investigation expenses, legal and accounting fees incurred for the startup, copyrights, etc. These would be nondeductible.

However, where there's a will, there's a lawyer. The IRS gives you an out. You may elect to amortize your preopening expenses over a period of at least 60 months. You must, however, elect to do so on your tax return. See your accountant about making a protective election for your startup expenses.

Question Number 3

I get this question a lot. Network marketers in particular frequently ask it. It applies, however, to any business. It entails one of the biggest myths that surround the tax law.

"I am in the network marketing business. I have some losses in my business during my first two years of operation. My accountant told me that I have to have a profit for three of the last five years in order to take the losses, so he won't allow me to deduct these losses against my salary. Is this true?"

Sandy's Answer

You need to get a new accountant immediately. As for needing a profit in three of the last five years, this is probably the biggest myth in tax law. Rightfully, you want to be construed as a business and not as a hobby. The implications are enormous.

If you're in business, you get to deduct all ordinary and necessary business expenses on a dollar-for-dollar basis. In addition, if your expenses exceed your income, you will have a tax loss that you can use against any form of income, such as wages, dividends, and pensions. You can even use it against your spouse's earnings.

Example: Scott earns $40,000 in salary from his job. If his side business generates a $10,000 loss, he may offset the salary with the loss and pay tax on only $30,000.

If the loss from your business exceeds your yearly income, you offset your current income with the loss. If the loss exceeds your current income, you carry forward the loss against future income and use it up to 80 percent of taxable income. This loss never expires until you use it up.

If you're a hobby, however, all expenses seem to be disallowed under the new law yet you must report your income from the hobby! Thus, there is no loss to use or to carry over to the future. Thus, you never want to be classified as a hobby.

The Internal Revenue Code notes that if you have a profit for three of five consecutive years (two of seven for businesses involving horses), you're presumed to be a business. However, even if you don't have the necessary profit in the three years, you can still have many years of losses *if you run your endeavor with a reasonable expectation of profit.*

There are a number of factors that the courts use in making this determination. One of the biggest and most important factors is whether you have a business plan. This is a five-year projection of income and expenses. The projection should at some year show a profit. I cannot overstate the importance of this. You also should have a marketing plan built into your business plan to show your projected marketing activities.

Another factor is documentation. Businesses have correct detailed records. Businesses keep tax diaries. Hobbies do not.

You also should work your business regularly. This means at least 45 minutes per day, four or five days a week. It's much more beneficial in establishing a business motive to work a business four hours a week than to put in eight hours in one week and none in the second week.

Business owners go to training that should be documented. In addition, if business owners don't have a profit in one year, they don't repeat the same mistakes. Insanity is expecting different results from doing the same thing from year to year. Business owners change marketing strategies if they don't work and they consult with experts.

There's much more that I can add to this answer, but it should give you a good review of what's necessary. See also the in-depth discussion of this subject in Chapter 8.

Question Number 2

This question deals with a major issue that is misunderstood nationwide. There are millions of people who take out home-equity loans unnecessarily because they don't understand this issue.

"I am self-employed and use the IRS mileage deduction for my vehicle. Therefore, I do not deduct gas, insurance, repairs, etc. However, my question is whether I can take the interest deduction incurred on my car loan and deduct a percentage for business."

Sandy's Answer

This is a great question and an example of one of the biggest misunderstandings in the tax law. You're allowed to deduct your car interest and/or sales tax to the extent that you use your car for business. Thus, if you use your car 80 percent for business, you can deduct 80 percent of the year's interest and 80 percent of any taxes incurred on the car for that year. This point is also true *regardless* of the method that you use to deduct your car, whether it's the IRS mileage approach or the actual expenses (such as deducting gas, repairs, insurance, etc.).

Sadly, many people don't understand that you can deduct interest on car loans to the extent that the vehicle is used for business. Thus they take out home-equity loans to accomplish this. This could be a bad mistake. If they fail to pay off the loan, they could lose their home. Moreover, home-equity loans do not provide deductible interest under the new tax law (Tax Cuts and Jobs Act). If you use a loan to purchase a car, this would reduce the available amount of the loan that you could use for other purposes.

I should note that employees who don't have a side business cannot deduct the interest and taxes incurred on their vehicles. You must use a car in business to get this benefit.

Question Number 1

This is the question I get most frequently. Someone asks this question on my Web site, www.taxreductioninstitute.com, almost every week. If you have a network marketing business, you probably have wondered about this yourself. However, this question also would apply to other businesses, such as franchises, where there may be a minimum purchase requirement.

"I have a multilevel marketing business. I am required to purchase $100 a month of product in order to receive any check. May I deduct the cost of this required monthly purchase?"

Sandy's Answer

In my opinion, and that of IRS personnel with whom I spoke, you cannot deduct your monthly purchases. The reason is that these items usually can be resold, so they would be nondeductible inventory, or you probably consume the products monthly, which would make these purchases personal and nondeductible.

However, as I'm fond of saying, "Where there's a will, there's a lawyer." There are a couple of ways that would entitle you to get a deduction for these purchases.

One way is to give them away to prospects as samples. You would have to note in your diary answers to the following questions:

- Who did you give the product to?
- What did you give?
- When (the date) did you give it?
- How much did it cost?
- Why did you give it (such as for samples or demonstration)?

If you write down the answers to these questions, you may deduct your monthly purchases to the extent that you gave the products away as samples. This all needs to be documented in a tax organizer such as Taxbot. (Go to www.taxbot.com)

A second method is to sell the products. As I mentioned, they're considered inventory, so they're not deductible until they're sold.

The third method is to donate them to charity, such as to your local college or religious organization. You then would take a charitable deduction for the donation as a nonbusiness deduction. Don't forget to get a receipt from the charity!

Author's note: There are tax professionals who disagree with my opinion on this issue. Their reason is that there is no case or IRS ruling on this issue. In addition, requiring product purchases in order to receive a check seems like it is ordinary and necessary to the network marketing business. I should note that this answer to question 1 is my opinion; however, it is also the opinion of IRS personnel whom I have questioned. If you try to take this deduction, be prepared to have to fight with the IRS about this issue. Who knows? You may win the case, and I can cite you in forthcoming books!

Author's note: In the American Taxpayer Relief Law, there is a little-known provision for donating food inventory. If you have food, such as diet bars and shakes that if properly labeled in accordance with federal and state rules and qualifies as inventory, your deduction to a qualified charity that donates food to the needy or sick, would be what you paid for the food plus one-half of the appreciation. Thus, if you purchased food bars for $2 that have a retail value of $3 and you meet the donation rules, you would get a charitable deduction of $2.50, which is your basis plus one-half of the gain. If you are a retailer of food, or wholesale supplier, you might benefit from this provision.

Appendix A

2018 Tax Rates

For Married Individuals Filing Joint Returns and Surviving Spouses:	
If taxable income is:	**The tax is:**
Not over $19,050	10% of taxable income
Over $19,050 *but not over* $77,400	$1,905.00 *plus* 12% of the excess over $19,050
Over $77,400 *but not over* $165,000	$8,907.00 *plus* 22% of the excess over $77,400
Over $165,000 *but not over* $315,000	$28,179.00 *plus* 24% of the excess over $165,000
Over $315,000 *but not over* $400,000	$64,179.00 *plus* 32% of the excess over $315,000
Over $400,000 *but not over* $600,000	$91,379.00 *plus* 35% of the excess over $400,000
Over $600,000	$161,379.00 *plus* 37% of the excess over $600,000

For Single Individuals (Other than Heads of Households and Surviving Spouses):	
If taxable income is:	**The tax is:**
Not over $9,525	10% of taxable income
Over $9,525 *but not over* $38,700	$952.50 *plus* 12% of the excess over $9,525
Over $38,700 *but not over* $82,500	$4,453.50 *plus* 22% of the excess over $38,700
Over $82,500 *but not over* $157,500	$14,089.50 *plus* 24% of the excess over $82,500
Over $157,500 *but not over* $200,000	$32,089.50 *plus* 32% of the excess over $157,000
Over $200,000 *but not over* $500,000	$45,689.50 *plus* 35% of the excess over $200,000
Over $500,000	$150,689.50 *plus* 37% of the excess over $500,000

For Heads of Households:

If taxable income is:	The tax is:
Not over $13,600	10% of taxable income
Over $13,600 *but not over* $51,800	$1,360.00 *plus* 12% of the excess over $13,600
Over $51,800 *but not over* $82,500	$5,944.00 *plus* 22% of the excess over $51,800
Over $82,500 *but not over* $157,500	$12,698.00 *plus* 24% of the excess over $82,500
Over $157,500 *but not over* $200,000	$30,698.00 *plus* 32% of the excess over $157,500
Over $200,000 *but not over* $500,000	$44,298.00 *plus* 35% of the excess over $200,000
Over $500,000	$149,298.00 *plus* 37% of the excess over $500,000

For Marrieds Filing Separately:

If taxable income is:	The tax is:
Not over $9,525	10% of taxable income
Over $9,525 *but not over* $38,700	$952.50 *plus* 12% of the excess over $9,525
Over $38,700 *but not over* $82,500	$4,453.50 *plus* 22% of the excess over $38,700
Over $82,500 *but not over* $157,500	$14,089.50 *plus* 24% of the excess over $82,500
Over $157,500 *but not over* $200,000	$32,089.50 *plus* 32% of the excess over $157,500
Over $200,000 *but not over* $300,000	$45,689.50 *plus* 35% of the excess over $200,000
Over $300,000	$80,689.50 *plus* 37% of the excess over $300,000

For Estates and Trusts:

If taxable income is:	The tax is:
Not over $2,550	10% of taxable income
Over $2,550 *but not over* $9,150	$255.00 *plus* 24% of the excess over $2,550
Over $9,150 *but not over* $12,500	$1,839.00 *plus* 35% of the excess over $9,150
Over $12,500	$3,011.50 *plus* 37% of the excess over $12,500

Appendix B

How to Find a Good Accountant

The question that I get asked most frequently at seminars is, "How do I find a good accountant?" Sadly, it is very tough finding the right, knowledgeable accountant.

First, not all accountants specialize in taxes. Many accountants perform audits, computer studies, and the like. Second, many accountants are timid! They would love for you to send in 100 percent of your income (less their accounting fee).

Accordingly, there are some questions that you can ask in order to see if an accountant is right for you. Here are some suggestions:

1. What designations or credentials do you have?

Look for enrolled agents (people who pass a special IRS examination), certified public accountants, ex-IRS agents, attorneys, etc. I like preparers with legal backgrounds, because they tend to be more aggressive.

2. Are you in practice full time?

Hopefully, the answer will be yes.

3. How many years' experience do you have in tax practice?

You don't want a rookie experimenting on you!

4. Do you prepare all returns by computer?

Handwritten returns ended with the '80s.

5. What are your fees, and do you have a written fee schedule?

Cheaper is not necessarily better. You may get what you pay for!

6. Can you provide references from other businesses similar to my own?

Many accountants, rightly, don't give out names of clients. However, all firms should have some happy clients who will be willing to speak to you. When you call

319

them, ask them, "What do you like about the accountant?" and "What would you improve about his/her services?"

7. Do you use any checklists to maximize my deductions?

8. Test your accountant.

Tell him/her that in a tax reduction book and seminar it was suggested "to hire your spouse and make that person the primary insured so you can deduct medical insurance premiums and set up a self-insured medical plan." Ask what the accountant thinks of this strategy.

9. Do you teach any tax courses, or have you written any tax publications?

The more, the better.

10. Are you conservative, aggressive, or somewhere in the middle?

11. What review process do you use in order to ensure a quality product?

12. May I look at your tax library?

Accountants need to look things up. The more sources, the better. They should have at least two separate tax research sources.

13. Do you specialize in taxes?

They should say yes!

14. What percentage of your practice relates to taxes? What other accounting services do you personally perform?

15. What is your attitude toward tax audits?

Unfortunately, many tax preparers recommend not taking legitimate tax breaks at all if it could possibly trigger an audit. These accountants are a "hazard to your wealth."

16. How do you treat gray areas?

The best advisors will tell you that the area is gray and give you your options. Stay away from advisors who say, "The area is not clear, so don't take the deduction."

17. What do you do after tax season?

You want to hear that he/she does other accounting work and also does marketing for new clients.

18. How often do you take tax courses?

19. Have you ever been disciplined by the IRS or any accounting society?

If an accountant refuses to answer this question or acts insulted, forget it!

20. How many other clients like me do you have?

You don't need hundreds, but more than 10 would be helpful.

21. Do you offer pre-year-end tax planning as part of your tax service? If so, is there an extra fee for this?

22. Do you offer any tax planning during the year?

23. How soon do you return calls from clients?

24. Give me a tax-planning tip based on a recent tax change that may benefit me.

If you need a firm to represent you before the IRS, as a rule, the firm's "Track Record" is the best objective indicator of how that firm will manage your case. Listed below are some of the additional key questions to be addressed:

25. How many years has the firm been in business?

26. Has the firm been designated as a Certified Tax Resolution Specialist?

27. Does the firm discuss all options available to the taxpayer to resolve their tax problem?

28. How many Offers in Compromise has the firm successfully settled?

29. What is the firm's success rate—total dollars negotiated in settlements divided by total dollars in tax, interest, and penalties owed?

30. What is the firm's rating with the Better Business Bureau?

31. What is the firm's Credit and Financial rating with Dun and Bradstreet?

Finally, there are certain other areas of concern that you should watch for in order to avoid unscrupulous firms. They are:

- Beware of organizations and telemarketers that are paid on an incentive basis for bringing your business to their firm.
- Be especially aware of unrealistic promises or improbable results. You want to be sure that you receive top-quality work and that you get the services that you pay for. I would avoid any firm that promises you that you will only have to pay pennies on the dollar to the IRS without first scrutinizing your complete financial situation.
- Beware of firms that charge you a fee exclusively based on the amount of money that you owe the IRS. Usually, the same amount of work is required to solve both large and small tax obligations.
- Ask the tax resolution firm direct questions about your case. If the firm is evasive or if their answers seem intentionally complex or unclear, it is possible that they are trying to cover up information about your representation or quality of service that they may or may not provide. You deserve straightforward answers.

Conclusion

These questions may not be all-inclusive. However, they will certainly "separate the wheat from the chaff" and enable you to make much better decisions as to whether an accountant is right for you!

Appendix C

Health Savings Account

Overview: A health savings account (HSA) requires a trust to be set up for paying qualified medical expenses. The contributions are deductible, and the payments for these qualified medical expenses are tax-free.

Qualifying: You must use the HSA proceeds for qualified medical expenses. In addition, you must have a high deductible medical policy.[1] A high deductible plan is one whose annual deductible and out-of-pocket expenses are as follows:[2]

2018 HSA Limits	Self Only	Family
Minimum Deductible	$1,350	$ 2,700
Annual Out-Of-Pocket	$6,650	$13,300
Maximum Contribution	$3,850	$ 6,900
Catch-Up Contribution	$1,000	$ 1,000 each

Caution: You can't have another medical plan that covers your deductibles. Thus, if you have a plan, such as Aflac, that pays for sickness and injuries, this may disqualify your HSA. However, you can have a plan that pays for specific types of diseases such as cancer, and you can have a plan that pays for daily stays in hospitals. In addition, you can have a self-insured medical plan, flexible spending account, or cafeteria plan in addition to the HSA *if* these plans have at least the same deductibles as the HSA.

Observation: In my opinion, the self-insured medical plan is still the better option since you don't need a high deductible policy, don't need to set up a trust with yearly fees paid to financial institutions, and don't have any dollar limitations on contributions other than the fact that the payments must be reasonable for the hours and work performed. An HSA, however, might be advisable if you are single and don't have a C corporation or you don't want to hire your spouse in your business in order to utilize the benefits of the self-insured medical plan for yourself. Frankly, I have an HSA setup for my family that works very well.

Notes

1. Section 223(b)(3)(A) of the IRC.
2. Section 223(c)(1)(A) of the IRC and Rev. Proc. 2008-66, 2008-45 IRB.

Index

A

ABLE accounts, 295
Accountant(s):
    at audits, 108
    how to find a good, 319–321
Actual expense method, IRS standard rate vs., 56–57, 70
Add backs, 60–63
Address:
    change of, 105
    of home office, displaying, 89
Adjusted gross income (AGI), 38, 173, 177
Adoption assistance, 165, 177
Advertising, 118
Advertising scams, 279–280
Affordable Care Act, 294–295
AGI (*see* Adjusted gross income)
Alabama Securities Commission, 281
Alcohol, 312
Alimony, 292–293
Alternative Minimum Tax (AMT), 295, 299
American Opportunity Credit, 240–244
American Opportunity Tax Credit, 238
American Taxpayer Relief Law, 59
    C corporations, 135
    transit pass limits, 201
Amortization, 223–224
AMT (Alternative Minimum Tax), 295, 299
Annual lease table rule, 66
Annual lease value method, 202–204
Annual Lease Value Table, 48
Annual share transaction statement, 255
Annuities:
    in tax-advantaged investments, 256–257
    tax-deferred, 248
Antiques, 93
Application for Taxpayer Assistance Order
    (IRS Form 911), 102
Appreciated property, 46–47, 50
Assets:
    LLC asset protection, 144
    tax-advantaged investments and, 256–257
    transfer of money and, 159–160
Athletic facilities, 166, 184–186

Auditors, IRS, 99–100
Audits/audit-proofing (IRS), 9, 98–110
    "audit lottery," 100, 102
    automobile mileage, 68–74
    average recommended additional tax following,
      101
    DIF (Discriminant Function System), 105
    documentation, 32–33, 107–108
    dressing appropriately for, 108
    evidence tampering, 109
    hasty agreement to adjustments, 109
    home office, 85–86, 88–90
    limiting scope of, 107
    meals and outings, 11–12
    most frequent, 53
    national revenue obtained from, 100
    preparing for, 107–109
    "rat fee," 109
    real estate universal exclusion, 227–231
    reducing chance of, 105–107
    special agents, 109
    tape-recording, 104
    taxpayer rights, 102–104
    and trusts, 109–110
Automobiles (*see* Vehicles)

B

Bank accounts:
    foreign, hiding income in, 274
    separate business accounts, 116
Basis:
    automobile adjusted, 64–66
    inheritance, 46
    mutual fund, 253–257
    partnership, 129–133
    stock, 140, 143
BBB (Better Business Bureau),
    119, 276
Below-market loan rules, exceptions to,
    187–188
Better Business Bureau (BBB), 119, 276
Bicycle, commuting by, 293–294
Boatner case, 265

Bonds:
    calculation process for, 248–250
    dealer definition and, 261–262
    entity types in purchasing, 261
    FIFO, 252
    holding strategy for, 252
    municipal, 247
    series EE/series I, in QTPs, 239
    Treasury, 248
Book scams, 281–282
Box seats, 9
Bridge loans, 188–189
Budgets, 115
Buffett, Warren, 277
Bush, George, 21
Business:
    classification as hobby vs. (*see* Business vs. hobby
      classification)
    combining fun with, 9, 27, 29
    courses and programs for, 235–236
    home-based, 3–7
    new, losses against income in, 312–313
    principal place of, 81–83
    promotion, 14
    (*See also* Home office)
Business days, 25–31
Business gifts, 10, 14–15
Business meals, 9–14
    documentation of, 10–12
    requirement for deducting, 10–11
Business mileage, 53–54, 66–67, 74
    flowchart for determining, 69
    personal mileage vs., 67–68
Business organization forms, 125–148
    C corporation, 134–138
    entity selection flowchart, 126
    general partnership, 129–131
    limited partnership, 132–133
    limited-liability corporation, 143–145, 153–154,
      162, 172
    Nevada corporation, 136, 145, 150–154
    S corporation, 39, 138–142, 155–157, 251
    sole proprietorship, 127–129, 172
Business travel (*see* Travel expenses)
Business vs. hobby classification, 112–121
    advance research into ventures, 118–119
    benefits from business losses, 112–113
    business plan/projections, 115
    business-like conduct of activities,
      116–117
    criteria for, 114–120
    history of income/losses, 119
    horse/dog breeding, 117, 310–311
    income from other sources, 119
    loss carryover/carryback, 113
    network marketing, 115–117
    operating like similar businesses, 117–118
    postponing determination of, 114
    presumption based on profit, 114
    prior business experiences, 118
    regularity of activity, 119
    suspicious activities, 120
    training and, 118
Business/business use, converting automobile to, 54–55
Buy-sell agreement, 131, 137

C

C corporations, 134–138
    advantages of, 134–136
    disadvantages of, 136–137
    who should operate as, 137–138
Cafeteria plans, 134–135, 168, 206–207
California, sales tax in, 153
California Public Research Group (CALPIRG), 285
Canceled flights, 27
Capital:
    for C corporations, 135
    for general partnerships, 129
    for limited partnerships, 132
    for S corporations, 142
    for sole proprietorships, 128
Capital gains, 251, 263–264
    avoiding consequences of, 46, 50
    corporate, 135, 251
    as investment income, 248–251, 263
    long-term, investor status and, 262
    losses and, 248–251
    from qualified small business stock, 140–141
    rates, 262
    S corporations and, 251
    set rate of, 248
    of traders, long-term, 267
Capitalization, 151
Car (*see* Vehicles)
Carryback/carryover, of losses, 113, 127
Cash method of accounting, 305
Casualty losses, elimination of, 290–291
Cents per mile method, 204
Cents per mile rule, 67
Chain letters, 278–279
Change of address form, 105
Charging order, 144
Charitable contributions:
    automobile, 64–65
    increased deduction limitation, 292
    as tax scam, 276
Charity events, 13–14
Charter boat operations, 117
Chauffeurs, tax free, 167, 196–197
Child tax credit, 289
Children:
    adoption assistance fringe benefit, 165, 177
    dependent child's business services/wage sheet, 44
    handicapped, 238
    hiring your, 289
    income shifting/splitting, 41–45, 47
    Kiddie tax, 47, 237, 290
Civic organizations, dues to, 17
Clients, in home office, 83
Closely connected spouse rule, 13
Colleagues, visiting, 28

Collectibles, 248, 249
College expenses, 234–245
    American Opportunity Credit, 240–244
    deductibility of, 235–237
    Economic Stimulus Law and, 237
    Lifetime Learning Credit, 241–244
    medical exceptions and, 238–239
    prepaid tuition, 236
    Qualified Higher Education Expenses, 237–244
    Qualified Tuition Programs, 234, 236–237
    rising tuition costs, 234
    series EE and series I bonds, 239
    student loan interest deduction, 243
    tax credits for, 240–244
College sports tickets, 292
Commuting, 196
    by bicycle, 293–294
    company-provided transit passes/parking/vanpools,
        168
    company-provided transportation/limos/chauf-
        feurs, 167, 196–197
    nondeductible costs example, 4
    qualified transit passes, 201
    (*See also* Vehicles)
Commuting valuation rule, 67
Commuting value method, 205
Company-provided benefits:
    adoption assistance, 165, 177
    corporate purchase of homes, 167, 194–195
    no/low-interest loans, 166, 186–189
    transit passes/parking/vanpools, 168
    transportation/limos/chauffeurs, 167, 196–197
    trips, 167, 192–193
    vehicles, 168, 202–205
Computers and peripherals, 301–302
Constitutional trusts, 110
Constitutionality, of taxation, 109–110
Consumer product testing, 174
Consumer Response Center, 285
Consumption taxes, 264
Continuity:
    in general partnerships, 130
    in limited partnerships, 132
    in sole proprietorships, 128
Control:
    in limited partnerships, 133
    in sole proprietorships, 127
Control employees, 67
Convenience of employer, 212
Conventions, 27, 31
Corker, Bob, 299
Corporate bond interest, 249
Corporate purchase of employee home that declined in
        value, 194–195
Corporate veil, 151–152
Corporate-provided transit passes/parking/vanpools,
        168, 200–202
Corporations, 106, 134–145
    C, 134–138
    capital gains/losses, 135, 140, 251
    definition of *incorporate*, 134
    Delaware, 152–153

disguised corporate ownership tax scam, 275
    flat tax rate for, 134, 136, 296–297
    limited-liability, 143–145, 153–154, 162, 172
    Nevada, 136, 145, 150–154
    new, property transfer to, 160–162
    "piercing the corporate veil," 151–152
    S, 39, 138–142, 155–157, 251
    sole stockholder in, 39
    transferring assets/money into, 159–160
Country club dues, 17–18, 167, 184–185, 190–192
Credit cards:
    identity theft and, 282–285
    "preapproved," 283, 285
Credit monitoring, 284–285
Credits (*see* Tax credits)
Cruise ships, 25–27

D

D'Arcangelo, David, 5
Day care, 84–85, 165, 175–177
Days in transit, 26
De minimis fringe benefits, 166, 180–182
    below-market loan rules, 187
    examples of, 180–182
Dealers, 261–262, 269
Defined-benefit plan, 216–217
Delaware corporations, 152–153
Dental expenses, 178
Department of Justice, on identity theft, 282–283
Dependent child's business services/wage sheet, 44
Depreciation, 48, 90–95, 249
    automobile/vehicle, 54–55, 57–60, 64–65
    equipment expensing vs., 300–301
    home office equipment, 93–95
    real estate, 230–231
    with simplified home office deductions, 88
    temporary 100 percent cost recovery, 302
    2018 limits of, 57–58
Desperation approach, 74
DIF (Discriminant Function System), 105 (*See also*
        Audits)
"Dirty dozen" tax scams, 273–276
Disability insurance fringe benefit, 166, 179–180
Discounts, for qualified employees, 166, 182–184
Discriminant Function System (DIF), 105
Discrimination:
    employee discount rules and, 183–184
    fringe benefits and, 165–170, 172, 174
    medical reimbursement and, 39–40
    relocation expense reimbursement allowed, 195
Dividends:
    dividends received deduction, 299
    as income, 261–262
Divorce, property transfer as part of, 231
Documentation, 116–117, 314
    audit, 32–33, 107–108
    automobile mileage, 68–74
    business meals, 10–12
    country club dues, 17–18
    hired relatives, 43–45
    home office, 88–90, 93

income shifting/splitting, 43–45
of incorrect Form 1099, 106
of IRS advice received, 99–100
lodging, 24, 32–33
lost, desperation or reconstruction approach for, 74
meals, 24
mileage logs as, 71–73
paper vs. electronic, 69
square footage, 87, 88
taxpayer service representative, 99–100
techniques for audit-proof, 32–33, (*See also* Audits/audit–proofing [IRS])
(*See also* Receipts; Record keeping; Tax diary)
Dog breeding, 117
Double taxation, 136, 138, 162
Double-category method, 253–254
Dry cleaning, 22
Dues, country club/health club, 17–18, 167, 190–192
Dumpster diving, 283

E

Economic stimulus:
college tuition under, 237
scams, 273
(*See also* American Taxpayer Relief Law)
Education:
assistance, 167, 189–191
business training, 118
college tuition, 234
deductibility of expenses for, 235–237
out of town, 28
paying for children's, 41–45, 47
tax credits for, 240–244
for traders, 265
training scams, 277–278
(*See also* College expenses)
Elections, 94
filing all entitled, 106
mark-to-market, 265
S corporation, 138
Employee discount rules, 183–184
Employees:
automobile provision for, 67
company-provided trips for spouses and, 167, 193
consumer testing of products by, 174
control, 67
corporate purchase of declined value home of, 194–195
discounts for, 166, 182–184
exempt from medical coverage, 40–41
highly compensated, 39–41, 165–170, 172–175
home office claims by, 92
IRS, 102–103
meals for, 17
part-time, 183–184
party invitations to, 17
qualified employee discounts, 166, 182–184
qualified move/relocation expense reimbursement for, 195–196
relocation loans, 167, 188–189
restaurant, tax-free meals for, 213–214
of sole proprietors, 128
spouses as, 23–24, 38
tax laws shafting, 5
working condition fringe benefit for, 173, 189–191
Employer, convenience of, 212
Enron, 150, 153–154
Entertainment (*see* Meals and outings)
Entities:
entity selection flowchart, 126
types of, 261
(*See also* Business organization forms)
Equifax, 285
Equipment, 47–49
automobile, 63
exercise, 166, 184–186
expensing vs. depreciating, 94–95, 300–301
home office, deductible, 94–95
home office, depreciation of, 93–95
purchase of $500,000 worth, 94–95
working condition fringe benefit, 165, 173
Estate taxes, 275, 296, 306–307
Evidence tampering, 109
Exclusive use rule (home office), 85–86
Exemptions, elimination of, 288–289
Exercise equipment:
deductions for, 184–186
as fringe benefit, 166
Exercising the option, 209–211
Expenses:
college (*see* College expenses)
dental, 178
home office indirect expense methods, 86–88
medical, 38–41, 322–323 (*See also* Health insurance)
on-the-road, 22–23, 25
relocation, 167, 188–189, 195–196
transportation, 22, 26, 167, 196–197
travel (*see* Travel expenses)
Expensing, equipment depreciating vs., 94–95, 300–301
Experian, 285

F

F. R. McDowell case, 214–215
Fabulous offer scams, 280
Fair Labor Standards Act, 196
Fair market value:
in leasing, 48–49
lower of cost or, 93
"Familiarization trips," 119
Family and medical leave, 304–305
Family estate trusts, 110
Family travel, 24
Federal Trade Commission (FTC), 285
FIFO (first-in-first-out), 252
Fifty percent rule, 10
exceptions to, 14–17
for meals, 14–17
Finger in the wind approach, 74
First-in-first-out (FIFO), 252
First-week rule, 73
Flagler, Henry, 306
Flat taxes, 264

Flights, canceled, 27
Flowcharts:
    automobile disposal decision, 64
    business mileage determination, 69
    business travel, 29
    entity selection, 126
Foreign bank accounts, hiding income in, 274
Foreign travel, 25, 30–31, 33
Foreign trusts, 109–110
Form 843, 275
Form 911, 102
Form 911, 102
Form 940, 45
Form 941, 45
Form 1065, 129, 133
Form 1065, 143
Form 1065, 143
Form 1099, 106–107, 275
Form 1120, 137
Form 1120, 137
Form 2553, 138
Form 2553, 138
Form 4852, 275
Form 4952, 263
Form 8822, 105
Form K-1, 133
Form SS-4/SS-5, 137
Form W-2, 44
Form W-4, 44
Four hour/one minute rule (travel), 27
401(k), 256, 310
Franchising, 115
Fraud Information Center (National Consumer League), 281
freecreditreport.com, 284
Fringe benefits, 171–217
    adoption assistance, 165, 177
    C corporation, 134–135
    cafeteria plan, 168, 206–207
    company-provided no/low-interest loans, 166, 186–189
    company-provided transportation/limos/chauffeurs, 167, 196–197
    company-provided trips for spouses/employees, 167, 193
    company-provided vehicles, 168, 202–205
    consumer testing of products, 174
    corporate purchase of employee home that declined in value, 194–195
    corporate-provided transit passes/parking/vanpools, 168, 200–202
    day care, 165, 175–177
    de minimis, 166, 180–182, 187
    defined-benefit plan, 216–217
    disability insurance, 166, 179–180
    educational assistance, 167, 189–191
    employee discounts, 166, 182–184
    exercise equipment/gym, 166, 184–186
    general partnership, 131
    health insurance, 166, 178–180
    health/country club dues reimbursement, 167, 190–192
    highly compensated employees, 165–170, 172–175
    and hiring your spouse, 37–38
    lodging, 168, 212–215
    meals, tax-free, 168
    no-additional-cost, 165, 175
    occasional supper money, 166, 180–182
    pension/profit-sharing plans, 215–217
    phantom stock, 168, 208–209
    profit sharing, 168
    relocation expense reimbursement, 167, 188–189, 195–196
    restricted property/restricted stock for services rendered, 207–209
    restricted stock, 168
    retirement advice, 186
    self-insured medical reimbursement, 166, 179
    simplified employee pension, 216
    small businesses and, 171
    stock options, 168, 209–211
    summary of, 165–170
    underused, 209
    working condition, 165, 173, 189–191
Frivolous arguments, tax scam, 273–274
FTC (Federal Trade Commission), 285
Fuel credit scam, 274
Furniture, depreciation of home office, 93–95

G

Gambling losses, 291
General partnership, 129–131
    buy-sell agreement, 131
    disadvantages of, 130–131
    who should operate as, 131
Gift tax, 306–307
Gifts:
    business, 10, 14–15
    leaseback technique, 47–49
    shift-the-tax technique, 45–47
Government bonds:
    in QTPs, 239
    Series EE/Series I, 239
Gross income limitation (home office), 90 (*See also* Adjusted gross income)
Gross profit percentage, 184
Guest book, 89, 91
Gym/exercise equipment:
    deductions for, 184–186
    as fringe benefit, 166

H

Handicapped children, 238
Health club dues, 17–18, 167, 190–192
Health insurance, 166, 178–180, 294–295, 308 (*See also* Self-insured medical reimbursement)
Health Reimbursement Arrangement (HRA) (*see* Self-insured medical plan)
Health savings account (HSA), 322–323
Heavy vehicles, 59–60
Heenan, Bobby, 272

Highly compensated employees, 39–41, 165–170, 172–175
Hobbies (*see* Business vs. hobby classification)
Home entertainment, 15–16
Home office, 78–95
    address/phone number display, 89
    administrative duties in, 81–83
    audits/audit-proofing, 85–86, 88–90
    day-care center qualification, 84–85
    deductions available with, 86–88
    depreciation and, 90–95
    documentation, 88–90, 93
    employee claims of, 92
    exclusive use rule, 85–86
    first-year tax refund, 80
    indirect expense methods, 86–88
    inventory/product sample storage as qualification, 84
    logbook for business visitors, 89, 91
    meeting or greeting clients in as qualification, 83
    photographing, 88–89
    principal place of business qualification for, 81–83
    problems with claiming, 90–92
    professionals denied deductions for, 81
    purchase of $500,000 worth of equipment, 94–95
    regular business use rule for, 85
    required record keeping, 93
    rules for deducting, 79–86
    separate structure qualification, 84
    simplified deduction method, 88
    Soliman case, 81–83
    square footage for, 86–88
    tax return election of, 94
    telephone, 89
    work-activity log, 90–91
    (*See also* Residence)
Home-based businesses, 3–7
Home-equity loans:
    interest deduction on, 291
    unnecessary, 314, 315
Hope Tax Credit (*see* American Opportunity Credit)
Horses, 117, 310–311
HSA (health savings account), 322–323

I

Identity theft, 282–286
    common means of, 282–283
    phishing scams and, 273
Improvements, real estate, 224–227
Income:
    adjusted gross, 38, 173, 177
    applying losses against, 5–6, 312–313
    business vs. hobby, 119
    dividends as, 261–262
    gross, home office limit on, 90
    investment, capital gains as, 248–251, 263
    offshore hiding of, 274
    ordinary, 261–262
    reasonable salary concept, 156–157
    reasonableness of wages, 43
    reporting, 106
    tax liability by type of, 249

of traders vs. investors, 267
    undistributed, 156
    unreported, 106
    yearly income statement, 116
    zero wages tax scam, 275
Income shifting/splitting, 37–51
    documentation, 43–45
    equipment protection, 47–49
    gift-leaseback technique, 47–49
    gift/shift-the-tax technique, 45–47
    hiring children for, 41–45
    hiring spouse for, 37–40
    IRS forms for, 44–45
    medical expenses and, 38–41
    real estate, 49
    S corporation advantage of, 139
    sale-leaseback technique, 50–51
Income Tax Act, 110
Incorporation (*see* Corporations)
Indirect expense methods, home office, 86–88
Individual Retirement Account (IRA), 310
    Roth, 42
    scams, 274
    SIMPLE, 217
Inflation, 290
Inheritance scams, 278–279
Inheritances, fair-market-value basis for, 46
Innocent Spouse Tax Relief, 104
Insurance:
    disability, 166, 179–180
    health, 166, 178–180
    self-insured medical, 38–41, 140, 166, 179
Intent test, 30
Interest, 166
    applicable federal rates, 18
    automobile loan, 314–315
    company-provided no/low-interest loan, 166, 186–189
    corporate bond, 249
    home office with mortgage, 80
    home-equity loan, 291
    income types with, 249
    mortgage, 291–292
    student loan, 243
Internal Revenue Code, 110
    "trader status" and, 265–268
    for travel, 34
Internal Revenue Service (IRS), 8
    agent promotions, 100, 110
    auditors, 99–100
    "business as hobby" weapon of, 112–121
    deductible weekends private ruling by, 25–26
    disability tax-planning strategy approved by, 179–180
    hierarchy of officers in, 99–100
    most frequent audits by, 53
    and phishing scams, 273
    publication on scams by, 276
    special agents, 109
    Sutter rule of, 13–14
    taxpayer service representative, 99–100
    training, 99–100
    (*See also* Audits/audit-proofing [IRS]; IRS Forms)

Inventory storage, home office qualification, 84
Investment:
    capital gains and, 248–251
    completely tax exempt, 247
    dealer status, 261
    expenses, 263–264
    fully taxable, 248
    mutual funds as distinct from, 249
    partially tax exempt, 247–248
    placing in right accounts, 256
    property, 303, 311–312
    real estate, fix-up, 312–313
    retirement account best options for, 256
    table/overview of taxes on various types of, 249
    tax implications of, 247–248
    tax treatment by type of, 269
    tax-advantaged accounts, 256–257
    taxpayer mistakes in taxes on, 252–253
Investment scams, 276–278, 280–281
Investors, 262–264
    problems for, 263–264
    tax treatment summary for dealers/traders
        and, 269
    traders vs., 265–268
IRA (*see* Individual Retirement Account)
Irrevocable trust, 48
IRS (*see* Internal Revenue Service)
IRS Forms:
    843, 275
    911, 102
    940, 45
    941, 45
    1065, 129, 133, 143
    1099, 106–107, 275
    1120, 137
    2553, 138
    4852, 275
    4952, 263
    8822/change of address, 105
    capital gains investment, 263
    K-1, 133
    LLC, 143
    partnership, 129–133
    Schedule C, 143, 265, 268
    Social Security Card application, 137
    SS-4/SS-5, 137
    for traders, 265, 268
    W-2, 44
    W-4, 44
IRS standard rate method, actual expense method vs.,
        56–57, 70
Itemized deductions, miscellaneous, 293

J

Job hunting, 28–29
Job scams, 280

K

Kiddie tax, 47, 237, 290
Kiplinger's retirement letter, 281

L

Laundry, 22
Lawsuits, statistics on, 128
Liability:
    in C corporations, 134
    in general partnerships, 130
    in limited partnerships, 132
    in limited-liability corporations, 143
    of Nevada corporations, 151–152
    of S corporations, 139
    of sole proprietors, 128–129
Lifelock, 284
Lifetime Learning Credit, 241–244
Like-kind exchange (investment property), 303,
        311–312
Limbs, loss of, 179
Limited partnership, 132–133
Limited-liability corporation (LLC), 143–145, 153–154,
        172
    advantages of, 143–144
    disadvantages of, 144–145
    property transfer with, 162
    who should operate as, 145
Limos, tax-free, 167, 196–197
LLC (*see* Limited-liability corporation)
Loans:
    automobile, interest on, 314–315
    bridge, 188–189
    company-provided, 166, 186–189
    employee relocation, 188–189
    home-equity, 291, 314, 315
    no/low-interest, 166, 186–189
    origination fees, 221–222
    processing fees, 221–222
    refinanced, 223, 224
    student, 243, 296
Local taxes, elimination of deduction for, 289–290
Lodging:
    documenting expenses for, 24, 32–33
    exclusion for meals, 213–214
    fringe benefit/tax-free, 168, 212–215
    receipts for, 32, 33
    with relatives, 32–33
Logbook, for business visitors, 89, 91
Logs:
    mileage, 71–73
    90-day, 73
    perfect one-day, 71–73
    work-activity, 90–91
Loss of limb/organ, 179
Losses (financial):
    applying income against, 5–6
    benefits of business, 112–113
    C corporation stockholders taking, 137
    capital gains and, 248–251
    carryback/carryover of, 113, 127
    new business, 312–313
    ordinary, 262
    passive, 133
    rental property, 309–310
    use of corporate, 140

Lottery, audit, 100, 102
Lower of cost or fair market value rule, 93
Luxury automobiles, 301

M

MACRS (modified accelerated cost recovery system),
   57–58
Madoff, Bernard, 276
Mailing, tax return, 105–106
Malpractice, 134
Management:
   money managers, 276
   specialized, 134, 139
Market, short-term swings in, 265, 267
Market value:
   automobile, 55
   fair, 48–49, 93
Marketing, network, 6–7, 16–17, 115–117, 279,
   313–316
Marketing plan, 116
Mark-to-market, 262
Mark-to-market election, 265
Master of business administration (MBA), 236
Mayer case, 267
Meals and outings, 8–18, 303–304, 312
   audit-proofing, 11–12
   business meals, 9–14
   business promotion, 14
   charity events, 13–14
   combining business with, 27, 29
   country club/health club dues, 17–18, 167,
      190–192
   employee meals, 17
   exceptions for meals, 214–215
   exclusion for meals, 213–214
   fifty-percent rule, 14–17
   gifts of, 14
   home entertainment, 15–16
   meals taken alone, 21
   occasional supper money, 166, 180–182
   100 percent deduction of, 9–10, 16–17
   with spouses, 13
   summary of strategies for deducting,
      18
   tax-free meals, 169
   See also Travel expenses
Medical expenses, 38–41
   and exceptions to Qualified Tuition Programs,
      238–239
   HSA for, 322–323
   receipts for, 39
   threshold reduction, 292
   (*See also* Health insurance)
Medical reimbursement plan, 38–41
   employees exempt from, 40–41
   self-insured, 38–41, 166, 179
Medicare:
   and LLCs, 144
   and S corporations, 139
Meet/greet test, 83
Middle America, 155

Mileage:
   business, 66–67, 74
   business vs. personal, 67–68
   cents-per-mile method, 204
   documentation, 68–74
   flowchart for determining business mileage, 69
Military, qualified, real estate deductions for, 230
Mirror test, 45
Miscellaneous itemized deductions, 293
Misuse of trusts, 275
MLM (multilevel marketing), 279, 315–316
Modified accelerated cost recovery system (MACRS),
   57–58
Moeller case, 266
Money, transfer of assets and, 159–160
Money managers, 276
Mortgage interest:
   deduction of, 291–292
   home office and, 80, 291
Mortgage loans, employee-relocation, 166, 188–189
Mortgage points, 221–224
   amortizing points paid, 223–224
   bulletproofing deduction of, 222–223
   paid by seller, 223
   recent changes on, 222–223
Motive, profit, 115, 117–119, 314
Moving expenses, 294
Multilevel marketing (MLM), 279, 315–316
Municipal bonds, 247
Musicians, home office claims for, 92
Mutual funds, 250, 252
   calculating basis of, 253–257
   investment as distinct from, 249
   record keeping of, 253
MYfico.com, 284

N

National Consumer League, 281
Net operating losses, 302–303
Net-square-footage method (indirect expenses), 88
Network marketing, 313–316
   advantages and disadvantages of, 6–7
   documenting intent in, 115–117
   entertainment deductions for, 16–17
   MLM scams and, 279
Nevada corporations, 136, 145
   advantages of, 151–152
   avoiding sales taxes and other liabilities with, 153–154
   Delaware corporations vs., 152–153
   forming, 150–154
   myths about, 150–151
Newsletters, job, 280
Nigerian scams, 278–279
90-day log, 73
No-additional-cost fringe benefit, 165, 174–175
No-hassle approach, 73
Nondisclosure agreements, 304
Nondiscrimination rules, for qualified employee
      discounts, 183–184
North American area, travel in, 31
Number-of-rooms method (indirect expenses), 88

O

Obamacare, 294–295
Occasional supper money, 166, 180–182
One-day log, perfect, 71–73
One-week loophole, 30
On-the-road expenses, 22–23, 25
"Ordinary and necessary," 17
Ordinary income, 261
Ordinary losses, 262
Owners, discrimination toward, 175
Ownership, disguised corporate, 275
Ownership vs. residence test, 228–229

P

Paperwork:
    with C corporations, 136–137
    cost of added, 137
    electronic vs. paper documentation, 69
    with LLCs, 145
Parents, giving appreciated property to your, 306–307
Parking, 168, 201–202
Parties, employee invitations to, 17
Partnership:
    basis, 129–133
    general, 129–131
    limited, 132–133
    limited-liability corporation, 143–145, 154, 162, 172
    startup checklist, 131
Part-time employees, 183–184
Passenger automobiles, 59, 63 (*See also* Vehicles)
Passive losses (limited partnerships), 133
Pass-through tax deduction, 127, 129, 133, 297–300
Peace limitation, 263
Pensions/pension plans, 215–217
    distribution, 310
    fringe benefits, 168
    qualified, 215–217
    simplified employee pension plan, 186, 256
    (*See also* Retirement)
Perfect one-day log, 71–73
Phantom stock fringe benefit, 168, 208–209
Phishing scams, 273
Photograph, home office, 88–89
Physicals, routine, 41
Piercing the corporate veil, 151–152
P-I-G rule, 14
Pollock v. Farmers' Loan & Trust Company, 110
Ponzi scams, 276
Preferred stock, 160
Prepaid college tuition, 236
Principle of duplication, 117
Privacy, corporate, 152–153
Private school tuition, 296
Prize scams, 280
Products:
    false advertising of, 279–280
    MLM, deducting purchase of, 315–316
    testing, 174
Professionals, denial of home office deductions for, 81
Profit:
    presumption based on, 114
    sharing, 168

Profit motive, 115, 117–119, 314
Profit sharing, 215–216
Promotion:
    of IRS agents, 100, 110
    of your business, 14
Property:
    appreciated, 46–47, 50
    corporate transfer of, 160–162
    fully depreciated, 48
    gifting, 45–47
    gift-leaseback of, 47–49
    investment, like-kind exchange for, 303, 311–312
    rental, 27–28, 49, 224–227, 309–310
    restricted, 207–209
    sale-leaseback technique, 50–51
    transfer, 160–162, 231
    working condition fringe benefit, 165, 173
Protest, tax, 110
Public offerings, 135
Pure trusts, 109–110
Pyramid scams, 279

Q

QSBS (qualified small-business stock), 136, 140–141
QTPs (*see* Qualified Tuition Programs)
Qualified employee discounts, 166
    limitations on, 183–184
    nondiscrimination rules for, 183–184
Qualified Higher Educational Expenses, 237–244
Qualified military, 230
Qualified move, defined, 195–196
Qualified parking, 201–202
Qualified pension plans, 215–217
Qualified relocation expense reimbursement fringe
    benefit, 195–196
Qualified Savings Plans, 237–244
Qualified small-business stock (QSBS), 136, 140–141
Qualified stock options fringe benefit, 168, 209–211
Qualified transit passes, 201
Qualified Tuition Programs (QTPs), 234, 236–237
    beneficiaries qualifying for, 238–239
    contributions to, 238
    medical exceptions to, 238–239
    Qualified Higher Educational Expenses, 237–244
    Qualified Savings Plans, 237–244
    series EE/series I government bonds, 239
Questions:
    about tax-advantaged accounts, 256
    to ask potential accountants, 319–321
    top ten tax questions, 308–316

R

"Rat fee," 109
Real estate, 49, 129, 221–232
    depreciation, 230
    fix-up investments, 312–313
    mortgage points, 221–224
    new tax laws on, 230–231
    repairs vs. improvements, 224–227
    tax-advantaged accounts and, 256–257
    transfer to regular corporation, 162

transfers as part of divorce, 231
universal exclusion for, 227–231
Real estate investment trusts (REITs), 257
Real Estate Tax Secrets of the Rich (Botkin), 231
Reasonable salary, 156–157
Rebate, fraudulent promises of, 272–273
Receipt of restricted property/restricted stock,
    207–209
Receipts, 9, 117
    educational assistance, 190
    medical expense, 39
    travel-related, 23, 32–33
Reconstruction approach, 74
Record keeping:
    home office, 93
    mutual funds, 253
    for your business, 116–117
    (*See also* Audits/audit-proofing [IRS]; Documenta-
       tion; Logs; Tax diary)
Record share transactions, 255
Reform:
    health reform law, 178
    tax, 264
Refunds:
    filing false claims for, 275
    first-year home office tax refund, 80
Registered mail (for tax returns), 105–106
Regular business stop, mileage and, 67
Regular business use rule (home office), 85
Reimbursement:
    of health/country club dues, 167, 190–192
    medical, 38–41, 166, 179
    of relocation expense, 167, 188–189, 195–196
REITs (real estate investment trusts), 257
Relatives:
    hired, 43–45
    and Kiddie Tax, 47
    lodging with, 32–33
    (*See also* Spouses or significant friends)
Relocation expenses, 167, 188–189, 195–196
Rental property, 27–28, 49, 224–227
    losses, 309–310
    repairs vs. improvements to, 224–227
Repairs (real estate), 224–227
Residence:
    company purchase of, 167, 194–195
    disqualifying use after home was principal, 231
    ownership vs., 228–229
Restaurants:
    deducting expenses related to, 312–313
    tax-free meals for employees, 213–214
Restricted stock fringe benefit, 168, 207–209, 212
Retirement:
    advice about, 186
    best investments for, 256
    defined-benefit plan, 216–217
    fringe benefit, 215–217
    Kiplinger's letter, 281
    profit-sharing plans, 215–216
    SIMPLE IRAs for, 217
    simplified employee pension plan, 186, 216, 256
    (*See also* Individual Retirement Account; Pensions/
       pension plans)

Retirement scams, 274
Retroactivity, real estate, 230
Return on investment (ROI), 247
Return-preparer tax fraud, 275
Revenue agents, 100, 109
Robbins, Tony, 28
Rockefeller, John D., 306
ROI (return on investment), 247
Ropfogel case, 266
Roth IRA, 42
Routine physicals, 41
Rowland v. Lepire, 151

S

S corporations, 39, 138–142
    advantages of, 138–141
    capital gains/losses for, 140, 251
    disadvantages of, 141–142
    election of, 138
    health insurance premiums paid by, 178–179
    taxation overview for, 155–157
    test for qualification as, 141–142
    who should operate as, 142
Salary, reasonable, 156–157 (*See also* Income)
Sale:
    automobile trade-ins vs., 64–66
    securities, 267–268
    wash-sale rule, 250, 251
Sale-leaseback technique, 50–51
Sales tax, 153–154
Savings account, health, 322–323
Savings Incentive Match Plan for Employees
    (SIMPLE), 217
Scams, 272–286
    advertising, 279–280
    book, 281–282
    fabulous offer, 280
    identity theft, 282–286
    inheritance, 278–279
    investment, 276–278, 280–281
    job, 280
    phishing, 273
    Ponzi, 276
    pyramid, 279
    seminar/investment, 281
    tax, 273–276
    telephone, 280–281
Schedule C:
    for LLCs, 143
    trader use of, 265, 268
Section 179 expense election, 94–95
Section 1244 stock, 135
Securities:
    dealer, 261
    short-term holding of, 267
    titles of, 267
    trader purchase/sale of, 267–268
    (*See also* Stock[s])
Self-employment tax, 156
Self-insured medical plan, 38, 39, 131, 140, 178, 320, 323
Self-insured medical reimbursement, 38–41, 166, 179
Seller, points paid by, 223

Seminar scams, 281
Seminars, 27, 31, 277–278
SEP (*see* Simplified employee pension)
Series EE bonds, 239
Series I bonds, 239
Sexual harassment, 304
Shares:
    annual transaction statement, 255
    record share transactions, 255
    tracking, 253–255
    traders' volume of, 267–268
Shift-the-tax technique, 45–47
Shoulder surfing, 283
Showing horses, 117
SIMPLE (Savings Incentive Match Plan for Employees),
    217
SIMPLE IRAs, 217
"Simplification," tax, 15, 30, 38, 57, 92
Simplified employee pension (SEP), 186, 216, 256
Simplified home office deductions method, 88
Single-category method, share tracking, 254–255
16th Amendment, 110
Slavery tax credits (tax scam), 276
Social Security card, 137
Social Security number, 284
Social Security taxes:
    for children, 42
    and LLCs, 144
    and S corporations, 139, 156
    for a spouse, 37
Software:
    mileage/expense, 17, 69, 73
    tax preparation, 106
    trading software scams, 277
Sole proprietorship, 127–129, 172
Soliman case, 81–83
Special agents, 109
Specialized management, 134, 139
Sports tickets, 9
Spouses or significant friends:
    closely connected spouse rule, 13
    company-provided trips for employees and, 167, 193
    as employees, 23–24, 38
    hiring, 37–40, 292
    Innocent Spouse Tax Relief, 104
Standard deduction, 288–289
Startup costs:
    for general partnerships, 129
    for limited partnerships, 133
    for sole proprietorships, 127
State taxes, elimination of deduction for, 289–290
States, corporate veil tests in, 151–152
Statistics:
    home-based business, 5
    identity theft, 284
    lawsuit, 128
Stock(s):
    basis, 140, 143
    buying back, 250–251
    C corporation and, 134–136
    calculation process for, 248–250
    control of voting, 160

dealer definition and, 261
double-category method for tracking, 253–254
entity types in purchasing, 261
FIFO, 252–253
holding strategy for, 252
phantom, 168, 208–209
preferred, 160
QSBS, 136, 140–141
qualified stock options, 168, 209–211
REIT, 257
restricted, 168, 207–209, 212
S corporation and, 38
tracking shares in, 253–255
traders' volume of shares, 267–268
transfer of property for, 160
(*See also* Securities)
Stockholders:
    C corporation, 137
    fights, 137
    LLC, 143
    meetings, 136
    protection/privacy of, 152–153
    tax efficient funds and, 255–256
Storage, home office and, 84
Strange bed rule, 22
Strike price, 209–211
Student loans:
    discharge due to death or disability, 296
    interest on, 243
Supper money, 166, 180–182
Supplies, automobile, 63
Sutter rule, 13–14
Swimming pools, 184–185

T

TAO (Taxpayer Assistance Order), 102
Tape-recording, audit, 104
TAS (Taxpayer Advocate Service), 102, 103
Tax:
    avoidance vs. evasion of, 111
    constitutionality of, 109–110
    disability tax planning strategy, 179–180
    first-year home office tax refund, 80
    frequent/top ten questions on, 256, 308–316
    protests, 110
    reforms, 264
    "simplification," 15, 30, 38, 57, 92
    2018 rates, 317–318
    (*See also* Fringe benefits; Medicare; Social Security
        tax; *specific topics*)
Tax credits, 240–244
    American opportunity, 238
    education, 240–244
    fuel tax, 274
    Lifetime Learning Credit, 241–244
    slavery, 276
Tax Cuts and Jobs Act, 287–307
    ABLE accounts, 295
    alternative minimum tax, 295, 299
    business losses, 113
    business meals, 9–10

casualty losses, 290–291
charitable contributions, 292
child tax credit, 289
elimination of certain deductions by, 292–294, 302–303
estate and gift tax lifetime exemption, 239
gambling losses, 291
hobbies, 113
home-office deduction, 79
individuals, tax changes for, 288–296
kiddie tax, 290
medical expenses, deduction for, 292
mortgage and home equity interest, deduction for, 291–292
net operating losses, 302–303
pass-through tax deduction, 127, 129, 133, 297–300
planning considerations with, 305–307
recommendations for businesses based on, 145–147
relocating expenses for employees, 195
restricted stock, income from, 212
school-related expenses and debt, 296
small business tax changes, 3, 296–305
standard deduction, increase in, 288–289
state and local taxes, deduction for, 289–290
tax rates under, 288, 296–297
vehicle purchases, 301
(*See also* Meals and outings)
Tax diary, 11–13, 117
company-provided vehicles, 202–205
home entertainment, 16
obtaining, 265
software, 17, 69
time sheets and, 43–44
"trader status" and, 265–268
travel expense, 34
(*See also* Documentation; Logs; Record keeping)
Tax efficient funds, 255–256
Tax laws, 109–110
American Taxpayer Relief Law, 59, 135, 201
Economic Stimulus, 237
employees shafted by, 5
Fair Labor Standards Act, 196
Income Tax Act, 110
new real estate laws, 230–231
Taxpayer Relief Act of 1997, 262
two sets of, 3, 260
(*See also* Tax Cuts and Jobs Act)
Tax liabilities/benefits:
for C corporations, 134–137
for general partnerships, 129–130
for limited partnerships, 132–133
for limited-liability corporations, 143–145
for Nevada corporations, 150–151, 153–154
for S corporations, 138–142, 155–157
for sole proprietorships, 127–128
Tax Reduction Institute (TRI), 28, 209, 214
Tax returns, 94–95, 275
IRS processing of, 104
method of mailing, 105–106
neat, 105–106
nonresident corporate, 150
preparer tax scam, 275

professional preparation of, 106
professional review of, 106
sales tax and, 153–154
use of software for, 106
Tax scams, 273–276
charitable contributions/organizations, 276
claiming zero wages, 275
disguised corporate ownership, 275
economic stimulus, 273
filing false claims for refunds, 275
frivolous arguments, 273–274
fuel credit, 274
hiding income offshore, 274
phishing, 273
retirement, 274
return-preparer tax fraud, 275
slavery tax credit, 276
Tax-advantaged accounts, investment and, 256–257
Taxbot, 17, 68, 73
Tax-deferred annuities, 248
Tax-deferred investments, 248
Taxpayer Advocate Service (TAS), 102, 103
Taxpayer Assistance Order (TAO), 102
Taxpayer Relief Act of 1997, 262
Taxpayers:
aggressive, 98–100
investment tax mistakes by, 252–253
as investors, 262–264
rights of, 102–104
taxpayer service representative, 99–100
Telemarketing fraud, 281
Telephone, 89
Telephone scams, 280–281
Temporary business stop, 67
Tennis courts, 184–185
Tests:
100 percent deduction, 33
consumer product, 174
corporate veil state, 151–152
intent, 30
meet/greet, 83
mirror, 45
ownership vs. residence, 228–229
principal place of business, 81
product, 174
relocation distance, 195
S corporation qualification, 141–142
Tickets, college sports, 292
Time sheets, 43–44
Top ten tax questions, 308–316
Trade-in, automobile sale vs., 64–66
Traders, 260–261, 264–268
advantages of, 264–265
deductible expenses for, 268
defining "trader status," 265–268
investors vs., 265–268
long-term gain allowed for, 267
securities purchase/sale control by, 267–268
short-term market swings and, 265
tax treatment summary for investors/dealers and, 269
transaction frequency for, 266
volume of shares for, 267–268

Trading software scams, 277
Training (*see* Education)
Transfer:
   of assets/money into corporations, 159–163
   property, 160–162, 231
   real estate, 162
Transit, days in, 26
Transit passes, 168, 201
Transportation expenses, 22, 26
   company-provided transportation/limos/chauffeurs,
      167, 196–197
   corporate-provided transit passes/parking/vanpools,
      200–202
   unsafe condition rule, 196
TransUnion, 285
Travel agents, 14
Travel expenses, 21–34
   automobile deductions in, 24
   business days, 25–31
   canceled flights, 27
   company-provided trips fringe benefit, 167, 192–193
   corporate-provided transit passes/parking/vanpools,
      200–202
   cruise ships and, 25–27
   documentation, 32–33
   driving distance per day, 24–25
   education, 28
   flowchart, 29
   foreign, 25, 30–31, 33
   four hour/one minute rule, 27
   and having fun, 23–32
   job hunting, 28–29
   laundry/dry cleaning, 22
   meals, 24
   North American area, 31
   100 percent deduction of, 14, 33
   one-week loophole, 30
   receipts for, 23, 32–33
   rental property, 27–28
   seminar/convention, 27, 31
   strange bed rule, 22
   tax diary, 34
   travel days/days in transit, 26–27
   visiting colleagues as, 28
Treasury bonds, 248
TRI (*see* Tax Reduction Institute)
Trips, company-provided, 167, 192–193
Trump, Donald, 287, 299, 306
Trusts:
   family estate trust (pure trust), 109–110
   foreign, 109–110
   gift-leaseback, 48
   misuse of, 275
   taxes and, 109–110
TRW, 285
Turbo Tax, 106
Two-car strategy, 54–55

U

Universal exclusion, real estate, 227–231
   audit-proofing, 227–228

ownership vs. residence test, 228–229
   prior depreciation, 230
Unsafe condition rule, transportation and, 196
Usable square footage method (home office),
   86–88

V

Vacation deductions (*see* Travel expenses)
Vacation offers, free, 280
Vanpools fringe benefit, 168
Vehicles, 53–75
   actual expense vs. IRS standard rate, 56–57, 70
   add back table for, 60–63
   adjusted basis, 64–66
   annual lease table rule, 66
   annual lease value method, 202–204
   audit-proof documentation, 68–74
   automobile disposal decision, 64
   bonus depreciation, 59
   business mileage rules, 53–54, 66–67
   business travel deductions for, 24
   buying vs. leasing, 60–63
   charitable deduction rules for, 64–65
   company-provided, 167, 168, 196–197,
     202–205
   converting to business use, 54–55
   depreciation of, 57–58, 64–65
   employee, 67–68
   fuel credit scam, 274
   gift-leaseback, 48–49
   heavy vehicles, 59–60
   interest on loans for, 314–315
   luxury automobiles, 301
   maintenance supplies/equipment, 63
   market value of, 55
   parking, 168, 200, 201–202
   passenger, 59, 63
   sale vs. trade-in of, 64–66
   two-car strategy, 54–55
   writing off trucks, 59
   (*See also* Mileage)
Visitors, business, 28, 89, 91
Voting stock, control of, 160

W

Wages, reasonableness of, 43
Wash-sale rule, 250, 251
Weddings, 41–45
Weekends, deductible, 25–26
Work-activity log, home office, 90–91
Working condition fringe benefit, 165, 173,
   189–191

Y

Yellow Pages, 118

Z

Zero wages claim (tax scam), 275